AFRICAN

**Becoming
Somaliland**

C000139774

AFRICAN ISSUES

Published in the US & Canada by Indiana University Press

Gender & Genocide in Burundi The Search for Spaces of Peace in the Great Lakes Region
PATRICIA O. DALEY

Guns & Governance in the Rift Valley Pastoralist Conflict & Small Arms
KENNEDY AGADE MKUTU

Becoming Somaliland
MARK BRADBURY

Diamonds, Dispossession & Democracy in Botswana*
KENNETH GOOD

Undermining Development The Absence of Power Among Local NGOs in Africa
SARAH MICHAEL

'Letting them Die' Why HIV/AIDS Prevention Programmes Fail
CATHERINE CAMPBELL

Somalia Economy without State
PETER D. LITTLE

The Root Causes of Sudan's Civil Wars
DOUGLAS H. JOHNSON

Asbestos Blues Labour, Capital, Physicians & the State in South Africa
JOCK McCULLOCH

Killing for Conservation Wildlife Policy in Zimbabwe
ROSALEEN DUFFY

Mozambique & the Great Flood of 2000
FRANCES CHRISTIE & JOSEPH HANLON

Angola: Anatomy of an Oil State
TONY HODGES

Congo-Paris Transnational Traders on the Margins of the Law
JANET MACGAFFEY & REMY BAZENGUISSA-GANGA

Africa Works Disorder as Political Instrument
PATRICK CHABAL & JEAN-PASCAL DALOZ

The Criminalization of the State in Africa
JEAN-FRANÇOIS BAYART, STEPHEN ELLIS & BEATRICE HIBOU

Famine Crimes Politics & the Disaster Relief Industry in Africa
ALEX DE WAAL

Published in the US & Canada by Heinemann (N.H.)

Peace without Profit How the IMF Blocks Rebuilding in Mozambique
JOSEPH HANLON

The Lie of the Land Challenging the Received Wisdom on the African Environment
MELISSA LEACH & ROBIN MEARNS (EDS)

Fighting for the Rainforest War, Youth & Resources in Sierra Leone
PAUL RICHARDS

* forthcoming

AFRICAN ISSUES

Becoming Somaliland

Mark Bradbury

PROGRESSIO

in association with

JAMES CURREY
Oxford

INDIANA UNIVERSITY PRESS
Bloomington & Indianapolis

JACANA MEDIA
Johannesburg

FOUNTAIN PUBLISHERS
Kampala

E.A.E.P.
Nairobi

Progressio
Unit 3, Canonbury Yard
190a New North Road
London N1 7BJ
www.progressio.org.uk

in association with

James Currey
73 Botley Road
Oxford 0X2 0BS
www.jamescurrey.co.uk

Indiana University Press
601 North Morton Street
Bloomington
Indiana 47404 USA
www.iupress.indiana.edu
Telephone orders 800-842-6796
Fax orders 812-855-7931

Fountain Publishers
PO Box 488
Kampala
www.fountainpublishers.co.ug

East African Educational Publishers
PO Box 45314
Nairobi
www.eastafricanpublishers.com

Jacana Media (Pty) Ltd
10 Orange Street
Sunnyside
Auckland Park 2092 SA
www.jacana.co.za

British Library Cataloguing in Publication Data
Bradbury, Mark
  Becoming Somaliland. - (African issues)
  1. Legitimacy of governments - Horn of Africa
  2. Sovereignty 3. Horn of Africa - Politics and government
  4. Somalia - politics and government - 1991 -
  I. Title II. Catholic Institute for International Relations
  967.7

ISBN 978-1-84701-310-1 (James Currey paper)
ISBN 978-1-84701-311-8 (James Currey cloth)

ISBN 978-9970-02-724-8 (Fountain Publishers paper)

ISBN 978-1-77009-532-8 (Jacana Media paper)

**Library of Congress Cataloging-in-Publication Data available
from the Library of Congress**
•
ISBN 978-0-253-21997-8 (Indiana University Press paper)
ISBN 978-0-253-35178-4 (Indiana University Press cloth)

Typeset by
Long House Publishing Services, Cumbria, UK
in 9/11 Melior with Optima display
Printed and bound in Malaysia

CONTENTS

v

TABLES, FIGURES, BOXES & PHOTOGRAPHS

Tables

Figures

Boxes

Photographs

ACKNOWLEDGEMENTS

This book is the product of a long engagement in the Somali region. In 1988, when working with the British charity ActionAid in London, I attended the screening of a video, filmed by fighters of the Somali National Movement (SNM), of Somali Airforce MiG fighters flying sorties over Hargeysa. The planes, which were taking off from nearby Hargeysa airport, were attacking the positions of SNM fighters who had briefly captured the city in May of that year. The SNM assault on Hargeysa and Burco marked the beginning of a war that is still being fought out in southern Somalia two decades later.

A few months later I was transferred to Mogadishu as head of Action-Aid Somalia, where one of my first tasks was to trace Somali colleagues who had fled the fighting in Hargeysa to refugee camps in Ethiopia. For two years, as the war inexorably spread through the country, we struggled to keep our operations running, but finally withdrew a couple of months before the regime of Siyad Barre was overthrown in January 1991. In late 1992, I flew for the first time to Hargeysa, in what people were calling the Republic of Somaliland. With ActionAid colleagues who had escaped by circuitous routes the mayhem in the south, I spent the next year helping to establish a recovery programme in Erigavo in Sanaag region. Initially perturbed by people's decision to break with Somalia and reject anything to do with it, I came to understand some of the anger they felt towards the former regime, and grew more conscious of the chimera that had been the former Somali state.

As Somalia descended further into civil war and famine, it seemed important to record the efforts of people in Somaliland to restore political, social and economic order and the role played in that by non-state institutions. The result was the *Somaliland Country Report* (Bradbury 1997) commissioned in 1996 by the Catholic Institute for International Relations (CIIR – the former name of Progressio) and published as a two-year civil war in Somaliland was ended through a national conference held in Hargeysa. When I was asked to update the report a few years later, it was clear that Somaliland had undergone some extraordinary developments, and it was not difficult to convince Progressio that Somaliland deserved a more comprehensive history of post-war reconstruction and state-building.

Over the years spent working in the Somali region I have had the privilege to meet and work with many people who have helped to shape my understanding of Somaliland and Somalia. I must first acknowledge the contribution to this book of Haroon Ahmed Yusuf who has been a friend and colleague since the late 1980s. Generously supported by ActionAid, we travelled throughout Somaliland to undertake research for this book in 2002. I trust he will recognise his influence here. I also owe a huge debt to Dr Adan Yusuf Abokor, Progressio's representative in Somaliland, not only for his insights on Somaliland, but also for his inspiration. Dr Adan's humanity and long-term dedication to the rights of all Somali peoples, stemming from his time as a member of the Hargeysa Group, is a story in itself.

I have benefited enormously over the years from working and talking with many Somalis. There are too many to name everyone, but I am particularly grateful to Sadia Musse Ahmed, Saeed Ahmed Mohamud, Ahmed Aden Mohamed, Omar Edleh Suleiman, Mohammed Hassan Gaani, Hassan Mohamed Ali, Ahmed Farah 'Wiwa', Adulrahman Jimale, Su'ad Ibrahim Abdi, Boobe Yusuf Duale, Roda Ibrahim, Amina Mohamed Warsame, Abdulkadir Jirde Hussein, Edna Adan, Mohamed Said Mohamed Gees, Zamzam Abdi, Rakiya Omar, Dr Saad A. Shire, Abdulrahman Raghe, Moe Hussein, Dr Tahlil Haji Ahmed, Abdirashid Duale, Ali Ahmed Ali, Ali Hersi 'Doy', Faiza Warsame, and Yusuf Abdi Gaboobe and Somali colleagues in ActionAid. Many thanks also to Mohamed Ali for checking the Somali glossary.

The influence of a number of scholars of the Somali people should be apparent from my liberal references to their writings. I have also benefited from discussions with many of them over the years, including Professor Ioan Lewis, John Drysdale, Matt Bryden, Ken Menkhaus, the late Ahmed Yusuf Farah, Andre le Sage, Roland Marchal, Peter Little, and Patrick Gilkes. I have also benefited from the insights of a new generation of scholars, including Anna Lindley and Peter Hansen. Although they may not immediately recognise it here, I also owe a debt to Mark Duffield, David Keen, Joanna Macrae, John Ryle and Alex de Waal whose writings and conversations have greatly influenced my own thinking.

Progressio commissioned this book and I am indebted to Pippa Hoyland, Judith Gardner, Shukri Abdullahi, Alastair Whitson and Steve Kibble for their patience and for keeping faith with the project. Progressio gratefully acknowledges funding from Comic Relief for this publication. I thank Lynn Taylor at James Currey for her assistance with editing.

The book has been informed by work I have undertaken for a number of international organisations in Somaliland, including ActionAid, VetAid, Oxfam, CIIR/Progressio, WSP International/Interpeace, the United Nations Development Programme, the United Kingdom Department for International Development, and the World Bank. Parts of Chapter 4 draw on work undertaken with ActionAid and Oxfam in 1993. Chapter 8 draws on experience of being an election observer in 2002, 2003 and 2005. Chapter 9 draws on fieldwork undertaken for DFID in 2003. During these assignments I have benefited from working with many people in Somaliland and Somalia including, among others, Bernard

Harborne, Randolph Kent, Robin le Mare, Pat Johnson, Simon Mansfield, Karin von Hippel, Paul Simkin, Chris Print, Simon Narbeth and Nisar Majid. Finally, this book would not have been completed without the patience and encouragement of Judith Gardner. And to Zara and Jak who suddenly came into my life and turned it upside down – in the nicest possible way – in case you should want to know where I was and what I was doing, this is part of it.

I dedicate this book to my mother Rosalind Bradbury and to the memory of my father, Robert Elwyn Bradbury.

Mark Bradbury

ACRONYMS

APD	Academy for Peace and Development
ASAD	Alliance for Salvation and Democracy
AU	African Union
EC	European Commission
EU	European Union
GED	German Emergency Doctors
ICRC	International Committee of the Red Cross
IGAD	Inter-governmental Agency on Development
IMF	International Monetary Fund
NEC	National Electoral Commission
NFD	Northern Frontier District (of Kenya)
NGO	Non-governmental organisation
NSS	National Security Service
RVF	Rift Valley Fever
SAHAN	Somali Alliance for Islamic Democracy
SNM	Somali National Movement
SNRC	Somalia National Reconciliation Conference
SOMRA	Somali Relief Association
SPM	Somali Patriotic Movement
SRRC	Somali Reconciliation and Restoration Council
SRRO	Somali Relief & Rehabilitation Organisation
SSDF	Somali Salvation Democratic Front
TFG	Transitional Federal Government
TNG	Transitional National Government
UAE	United Arab Emirates
UCID	Justice and Welfare Party
UDUB	United Democratic People's Party
UIC	Union of Islamic Courts
UNDP	United Nations Development Programme
UNHCR	United Nations High Commissioner for Refugees
UNOCHA	United Nations Office for the Coordination of Humanitarian Affairs
UNOSOM	United Nations Operation in Somalia
USC	United Somali Congress
WSLF	Western Somali Liberation Front

GLOSSARY OF SOMALI WORDS

Note on Somali spellings and names
A standardised Somali orthography, based on the Latin script, was first introduced in 1972, as part of a mass literacy campaign. In this book the spelling of Somali words follow the Somali orthography, in which 'c' is pronounced like the Arabic 'ayn', as in *caano* (milk), and 'x' is 'ha', as in *xawaala*. For names and places commonly used anglicised spellings are preferred. It is common for Somalis to have nicknames and some people are better known by their nickname than their proper name. When a nickname is used, this is indicated on first mention, and subsequently when required for clarity, by inverted commas (e.g. Abdirahman Ahmed Ali 'Tuur').

abbaan	'protector', security escorts or middlemen
af-maymay	Somali dialect spoken by agro-pastoralist groups in southern Somalia
af-maxaa	Somali dialect spoken by the nomadic clans
af-Somaali	Somali language
amaano	trust
aqal	nomadic house constructed of woven branches
Ahmadiya	Islamic sufi sect
bagaash	non-food consumer items
beel	community, clan
berkad (pl. *berkado*)	cement-lined water reservoir
bilis	noble pastoralist lineages
biri-ma-geydo	'spared from the spear', a code of war, refers to people who are protected in war
Boqor	highest ranking traditional leader among the Darod
caaqil (pl. *caaqilo*)	chief, elder
calan cas	'red flag', radical SNM faction
col iyo abaar	conflict and drought
cuquubo	divine retribution
daba-dheer	'long-tailed' or 'endless' drought of 1974–5
dabar-goynta Isaaqa	'Isaaq exterminating wing' of Somali military forces

Daraawiish	dervish movement of Sayyid Mahammed Abdalla Hassan
Dariiqa	sufi order (from the Arabic 'The Way')
degaan	territory and its resources controlled by a clan/land tenure
deydey	armed bandits
deyr	November–January rainy season
dhaameel	the seed of an acacia tree used to feed goats, but also refers to a bribe
dhabar-jebinta	'back breakers', nickname of military counter-intelligence
diya	blood compensation (Arabic)
Gabooye	occupational castes
Garaad (pl. *Garaado*)	traditional leader among Darod and Dir
goodhi	tea stalls
gu'	spring rainy season
Guulwade	'Victory Pioneers', a party militia that provided a system of surveillance
Guurti	assembly of traditional clan leaders, also the House of Elders
hagaa	August–October dry season
Hangash	military intelligence
ilaalo	rural police force
Islaan	traditional leader among Majeerteen
jameeca	religious community (Arabic *jama'a*)
jareer	'hard hair', derogatory name for Somali Bantu peoples
jihad	holy war (Arabic)
jiilaal	January–April dry season
jiri	armed bandits (north east Somalia)
karin	summer coastal rains
laan-gaab	smallest or shortest lineage
laan-dheere	largest or longest lineage
mag	blood compensation (Somali)
Malaaq	traditional leader among Rahanweyn
mandeeq	she camel
mefrish	place for chewing *qaad*
Midgaan	occupational caste (leatherworkers)
moryaan	bandits (southern Somalia)
mugadas	sacrosanct
nabad iyo caano	'peace and milk' meaning 'peace and prosperity'
nabad-doon	peaceseekers
oday (pl. *odayaasha*)	elder
qaad (also known as *gaat/khat/chat*)	narcotic plant (*cathula edulis*) that is chewed ubiquitously by Somalis
Qaadiriya	Islamic sufi sect

qaadiro	hangover from chewing *qaad*
qaadiyo	judges
reer	domestic camp
reer magaal	urban people
reer miyi	rural people
Saalahiya	Islamic sufi sect
shariica	Islamic law (Arabic *shari'a*)
sheegad	adoption into a lineage not of one's birth
shifta	bandits
shir	meeting or council of elders
shir beeleed	clan conference
shir-gudoon	chairing committee of a clan conference
shir qarameed	national conference
shir nabadeedka	peace meeting
somalinimo	Somali nationalism
Suldaan (pl. *Suldaano*)	titled traditional leader among Isaaq
tawfiq	understanding or consensus
tol	kinsmen
Tumaal	an occupational caste (blacksmiths)
Ugaas (pl. *Ugaasyo*)	titled traditional leader among Hawiye and Gadabursi
Ulema	committee of religious scholars
Uwayisiya	order founded by Sheikh Uways Mohamed el Baraawi
wadaad (pl. *wadaado*)	man of god, religious leader
Wahaabi	conservative Islamic tradition of central Arabia
waranle	warrior (spear holder)
Woqooyi Galbeed	north west region
Xaarame Cune	the 'time of eating filth' (1911/12 famine)
xawaala	remittance or money transfer company
xawilaad	money transfer
xeer beegti	experts in customary law
xeer caado	customary values
xeer dhagan	social conduct
xeer dhiig	blood code
xeer gar	customary law regarding economic relations
xeer guud	customary law regarding domestic matters
xeer somali	Somali customary law/political treaty
xeerka biri-ma-geydada	rules or codes of war
xidid	affinal marriage ties
Yibir	an occupational caste (hunters)
Zakaat	alms

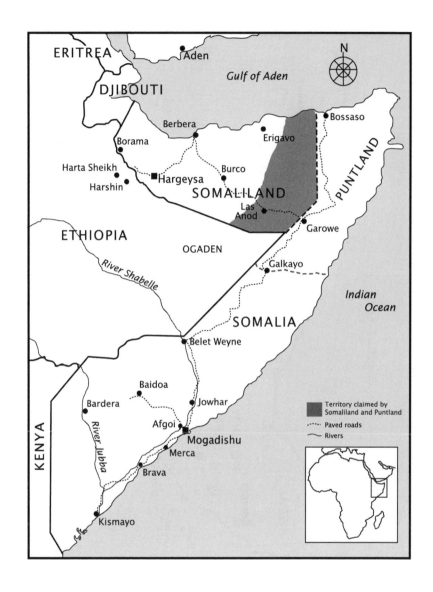

Map 1 Somalia (showing Somaliland & Puntland)

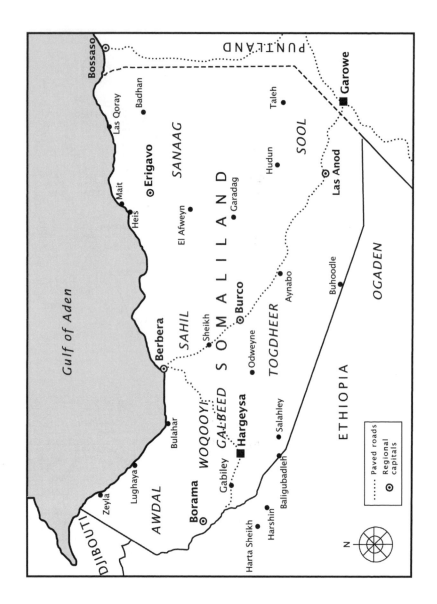

Map 2 Somaliland

Introduction

On 18 May 1991, leaders of the Somali National Movement (SNM) and elders of the northern Somali clans, meeting at the Grand Conference of the Northern Peoples in the war-scarred town of Burco, bowed to public pressure and announced that the people of north-west Somalia were withdrawing from the union that had joined the colonial territories of Italian Somalia and the British Somaliland Protectorate in 1960. Intent on re-establishing the sovereign independence granted to them by Britain, they proclaimed the formation of a new state – the Republic of Somaliland – whose borders were to follow those of the former British Protectorate, with Djibouti to the north, Ethiopia to the south-west and Somalia to the east.

Severing political ties with Somalia helped to distance the north-west regions from the civil war that was intensifying in southern Somalia and in the intervening years people in Somaliland have rebuilt their country and forged an alternative path to recovery and development. Located on the northern edge of the Horn of Africa, Somaliland has emerged as one of the most stable polities in the Horn, and by 2006 could boast a popularly elected government and a political system with democratic credentials to rival any in the region and most Muslim states. As such, Somaliland challenges the image of war, disaster and social regression that has been associated with this part of Africa since the early 1990s.

In the early 1990s, the end of the Cold War precipitated democratic transitions and created opportunities to resolve proxy wars. But the optimism with which the then United States President, George Bush Senior, proclaimed a new liberal 'world order' was soon dashed by the outbreak of wars in Somalia, West Africa and the Balkans, and the continuation of long-running wars elsewhere in Africa, Asia and the Middle East. As forces from twenty nations combined under a United Nations flag to evict Iraq from Kuwait in the First Gulf War,[1] the war and

---

[1] The US-led and UN-mandated coalition began its offensive against Iraq in January 1991, the same month that the President of Somalia was overthrown.

famine that engulfed Somalia heralded an era of 'new wars', 'failing states', global insecurity and, since 2001, a 'war on terrorism'.

Straddling the end of the 1980s and the beginning of the 1990s, civil war and state collapse in Somalia were both a consequence and reflection of many of the changes occurring in the international order. The Somali state failed before it collapsed, as the number of people benefiting from state policies diminished and security declined. But, when the government of General Mohamed Siyad Barre was overthrown in January 1991, society and political authority fragmented and the Somali state as a unitary administrative, ideological and territorial entity ceased to function. All legislative and judicial state institutions collapsed, along with all other state bodies such as the army, banks and educational institutes. The human cost was enormous. A quarter of a million people died in the famine that raged between 1992 and 1993, some 90,000 were killed in fighting and many more became refugees or were internally displaced (Hansch *et al.* 1994: 24).

Buoyed by the allied victory over Iraq in the Gulf another international coalition was assembled to respond to the crisis in Somalia, which became a theatre for trialling new international institutions and mechanisms for managing global crises. The United Nations Operation in Somalia (UNOSOM) which intervened in Somalia to end hostilities and restore political order was one of the first UN-led, multi-mandated international peacekeeping operations that were to become a hallmark of international governance in states in crisis in the 1990s, including in the Balkans, Sierra Leone and, belatedly, Rwanda. The military and humanitarian operation helped to alleviate the famine, but it failed to reconstitute a functioning state in Somalia before withdrawing ignominiously in 1995. Since then, fourteen internationally sponsored peace conferences have also failed to resolve the political conflict and restore to Somalia a government whose authority is accepted throughout the territory. Consequently, Somalia has the dubious reputation of being the longest-running case of 'state collapse' in post-colonial Africa and the 'world's most comprehensively collapsed state' (ICG 2005b: 27).

In the 1990s, as other states that had been sustained by Cold War patronage began to implode, failed states, collapsed states and fragile states became a focus for international – largely Western – geostrategic concerns. In the post-9/11 world, such states have re-emerged as a focus of concern for Western governments and development agencies because of the threat they are thought to pose to human life and international security. States, however, are a relatively recent approach to managing social order. The Somali Republic that joined the world of nation-states in June 1960 was a product of nineteenth-century European colonialism. Prior to colonisation, the Somali people lived in a stateless, largely nomadic pastoralist society that was organised politically around clan lineages with no centralised governing institutions. The state of Somalia only functioned for thirty years and analysts have questioned whether it ever existed as a meaningful polity before it collapsed (Little 2003: 14). The impact of state collapse in Somalia varied from region to region, but, in the absence of a single central government, politics, economics and development have not ground to a halt. Somalis have fashioned diverse forms of governance and revitalised economies within the territory of the Somali Republic (UNDP 2001; ICG 2002: 11). These include military administrations, long-distance trading enterprises, civic structures, religious authorities that govern through Islamic law (*shari'a*), and putative state-like polities where a degree of consent has been established between authorities and the public. The latter include the breakaway Republic of Somaliland, created in 1991, and Puntland State of Somalia, formed in the north-east in 1998. There were also faltering attempts to establish a regional administration in the south-western regions of Bay and Bakool by the Rahanweyn Resistance Army in 1992, and a Transitional National Government (TNG) in Mogadishu in 2000, the product of a national peace conference in Arta, Djibouti. The TNG was replaced in October 2004 by the Transitional Federal Government (TFG), formed at the Somalia National Reconciliation Conference held in Kenya, the fourteenth internationally sponsored Somalia peace conference. The TFG was accorded conditional diplomatic recognition, with seats in the United Nations, the African Union, the Arab League and the regional Inter-Governmental Agency on Development. In 2006 the TFG was challenged by the dramatic rise of the Union of Islamic Courts (UIC),[2] which ejected the 'warlords' from Mogadishu and took control of large swathes of southern Somalia, only to be ousted six months later by the TFG backed by Ethiopian and US military forces. Since 1991, Somaliland has been the most developed and stable of these polities.

In 1991, the SNM government, which had been fighting the regime in north-west Somalia since 1982, inherited a devastated region. Tens of thousands of people had been killed in the war and hundreds of thousands had fled abroad. The main cities of Hargeysa and Burco had been reduced to rubble and all public utilities and services had been destroyed. In 1991, Hargeysa from the air resembled a city of dry swimming pools, which on closer inspection were shells of houses whose roofs had been systematically looted during the war. Many villages had suffered similar fates and both urban and rural areas were littered with landmines and unexploded ordinance. Landing at Hargeysa airport in 1991 one had to gamble on surviving the drive to the centre of town without losing one's luggage or car to armed men.

Today, the scene could not be more different. Flying over the city, sun glints off the roofs of new buildings. The airport – renamed Egal International Airport – has been rebuilt and expanded and receives international flights. The city has been rebuilt and expanded with new

---

[2] The most common name for the alliance of Courts – the Union of Islamic Courts – is used throughout this book, although the more correct name was the Council of Somali Islamic Courts (*Golaha Maxakiimta Islaamiga Soomaaliyeed*). Matt Bryden, personal communication.

houses, shops, offices and hotels. Telephone services link Hargeysa to other towns and villages in Somaliland and overseas. Hargeysa's streets bustle with vendors openly hawking everything from money and clothes to frankincense and food, a scene repeated in most of Somaliland's towns. In Hargeysa, as in any capital, shops are stacked with a huge range of imported luxury food items and the latest electronics and computer technology, and the roads are feeling the strain of an increased number of vehicles. Over the past decade, without assistance from international financial institutions, people in Somaliland have built telecommunications and airline companies, universities, hospitals and money transfer businesses. Outside of the urban sprawl, where perhaps half of the people live, the other half of the population continues the age-old life of nomadic pastoralism, herding camels, sheep and goats. For the past decade the only guns visible on the streets of Somaliland's cities are those carried by uniformed police or the occasional soldier, and in the rural areas by the occasional pastoralists protecting their herds.

Since breaking with Somalia, the people of Somaliland have successfully managed a process of reconciliation and created a constitutionally based government and public administration that has restored law and order, overseen demobilisation and held three democratic elections. Much of the urban infrastructure, municipal services and systems of education and health that were destroyed during the war have been re-established. Throughout Somaliland civic organisations have emerged to provide welfare services or to advocate for political rights. The restoration of security means that Somaliland has ceased being a refugee-producing area: there is evidence that more people are returning to Somaliland from overseas than are leaving, and thousands of people from some of the poorest communities in southern Somalia and Ethiopia have migrated to Somaliland for physical and economic security.

Today Somaliland has many of the attributes of a sovereign state, with a constitution, three political parties and a popularly elected government that provides security for its population, exercises some control over its borders, manages some public assets, levies taxes, issues currency and driving licences, and formulates development policies. In December 2002 Somaliland staged the first multi-party democratic elections in this region for thirty years to establish district councils. To bolster Somaliland's sovereign identity, many of the symbolic trappings of a state have been adopted, including its own flag, a national anthem, vehicle licence plates and national holidays. The political system created in Somaliland that incorporates clan elders into the Upper House of the legislature means that government is more representative than it has been in the past, and contrasts favourably with several other countries in the region.

Constructing a state from scratch has brought many challenges. Between 1992 and 1996 Somaliland experienced two civil wars. An embargo imposed in 2000 on imports of Somali livestock by Gulf countries has deprived the country of a key source of revenue. The absorption of former refugees, sedentarisation and urban drift have placed new strains on infrastructure and the environment and created tensions over the ownership and management of resources, particularly land. Despite the many achievements in restoring political order, human development indicators remain poor, and marked disparities in wealth and well-being persist between social groups, between men and women, between the east and west of the country and between urban and rural populations. The achievements in creating an electoral democracy are marred by a government bureaucracy that is ineffective and corrupt and the government's failure in recent years to uphold its stated commitment to human rights. Somaliland's growing reputation as a haven of security in a troubled region was tarnished when four foreign aid workers were murdered in 2003 and 2004 by members of an Islamic *jihadist* network with links to southern Somalia.

Most fundamentally, after a decade and a half Somaliland's sovereignty claim remains unrecognised by Somalis in Somalia or any foreign government, and is contested by a significant proportion of the people populating eastern Sanaag and Sool regions of Somaliland.[3] Once 'Africa's best-kept secret' (Jahzbahy 2006), recognition is growing of what has been achieved in Somaliland. Since the late 1990s there has been an increasing acceptance of the Somaliland administration as a responsible authority by international bodies like the UN, the European Union and the World Bank. In 2005 the British government's Commission for Africa recognised Somaliland as a place of 'modest but ordered prosperity' (Commission for Africa 2005: 30). In the same year Bob Geldof began his series of 'Live8' documentaries in Somaliland, in order to demonstrate some of the positive developments in Africa. While existing in a diplomatic no man's land, the government has developed functional relations with Ethiopia, which has posted a trade delegate to Somaliland, and several European governments have signed formal memorandums with the government in Hargeysa on the repatriation of asylum applicants. Ethiopian Airlines has scheduled flights to Hargeysa, and Somaliland ministers and government employees now travel on Somaliland passports. But these functional relationships have not translated into legal recognition. In spite of a positive recommendation by an African Union fact-finding mission to Somaliland in 2005 to investigate further its application for membership, Somaliland's sovereignty in 2006 remained unrecognised beyond its borders (ICG 2006a). It is a deep irony that Somaliland – which has many of the empirical attributes of a state – has no legal status or representation in international fora, while Somalia – despite the absence of effective government since 1991 – continues to be accorded *de jure* sovereignty, with the TNG and TFG purporting to represent all the people of Somalia in a number of international bodies. As the territorial definition of the

[3] Certainly not all the Harti people of these eastern regions are against the independence of Somaliland, but over time, as will be discussed in later chapters, many have thrown their support behind Puntland and Somalia.

Somali state is recognised in preference to the existing political authorities and the borders of Somalia remain the reference point for the policies of the UN and other international bodies.

International aid strategies are handicapped by international conventions that privilege only 'legitimate' states with development assistance and are ambivalent over how to work with 'weak' or 'quasi-state' formations. The relative stability sustained over the past decade in Somaliland has enabled international aid organisations to support the restoration of basic services and infrastructure, clear landmines, reintegrate displaced populations, demobilise militia and support the development of new civil society organisations. However, its ambiguous diplomatic status has denied Somaliland access to forms of support that many post-conflict countries receive – support that would enable it to rebuild its infrastructure and services and develop its institutions of governance. For example, Somaliland government institutions have not received the same type of institutional support that the international community immediately granted to the TFG of Somalia in 2004. Interestingly, the consequences of this have not necessarily been negative. While the limited scale of assistance has perpetuated hardships and perhaps imposed a slow pace of recovery, it has meant that the process of establishing security and constructing a nascent democratic political system has largely been internally driven and financed by the people of Somaliland. This internally generated process of recovery has served increasingly to forge a separate identity, a feeling of self-reliance and a belief amongst Somalilanders that 'Somaliland is becoming a reality' (Somaliland Ministry of Foreign Affairs 2002).

Why write a book about Somaliland, a lightly populated region on the edge of Africa which, if the international community had its wish, would be reincorporated into a federal Somali state? Part of the answer is that Somaliland offers important insights for current policy concerns about 'failed' and 'collapsed' states in Africa and elsewhere. Since the early 1990s, some fundamental changes to the state system created in Africa during colonisation have been taking place that have produced new political formations. Somaliland is one of several polities that have emerged since the end of the Cold War that do not fit the normative world of juridical states and have been variously described as 'non-state entities', 'quasi-states' and 'states-within-states' (Spears 2001). These political entities challenge the basis of international law and the territorial integrity of states, while their large diaspora communities are altering notions of citizenship and changing the relationship between states and their citizens, as well as the ways in which livelihoods are generated. For many people living in these non-states, the local political arrangements provide better security than was previously provided by formal state structures.

Somaliland challenges international efforts at state-building in Somalia, by questioning the basis for and the nature of that state and by demonstrating an alternative route to state-building than has been determined by foreign diplomats and aid programmes to date. Somaliland's break with Somalia has been criticised harshly by some Somalis as a regressive step that serves to reinforce clan-based politics. However, the restoration of political order in Somaliland does much to challenge the image of social regression typically associated with collapsed states, and an international order that assumes a certain dependence of countries in the South on the North. It also challenges the conclusion that Somalis are incapable of governing themselves, a view the international community holds, perhaps not surprisingly, after fourteen internationally sponsored peace conferences. The state of Somalia was in many respects an external construct sustained by external resources, even if it was adapted and reappropriated by the local political culture. The formation of Somaliland has involved a process of state reform or redesign. Limited international engagement with Somaliland since 1991 means that people in Somaliland have crafted a system of representative politics suited to their own needs. Uniquely in Africa, this has involved the incorporation of traditional institutions and practices into the system of governance. Thus Somaliland offers an alternative path to state reconstruction in the Somali region – one that, for all its weaknesses, provides a more representative, more participatory and less violent form of politics than Somalis have experienced for the past quarter of a century, and therefore a potentially more robust and sustainable state.

State-building in Somaliland also reflects important global developments. In Somaliland the most significant source of finance for rebuilding has come from money remitted by Somalilanders living overseas. These migrant communities have played a critical economic and political role in constructing and sustaining Somaliland. In many respects, therefore, Somaliland is a 'transnational state', with many of its citizens living outside the geographical country and much of its economy generated externally. The dynamic relationship between Somaliland and its diaspora has a crucial influence on the type of state that is emerging. In an era of globalisation, understanding the dynamic relationship between large migrant communities and the states that claim to represent them should critically inform international development policy, and in this regard Somaliland also has important insights to offer.

Somaliland's experiences of post-war recovery and state reconstruction are not easily transferable to southern Somalia. Nevertheless, the experiences from Somaliland of peacemaking and reconciliation, the demobilisation of militia and restoration of law and order, constitutional development and the creation of a parliamentary democracy, the management of a deregulated economy and the role of the diaspora, do provide insights for people in Somalia and in other countries emerging from war.

International aid policy-makers and bureaucrats often lack a historical perspective. International efforts at state reconstruction in the Somali region need to be cognisant of the reasons for the collapse of the state of Somalia and of the processes of development that have subsequently taken place. This book seeks to fill a gap in the literature on the Somali people since 1991 by describing the recovery of a society after war and the efforts of its people to construct a new state in the Horn of Africa. The book provides a general introduction to Somali society and a brief history of state-building and state collapse in Somalia, before focusing on Somaliland. Since 1991 aid programmes have been the main prism through which the international community has engaged with Somaliland and has sought to understand it. But the assumption that state-building can be controlled through aid projects, logical frameworks and set timeframes is simplistic, if not delusional. State formation involves more than demobilisation, re-establishing the rule of law, or rehabilitating services and infrastructure. States are 'the outcome of complex sets of practices and processes [and] the result of myriads of situations where social actors negotiate power and meaning' (Krohn-Hansen and Nustad 2005: 12). And states in the making are subject to a range of internal and external political, social and economic forces that can affect the trajectory of development. This book looks beyond the aid programmes to describe some of the events and processes in the creation of Somaliland between 1991 and 2006. The SNM and its war against the Somali government, the large-scale post-war clan peace conferences, the civil wars and the democratic elections are a few of the key events and processes described. Around these the people in Somaliland and in the diaspora debated, defined and created a new polity. The processes of state formation can also transform the way people live and think. Despite its uncertain beginnings and many weaknesses, Somaliland has developed into a functional polity and its public aspiration for international recognition deserves serious attention.

The creation in October 2004 of a transitional government for Somalia that was accorded international recognition by foreign governments posed a threat to Somalilanders' own aspirations for their country to be recognised as a sovereign state. However, for its first two years the long-term survival of the TFG was in serious doubt, divided within itself and rapidly losing territory and influence to the UIC in 2006. The religious and nationalist rhetoric of the leadership of the Islamic Courts also threatened the stability of Somaliland, where the movement had some sympathisers. There were renewed calls for the recognition of Somaliland to offset this threat (Schraeder 2006). The retreat of the Islamic Courts in early 2007 and the forcible entry into Mogadishu of the TFG backed by Ethiopia heralded another sudden swing in the politics of the region that will inevitably have ramifications for Somaliland. With Ethiopia, Eritrea and other countries picking sides and arming their allies, the prospect of warfare once again engulfing the Somali region was a grim possibility in early 2007. State building, however, is never a completed process; states are in a perpetual state of becoming. Whatever the fortunes of the TFG or the UIC, the place people call Somaliland will change. This book is a modest contribution to recording its history so far.

1
The Somali People & Culture

Behind the notion of a 'failed state' lies an assumption that there is an optimal model of a state. But historically states have taken different forms and the contemporary, modern state is a relatively recent invention that also exists in diverse forms reflecting the society that it incorporates. The majority of people in Somaliland are ethnic Somali and their aspiration to independence is not based on a strong sense of cultural or ethnic difference from other Somalis, with whom they share a common language (*af-Somaali*), an adherence to *sunni* Islam, a common ancestry and lineage-based social system and a livelihood system traditionally based upon nomadic pastoralism. These cultural traits profoundly influence Somali life, politics and development and are important for under-standing political trends and processes of state building in post-war Somaliland. This chapter therefore provides a brief introduction to the history and culture of the Somali people.

The Somali people

The people of Somaliland are part of the Somali 'nation' of peoples who inhabit a large contiguous area in the Horn of Africa, from the Awash Valley, through the Ethiopian Ogaden and into northern Kenya as far as the Tana River. The origin of the Somali people is a subject of debate among scholars. Brilliantly preserved paintings of cattle and herdsmen in the Laas Geel caves near Hargeysa in Somaliland, which may date as far back as 9,000 BC, illustrate that the herding of livestock existed in the peninsula for several millennia before Somali-speaking people appeared there (Gutherz, Cros and Lesur 2003). Linguists suggest that the Somali people are descended from a stock of Cushitic peoples, related to the Afar, Oromo, Saho and Beja peoples in the Horn of Africa (Lewis 2002 [1965]: 4), who began migrating northwards from an area on the present-day Ethiopia–Kenya border into the peninsula around the fifth century

9

BC (Said Samatar 1991: 10). They date the appearance of speakers of modern-day Somali to the sixth or seventh century AD, and the presence of Dir Somali (considered the most ancient Somali lineage) in the northern part of the peninsula to the tenth century (Ehret 1995: 246). There, Somali-speaking people would have come into contact with Muslim Arab and Persian merchants who had established a string of settlements in Zeyla, Berbera, Heis and Mait along the northern coastline. Conversion to Islam is linked to the arrival from Arabia of the eponymous clan ancestors Sheikh Darod and Sheikh Isaaq, some time between the tenth and thirteenth centuries, who married local women (Lewis 2002: 22).[1]

Somali genealogies and oral history record this union between indigenous Africans and migrants from Arabia descended from the noble Hashimite Qurayshi lineage of the Prophet Mohamed and his companions, thus firmly anchoring Somali culture in Islam (Lewis 1961: 11; Samatar 1988: 9). It is thought probable that in this period camel herding and nomadic pastoralism also became established as a way of life and the southward and westward expansive movement of the northern Somali clans began (Ehret 1995: 249). In this way the distinct characteristics of the Somali people began to take form through a common language, descent, faith and mode of livelihood.

The Somali 'nation', although united through common descent and cultural characteristics, is divided into clan-families, which sub-divide into smaller kin-based groups of clans, sub-clans and primary lineages.[2] The Somali nation is conventionally described as consisting of six clan-families[3] known as Dir, Isaaq, Darod, Hawiye, Digil and Rahanweyn[4] (see Appendix 2). These are divided into two groups, reflecting a difference in economic vocation among Somalis. The Dir, Isaaq, Darod and Hawiye are predominantly nomadic pastoralist clans and are sometimes referred to as the 'noble' (*bilis*) lineages. The Digil and Rahanweyn (also known as Digil-Mirifle) are cultivators and agro-pastoralists inhabiting the relatively fertile regions between the Shabelle and Jubba rivers in southern Somalia.

[1] Tradition explains that the founding father of Darod, Sheikh Ismael Jabarti, arrived between the tenth and eleventh centuries, with Sheikh Isaaq arriving two centuries later.

[2] Anthropologists refer to this as a 'segmentary lineage' system. The classic exposition of this can be found in I. M. Lewis's ethnography of northern Somali pastoralists (1961). This seminal work has had a profound influence on the way Somali society is understood.

[3] Clan-families are broad confederations of clans that are genealogically related by descent (*tol*) through the male line from a common ancestor, and represent the highest level at which collective political action takes place. The term was coined by I.M. Lewis (1961) in his study of northern Somali pastoralism and has been commonly adopted. However, the designation of 'clan-family' is politically contentious, as it can determine forms of political representation at local and national levels. For example, the national reconciliation conferences of Arta in 2000 and Mbgathi in 2003 used a formula of '4.5' clan-families to apportion voting rights and seats in the transitional national assemblies. These are the Dir, Darod, Hawiye, Digil-Rahanweyn, with minority groups holding half as many seats. In this formula, the Isaaq are included with the Dir, although the Isaaq rarely consider themselves to be part of the Dir.

[4] They call themselves Rewiin.

The social organisation of these settled communities differs from that of the nomadic pastoralists and they speak a dialect of Somali (*af-maymay*) that is distinct from the *af-maxaa* Somali spoken by the nomadic clans.

When the state of Somalia was formed in 1960, pastoral society became the dominant political culture: Somali nationalism (*somalinimo*) glorified the nomadic tradition and the she camel (*mandeeq*) was promoted as a symbol of unity and independence (Mansur 1995: 112). However, Somalia also encompassed several other smaller ethnic communities whose traditions, histories and political rights were largely neglected by the state. One impact of the civil war has been to highlight and reinforce the identities of these groups in a way that challenges the ideology of a Somali state founded on an ethnically homogeneous society – a challenge underlined by several Somali and non-Somali scholars (Ahmed 1995). These communities include the Barawani and Benadiri people of mixed Arab, Persian, Pakistani and Portuguese descent, whose communities in the coastal towns of Mogadishu, Merca, Brava and Kismayo predate the urbanisation of Somalis. Another group are the Bajuni people, who live in fishing communities on the islands and coast of southern Somalia. The most numerous group are the so-called 'Somali Bantus', a term that has come to refer to a number of distinct groups living in farming communities along the southern rivers, some of whom are descended from pre-Somali Bantu populations and others from slaves freed in the nineteenth century (Lewis 2002: 7). Until the 1990s these riverine farming communities had little sense of a common identity (Menkhaus 2003).

Another social group of note are occupational castes associated with specialised tasks that were looked down on by nomads and are treated as outcasts. These include the *Yibir* (hunters), *Midgaan* (leatherworkers) and *Tumaal* (blacksmiths), collectively referred to as Gabooye in Somaliland. By tradition they are bonded to the 'noble' Somali lineages, but are prevented by taboo from marrying into them. Yet another social group comprises people who have been 'adopted' (*sheegad*) into the major lineages, a practice that is particularly common among the Rahanweyn, but occurs within all the major Somali lineages.

Politically marginalised in a state that was dominated by the major Somali clans, smaller in numbers and lacking adequate military force, these communities, along with Rahanweyn farming communities, suffered disproportionately in the war and the famine of the early 1990s. In 2002 minority groups still comprised the largest proportion of the internally displaced populations in Somalia (UNOCHA-Somalia 2002). Vulnerable to exploitation and predation, they have been forced to organise politically and militarily to survive and as a result some have gained recognition and representation in the parliamentary forums of the different Somali administrations. Recognition of their political vulnerability has also gained some of them preferential treatment in asylum and resettlement programmes overseas.

Pastoral society & culture

The Somali-inhabited region of the Horn of Africa is, in the main, a semi-desert region with an ecology that is best exploited by pastoralism. At the beginning of the last century colonial authorities estimated that some 75 per cent of the population of Somalia was nomadic. At independence Somalia had the highest percentage of pastoralists per population and largest area of rangeland[5] of any country in the Horn. In the arid regions of the north, centre and south-west, nomadic pastoralism has been the dominant mode, while between the Shabelle and Jubba rivers, and in parts of the northern escarpments, perennial water, higher precipitation and richer soils provide conditions for cultivation and agro-pastoralism. The varied environmental conditions and modes of production are reflected in different land tenure practices, resource management systems and forms of social and political organisation.

Nomadic pastoralism is a sophisticated land-use system, utilising mixed species: herds of camels, sheep and goats. The symbiotic relationship between the environment and livestock production is recognised in the words of the Somali poem: 'livestock are the growing grass' (Lewis 1961: 37). The health, nutrition and productivity of livestock – and, therefore, the livelihood security and health of pastoralists – are conditioned by the availability and quality of pasture and water and their access to those primary resources. Production is also influenced by disease, herd management, marketing and trading strategies. Ultimately the effectiveness of pastoral production is linked to the social organisation of pastoralists. Social structure determines resource entitlements, the division of labour and the exercise of authority. Social institutions and organisational strength affect a group's ability to cope with change and to secure a livelihood. Collective action through kinship, for example, provides physical and economic security, as illustrated in a Somali saying that 'He who does not own a camel lives under the protection of others.' To move with the nomadic hut (*aqal*) requires a burden camel, but as not all families possess camels the most basic requirement of nomadic pastoralists – mobility – requires cooperation. The well-being or the vulnerability of people is, therefore, not just a measure of relative economic wealth, but of socio-political organisation.

State formation changed the nature of pastoral production and the relationship between nomadic, sedentary and urban communities. The integration of pastoral production into a global economic system through livestock exports and state economic and political policies created economic stratification and affected systems for managing communal

---

[5] 'Rangelands' are the whole natural resource base – including pasture, water, wild foods and construction materials – upon which pastoral livelihoods are based.

resources. Urbanisation, the development of new economic sectors, state settlement schemes for nomads, international migration and civil war have all reduced the percentage of the population who live a nomadic way of life. In 2003 demographic data suggested that only 66 per cent of Somalia's population today is rural – a figure that includes both nomadic and settled populations (World Bank/UNDP 2003). But while the numbers of people practising pastoralism throughout the Horn are declining, nomadic pastoralists are still thought to make up the largest percentage of the population of Somaliland.

The relevance of kinship

In Somali society kinship has been described by the anthropologist I.M. Lewis (1993: 47) as the principle of social organisation and the key to understanding politics, organised violence, trade and conflict management. All Somalis are born into this social structure and because it defines a person's relationship to other Somalis and non-Somalis, kinship is a critical source of an individual's identity. Knowledge of a person's clan can enable one to identify their elders, deduce where they reside and whom they are likely to vote for in an election. Genealogies are not simply family trees and clans are not static forms of social organisation. Kin groups form alliances, divide and realign in response to internal and external events and processes. The clan or sub-clan that a person identifies with (or is identified with) will depend on the prevailing context and issue at hand, such as access to environmental resources, the control of real-estate, competition for political office or a collective response to security threats. The tradition of exogamous marriage means that Somalis can have relatives in several clans dispersed over large geographic areas and individuals can adopt the identity of another lineage. Clans and genealogies are therefore dynamic social constructs that can be subject to different interpretations and are used to describe and validate changing social and political relationships. They are, as Luling (2006) has described, 'not only good to fight with (or play politics and do business with) but good to think with'.

Historically, this particular form of lineage-based social organisation has been associated with a way of life that revolved around nomadic pastoralism. But it is, as noted, a way of life that has been undergoing profound changes since the advent of colonialism. The emergence of a state has affected the relationship between pastoral, sedentary and urban communities. Sedentarisation, urbanisation and new economic livelihoods have increased attachment to territory and created new social groups and sources of identity. In addition to kinship, a person's social standing and authority can be influenced by their wealth, educational qualifications, gender, age, or their religious learning. Age-groups, school friendships, neighbourhoods, workplaces, or affiliation to a religious sect can all provide bases for social bonds between people of different lineages and alternative forms of individual and group assurance and security. Many Somalis therefore reject categorisation by clans, and individuals may choose not to act as a member of his or her clan. This can, however, incur social costs because kinship ties also define an individual's rights and obligations to give and receive assistance and protection.

The primacy that Lewis and others[6] give to the segmentary kinship system in explaining political dynamics in Somalia has been criticised by some Somali and non-Somali scholars as too reductionist, to the neglect of other factors such as individual agency, class and political and economic forces. Abdi Samatar (1989), for example, argues that the politicisation of genealogy (or 'clanism') is a product of the political and economic intrusions of colonialism and post-independence state policies, and is a symptom rather than a cause of state collapse. Besteman and Cassanelli (2000) argue that underdevelopment and elite class competition over land and resources in southern Somalia were important in the genesis of the war. Barnes (2006) suggests the emphasis on kinship as a non-territorial form of organisation underplays the importance of territorial identity. In the course of the civil war, territory in Somalia and Somaliland has become a highly charged political issue, with clan groups asserting historical rights over territory and new claims through conquest. The growth of Islamic militancy in the 1990s has suggested to other scholars that the emphasis given to kinship has also neglected the potency of religion as a force for supra-clan social organisation and identity (Le Sage 2004). The attention given by scholars to Somali pastoralist lineages has also been criticised for underplaying the ethnic heterogeneity of the people who live in Somalia (Ahmed 1995). There is, as Little (2003: 46) rightly argues, a need to move beyond narrow debates over the role of kinship to appreciate the influence that trade, religion or regional and global politics have on inter-group politics and developments in Somalia.

No single factor can adequately explain the cause of state collapse in Somalia. The legacies of European colonialism, the contradictions between the centralisation of state power and the traditionally uncentralised political culture of Somalis, Cold War politics, militarisation, autocratic government, oppression, and economic and social injustices all played a role. In post-independence Somalia, kinship was used by the political elite as a mechanism to access state resources and other assets, and for disbursing political patronage. General Mohamed Siyad Barre instrumentalised and manipulated genealogy to hold on to power. The civil war in the 1990s was not a 'traditional' war between nomadic clans, but one where 'clanism' was manipulated by elites and political entrepreneurs vying to control diminishing state resources in the context of declining aid flows and new trade flows and Somalia's (and Africa's)

---

[6] See also Schlee (2001).

marginalisation in the world economy. It is, therefore, to the specific nature of Somali society and its interaction with global processes that one needs to look to understand the war and the protracted nature of state collapse.

The kinship system remains an important feature of Somali social, political and economic life, despite more than forty years of state-building, urbanisation, industrialisation, civil war and international migration, and an appreciation of this lineage-based form of social organisation is essential for understanding many aspects of contemporary Somali society. During the war kinship affiliation affected an individual's access to assistance and protection from other Somalis and, in many instances, whether the person lived or died. In the context of state collapse and in the absence of state institutions and other forms of political organisation the kinship system provided a structure for inter-group relations and governance, for organising and managing violence and for organising trade. The continuing significance of kinship is apparent in many aspects of private and public life, such as in the proportional distribution of parliamentary seats and cabinet posts in the governments of Somaliland, Puntland and the TFG, in the formation of *shari'a* courts in Mogadishu, or in the hugely significant remittance economy, in which kinship relations have taken on a global dimension. And, as will be seen in later chapters on Somaliland, in the absence of a functional government, this form of socio-political organisation has been vital in providing a basis for governance, the restoration of law and order and economic recovery.

Stateless order

Prior to colonisation Somali nomadic pastoral life was a classic example of a 'stateless' society. Unlike 'primitive state' societies described by anthropologists elsewhere in Africa (Fortes and Evans-Pritchard 1958), Somali pastoral society is acephalous, with no hierarchy of political units or administrative offices. As Lewis wrote in his study of northern Somali pastoralism: 'Few societies can so conspicuously lack those judicial, administrative and political procedures which lie at the heart of the western conception of government' (1961: 1). This does not mean that no states previously existed in the territories that the European colonial powers came to call Somalia and Somaliland. From the thirteenth century until the arrival of European colonialists in the nineteenth, the history of the Somali region is marked by the rise and fall of Arab city states and Ottoman sultanates in coastal settlements like Zeyla and Berbera in the north and Mogadishu, Merca and Brava in the south. In these city states the first forms of government in the Somali region were established where an urban culture and civic identity rather than genealogy formed the basis of communal identity (Kapteijns 1994). Their influence on the pastoralists of the interior is unclear, but they connected the pastoral economy into international trade networks and there is evidence that prior to the European colonisation of the region an unequal relationship had developed between the pastoralists and the urban mercantile class that inhabited the cities (Ahmed Samatar 1988: 14–15). The Ajuran Islamic state in southern Somalia (1400–1600), the Geledi Sultanate along the Shabelle, and the nineteenth-century Majeerteen sultanates in the north-east, are evidence that Somali society and state structures are not necessarily inimical. It is important to appreciate that Somali pastoralist society is not constituted on the basis of centralised institutions, but it is not without governance or rules. Historically, Somali pastoralists lived in what has been described as a state of 'ordered anarchy',[7] whereby political order and social relations are maintained through the kinship system, through collective social institutions and through reciprocal, rule-bound behaviour delineated in customary law (*xeer*).

While clan-families represent the highest level of political solidarity in Somali pastoral society, numerically they are too large to act as collective political units. Amongst northern pastoralists the smallest unit where effective cooperation, political action and collective security are feasible is the *diya*-paying group (Lewis 1961). This comprises a number of families[8] who are united through genealogy (*tol*) and marriage ties (*xidid*) and who are obliged to protect one another and to pay and receive 'blood compensation' (*diya*)[9] for murder and other injuries. As *diya* is traditionally paid in the form of livestock (in the case of murder at 100 camels for a man and 50 for a woman), it provides a sanction against violence and reinforces collective responsibility.

Traditionally in Somali pastoral society governance is decentralised and based on consensus. Authority is exercised by lineage elders (*odayaasha*), who assemble in councils (*shir*) to deliberate on matters affecting the clan, such as the payment of *diya* or the declaration of war. Historically, these clan councils have not been permanent institutions, but *ad hoc* gatherings formed in response to particular needs and, depending on the issue at hand, might last for days or weeks. When a conflict arises a special committee, called a *Guurti*, may be formed to facilitate its resolution.[10] In this acephalous society any adult male can be considered an elder (*oday*) with an equal right to speak in a council. As representatives rather than leaders with executive authority, they are chosen by their clans for their particular

---

[7] This phrase was applied to another stateless society – the Nuer – by the anthropologist Evans-Pritchard, but well describes Somali society (Evans-Pritchard 1974 [1946]).

[8] A *diya*-paying group may comprise several hundred families.

[9] Arabic for blood, known as *mag* in Somali.

[10] In Somali pastoral society, *a guurti* is traditionally the highest political council, comprising titled and non-titled clan leaders selected for their knowledge and wisdom (Farah and Lewis 1993: 17).

attributes, which may include age, experience, powers of oratory and wealth. Some lineages have a titular head known variously as a *Suldaan* (Sultan) among the Isaaq, *Garaad, Islaan* and *Boqor* among the Darod, *Ugaas* among the Hawiye and Gadabursi, and *Malaaq* among the Rahanweyn. Although their titles can be inherited, they traditionally lack the executive power of chiefs, and act instead as arbiters and peacemakers within their clans and for others. In a peace meeting (*shir nabadeedka*) it is the elders who undertake the negotiations, while the Sultan approves the outcome.

The acephalous structure and diffused authority give Somali society an egalitarian ethos. But inequalities do exist, such as between genders and between generations, or between Somali nomads and agriculturalists, or Somalis and non-Somalis. Demographic growth also means that lineages grow and over time divide into sub-lineages of unequal size; some even die out. Somalis distinguish between smaller branches (*laan-gaab*) and larger branches (*laan-dheere*) of lineages. The *laan-dheere*, which trace a longer line of descent from the founding ancestor, are numerically larger and, because they can call on more kinsmen, are potentially stronger and politically more powerful than the *laan-gaab*. Consequently, they are often favoured in terms of political representation.

Kinship ties alone are insufficient to achieve social cohesion and cooperation. This requires rules of behaviour and agreements between groups that define collective rights and responsibilities and further common interests. In Somali society these rights and obligations are laid down in unwritten agreements or contracts between clans, known as *xeer*, that are transmitted orally through generations. In addition to *xeer*, traditional values (*xeer caado*) and a code of social conduct (*xeer dhagan*) also serve to mitigate conflict and maintain public order. The precise nature and application of *xeer* is debated among Somalis and cannot be dealt with adequately here,[11] but they exist at different levels of lineage segmentation, between members of particular sub-clans, clans, and clan families. Collectively they form a repository of customary law (*xeer somali*), which includes elements of *shari'a* law, that defines basic social norms and values. This body of customary law is comparable to the Western political notion of a 'social contract', regulating political relations between groups.[12] The interpretation and application of *xeer* are the responsibility of particular lineage elders (*xeer beegti*) whose knowledge of *xeer* is respected. Traditionally, judicial proceedings are normally held in public, and emphasis is placed on arbitration and the production of a

[11] For discussions of *xeer* see, for example, Lewis 1961; Ahmed Samatar 1994; Puntland Development Research Centre 2003; Le Sage 2005.

[12] One broad category (*xeer guud*) defines the reciprocal rights and obligations of kin in domestic matters, such as the payment of *diya* or dowry, political relations between groups, and the conduct of warfare such as the protected status of certain social groups, including women, children, religious leaders, guests and in-laws. Another category (*xeer gaar*) covers economic relations, among the most important of which are those dealing with entitlements to pasture and water and the management of environmental resources.

consensual agreement. Together, the collective councils of elders, the office of *Suldaan* and *xeer* provide institutional mechanisms for managing turbulent change and conflict.

As ecological and demographic pressures, together with external and political forces, can give rise to competition over natural resources, conflict was never far from the surface in nomadic pastoral society. Traditionally, the role of men was to be a spear-bearing warrior (*waranle*) or a man of God (*wadaad*) (Lewis 2002: 15). Anthropologists have argued that under subsistence conditions feuding and warfare can serve a political function, either by regulating relations between groups and enabling them to adjust to demographic, economic and environmental change (Turton 1989), or by symbolically delineating the political and cultural boundaries of ethnic groups (Fukui 1994). But warfare can only serve such functions when rules exist to condition its scale and nature, and mechanisms exist for its resolution. It has been argued that as semi-subsistence economies in Africa were transformed by their integration into market economies and the creation of new forms of exchange relations, a shrinking resource base, decaying governance and the spread of automatic weapons, such reciprocal systems collapsed and warfare changed 'from a means of adaptation to an agent for destruction' (Duffield 1990: 18).

Historically, in subsistence societies the aim of warfare was not to vanquish the enemy completely, but to establish political ascendancy that ensured access to resources. Disputes over grazing land or water, although often violent, typically involved negotiation and the formation of alliances. Somali society has strong traditions of mediation, reconciliation and consensus-building alongside customary institutions of law and order, and feuding and warfare in Somali society was traditionally regulated by rules and social conventions. For example, women, children, religious leaders, guests, community leaders, the elderly, enemy captives, war wounded, the sick and peace delegates were traditionally immune to attack and were 'spared from the spear' (*biri-ma-geydo)* (ICRC/SRCS 1997). Titled heads of clans were not supposed to participate in or encourage war, but counsel against it, and certain weapons and violent practices were prohibited. The theft of camels and horses was permissible, but to limit the economic impact of warfare the looting of small stock and household assets that were essential to the sustenance of women and children was prohibited. Public utilities such as wells that benefited all were also protected. Such codes of war (*xeerka biri-ma-geydada*) were enforced through a sense of honour, agreed methods of compensation, and a fear of divine retribution (*cuquubo*) for attacks on the weak and vulnerable, who are protected by God.

The introduction of secular law by colonial authorities, the practice of investing lineage elders with an authority that they did not possess previously, and efforts by Somali governments to codify customary law and to modernise it, have all impacted on Somali *xeer*. But the weak presence of the state in most rural areas means that, for many people, *xeer* remained the main source of law and the first recourse for settling disputes and hostilities. The civil war in the 1990s has impacted on *xeer* in several ways. On the one hand, social norms were violated and crimes were committed for which there was no precedent, and *xeer* could not deal with these breaches. Armed militia rejected clan authority, and the standing of elders as trusted neutral parties was often compromised. On the other hand, with the collapse of formal judicial institutions *xeer* regained significance in regulating and restoring social relations. It has been observed that in many places state collapse served to re-invigorate these institutions (Menkhaus 2005). As will be seen in later chapters, in Somaliland the social institutions of elders and clan councils and time-honoured cultural practices of mediation, arbitration, consensus decision-making, and the restoration of *xeer* between clans, far from being an anachronism, played a critical role in post-war governance and state-building.

Islam

Adherence to Islam is a fundamental pillar of Somali society. Reinforced by a belief in their common descent from the lineage of the Prophet,[13] it provides a common thread of identity that can cut across clan divisions and kinship loyalties. Somali children are raised into the practice and morality of Islam through Qur'anic education and Islam informs many aspects of cultural life and attitudes.

Islam probably arrived in the Somali peninsula, brought by Arab and Persian traders, soon after the faith emerged in the deserts of Arabia (Lewis 2002: 20). Somalis traditionally adhere to the *shafi'i* school of *sunni* Islam and historically the majority of Somalis have belonged to one of the three *sufi* orders (*Dariiqa*): the Qaadiriya, the oldest order founded in the twelfth century which has the largest number of followers; the Ahmadiya founded in the eighteenth century and influenced by the *Wahaabi* reformist movement; and its offshoot, the more puritanical Saalahiya. The latter became the inspiration for the religious and proto-nationalist warrior sheikh, Sayyid Mahammed Abdalla Hassan, whose Dervish (*Daraawiish*) movement fought a holy war against the colonial powers in the late nineteenth and early twentieth centuries.

Islam as practised by Somalis has had a distinctive character, fusing local traditions and beliefs with Islam. The founding ancestors of Somali clans have been assimilated as saints whose graves are venerated sites of pilgrimage; Somali customary law incorporates elements of *shari'a*; and, against the tendency in many Islamic societies, sheikhs (*wadaad*) have

---

[13] The Darod, Dir and Hawiye trace their descent from Aqil Abu Talib, son of the Prophet's nephew Abu Talib and married to the Prophet's daughter Fatima. The Isaaq trace their descent from Aqil Abu Talib's brother Ali.

traditionally not held political power in their communities, other than at exceptional times. Instead, their typical role has been a pastoral one, caring for the religious needs of their people. At certain periods in history and in different locations Islam has played a more decisive organisational and political role among Somali communities. The theocratic Ajuran state in the fourteenth and sixteenth centuries is one example. At certain times charismatic religious leaders have emerged and founded religious communities (*jameeca*) which have drawn together people of different clans. The nineteenth century was a period of European colonisation and Islamic revivalism in the Horn of Africa, which produced a proliferation of religious settlements across the Somali peninsula, and the emergence of two charismatic leaders – Sayyid Mahammed Abdalla Hassan and Sheikh Uways Mohamed al Baraawi from Brava whose followers founded the Uwayisiya order (Said Samatar 1992b). The emergence of these Islamic movements was part of a wider phenomenon occurring in the Islamic world, caused by the decline of the Ottoman Empire and what Muslims perceived as the subjugation of their lands and co-religionists in Africa and the Middle East to European-Christian rule (Said Samatar 1992a; Ahmed Samatar 1988: 24–5). The crisis in the Muslim world gave rise to new *sufi* orders and the emergence of more puritanical and militant forms of Islam. In Africa it sparked the *jihad* of the Mahdi in Sudan in the 1880s, the Dervishes in Somalia from the late 1890s, and the Sanussi movement in Libya in the early 1900s. These reformist movements advocated that the only way to regain divine favour was to live in strict accordance with God's laws and resist foreign rule through a *jihad*.

After the Sayyid and the Dervishes were defeated in 1920, Islam as a political force in Somalia remained largely dormant until the 1990s. Political developments in the Islamic world did not go unnoticed, but religious activism found little support during the period of civilian government in the 1960s, or under the military regime of Mohamed Siyad Barre which sought to marry socialism and Islam (Lewis 2002: 220). This changed in the 1990s. The social, economic and political dislocation caused by the war and the absence of secular state institutions led to a revival of religious practice and the adoption of new Islamic creeds (Marchal 2004; ICG 2005b). New commercial networks with Islamic states, funding from Islamic countries and the opportunistic strategies of factional leaders have all encouraged the proliferation of Islamic organisations, including welfare charities, courts and militant *jihadist* groups with both a local and a global political agenda (Le Sage 2004). The latter have also been stimulated by political developments elsewhere in the Islamic world and the so-called 'war on terrorism'. Indeed there are certain parallels here with the rise of reformist movements in the nineteenth century in response to a world crisis in Islam. As we have seen, in 2006 this tendency gave rise to the powerful Union of Islamic Courts, which took control of large areas of southern Somalia.

The political impact of these developments has, to date, been felt most keenly in southern Somalia, where in the absence of any organised government, Islamic courts, Islamic charities and militant Islamic groups have been politically active. Religious groups did play a role in the early military struggle of the SNM against the Barre regime, but their influence in post-war Somaliland has mostly been limited to social programmes, such as in education, and some changes in social and cultural practices. The growing influence of *Wahaabism*, for example, has led to a decline in the practice of venerating Somali saints. Since 2001, however, the threat posed by militant Islamic groups in Somaliland has become clearer. After the targeted killing of several foreign aid workers in 2003 and 2004, Somaliland finds itself being drawn into the conflict between the forces of militant Islam and the so-called 'war on terror'.

2

The Rise   of the State
& Fall   of Somalia

The collapse of the state of Somalia in 1991 signalled the end of a long state-building endeavour. The decision of the clan elders and the Somali National Movement (SNM) leadership to withdraw Somaliland from the union with Somalia was not based on an established SNM policy, but was a response to events unfolding in Mogadishu and grievances felt by the people of Somaliland after a decade of war. Since then, Somalilanders have further justified their actions by pointing to the existence of Somaliland as a political entity before 1960 and stating their belief that the union with Somalia was a failure. They trace this failure to several factors: the incomplete integration of two polities that had developed under different colonial administrations; the unequal political and economic relationship between the territories; the failure of the union to unite all the Somali territories in the Horn of Africa and the unravelling of Somali nationalism; the oppressive authoritarianism of Mohamed Siyad Barre's government in the 1970s and 1980s; and the increasing margin-alisation of the Isaaq within the state.

To understand the reasons for state collapse and the withdrawal of Somaliland from the union, it is necessary to reflect briefly on the history of modern state formation for the Somali people. This falls roughly into three periods. The first and longest (1827–1960) covers the period of European colonisation of the Horn of Africa and the division of the Somali people into five states. The second period (1960–9) covers the first nine years of the independent Somali Republic, when the Somali people under a civilian government joined the world of independent nation-states. In the third period (1969–91) democratic government was replaced by the military-led regime of General Mohamed Siyad Barre, who held power for twenty-one years until violently overthrown.

Although state collapse is today commonly identified as an outcome of war, historically state formation has often been a violent process. Somalia was no exception. In the first two decades of the twentieth century British and Italian colonists fought the Dervish armies of Sayyid Mahammed

Abdalla Hassan. In the 1920s and 1930s, Somali people were subjected to Italian fascist rule and during the Second World War Britain and Italy fought over the territory. After independence nationalist efforts to reunite the 'lost' Somali territories became a source of regional conflicts with Kenya and Ethiopia, culminating in the Ogaden war of 1977–8. Then, between 1988 and 1991, after more than one hundred years in the making and thirty years of independence, the Somali state was dismantled in four years of internecine warfare.

In tracing this history of state formation, it is important to recognise that both Somaliland and Somalia are a legacy of the territorial division of the Horn of Africa by European colonial powers. Although at independence the Somali Republic was considered to be unique among Africa's multi-ethnic states – as a nation-state founded upon a single ethnic group, the Somali – in fact the nation was divided and the nation-state incomplete. The consequences of this resonate today in the separatist aspirations of people in Somaliland, in the nationalist and irredentist aspirations of people in Somalia, and in the regional politics of the Horn. The civil war and the break-up of Somalia also challenge the assumption that common ethnicity and culture is a 'natural' basis for nationalism and a secure basis on which to construct a state. It is also important to recognise that colonial rule implanted a model of centralised state governance into a stateless society of nomadic pastoralists, whose political system was uncentralised. From its foundations, the state of Somalia, although shaped by local culture, was largely a foreign construct sustained by foreign resources and subject to foreign strategic interests. The outcome by the 1980s was an ineffective and predatory state that, in the words of Luling (1997: 289), was 'suspended above a society that would never have produced it and did not demand it'.

The Somaliland Protectorate

Over a hundred years of European commercial and political engagement in the Horn of Africa, from 1827 to 1960, has had a profound influence on the development of Somalia and Somaliland. When the Europeans arrived in the Somali region in the nineteenth century they encountered several cultures: an interior populated by stateless nomadic pastoralists; sedentary farming and agro-pastoral cultures along the southern river valleys; and rudimentary city states along the northern and eastern coastlines. The historian Cassanelli (1982) has argued that European colonialism accelerated the emergence of what was already an 'embryonic nation'. But, while there may have been a sense of common cultural identity among Somali-speaking peoples, prior to colonisation they lived in a stateless society. Arab and Asian traders had long inducted Somalis into a world religion and regional trade networks. It was European colonisation that integrated the Somali people, territorially, politically and economically, into an international political system constructed on the basis of nation-states. If an embryonic Somali nation did exist prior to European colonisation, then one of the consequences of colonial engagement was to divide it. Between 1827 and 1900, Britain, Italy, France and Abyssinia carved up the Somali-inhabited regions into five states: the British Somaliland Protectorate, Somalia Italiana, Côte Français des Somaliens (now Djibouti), the Northern Frontier District of Kenya, and the Abyssinian Empire of Menelik II.

The impact of this has been profound and long-lasting. First, the international borders between Ethiopia, Djibouti, Kenya and Somalia cut through the pastoralists' rangelands, leaving Somali clans living in more than one state. Aspirations of Somalis to re-unite the 'lost' Somali territories in a Greater Somalia have subsequently driven national politics and regional conflicts. These include the religious and proto-nationalist struggle of Sayyid Mahammed Abdalla Hassan in the first two decades of the twentieth century, Somalia's clashes with Kenya and Ethiopia in the 1960s, and its war with Ethiopia over the Ogaden in the late 1970s. The tensions involved in delineating the Somali nation-state continue to permeate the current political dynamics. The different attitude among Somalis to Somaliland's claim of independence is one example. The claims in 2006 of pan-Somali support by the leaders of the UIC who revived the spectre of Somali irredentism and animosity to Ethiopia are other examples.[1]

Second, the countries that colonised the region in the nineteenth century had diverse reasons for doing so and intervened in different ways in the territories that they ruled. While the creation of a state with a centralised and hierarchical system of government was a common legacy of European colonisation, the process by which this was accomplished differed. This affected the kind of colonial state that emerged in Somaliland and, as will be suggested, the trajectory of the civil war in the 1990s and the make-up of Somaliland today owe much to the particular form taken by British colonial engagement. Several features of British colonisation are noted here: the reluctance of Britain to invest in Somaliland; the system of 'indirect rule' to govern the territory; the development of a mixed economy; and the development of an urban-based governing class.

The British were in many respects reluctant colonialists. Britain had no grand designs to occupy and develop a colony in Somali territory. Within the imperial empire Somaliland was always a 'peripheral' colony, subject to Britain's broader colonial strategy (Abdi Samatar 1989: 31). The territory, without resources to exploit or a settler population to protect, did not require the development of a colonial administration, and in any

---

[1] The animosity in 2006 between the UIC and the Ethiopian government is the latest in a very long history of hostilities between Somalis and Ethiopia that stretches back to the sixteenth-century wars between the Ethiopian empire and the Islamic forces of Ahmed Gran (the 'left handed') (Lewis 2002: 25–6).

case offered a tax base of limited potential on which to finance a state bureaucracy. Britain's interest in the region was driven by commercial and geopolitical interests and it only incrementally increased its engagement because of imperial interests elsewhere, or in response to particular events in the region. Indeed, British, French and Italian interests in the region were all initiated by commercial companies. The need to protect the valuable trade routes to Asia and the Far East gave the Somali-inhabited region on the Gulf of Aden and the Indian Ocean a strategic importance. The first formal treaty between a Somali clan and a European country was signed in 1827 by a representative of the British East African Company (Lewis 2002: 33).[2]

The importance of the Somali region for Britain increased significantly after 1839, when it occupied the Red Sea port of Aden in present-day Yemen and established a coaling station and a garrison there to safeguard the sea routes of its eastern trading empire and the imperial 'jewel', India. In order to feed Aden's garrison Britain entered into a series of treaties with northern Somali clans to provide a supply of meat, mainly sheep. The opening of the Suez Canal in 1869 increased Aden's strategic significance and with it the importance of the Somali coast, but did not warrant the establishment of a British presence there. Between 1870 and 1884 Britain reluctantly accepted Egyptian occupation of the coast as long as it did not interfere with the meat supply to Aden.[3] British political interest increased after 1883 when Egypt came under its control and in response to the Mahdist revolt in Sudan Egyptian forces were withdrawn from the Horn of Africa. As European powers were drawn into a scramble for political influence in the region, the 'protection' treaties that Britain had signed with Somali clans gained greater significance in pre-empting the territorial ambitions of Italy, France and Abyssinia. Nevertheless, it took further pressure from the government of India before the British government finally authorised the occupation of Somaliland (Abdi Samatar 1989: 30). Britain's lack of imperial ambitions was underlined by the fact that it assigned responsibility for the administration of the territory to the government of India, which used customs duties raised in Somaliland to pay for the patrol of the Red Sea (Federal Research Division 1993: 160). In 1886, after entering a series of protection treaties with clans of the 'Iise, Gadabursi and Isaaq, British vice-consuls were posted to Berbera, Zeyla and Bulahar. The Indian government, which was adamant that Somaliland would only be a coastal colony, spelled out what the nature of the colony was to be:

> The primary objectives of Government are to secure a supply market, to check the traffic in slaves, and to exclude the interference of foreign powers. It is consistent with these objectives, and with the protectorate

---

[2] The treaty was to provide safe passage for cargo ships plying the Somali coast following an attack by Somalis on a British vessel, the *Mary Ann*, in 1825.

[3] In 1887 Britain recognised Egyptian jurisdiction as far south as Ras Hafun (Lewis 2002: 42).

which the Indian Government has assumed, to interfere as little as possible with the customs of the people, and to have them administer their own internal affairs. (quoted in Abdi Samatar 1989: 31)

While the colonial government professed not to want to interfere with the people's internal affairs, Britain's geopolitical interests did have an impact. The territory of Somaliland was delineated in a series of political treaties with France in 1888, Italy in 1894, and Ethiopia in 1897 and 1954, in which Somalis were not consulted. At stake were British rather than Somali interests. The Anglo-Ethiopian treaty of 1897, which established the boundaries of the Protectorate, was as much concerned to protect British interests in Sudan as to address relations in the Somali territories.[4] This treaty, which gave Ethiopia control over the Ogaden and parts of the important wet season grazing lands of the Haud, had long-term ramifications for Ethiopian-Somali relations. A more immediate impact was to make it easier for the Ethiopian state to exact tribute from Somalis in the Ogaden, which galvanised support for the *jihad* of Sayyid Mahammed Abdalla Hassan in 1899, an event that forced Britain to deepen its engagement in Somaliland.

Born near Buhoodle on the current border of Somaliland and Ethiopia in 1856, Mahammed Abdalla Hassan was a convert to the puritanical *sufi* Saalahiya brotherhood.[5] His efforts to convince his fellow Muslims to join the Saalahiya path found little support among Somalis, who were mostly adherents of the Qaadiriya order, until he added a nationalist fervour to his preaching and launched an anti-colonial uprising in the late 1890s. This was precipitated by raids on Somali communities in the Ogaden by Christian Ethiopians who were fleeing famine in the highlands, during which hundreds of thousands of livestock were lost and several Islamic religious centres were sacked (Bemath 1992). Abdi Samatar (1989: 35–7) argues that the crisis this created among Somali communities required a supra-clan response. Using his religious authority and his skills as an orator and poet – an art much revered in Somali society – Sayyid Mahammed Abdalla Hassan mobilised Muslim fighters (known as the Dervishes or *Daraawiish*) to defend Somali communities. In 1899 the Sayyid, as he had become known among his followers, forced the British to take notice when he declared a *jihad* against all Christian colonisers and his Dervishes sacked the towns of Burco and Sheikh, the latter being an important centre of the Qaadiriya order. Alarmed at this new *jihad* so soon after the Mahdist revolt in Sudan, the British responded with force. However, they underestimated the support for the Sayyid, whom they mockingly nicknamed the Mad Mullah, and found themselves embroiled in a war that was to last two decades.

---

[4] At the time, Emperor Menelik of Ethiopia was threatening to enter an alliance with the Khalifa in Sudan (Lewis 2002: 56–62).

[5] For descriptions of Sayyid Mohamed Abdullah Hassan and his holy wars see Lewis 2002: 65–85; Ahmed Samatar 1988: 24-40; Said Samatar 1992b; Bemath 1992.

Twenty years of warfare at the beginning of the twentieth century devastated the Somali territories in a way that has some resonances with events in Somalia in the closing decade of the century. The mobilisation of the Dervishes and the arming of 'friendlies' by the British introduced new weaponry into the region that fermented inter-clan conflicts. The war precipitated a famine in 1911 and 1912 during which as many as one third of the Protectorate's population died (Lewis 2002: 77), a period remembered as *Xaarame Cune* (the 'time of eating filth'). The war, which affected both the northern and southern regions of the peninsula, only ended in 1920 when the British were able to commit sufficient forces after the First World War to a combined land and air offensive against the Dervishes. During its first foray into Africa, the Royal Air Force bombed the Dervish headquarters in Taleh, in the present-day Sool region.[6]

The impact of the Dervish uprising on state formation is complex. For resisting the foreign armies for two decades and mobilising cross-clan support, and for his poetry which extols a great pride in Somali culture, Sayyid Mahammed Abdalla Hassan was subsequently adopted by Somalis as a symbol of putative Somali nationalism. However, except for a short period between 1905 and 1909 when the British and Italian authorities granted him control over an area of territory in northeast Somalia which he ruled as a theocracy, the Sayyid failed to establish a pan-Somali state. Brons (2001: 139–41) suggests that a combination of the Sayyid's use of clan politics, competition between the religious orders and the diverse experience of Somalis under the different colonial powers prevented the formation of a pan-Somali state based on consent, and the Dervishes were unable to impose one through force.

The legacy of this period has contemporary resonances in Somaliland. The Sayyid drew much of his support from the Dhulbahante and Ogaden clans of his maternal and paternal lineages (and to a lesser extent from the Warsengeli), with whom the British had no treaties (Lewis 2002: 68). His attack on the Qaadiriya settlement in Sheikh, which was aimed at disrupting the political and economic relationship between the Isaaq leaders and the British administration, encouraged many Isaaq to side with the colonialists. This history is vividly recalled in Somaliland when tensions arise between the Isaaq and the Dhulbahante.[7]

A more immediate consequence for state formation was to expand Britain's colonial administration in Somaliland. For a long period of the war the British had remained in the coastal towns, leaving the Dervishes in control of much of the interior. In order to prosecute the war effectively, however, they were eventually forced to venture inland and, after the Dervishes were defeated, Britain gradually extended its control over the territory. The pace of colonial expansion nevertheless remained slow. Britain still had no interest in creating a colony and therefore placed little emphasis on creating a large administration. In 1911 the

---

[6] Mohamed Abdallah Hassan died through illness in December 1920.
[7] Interviews by the author in Las Anod, September 1993.

colony had established only one municipality – in Berbera – and employed only thirty-six Europeans (Abdi Samatar 1989: 42). By 1920 five administrative districts had been established (in Berbera, Hargeysa, Zeyla, Burco and Erigavo) each with a district commissioner (*ibid.*: 48). However, as late as 1955, when I. M. Lewis arrived in Hargeysa, the entire Protectorate was run by fewer than two hundred expatriate officers (Lewis 1994a: 5). Despite the expanse of territory, it was feasible to administer it with a light touch owing to the small scale of the population, estimated at 350,000 in the 1930s, and the relatively 'compact and homogeneous' nature of the clans (Lewis 2002: 104). Minimal government was accomplished by incorporating local political structures through a system of 'indirect rule'.

Indirect rule – the key doctrine for British colonial administration in Africa – was intended to create a system of stable governance and limit resistance to colonialism by reinforcing traditional forms of authority (Willis 2003). In most colonies this approach rested on the presence of chiefly authorities. As these did not exist in Somali society a different strategy was required. In Somaliland the British made senior elders of *diya*-paying groups – understood to be the basic political institution in Somali society – part of the state system by bestowing upon them the title of 'chief' (*caaqil*), providing them with a government stipend, and giving them limited judicial and revenue-collecting powers.[8] Some elders were also incorporated into the administration as judges (*qaadiyo*) in local courts. As the 'chiefs' were entitled to a proportion of fines that were collected they had a stake in enforcing colonial ordinances, and their authority was reinforced with rural police (*illaalo*) attached to the office of the district commissioner.

The impact of this imperial intrusion on Somali society is contested by scholars. Some argue that the colonial system of governance affected the political structure of Somali pastoral society in important ways (Abdi Samatar 1989: 44; Jimcaale 2005). By elevating the authority of elders from solely managing kinship relations the relationships of authority within the clan changed. The presence of a district commissioner with executive decision-making power may have weakened the role of elders in the management of environmental resources, for example. The introduction of a Western judicial system that emphasised individual responsibility challenged the system of customary law, and district courts may have diluted the function of the *shir*. It is argued that clan identity was politicised in new ways, as the arming of 'friendlies' altered the balance of power between some clans and the state's allocation of rights to pasture and water to certain lineages reinforced communal identity and territorial exclusivity. As new forms of wealth accumulated in the state, the role of clan leadership changed from managing kinship relations and

---

[8] The position and title of *caaqil* was introduced by the Egyptians and expanded by the British. The *caaqil* were mostly drawn from the *laan-dheere* (long) lineages, although a few came from the *laan-gaab* (Jimcaale 2005: 119 fn 4).

entitlements to pastoral resources to also managing access to the political and economic benefits of the state, such as the right to export licences, the collection of taxes or the ownership of wells. The practice of incorporating elders and titled heads of clans into the structures of the state was followed to varying degrees by Somalia's post-independence governments and became a means of distributing state patronage.

Others suggest that the limited investment in the Protectorate by Britain left rural society largely untouched and did not significantly alter the political structure of pastoral society (Lewis 2002). The system of indirect rule served to reinforce indigenous political institutions in a way that contrasted with southern Somalia, where Italy sought to create a colony as a source of primary goods and a place for settling Italy's burgeoning population. This involved a much more brutal assault on society. In 1900 the Benadir Commercial Company, which administered the territory before the imposition of fascist rule in 1923, was accused of perpetuating slavery in contravention of Italy's treaty obligations (Pankhurst 1951). In order to facilitate land alienation for plantation agriculture lineage authority was undermined (Ahmed Samatar 1988: 49). It has been suggested that the consequent weakening of traditional institutions can help to explain the protracted nature of the conflict in southern Somalia since the 1990s and the difficulty of restoring political order there. In contrast, as will be suggested in later chapters, one legacy of indirect rule in Somaliland was to reinforce indigenous political institutions in a way that has proved vital to the ability of people in Somaliland to reconstitute a polity in the aftermath of the civil war.

Colonisation also brought some significant economic developments, laying the foundations for a mixed economy comprising livestock production and export, a small rain-fed agricultural sector, an urban entrepreneurial sector, and a public sector of salaried officials and civil servants. With the British occupation of Aden in 1839, trade in live animals and hides had come to dominate exports and to underpin Somaliland's economy. The expansion of trade and the commercialisation of livestock production had important socio-economic impacts on what previously had been a family-centred, semi-subsistence economy, and on customary resource management systems. One important impact was to create a new trading structure with internal marketing centres. Hargeysa, Berbera and Burco became the hubs of the trade and to this day they remain the centre of economic development in Somaliland. The trade gave rise to a new urban mercantile class and embryonic urbanisation, and created a new set of economic relationships between pastoralists, merchants and the state (Swift 1979). A politically egalitarian Somali pastoral society became economically divided.

As in other spheres, the intervention of the colonial state in the rural economy was limited. But as export tariffs were one of the main sources of revenue, the administration invested in boosting production by building water reservoirs in the Haud and introducing veterinary services.

The water reservoirs prolonged the period that pastoralists could graze their stock in the Haud and encouraged sedentarisation, while the veterinary services supported an increase in herd sizes. As land use changed from raising livestock for subsistence to rearing livestock for the market, the exploitation of rangelands intensified, giving rise to fears of environmental degradation as early as the 1930s (Abdi Samatar 1989: 17), and increasing the vulnerability of the pastoralist families to drought. The political treaties between the colonial powers created borders that did not respect clan territories and curbed the mobility of pastoralists, leaving them more vulnerable to seasonal variations in climate and pasture. The pace of transformation of the rural economy increased significantly from the 1950s, when new oil wealth in the Gulf States generated a huge demand for Somali livestock. This economic boom in the Gulf States also encouraged economic migration from Somalia and the development of a remittance economy that plays a crucial role in Somaliland's economy today.

Although, as a result of the war with the Dervishes, Britain had expanded its engagement in Somaliland, its investment in the development of the territory remained minimal. The military operations against the Dervishes had consumed considerable resources and the British Foreign Office, which had taken over responsibility for administration from India in 1898, remained ill-disposed to invest in Somaliland's development. Taxation on imports and exports was the main source of revenue.[9] The administration therefore relied heavily on the imperial treasury for grants and loans; grants were provided for military expenditure, while loans for development had to be paid back through taxation. Consequently between 1920 and 1940 the colony stagnated: a few roads were cleared, some agricultural projects were started, a few schools were built and some students were sent to Sudan for education (at their parents' expense). The slow pace of development was interrupted by the onset of the Second World War and Italy's brief occupation of Somaliland in 1941. After the war, when Somaliland reverted to the status of a British Protectorate, Britain took a few measures to bolster its authority by strengthening law enforcement and improving public services and infrastructure, but it continued to eschew major investment. Between 1951 and 1955 annual internal revenues in British Somaliland averaged only £860,000 and the Protectorate's budget was subsidised by the British exchequer to the tune of £1.2 million per year (Reno 2003: 13). This was a meagre sum, but it nevertheless established a pattern of financing Somali state structures with foreign subsidies that continues today. One of the main beneficiaries was a new class of urban-based salaried officials.

One important legacy of colonialism was the creation of an urbanised class of bureaucrats, civil servants and traders. In Somaliland this

---

[9] In 1920 an attempt to introduce a head tax provoked violent disturbances during which the district commissioner of Burco was killed, thus limiting options for increasing state revenue.

constituted a small educated elite. Religious resistance to foreign educa-tion[10] and the limited demand by the Protectorate for an educated cadre meant that Britain invested as little in education as it did in other spheres. Consequently, only a small number of schools were established offering a high standard of education, the best pupils from which were sent to Sudanese or British universities. As late as 1956 there were only 60 places available in the Protectorate's two secondary schools (Abdi Samatar 1989: 72). By the 1950s the educated elite was caught up in the wave of anti-colonial sentiment that was sweeping Africa and they provided the cadre for emerging Somali nationalist organisations. The most prominent of these were the Somalia-wide Somali Youth League, established during the British Military Administration of 1943, which dominated Somali politics up to and after independence, and the Somali National League, which became the leading nationalist party in Somali-land. These parties and others, such as the National United Front and the United Somali Party, all supported independence and the union of the Somali territories. Only one party, the Hizbi al Dastuur Mustaqil al Somali (Somali Independent Constitutional Party) representing the Digil-Mirifle, took a different stance, advocating regional autonomy and federalism. The general lack of education in-country meant that the new political parties were founded by and represented the urban class of merchants, military officers, civil servants, religious leaders and Somalis living abroad.[11] Influenced by a Western discourse that promoted the state as the natural and appropriate form of political community, they delegiti-mised other forms of non-state political community. Control of the state therefore became central to the anti-colonial struggle (Dixon 2002: 72). Clanism was considered an anathema to the nationalist cause and aspirations to create a Greater Somalia. This small elite that was educated during the colonial period and their network of relationships has had a long and significant influence on Somali politics. The first two presidents of the Republic of Somaliland – Abdirahman Ahmed Ali 'Tuur' and Mohamed Haji Ibrahim Egal – both began their political careers during this period.

After the Second World War, the UN General Assembly placed Somalia under a UN trusteeship to be administered by Italy until independence, scheduled for 1960. Under the eye of the UN the pace of development in southern Somalia and the 'Somalisation' of state institutions outpaced that in British-administered Somaliland. In 1954 Britain controversially ceded the Haud to Ethiopia.[12] This boosted pan-Somali nationalist

---

[10] It was assumed that the real intention was to spread Christianity.

[11] The first Somali society, the Somali Islamic Association, was formed by the Somaliland Protectorate community in Aden in the 1920s. This was not a political organisation, but took an interest in developments in the Protectorate and frequently petitioned the British government on Somali affairs. This Association was followed by the Somali National Society which emerged immediately after the Second World War.

[12] Ethiopia had gained these lands under the Anglo-Ethiopian treaty of 1897, which also preserved Somali grazing rights. By the second Anglo-Ethiopian Treaty of 1954 the British

sentiments in Somaliland, which held that Somali control and grazing rights in the Haud and Reserved Area could only be achieved through unity and independence. Unification also held out the promise of reaping greater development gains. Britain's 'benign neglect' of its colony (Prunier 1998: 225) meant that Somaliland was woefully underdeveloped. Following India's independence in 1947, the strategic value of the Protectorate to Britain diminished. Unwilling to sustain the financial burden, Britain responded to nationalist agitation by accelerating the timetable for self-government. In 1957 the first Legislative Council of Somaliland was formed and Somalis began to replace expatriate officials in government. In February 1960 elections were held for the Legislative Assembly and two months later Britain formally agreed to grant the Protectorate independence, a move approved by the Somaliland Council of Elders on 19 May 1960. On 26 June 1960, after seventy-six years under colonial administration, Somaliland was formally granted independence by Britain. For the next five days Somaliland existed as an independent sovereign state until it united with the Italian-administered UN Trust Territory of Somalia on 1 July 1960.

Unification & the democratic state

If Somalilanders today repudiate the union with Somalia, in 1960 Somaliland's politicians pursued it with enthusiasm. Smitten with the notion of bringing all Somali-speaking communities together within a Greater Somalia, the unification with Italian Somalia was also viewed as an essential step in securing Somalilanders' grazing rights in the Haud. At that time, the growth in the livestock trade was generating a modest economic boom and, with a qualified civil service and judiciary, Somali-landers were confident in their ability to engage with Somalia (Drysdale 1994: 132). But the leadership entered the post-colonial era with no agenda for addressing the scourges of underdevelopment and their 'blind faith' in the benefits of union meant no attention was given to the mechanics of integrating the two territories (Ahmed Samatar 1988: 48). Although a decision to unify the territories had been made by northern and southern leaders as early as April 1960, there was no agreed arrangement for amalgamating their institutions (Adam 1994: 3). The former colonies had developed different administrative systems, police forces, taxes, currencies and education systems, and they conducted official affairs in different languages. The new Republic also inherited four distinct legal traditions – British common law, Italian law, Islamic *shari'a* and Somali customary law. Almost immediately the 'dual colonial heritage' became an obstacle to integration (Lewis 2002: 170).

12 (cont.) Military Administration withdrew from the Haud and Reserved Area. Although Somali-landers' grazing rights were reaffirmed, they were subsequently abrogated at independence in 1960.

In Somaliland enthusiasm for the union began to wane as people were confronted with its consequences. Under British colonial rule the Isaaq clan had held a preponderance of administrative posts in Somaliland. With unification they became a minority in government. The President of Somalia, Adan Abdalla Osman, and Prime Minister, Abdirashid Ali Sharmarke, were southerners and the fourteen-member cabinet included only four northern ministers. The former Premier of Somaliland, Mohamed Ibrahim Egal, became the Minister of Defence. Only 26 per cent of parliamentary seats were allocated to the north and, with the senior ministries and senior army posts held by southerners, northerners felt politically marginalised within the new state. Economic contacts between the two regions were also constrained by the distance between the north and the capital in Mogadishu. People in the northwest saw their former capital Hargeysa reduced to a regional headquarters, while Mogadishu became the seat of the government, and national affairs. This imbalance in power sharing between the former colonies was in part a consequence of Britain's lack of investment in the Protectorate (Ahmed Samatar 1988; Samatar and Samatar 2003). Southern politicians were generally more advanced in the mechanics of government, having experienced a measure of self-rule under the Italian trusteeship since 1956, and the distribution of political posts reflected this. Nevertheless, as Lewis observes, 'northern pride found it hard to stomach this reduction in prestige' (2002: 172). Consequently, northerners in general and Isaaq in particular began to lose faith in the union and to dispute its legality.

In advance of unification the respective Somalia and Somaliland legislatures had approved two separate acts of union. However, because a joint Act of Union was not ready in time for unification on 1 July 1960,[13] it was retrospectively approved by Somalia's new national assembly a year later. Northerners who were becoming dissatisfied with the progress of the union argued that the act carried no force in the north because it had not been approved by the Somaliland legislature. A constitutional referendum in June 1961 highlighted the level of discontent, when more than half of the electorate in the former Protectorate voted against the provisional constitution (*ibid.*; Drysdale 1994: 133). The vote was carried by a majority in the south,[14] but in December of the same year a group of British-trained junior military officers in the north attempted an abortive coup, the purpose of which appeared to be to end the union. Charges of treason against them were dismissed by a judge on the grounds that, in the absence of an Act of Union, the court had no jurisdiction over Somaliland. The rejectionists took this as a vindication of their case.

Today people in Somaliland question the historic legality of the Act of

---

[13] In Somaliland 'the Union of Somaliland and Somalia Law' had been approved on 27 June 1960, a day after independence.

[14] The validity of the vote has been contested. Allegations of vote rigging in the south (Adam 1994: 6) are countered by arguments that the rejectionists in the north came from a narrow sectarian base (Samatar and Samatar 2003).

Union to support their independence claim (Rajagopal and Carroll 1992). In reality the union was not seriously challenged again and when Mohamed Ibrahim Egal, an Isaaq and Somaliland's former Premier, became Prime Minister of Somalia in 1967 integration appeared to be an accepted fact (Lewis 1993: 29). Northern discontent with the union did not disappear entirely, as we shall see, but many Somalis look back on the early years of independence as a period of hope and a time when Somalia gained a reputation for democratic rule in Africa by holding three elections within its first decade of independence. Nevertheless, during this period one can trace several developments that would contribute to the collapse of the state three decades later.

When the Somali Republic joined the world of independent nations in 1960 it did so as a nation-state that was poor, not entirely independent, and incomplete, with ill-defined borders and many Somalis living under 'foreign rule' in Ethiopia, Djibouti and northern Kenya. Colonialism bequeathed Somalia the political accoutrements of a modern state, but not an economy to sustain it. At independence some 65 per cent of the population were involved in subsistence herding and the country had no industrial base or mineral reserves. The GNP was estimated to be only US$56 million, *per capita* income US$28, and the literacy rate in urban areas as low as 4 to 8 per cent (Ahmed Samatar 1988: 77 fn3). Colonial state structures had been sustained by copious amounts of foreign finance and this continued after independence. In the British Protectorate the scale of the state bureaucracy and investments in development had been limited by a meagre revenue base and a reluctance to develop the colony. After independence the structures of the newly unified state were expanded and centrally orchestrated development programmes were initiated. To pay for this the government had to attract foreign capital. In the first three years of independence, some 31 per cent of the national budget was paid for by Italy and Britain (Abdi Samatar 1989: 87). A failure to invest in and develop a productive domestic economy meant that food imports increased, as did the country's reliance on foreign aid to sustain the state. Consequently, the scale of the post-colonial state in Somalia bore little relationship to its economy. In the words of Abdi Samatar, 'rather than being embedded in the productive fabric of the Somali economy, [it] was suspended over it' (*ibid.*: 83).

During the Cold War, Somali leaders proved adept at soliciting foreign finance, and from the 1960s to the 1980s Somalia was one of the highest *per capita* recipients of foreign aid in Africa. Somalia's Italian- and British-educated leaders initially favoured the West, but the non-aligned position that Somalia adopted at independence and its irredentist claims over the 'lost' Somali territories led it to into a relationship with the Soviet Union and China. In 1963 Britain granted independence to Kenya, which incorporated the Somali-inhabited Northern Frontier District (NFD). Britain's disregard for the results of a referendum in the NFD in which the majority voted for union with Somalia, provoked a four-year insurgency (known as the '*shifta* war')[15] and pushed Somalia into a relationship with the Soviet Union (Lewis 2002: 201). In 1964, Somali irredentism received a further blow when Somalia was defeated by Ethiopia in a clash over the Somali-inhabited Ogaden region of Ethiopia. Under the Premiership of Egal Somalia restored its relations with the West. But two important consequences of Somali irredentism and these Cold War manoeuvrings were the inauguration of an arms race in the Horn of Africa[16] and a deepening relationship between the Soviet Union and the Somali military.

European colonialism not only created a state in Somalia, but also fostered the development of the social classes that controlled it (Abdi Samatar 1989: 82). After independence the expanding state, resourced through foreign aid, became a focus of competition between the political and mercantile elites. As competition was mobilised along clan lines, politicians and their parties became increasingly fragmented and 'clanist' in their orientation, and parliamentary democracy progressively opaque. Only a handful of political parties had fought the first post-independence election. In 1969, 1,002 candidates from sixty-two parties competed for 123 seats in the National Assembly. As Samatar notes, that election, which was to be the last 'democratic' election for thirty years, 'was not a contest between competing ideologies, but a race for the greatest personal access and use of state resources' (*ibid.*: 111). Prospective candidates spent excessively during their campaigns, with the Prime Minister allegedly spending huge sums of public money to secure his victory. Following the election all but one of the members of the Assembly crossed the floor to join the ruling party, effectively turning Somalia into a one-party state. Somalia's parliament, once a symbol of democracy, had become a 'sordid marketplace where deputies traded their votes for personal rewards with scant regard for the interests of their constituents' (Lewis 1972: 399). The increasingly venal struggle among the elite eventually led to the collapse of Somalia's parliamentary democracy. In October 1969 Somalia's President, Abdirashid Ali Sharmarke, was killed by one of his security guards. On 21 October, as Parliament prepared to vote in his successor, the military took control of the state. Somalia's experiment with political democracy had lasted only nine years.

The military state

The 'bloodless revolution'

On taking power the military suspended the constitution, imprisoned

---

[15] The *shifta* war between 1963 and 1967 was a secessionist conflict in which the Somali people of the NFD fought to become part of a Greater Somalia. The conflict was given the name '*shifta*' by the Kenyan government after the Somali word for 'bandit'.

[16] To counter Soviet influence in Somalia, the US provided Ethiopia with development and military aid.

leading politicians and banned all parties. For the next twenty-one years the country was to be governed by a military regime, first in the guise of the Supreme Revolutionary Council and after 1976 as the Somali Revolutionary Socialist Party, led by the army commander and new head of state, Major-General Mohamed Siyad Barre. Given the dismal state of Somalia's parliamentary democracy in the late 1960s, the military coup was not entirely unexpected, nor entirely unwelcomed.[17] The military's pronouncement, articulated in the 'First Charter of the Revolution', that it intended to build a society based on justice and the right to work, to end corruption and tribalism, and to tackle the country's underdevelopment initially won broad public support. Within a year the coup was being recast as a 'bloodless revolution' and Scientific Socialism was adopted as the ideological framework for the country's development. Blending concepts of wealth-sharing and self-reliance with Marxism-Leninism, Islam and anti-imperialism, the revolutionary agenda struck a sympathetic chord with the Somali public. But if the takeover was bloodless the revolution was to produce one of Africa's most repressive governments. The concentration of political and economic power in the Somali state reached its zenith under Siyad Barre and under his management the seeds of state collapse were sown. It is in the context of this repressive state that claims for Somaliland's independence also need to be understood.

With public support the government set about addressing the country's problems with some energy. One of the first tasks was to deal with what were perceived as the divisive and debilitating effects of 'clanism'. This was not a new concern. Before independence the nationalist parties had sought to eliminate 'tribalism' in pursuit of unity. In the 1960s the governments had unsuccessfully sought to excise all public references to clans as being antithetical to the unity of the nation. The difference with the military regime was the rigour with which it approached the task when it launched its 'Campaign Against Tribalism' in 1971. Effigies of tribalism were ceremonially burnt and buried; the payment of *diya* (blood compensation) was outlawed and the death sentence introduced to replace it; *xeer* was to be replaced by secular law; marriages were henceforth to be celebrated at orientation centres and stripped of clan significance; *caaqil* were replaced, renamed 'peaceseekers' (*nabad-doon*) and integrated into the state machinery; the country was reconstituted into new regions which were renamed where necessary to exclude reference to clans; and place of settlement replaced lineage as the means of personal identification (Lewis 2002: 209–11). The intention was to turn a 'nation of nomads' into a modern state, to which people would look for leadership, security and welfare instead of the clan. Embodying the nation was its 'father', President Mohamed Siyad Barre.

Under the guidance of the Supreme Revolutionary Council the public

---

[17] An example had been set in Sudan only five months earlier, when Colonel Gaafar Numeiri took power and installed a socialist-leaning regime.

was mobilised through 'crash' development programmes and in the first few years considerable progress was made. A standard Somali orthography was introduced in 1972 and a national campaign to raise desperately low levels of literacy was launched which won international plaudits.[18] The socialist and non-aligned stance of the regime lost Somalia the support of the US and other Western countries, but won the backing of the Soviet Union. Under the 1974 Somalia Treaty of Friendship and Cooperation, the USSR provided Somalia with military and financial aid in return for access to the port of Berbera on the Gulf of Aden. Somalia also attracted support from China, whose construction of an all-weather road linking Mogadishu to Hargeysa was the second largest Chinese project in Africa at that time (Ahmed Samatar 1988: 127).

On the social front, women were empowered to take on greater political and economic roles outside the household, and amendments to the Family Law in 1974 enhanced their legal and economic rights, particularly in relation to inheritance. These progressive reforms were generally popular. However, the adoption of the Latin alphabet for the Somali script and the advancement of women's rights drew vocal opposition from Islamic scholars. In 1975, in a demonstration both of the regime's secular stance and of its intention to defy all opposition, ten Islamic leaders were executed for sedition and anti-revolutionary activities. This incident served to radicalise Islamic groups in Somalia, some of whom were to resurface in new Islamic movements in the civil war three decades later (Le Sage 2004; Marchal 2004).

The social transformation of society was coupled with a reform of state institutions. The declared policy of the government was to decentralise state authority in order to facilitate grassroots participation in development. However, the structures through which development was instituted were subject to state control, with military or party functionaries appointed as district and provincial officials (Abdi Samatar 1985). Mass participation in development was ordered from above rather than mobilised through consensus, so that far from being brought into the political process the population was alienated from it. In addition, all non-governmental forms of association were banned or brought under state control. Freedom of expression was also controlled by strict media censorship, which in the end negated the benefits of a standardised Somali script and the mass literacy campaigns.

Militarisation
The ease with which Siyad Barre assumed power in 1969 demonstrated that the army had become the most powerful and organised force in Somalia. Compulsory military training impressed on the public the supremacy of the military. Its domination was reinforced by the legislation that established the military's legal control over state affairs

[18] By the end of the 1970s the adult literacy rate had reportedly risen from 7–10 per cent to 60 per cent (Ahmed Samatar 1988: 103).

and by an array of new security forces. The principal security agency, the National Security Service (NSS), was given unlimited powers to arrest and detain opponents without trial. The military police (nicknamed *dhabar-jebinta* – 'back breakers') and the paramilitary Guulwade ('Victory Pioneers'), which provided a system of community-based surveillance, both instilled a culture of fear and silence. *Habeas corpus* was annulled at the time of the coup and thousands of people fell foul of national security legislation, which overrode any rights that had been guaranteed by the constitution. Political prisoners and their relatives were routinely tortured to extract confessions and extrajudicial executions were commonplace. Rather than providing protection for its citizens, the state became a tool of repression.

The militarisation of the state had begun in the early 1960s, when Somalia solicited foreign assistance during its border disputes with Kenya and Ethiopia. By the early 1980s, security was consuming nearly three-quarters of government spending and exceeded the country's export revenues (Ahmed Samatar 1985: 37). Indeed, in terms of the expenditure of state resources, state-building largely consisted of the development of security institutions rather than investments in social and economic development. Barre was able to sustain this level of military expenditure by using Cold War tensions to obtain a vast array of armaments, first from the Soviet Union and later from the United States. Other sources of military assistance to the regime included Italy, Romania, East Germany, Iraq, Iran, Libya, South Africa, Saudi Arabia and China. Barre used this military assistance to go to war with Somalia's neighbour and to suppress internal opposition, and the largesse of the Cold War superpowers became readily apparent in the huge arsenals of weapons that were bequeathed to Somalia's 'warlords' to fight the internecine war in the 1990s.

By the mid-1970s, with Soviet assistance, Somalia had built one of the most powerful armies in sub-Saharan Africa and in 1977 Barre took his country into a fateful war with Ethiopia over the Ogaden. The coup of 1969 had been motivated in part by the military's opposition to Egal's policy of detente with Kenya (Lewis 1993: 31). In the mid-1970s, having consolidated his authority at home, Barre sought to project Somalia onto the international stage by joining the Arab League and hosting the Organisation of African Unity in Mogadishu. Despite Somalia's earlier military defeats by Ethiopia, in the mid-1970s the regime also began to provide clandestine support to the Western Somali Liberation Front (WSLF) which was seeking to liberate the Ogaden region from the rule of Addis Ababa. Djibouti's independence in June 1977 focused attention on the pan-Somali issue. Tapping into a rich vein of Somali nationalism and taking advantage of the political turmoil in the Ethiopian state following the overthrow of Emperor Haile Selassie in 1974, Barre ordered a full-scale offensive in support of the WSLF to reclaim the Somali-inhabited Ogaden for Somalia. The Somali army's rapid advances in Ethiopia became a high point of Siyad Barre's popularity at home. But within a year his army was forced into a humiliating retreat after the Soviet Union switched its support to the new Marxist regime of Mengistu Haile Mariam in Ethiopia.

Defeat in the Ogaden was a turning point for the Barre regime and the beginning of its demise. The war was costly in lives and was a massive drain on national resources. In the wake of the defeat, national unity began to dissipate as opposition groups took up arms against the regime. A failed coup attempt in 1978 led to the creation of the Somali Salvation Democratic Front (SSDF), which launched a guerrilla campaign in the central regions of Somalia. In 1981 the SNM was formed and launched an insurgency in the north-west. The regional and clan-based support for these insurgencies, and the fact that they were based in Ethiopia, was indicative both of the lack of opportunity for expressing internal opposition and the demise of national unity. As the political and economic crisis developed in the 1980s, and as Somalia became more indebted to military and financial assistance from the West, the regime's socialist ideology began to wear thin and the reality of political autocracy became apparent (Ahmed Samatar 1988).

Economic mismanagement & underdevelopment
Hot on the heels of the Somali army's retreat, Somalis from the Ogaden sought refuge in Somalia, leaving the country host to Africa's largest refugee population at that time. The government estimated that there were 1.5 million refugees, equal to 40 per cent of Somalia's total population. The United Nations High Commission for Refugees (UNHCR) estimated the real number to be half that, but the refugee crisis had huge political, social and economic consequences as the country opened its doors to a deluge of international aid and Western aid organisations. This presaged a long history of engagement by Western aid organisations in Somalia, many of whom are still working in the country three decades later. On taking power the regime had proclaimed its intention to tackle the scourge of underdevelopment, hardly addressed since independence, and to release the country from external dependence by utilising its own resources (Ahmed Samatar 1988: 85). The need to solicit foreign assistance also signalled a further failure by the regime. Two decades of economic mismanagement by the regime became one of the contributory causes of state collapse (Mubarak 1996).

Under Scientific Socialism most areas of the economy were brought under state control, with the exception of Somalia's two major export sectors and sources of state revenue: bananas and livestock. Banana production was allowed to remain in private hands although a state agency was established to control exports. In the case of livestock, the subsistence nature of the economy made it difficult to nationalise. In the early 1970s the rural sector – comprising pastoralism, agriculture and fisheries – accounted for over 60 per cent of GNP, 80 per cent of the labour force and 98 per cent of exports (Ahmed Samatar 1988: 89). A series of national development plans emphasised the need to develop the productive sectors in order to reduce external dependence and increase self-reliance. The regime largely failed in this task.

Somalia had never been self-sufficient in grain production and efforts by the Barre government to modernise and expand peasant agriculture failed to change this. Experiments in cooperative production and state farming proved disastrous. Agricultural productivity declined, as a combination of state control over producer prices, an overvalued currency (which subsidised imports) and food aid removed any incentive for production. As a consequence, poverty among smallholders increased, as did import dependence, inflation and the country's external debt. In the north-west the crisis in peasant production encouraged farmers to expand the production of *qaad* (*Cathala edulis*), a mild stimulant whose green leaves are chewed throughout Somali-inhabited regions in the Horn of Africa (Abdi Samatar 1989: 139).[19] Services and industry fared little better. Although these grew in the early years of military rule, by the end of the 1970s manufacturing had stagnated and improvements in social services, such as education and health, could not be sustained due to declining revenues.

Pastoralism, which provided some 60 per cent of the population with a livelihood, fared better than the other sectors. Since the 1950s the demand from the new oil-rich Arabian peninsula had stimulated the growth of livestock exports from Somalia, and by the late 1980s these accounted for some 80 per cent of all exports (Mohamoud and Hashi 1988). Abdi Samatar (1989) has argued that the commercialisation of pastoral production since colonial times had profoundly affected the social, political and economic life of pastoralists, and their relationship with the environment. As livestock became the major source of revenue for the state, the socio-economic functions of pastoralism shifted from supporting producers to supporting the state and merchants. As the revenues from the livestock trade were appropriated by a small number of trading families and the state, new inequalities of wealth between pastoralists, merchants and the state emerged.

Despite its economic value and the cultural significance accorded to it in representations of the country, pastoralism was consistently viewed by Somalia's governments as an outmoded and unproductive economic activity. The Land Registration Act of 1975, which nationalised Somalia's rangelands, in theory nullified customary property rights and brought all land formally under state control. In an effort to modernise the sector, the government encouraged pastoralists to settle and intensify production through ranching. This contributed to a spread of rangeland enclosures which restricted pastoralists' movements and access to resources and degraded the environment. Despite the contribution of pastoralism to the

---

[19] See Chapter 7 for a further discussion of *qaad* in Somaliland.

economy the benefits were not passed down to the producers. As in other sectors, efforts to boost production were never realised. Government investment in the sector was minimal and the two major state-funded interventions in pastoral production – the Northern Range Project and the Central Range Project – did nothing to advance production and in most respects were judged to be failures.

Under the management of Siyad Barre's government, livestock exports actually declined. Although demand in Saudi Arabia kept prices elevated (Ahmed Samatar 1988: 125), dependence on a single market left pastoralists vulnerable to market forces. Swift (1979) argues that the commercialisation of pastoralism and the volatility of the market help to explain why pastoralists were vulnerable to the *daba-dheer* ('long-tailed') drought of 1974–5, during which an estimated 20,000 pastoralists in northern Somalia died. After 1983/4, when Saudi Arabia banned imports from Somalia on the grounds of alleged rinderpest, livestock exports declined further and pastoralists were forced into illicit trade with Yemen and Kenya, causing terms of trade to decline. The economist Vali Jamal (1988) nevertheless provides a compelling analysis which suggests that poverty among pastoralists (and by extension a large part of the population) had been overstated due to a failure to understand the subsistence nature of the economy. The regime's attempt to regulate the export trade brought it into conflict with the livestock traders, who were predominantly northerners. As will be described later, this contributed to the discontent among the Isaaq during the SNM insurgency.

In 1969 the country had been one of the largest recipients (*per capita*) of aid in Africa. Efforts by the government to wean Somalia from foreign dependence through developing local production largely failed. Although the sources of aid varied, the high level of state dependence on foreign assistance did not change until it was withdrawn in the 1980s.

Collapsing the state
State-building in Somalia reached its apogee under Siyad Barre's military regime, with all political and economic power concentrated in the state and the office of the president. Nationalism and loyalty to the state was sustained through the adoption of a common Somali orthography and by stoking the popular dream of a 'Greater Somalia'. The failure to achieve the latter through a war with Ethiopia over the Ogaden and the decision of people in Djibouti the previous year to opt for independence rather than unity with Somalia, served to fracture national unity. Although the overthrow of the Barre government in 1991 appeared sudden, state collapse did not happen overnight. As Brons (2001) has pointed out, if a primary purpose of a state is to contain violence and provide security for its citizens, then the Somali state under Barre had 'failed' before it 'collapsed'.

It is a mistake, however, to locate Somalia's crisis solely in local mismanagement of the state, and important to understand the war and state collapse in the context of, and as a response to, global political and economic transformations that were occurring in the 1970s and 1980s. The armed insurgencies against the regime occurred at a time when it had been weakened by the loss of Soviet Union patronage. And it was only able to survive for a further ten years because of the patronage from the West that replaced it. Various figures illustrate the level of Somalia's dependence on foreign aid. Sommer (1994: 7), for example, reports that between 1972 and 1989 Somalia received US$2.8 billion in foreign aid, and was the largest *per capita* beneficiary of aid in Africa; Menkhaus and Ortmayer (1999) state that by 1985 official development assistance constituted some 57 per cent of its GNP; Abdi Samatar (1989: 160–1) records that in the mid-1980s foreign assistance funded 75 per cent of the operating budgets of all the social and economic ministries; and according to Lewis (2002: 330) in the last decade of the regime 75 per cent of Somalia's resources came from foreign aid. For hosting Ethiopian refugees, the country reaped a windfall of humanitarian assistance from Western donors estimated at US$120 million per year. This became an important source of funding for the government and the military. While very little development assistance trickled down to the ordinary citizens, government employees, business people and residents near to refugee camps did benefit from access to cheap food diverted from the camps.

Up to the Ogaden war Somalia's main benefactors were the Soviet Union, China and the Arab states. In the 1980s the main sources of finance came from Western donors, in particular the United States and Italy. In the 1980s US policies in the Horn of Africa were shaped by the fall of the Shah of Iran, fears that the Iran–Iraq war could jeopardise access to Middle East oil and the threat presented by the Soviet Union's alliances with Ethiopia, Libya and South Yemen. In this context Somalia's location on the Gulf of Aden and the Indian Ocean, as in the nineteenth century, gave it strategic importance. By 1982 Somalia was the third largest recipient of US aid in Africa (Simons 1996: 76). In return for US$100 million a year in development, military and refugee assistance, the US gained access to the facilities of the port of Berbera for its Rapid Deployment Force.[20] At the same time US companies invested in oil and uranium exploration and fisheries. Italian aid was even greater[21] and was more open to directly supporting Barre's patronage system (Reno 2003: 19).

Western aid was conditional on an agreement to liberalise the economy and in 1981 Somalia duly signed a deal with the International Monetary Fund to implement a package of economic structural reforms. Deregulation of the economy and lifting of mandatory sales to state marketing boards boosted agricultural production, but at a cost for the peasant producers (Abdi Samatar 1994). Land prices rocketed and much of the irrigable land along the Shabelle Valley was expropriated by wealthy military and political figures associated with the regime (Beste-

---

[20] There was also a scheme to build an emergency landing facility at Berbera for the space shuttle.
[21] Lewis (2002: 330 fn 1) gives a figure of US$1 billion in the 1980s.

man and Cassanelli 1996). Economic liberalisation also stimulated the growth of an illicit parallel economy as low wages forced civil servants and others to seek incomes outside their official employment. As public-sector investment declined, the illicit shadow economy grew in importance as a source of livelihoods (Miller 1981). For many people, the gap between wages and needs was filled by remittances from relatives working abroad, estimated at US$338 million in 1985 and fifteen times the entire wage bill for the country's formal sector (Jamal 1988). When oil prices dropped and employment opportunities in the Gulf declined remittances decreased, but other extra-legal activities proliferated, including trade in *qaad*, which had been banned in 1983. As the formal economy and banking system atrophied, the significance of the informal economy further increased.

The regime's agreement to liberalise the economy was not matched by political liberalisation. In response to internal military threats Barre abandoned any pretence of national unity and simply strengthened his monopoly on power by progressively restricting state patronage to his immediate and extended family. In spite of the regime's anti-tribal rhetoric, its top echelons had for some time been drawn from the main clans of the Darod clan-family – the Marrehan, Ogaden and Dhulbahante. This alliance, to which Somalis aptly gave the acronym MOD, provided the regime with a degree of internal and external security (Lewis 2002: 221–2).[22] In the face of mounting insecurity, government increasingly came to be dominated by Barre's Marrehan clan.

As the regime became increasingly autocratic, the human rights situation worsened (Amnesty International 1988). In the regime's first seven years its targets had been individual ideological opponents. After 1978, whole clans and economic groups associated with the insurgencies were targeted: first the Majeerteen from Mudug region, for supporting the SSDF, and later the Isaaq in the north-west, from whom the SNM drew support. The level of state violence went largely unreported and un-challenged outside of Somalia for much of Siyad Barre's tenure in power. Despite the West's championing of democracy and political and civil rights, its strategic interests took priority. In the 1980s Western aid became complicit in buttressing an increasingly predatory regime that siphoned off foreign assistance to sustain its patronage networks. The US government ignored its own legal restrictions on providing financial assistance to regimes engaged in human rights violations. Foreign military assistance that was given on the principle of protecting the country against foreign aggression was used to support internal repression. As the Cold War *realpolitik* gave the principle of sovereignty primacy over concern for individual human rights, the international human rights regime was

---

[22] Barre's paternal clan was the Marrehan; the Ogaden was the clan of his mother; and a son-in-law, Ahmed Suleiman 'Daffle', the head of the powerful National Security Service, was Dhulbahante. Internally, the Dhulbahante gave the regime some leverage in relations between northern and southern Somalia, while the Ogaden gave it a channel for relations with Ethiopia.

mostly confined to the protection of refugees outside the borders of their countries. In the 1980s international relief and development agencies in Somalia were, therefore, more focused on the rights of refugees than on those of Somali citizens in their own country.

Somalia's crisis finally gained international recognition with the outbreak of full-scale civil war in the north-west. In May 1988, Ethiopia and Somalia signed a peace agreement ending ten years of hostilities. Fearing the loss of its bases in Ethiopia, the SNM attacked the Somali army in the northern cities of Hargeysa and Burco, which they briefly held. The army's retaliation caused the flight of hundreds of thousands of Somalis abroad. The presence of refugees in neighbouring countries and the evacuation of international aid agencies from the north-west made the documentation of human rights violations easier (Gersony 1989). As the Cold War drew to a close, Somalia began to lose its strategic importance and Western concerns for civil and political rights rose higher on the international agenda. From 1988 there was a steady stream of reports by Amnesty International, Africa Watch, the US State Department and the General Accounting Office of the US Congress on the civil war in Somalia, the situation of refugees and on human rights. These reports brought international pressure to bear on the regime and in March 1989 300 long-term prisoners were released, including members of the 'Hargeysa Group' who, as will be described in Chapter 3, have an important place in Somaliland's recent history. Following anti-government riots in Mogadishu in July 1989, the US Envoy for Africa declared that 'the people of Somalia were tired [of] military rule' and urged the regime to restore democratic government.

As Somalia's strategic importance dwindled, the incentive for the West to continue aid diminished. Most relief and development work in the north-west halted following the evacuation of aid workers from Hargeysa in 1988, except for the International Committee of the Red Cross (ICRC) in Berbera hospital, the provision of food for refugees and a handful of international non-governmental organisations (NGOs) running medical programmes on the SNM side of the lines. In response to the intensification of fighting in the north-west, the US Congress blocked further aid to Somalia (Simons 1995: 78). In November, in response to the Somalia–Ethiopia peace agreement, the UNHCR announced it was to scale down the refugee assistance programme in Somalia, halve its annual budget and develop 'durable solutions' for the refugees (*ibid.*: 74). Things got worse for the Somali government in January 1990 when the US Congress invoked the 'Brooke Amendment' halting any non-humanitarian aid to Somalia. Bilateral aid was cut from US$30 million in 1988 to $740,000 for 1990, although some military and financial aid to the regime continued up to and after the outbreak of war.[23] Germany, the Netherlands and

---

[23] As late as June 1988 a US arms shipment was unloaded in Berbera. In mid-1989 the US supported the disbursement of World Bank and African Development Bank loans to Somalia. And during the early months of war US technicians reportedly helped repair the military's

Finland suspended their bilateral aid programmes and even Italy reduced its aid following the arrest of 45 signatories of a manifesto appealing for the regime to reform (see below). Oil companies also began to scale down their operations. The phasing out of the UNHCR programme increased armed banditry as local inhabitants found a major source of livelihoods drying up. As insecurity spread through the country, NGOs withdrew to Mogadishu or left the country. The reduction in Western aid forced the Somali government to turn elsewhere for economic and military aid, including Libya, China, the United Arab Emirates and Iraq.

In the 1980s the adoption of structural adjustment programmes had undermined the regime's ability to control sources of patronage. As government provision of public services ceased, the state took on the character of a privatised enterprise managed for the ruling elite (UNDP 2001:139–57). Clan identity, officially proscribed since the 1970s, resurfaced as the main channel for political and economic security. Clans privileged by the regime received preferential disbursements of development aid. The response of those excluded from the regime's patronage networks was to move outside the formal economy, further undermining the legitimacy of the state and its institutions. As trade balances deteriorated in the 1980s, the economy revolved around three main pillars: foreign aid, which was a key source of finance for the state; livestock production, which continued to provide a subsistence livelihood for most of the population; and an informal or illicit economy, on which much of the urban population depended. At the end of the 1980s, in the context of general economic decline, there was a growing struggle within the (largely urban) political and economic elite for control over economic resources in the formal and informal economy. In the absence of alternative civil structures that might have provided pressure for reform, political and military leaders marginalised from power turned to their clan constituencies to organise rebellions. As Siyad Barre's divide-and-rule tactics facilitated the spread of weapons, the power struggle became increasingly violent and was projected along clan lines. The fragmentation of patronage networks laid the foundations for the violent warlord politics that took hold of Somalia after the regime was overthrown. Foreign assistance had helped the Barre regime to maintain its grip on power for twenty-one years. At the end of the Cold War, as Somalia lost its strategic importance and the international community began to disengage from the region (and Africa in general), the regime's authority dissipated and the state collapsed.

Civil war

The SNM's attacks on the northern cities of Hargeysa and Burco in May 1988 proved to be the opening skirmishes of a civil war that is continuing in Somalia at the time of writing eighteen years later. The savage

[23] (cont.) communications system in the north.

government counter-offensive killed tens of thousands of civilians, forced hundreds of thousands to seek refuge in Ethiopia, served to unite the Isaaq behind the SNM. The SNM in turn encouraged other groups to take up arms against the ailing regime. The Somalia–Ethiopia peace agreement also had an impact on the Ogaden, because in theory it rescinded Somalia's claims to the territory. In 1989 the Somali Patriotic Movement (SPM) and the United Somali Congress (USC) were formed to mobilise the Ogaden people and the Hawiye against the government.

In July 1989, these troubles were brought home to Mogadishu when the Catholic bishop was assassinated and the subsequent arrest of several Islamic leaders sparked anti-government riots in the capital. The ruthless suppression of the riots with mass arrests and summary executions of some 450 civilians shattered any remaining loyalty to the regime. Even Marrehan elders petitioned the President to restore democracy. In another indication that the state was imploding, the Central Bank ran out of money. In May 1990, more than one hundred prominent Somali citizens (from all clans) signed an open letter, known as 'Manifesto No. 1', condemning the government's policies and calling on it to hold discussions with opposition groups to end the political turmoil. Forty-five of the signatories were arrested, but later released under pressure from the Italian government and the threat of further demonstrations. The regime lamely offered political reforms and dialogue, but these were rejected by the opposition groups who viewed them as a last-ditch attempt by the regime to cling to power. Its promises to improve the human rights situation were contradicted by the government's brutal military campaign. On 6 August 1990, the SNM, USC and SPM, meeting in Ethiopia, agreed to form a united front against the regime. Rejecting offers by Italy and Egypt to mediate, the USC, led by General Mohamed Farah 'Aideed', fought its way into Mogadishu on 3 December 1990.

Little was done by the international community to prevent the impending catastrophe. The build-up to the First Gulf War that followed Iraq's invasion of Kuwait consumed international attention, although the lack of international will to intervene in Somalia contrasted markedly with the US mediation efforts in Ethiopia six months later. In early January 1991, during intense fighting in Mogadishu, the US aircraft carrier *Guam* was diverted from its duties in the Gulf to evacuate remaining foreign nationals from the country. In the words of the US Ambassador to Somalia, the US then 'turned out the light, closed the door and forgot about Somalia'.

On 27 January 1991 Siyad Barre fled from Mogadishu. Two days later, one faction of the USC appointed Ali Mahdi Mohamed as President of Somalia for an interim twenty-eight-day period, with Omar Arteh Ghalib as his Prime Minister.[24] This unilateral action broke a deal between the

[24] Ali Mahdi was a member of the Manifesto Group of political leaders that had called for a peaceful transfer of power in the south in 1990. A rich hotelier, he is from the Abgal clan of the Hawiye that are predominant in Mogadishu. The SNM and SPM had been allied with General

USC, SNM and the SPM to form a joint administration and precipitated an irrevocable rift within the USC. The SNM chairman and General Aideed denounced, unfairly, the self-appointed government as an extension of the deposed administration (Drysdale 1992: 21). In May the SNM declared Somaliland's independence. Attempts by the Italian and regional governments of the Inter-Governmental Authority on Development (IGAD) to reconcile the factions at two conferences in Djibouti in May and June failed. The second Djibouti conference was probably the last and best opportunity to avert an escalation of the crisis. But Aideed refused to attend and Somalia slipped into a bloody civil war between clan-based military factions who were fighting over the remnants of the state.[25] Militias, mobilised by political entrepreneurs such as Aideed, Ali Mahdi Mohamed, Colonel Omar Jess, General Aden 'Gabiyo' and General Mohamed Hersi 'Morgan' – a mixture of soldiers, politicians and businessmen who were given the nomenclature of 'warlords' by journalists – embarked upon a spree of killing, rape, population eviction and the looting of public and private property.

For some sixteen months, from December 1991 to March 1992, there was almost continual warfare in the south. Some 25,000 people are estimated to have been killed in Mogadishu alone between 1991 and 1992, as a result of indiscriminate shelling between the forces of General Aideed and Ali Mahdi. So-called 'clan cleansing' caused massive population movements as armed groups sought to wrest control of urban and rural assets. Forced displacement, drought and the disruption of food supplies led to mass deaths from starvation and disease in the arable riverine areas. It is estimated that between 1992 and1993 war-induced famine claimed the lives of some 250,000–300,000 people (Hansch *et al.* 1994: 24). Tens of thousands were killed in fighting, over a million people fled the country, nearly two million people were displaced internally and there was widespread destruction of public services and economic infrastructure. Those who died in the greatest numbers in the inter-riverine agro-pastoral regions of southern Somalia were from historically marginalised groups such as the Rahanweyn, Digil, Bantu and Bravani, whose livelihoods were disrupted and who lacked organised forces and weaponry to fend off other marauding clan militia.

The ICRC and international humanitarian NGOs formed the first international response to the crisis, establishing emergency medical and feeding programmes as early as January and February 1991. It took eighteen months for the UN to respond in any meaningful way. In April 1992, having secured a ceasefire agreement from General Aideed and Ali Mahdi,

---

[24 (cont.)] 'Aideed', who took on the military leadership of the USC after the death of Ali Mohamed Ossobleh. Aideed was a member of the Habar Gedir clan of the Hawiye, who traditionally hail from Somalia's central regions. Rivalry between Ali Mahdi and Aideed and between their respective clans dominated the conflict in the south until Aideed's death in 1995.

[25] The SNM, which had declared Somaliland's independence, stayed away from both conferences.

the UN Security Council, under Resolution 751 (24 April 1992) authorised the establishment of the United Nations Operation in Somalia (UNOSOM). Conceived as an observer mission, UNOSOM initially comprised fifty unarmed military observers and a six-month Plan of Action to provide US$23 million in humanitarian aid. Attacks and looting of aid convoys by predatory militia led the UN Security Council to authorise an offer by the outgoing US President George Bush to deploy 28,000 US troops in Somalia. US marines landed on Mogadishu's beaches on 9 December 1992 in the full glare of the foreign press. Codenamed Operation Restore Hope, the limited objective of the US-led UN International Task Force (UNITAF) was to 'create a secure environment for the delivery of humanitarian relief' throughout the country. For President Bush, buoyed by the allied victory in the Gulf, the military and humanitarian operation provided an opportunity for the US to demonstrate its role of global policeman in the 'new world order'. By February US forces were supplemented with a further 5,000 troops from other countries. This unprecedented 'military humanitarian' intervention is credited by some with having halted the famine. Others argue the famine had already peaked (African Rights 1993a).

The intervention was followed by two hastily arranged national reconciliation conferences in Addis Ababa in January and March 1993. The purpose of these conferences was to agree a ceasefire and procedures for disarmament, and to form a Transitional National Council to guide the country to elections within two years. Some 15 factional leaders signed the March 1993 Addis Ababa Agreement (Bradbury 1994a). In support of the agreement, the UN Security Council passed Resolution 814 (1993), which authorised the establishment of a large civilian and military peace support operation – UNOSOM II – to be responsible for the political, economic and civil reconstruction of Somalia. Comprising 20,000 peacekeepers and an additional 11,000 logisticians and civilian administrators, UNOSOM II took over on 1 May 2003, supported by US military and financial resources. The US Permanent Representative to the UN Madeleine Albright announced the intervention was 'aimed at nothing less than the restoration of an entire country as a proud, functioning and viable member of the community of nations' (Jan 1996). Within a few months, however, UNOSOM had become embroiled in the conflict and after eighteen US servicemen (and hundreds of Somalis) were killed, the US withdrew its troops from Somalia in March 1994. Other countries followed and UNOSOM finally withdrew from Somalia in March 1995, having failed to engender a process of reconciliation or to restore a national government.

UNOSOM was a poorly considered, poorly informed and poorly managed operation that had a profound effect on Somalia and on international responses to other crises. Bush's vision of a new world order was buried on the streets of Mogadishu and the reluctance of the US to respond to the genocide in Rwanda was a direct consequence of this. The legacy of UNOSOM in Somalia has been a long one. Critics of the intervention argue that it served to deepen and prolong the crisis in Somalia by shoring up the power structures of the warring factions. Another unintended effect was that the vast resources poured into the Somalia economy also served to provide capital for a vibrant economy in Mogadishu (UNDP 2001). The US government, somewhat unconvincingly, also traces the involvement of Al Qaeda in Somalia to this period (Bradbury 2002).

Between 1993 and 2003, thirteen internationally brokered peace talks failed to restore an effective central government to Somalia, as political and economic interests within Somalia and the region conspired to perpetuate state collapse (Le Sage 2002; Menkhaus 2004). The installation of a Transitional National Government (TNG) in Mogadishu in 2000 generated much optimism among many Somalis and foreign diplomats. This proved short-lived. Despite gaining acceptance in the UN,[26] the African Union, IGAD and the League of Arab States, the TNG failed to establish any meaningful authority in Somalia. The successor Transitional Federal Government (TFG) that emerged from the Somalia National Reconciliation Conference (SNRC) in the latter half of 2004 faced an equally challenging task in forging a meaningful government in Somalia that has the support of the Somali people. In early 2007 the prospects were not good, when an increasingly beleaguered TFG had to rely on Ethiopian and US military support to defeat the Union of Islamic Courts in southern Somalia and to establish its presence in Mogadishu.

The end of a political regime and the collapse of state institutions should not automatically be equated with the collapse of social order or the end of politics. Social organisations exist beyond the state. In the civil war, genealogy rather than nationalism was a source of unity and division. In the absence of a single central government Somalis have fashioned a range of governance systems within the territory of the Somali Republic. These have included warlord fiefdoms, long-distance trading enterprises, Islamic-based organisations and nascent state-like polities where a degree of consent has been established between the authorities and the public (Brons 2001: 244). The latter include the Republic of Somaliland, formed in 1991, and Puntland State of Somalia, formed in 1998 from the north-east regions of Somalia.[27] During this time Somaliland has emerged as the most stable polity within the territory of the former Somali Republic – and indeed, since 1996, one of the most peaceful places within the Horn of Africa. The next chapter explores the basis of this stability by examining the decade-long insurgency and civil war in north-west Somalia and the events that led up to the declaration of Somaliland's independence in May 1991.

[26] The TNG reclaimed Somalia's seat at the UN in 2001, ten years after the Barre regime fell. In 2004 it passed to the TFG, but as its dues have not been paid Somalia is a non-voting member.
[27] Efforts in 1994 by the Digil-Mirifle Governing Council and in 1999 by the Rahanweyn Resistance Army to establish administrations for Bay and Bakool proved short-lived.

3
The Political Foundations of Somaliland

Somaliland has its origins in the war that led to the collapse of the Somali state. The civil war and the appalling human suffering that wracked Somalia in the early 1990s was widely reported by the international media and humanitarian agencies and has been analysed extensively since.[1] Much less has been written about the ten-year conflict between the SNM and the government of Somalia during the 1980s. Yet this period was formative in creating a 'political community' of shared interests, particularly among the Isaaq people, that broke away from Somalia in 1991. Shaped through a decade of insurgency, a common 'struggle' against repression and life in refugee camps, the existence of a political community provided a foundation for political and social recovery that other areas of Somalia have lacked. The particular nature of the SNM as a politico-military movement also influenced the form of polity that emerged in Somaliland after the war. This chapter considers the political genesis of a new Somaliland. It begins with a description of the territory and its people.

The land

The territory over which the Somaliland government and people claim sovereignty comprises about 20 per cent of the landmass of the Somali Republic, and, at some 137,600 square kilometres, is roughly the size of England and Wales. It incorporates the former regions of north-west Somalia – Awdal, Woqooyi Galbeed (Hargeysa Region), Togdheer, Sool and Sanaag – which were the designated districts under the British Somaliland Protectorate (see Map 2). A sixth region – Sahil – was created in 1996 with the port town of Berbera at its centre. Somaliland is

---

[1] For a small selection of writings see, for example, Drysdale (1994); Sahnoun (1994); Clarke and Herbst (1997); Lyons and Samatar (1995).

mostly a semi-arid savannah region with three distinct topographical zones.

Along its northern edge on the Gulf of Aden runs a narrow coastal plain known as the *Guban* (meaning 'scorched'), where temperatures can reach over 40°C between the months of June and August. This sandy scrubland, stretching only twelve kilometres inland at its widest point, is criss-crossed by dry watercourses. In the short rainy seasons pastoralists graze their livestock on the sparse seasonal bushes and grasses. The ancient settlements of Zeyla, Lughaya, Berbera and Mait are located along this coast and their ports vouch for the historical importance of trade for the region.

The inhospitable terrain and climate keeps the region thinly populated and to escape the summer heat many people migrate southwards to the cooler highland areas of the Ogo plateau. The highlands, the second geographic zone, are dominated by the Gollis Mountains that traverse Somaliland from Ethiopia in the north-west to Somalia and the tip of the Horn of Africa in the east. The mountains reach their highest peak (over 2,000 metres) at Shimber Berris, just north of the town of Erigavo in Sanaag Region. The northern slopes of the escarpment are wooded with juniper forests and species of frankincense and myrrh, whose resins have long been collected and exported. Some scholars believe the northern Somali coastline to be the mythical Land of Punt, from where ancient Egyptians obtained frankincense (Farah 1994). In the south-facing valleys of the escarpment small-scale irrigated agriculture is feasible. Moving southwards and eastwards from the escarpment the Ogo plateau is characterised by vast plains, such as the Saraar plain in Sanaag and the Sool plateau, covered with acacia bush and grass rangelands which provide rich grazing and water for livestock. There are no permanent water courses, but a more temperate climate and underground aquifers support human settlement and Somaliland's main towns – Hargeysa, Borama, Sheikh, Burco and Erigavo – are all located in this area. These plains extend southwards and westwards into the Somali-inhabited area of Ethiopia, known as the Haud, which constitutes a third zone. The Haud provides some of the best wet-season grazing land in the region and some arable land, though lacking in permanent water sources. The construction of water harvesting reservoirs (*berkado*) by the British colonial administration in the 1950s enabled year-round grazing. The spread of *berkado* over the past fifty years, financed by the growth in the livestock trade and foreign remittances, has increased permanent human settlement in the zone and affected the delicate environmental and ecological balance.

With the sun passing vertically over the territory twice a year, Somaliland experiences two rainy seasons – the *gu'* (May–July) and *deyr* (November–January) – brought by the north-east and south-west monsoons respectively. The rains bring a welcome respite following two dry seasons – the *jiilaal* (January–April) and *hagaa* (August–October).

These rains are augmented along the coast by shorter rains (*karin*) in the summer months. But with annual rainfall ranging from as little as 200 mm to 800 mm per annum, and temperatures between 25°C and 40°C, the region is subject to periodic drought.

The ecology and climate have meant that nomadic pastoralism – with wide-ranging transhumance between rainy and dry season pastures and water points – has been a dominant way of life for hundreds of years. In the escarpments and valleys of the Gollis Mountains in Sanaag Region and in Awdal Region and the plateau west of Hargeysa higher precipitation allows for some limited irrigated and rain-fed farming. Since the end of the war there has been an expansion of horticulture along Somaliland's seasonal watercourses, but the yields of sorghum, maize, vegetables and fruit are small, and any surplus is sold in local markets. In the farming areas west of Hargeysa *qaad* is also grown, although the production cannot compete with the *qaad* imported from the Ethiopian highlands. Somaliland has 850 kilometres of coastline and its northern coastal waters are rich in marine life. But this resource is largely underdeveloped, with small artisanal fishing communities supplying the urban markets of Berbera, Hargeysa and Burco.

Hargeysa is the capital of Somaliland and its largest city. According to the government of Somaliland the majority of the population are still nomadic (Somaliland Ministry of National Planning and Coordination 2004).[2] However, since the war there has been a significant growth in Somaliland's urban population and, depending on which figures one uses, anywhere between 15 and 30 per cent of the population now live in Hargeysa.

The people of Somaliland

The majority of the people in present-day Somaliland come from one of five main clans: the Isaaq, Gadabursi,[3] 'Iise, Dhulbahante and Warsengeli. The Isaaq clan-family is the most populous group in Somaliland. Isaaq formed the backbone of the SNM and continue to be politically and economically dominant in Somaliland. Genealogically, the Isaaq divide into six main sub-clans descended from the sons of the eponymous ancestor Sheikh Isaaq: the Habar Yunis and 'Idagalle (collectively known as the Garhajis), Habar Tol Ja'lo, Habar Awal (that includes the 'Iise Muse and Sa'ad Muse lineages), Arab and Ayuub.[4] Historically, the largest sections of

[2] See Chapter 6 for a more detailed discussion of the population.
[3] The Gadabursi include the Samaroon, increasingly differentiated from the Gadabursi in recent years.
[4] Sheikh Isaaq had eight sons by two wives. The first level of division within the Isaaq operates at the maternal level, between the four sons of Magaado and the four sons of Habuush. Ayuub are sometimes included with the Habar Awal and Arab with the Habar Yunis. The four sons of Habuush are collectively referred to as Habar Tol Ja'lo.

the Isaaq have been the Habar Awal, Habar Garhajis (especially the Habar Yunis) and Habar Tol Ja'lo (commonly shortened, as below, to Habar Ja'lo), and the ebb and flow of Somaliland's politics is often reflected in the dynamic divisions and alliances between these three (see Appendix 1).

The Gadabursi and 'Iise form part of the Dir clan-family.[5] The Warsangeli and Dhulbahante, together with the Majeerteen of north-east Somalia, form part of the Harti federation, a sub-section of the Darod clan-family. Prior to the civil war the Harti was not commonly recognised as a politically significant grouping, but became so during the war (see, for further detail, Chapter 5).

Before the civil war individuals from these clans could be found disbursed throughout Somalia. During the war, however, many people who had been living in Mogadishu or elsewhere in Somalia returned to the territories traditionally associated with their lineages for safety. In Somaliland, the land of the Isaaq traditionally falls within the regions of Woqooyi Galbeed (Hargeysa Region), Togdheer, western Sool and western Sanaag. The Gadabursi and 'Iise reside in Awdal Region in the west, the Dhulbahante in Sool, Sanaag and eastern Togdheer, and the Warsengeli in eastern Sanaag Region. All these clans, however, straddle the borders of Somaliland. The 'Iise, for example, are the dominant Somali clan in Djibouti, while significant numbers of Isaaq and Dhulbahante live in Ethiopia. As will be discussed in later chapters, the areas of Sool and eastern Sanaag mostly inhabited by the Dhulbahante and Warsengeli are contested between Somaliland and Puntland. The existence of cross-border relationships played a very important role during the war and afterwards, providing sources of refuge, assistance and political support for Somaliland's people.

There are fewer 'minorities' in Somaliland than in the south. The most common are small lineages attached to the major clans through a form of adoption. In Somaliland the specialised occupational castes – the *Tumaal, Midgaan* and *Yibir* – are collectively known as Gabooye. A sizeable population of Rahanweyn and a smaller number of Bantu peoples are also currently resident in Somaliland, being displaced or economic migrants from the south.

Looking back in anger: origins of the SNM insurgency

People in Somaliland explain that the decision to break with Somalia was more than a whim or an emotional reaction to events in 1991, but instead grew out of a long-term discontent among northerners with the union of the former territories (WSP International 2005: 10). Following the 1961 coup attempt by junior military officers, northern, and in particular Isaaq, dissidence against the union became muted, especially as northerners gained a stronger economic and political stake in the state. This culminated

[5] As already noted some non-Isaaq include the Isaaq as part of the Dir.

in 1967 in the premiership of Mohamed Haji Ibrahim Egal, who had led an independent Somaliland into the union in 1960. Nevertheless, some northern discontent continued over the loss of autonomy. The size of the new republic was vast and its population of only 2.5 million was widely dispersed. The concentration of government in the capital gave rise to the popular jibe among northerners that even 'the electric light has to be switched on from Mogadishu' (Jimcaale 2005: 56). Northern citizens who needed trade licences, legal services, passports and higher education, or who sought employment in the civil service, were obliged to travel 1,500 kilometres of dirt roads to Mogadishu. This was a journey of considerable expense and northerners who undertook it found that their weak political connections in Mogadishu meant they had difficulty finding employment and accessing the services they required. The growth in livestock exports kept the economy in the north relatively buoyant and investment by the state in the north did increase. The expansion of the port of Berbera, Togwajaale wheat farm, Las Qoray fish factory and the modernisation of Hargeysa airport were all projects that were started in the 1960s. Nevertheless, development expenditure in the north was less than 10 per cent of investment in the south (*ibid.*: 56), reflecting a growing centralisation of the state.

Like other Somalis, many northerners initially welcomed the military takeover of the state in 1969, after the disappointments of civilian rule. The Isaaq held the relatively powerful portfolios of Vice-President and Foreign Minister in the new military regime. But as the popularity of the regime faded, concerns over unequal and undemocratic political representation, unfair economic practices, and uneven distribution of development resources resurfaced. The government's response to the 1974–5 *daba-dheer* drought, in which thousands of northern pastoralists were relocated to agricultural cooperatives in the south or fishing cooperatives along the coast, also increased disaffection with the regime.

The Ogaden war had a critical impact on the lives and attitudes of people in the north. At independence in 1960 people in Somaliland had surmised that unity with the south would be the first step towards the realisation of a Greater Somalia and the re-establishment of control over the wet season grazing lands in the Haud. Many, therefore, supported the war to reclaim the Ogaden (Brons 2001: 185). After going to war, however, many northern officers blamed Siyad Barre for the debacle that ensued, contending that if the Somali army had not tried to advance beyond Jijiga they could have held on to the Ogaden and the Isaaq grazing lands (Gilkes 1993:4).

Prior to the war, Somalia's military support for the WSLF had aggravated competition between the Isaaq and Darod pastoralists over pasture and water in the Haud. The military assistance given to the WSLF was often used against civilians in the Haud rather than the Ethiopian government. The mass influx of Ogaden and Oromo refugees from Ethiopia into the north-west following the war generated considerable tension. As branches of the Darod clan family, both these groups were perceived to be allied to the Barre regime. Grievances began when the government appropriated land for refugee camps and they were further fuelled by the provision of international assistance to the refugees and the preferential treatment they received in terms of access to services, business licences and contracts. The National Refugee Commission, financed by international aid to administer assistance to refugees, became a huge bureaucracy and those who benefited from the resources and jobs that passed through it were perceived to be government supporters. According to Omaar (1994), the preferential treatment accorded to refugees left Isaaqs feeling they were second-class citizens in their own land.

Isaaq disaffection increased further when the army began recruiting refugees and using the WSLF to maintain security in the north. As well as violating international refugee law, the arming of refugees was perceived by Isaaqs to pose a direct threat to their lands. In response to this Isaaq military officers formed a militia known as the Afaraad (Fourth Brigade) which, while officially part of the WSLF, was intended to protect the Isaaq population from WSLF aggression (Bryden 1994a). The growing disaffection with the regime was powerfully expressed in a poetry campaign that satirised the government, led by the most prominent Isaaq poets Mohamed Ibrahim Warsame 'Hadraawi' and Mohamed Hashi Dhama 'Gaarriye'. In 1980, fearing that he could no longer rely on the loyalty of his defeated national army in the north, Siyad Barre declared a state of emergency, appointed General Mohamed Hashi Gani as military governor in the north and transferred Isaaq officers to the south. The Afaraad was disbanded and militia from the Dhulbahante and the Gadabursi were armed by the government. Under the emergency laws harsh military rule was imposed on the region. On visiting Hargeysa in the mid-1980s, Lewis (1990: 59) observed that it looked and felt like a city under foreign military occupation. Ogaden refugees had been conscripted to fight the SNM and:

> ... encouraged to take over the remains of Isaaq shops and houses in what are now ghost towns. Thus those who were received as refugee guests have supplanted their Isaaq hosts, many of whom – in this bitterly ironic turn of fate – are now refugees in the Ogaden.

In the late 1970s, in the wake of the Ogaden war, the repressive methods used by Siyad Barre to remain in power persuaded many Somalis to leave the country. In exile some began to produce anti-government literature and to formulate strategies to change the regime. In April 1981 two groups from émigré Isaaq communities in Saudi Arabia and Britain met in London, announced the formation of the Somali National Movement and declared war on the Barre regime. The SNM's objectives were published in the journal *Somalia Uncensored*. On 24 February 1982, frustrations within the Isaaq community exploded into riots in Hargeysa following the arrest and trial of twenty-eight professionals who had organised a self-help initiative to improve Hargeysa's public hospital. Several students were killed in the rioting and some 200 people were arrested. Emergency regulations were invoked and curfews imposed across the north. Somalilanders remember this day as the beginning of the civil war.

The Hargeysa Group

The actions of the young professionals – the 'Hargeysa Group' as they became known – were pivotal in the uprising against the dictatorship of Siyad Barre in the north. In the late 1970s these professionals had individually decided to return from abroad and from Mogadishu to contribute to the development and welfare of their communities. Dr Adan Abokor, a member of the Group and Director of Hargeysa Hospital at the time, recalls that these professionals who had been exposed to the outside world were appalled at the region's underdevelopment and were convinced that something could be done to help their people.[6]

The Group concluded that the most immediate need was to revive social services like health and education, and they chose Hargeysa Hospital as their first project. The hospital, which in the 1960s had a reputation as one of East Africa's finest, had been neglected by the government. The Group formulated a plan to rehabilitate it through a self-help scheme and attracted a lot of volunteers and financial support from business people and from the support of the German Emergency Doctors (GED), an emergency medical organisation that was assisting refugees. In less than a year Hargeysa Hospital was again one of the best hospitals in the country.

News of the self-help scheme spread quickly. The regional administration was uncertain how to react, because self-help projects were supposed to be a pillar of the community development approach promoted by Scientific Socialism. However, the Group's public meetings, at which the challenges facing the northern regions and the futility of relying on the government in Mogadishu were openly discussed, gave the authorities a reason to respond. The government sought to re-impose its authority by instructing the GED to transfer its activities to Mogadishu, which it refused to do. To test the level of public support for the Group, the government also dispatched a delegation of northern government ministers and elders of Siyad Barre's own (Marrehan) clan to speak with community leaders. The latter responded by nominating the Hargeysa Group to represent them in the meetings. According once again to Dr Abokor, the delegates from Mogadishu were then 'forced to listen to the people's grievances, presented by professionals who had facts and figures at hand and could demonstrate the unequal development between the

[6] Personal communication. This section also draws on Abokor (2002).

north and the south of the country'. Realising how popular the Hargeysa Group had become, the regime instructed the National Security Service and the *Hangash* (military intelligence) to construct a case against them.

In mid-1981, two members of the Group began writing a newspaper called *Ufo* (a name for the whirlwind that precedes rain), by which the Hargeysa Group became known. This drew attention to discrimination against the people of the north and accused a colonel from Siyad Barre's clan of using force to secure preference for the livestock of his clansman on a cargo ship to Saudi Arabia. For several months members of the group also distributed anti-government leaflets signed with the by-line *Ragga u Dhashay Magalada* ('Men Born of the City'). On 26 June 1981, the anniversary of Somaliland's independence from Britain, several members of the group gathered for a secret flag-raising ceremony. In a further provocative move, the flag they used retained only one point (representing Somaliland) of the five pointed star that appears on Somalia's flag.[7]

In January 1981 several members of *Ufo* were detained and after four months of torture and interrogation were taken before the courts to answer accusations that they were planning to overthrow the government. It was strongly rumoured that several of the Group, if found guilty, would face capital punishment. Their lives were saved by the students in Hargeysa, who held a protest on the day of the trial (20 February 1982). When the students began throwing stones, heavily armed soldiers responded with live ammunition, killing several students and wounding many others. Eighteen female and 200 male students were arrested.

The riots delayed the trial and when it ended the death sentence was commuted to life imprisonment for three of the group, while eleven others were sentenced to between twenty and thirty-five years in prison. Fourteen of the group were later transferred to Labaatan-Jirow maximum security prison near Baidoa in southern Somalia, where they spent six and a half years in solitary confinement. The last of the Hargeysa Group were released in 1989 thanks to campaigning by Amnesty International and other human rights organisations, and thanks also to the northern students in Burco and Hargeysa who continued to celebrate 20 February every year as the day of the *Dhagax-Tuur* ('stone-throwing'). By the time they were released much of Hargeysa had been destroyed and the SNM controlled most of the north-west. Soon after their release, several members of the Group joined their relatives in the refugee camps in Ethiopia. There they resumed their humanitarian activities by founding a relief organisation.[8] In Dr Adan Abokor's words, they really had 'no time to cry and reflect on the sufferings of their people'.

---

[7] The five points of the star on Somalia's flag represent the five territories of 'Greater Somalia': Somalia, Somaliland, Djibouti, the Somali region of Ethiopia, and Kenya's Northern Frontier District.

[8] The Somali Relief and Rehabilitation Organisation was one of the first Somali NGOs created in Somaliland.

Economic marginalisation

The public events surrounding the arrest and detention of the Hargeysa Group emboldened several Isaaq elders to compose a memorandum to the head of state with a list of economic grievances. These referred to trade policies which they believed discriminated unfairly against northern traders, the seizure of imported goods by the government without compensation, and a lack of investment in livestock production, agriculture, public works and industry in the north (Africa Watch 1990: 35–7). Barre's response was typically draconian. He arrested his Foreign Minister and a Vice-President in his government – both Isaaq – on unsubstantiated charges of plotting against the regime (Lewis 1994b: 206).

The memorandum by Isaaq elders served to highlight some of the underlying economic causes of the nascent insurgency and a growing struggle between elite groups within the state over the economy and economic networks. On assuming power the military government had taken measures to bring most aspects of the economy under central state control. Trade, however, largely remained in private hands and was dominated by Hawiye and Isaaq merchants in Mogadishu and Berbera. Mogadishu was the main port of import and export in the south, particularly for bananas, while Berbera was the main channel for the export of livestock and the main entry port for goods from the Persian Gulf. A high proportion (90 per cent) of all Somali livestock was exported through Berbera, accounting, along with skins and hides, for over 80 per cent of Somalia's export earnings (Brons 2001: 191). Isaaq merchants were prominent in the livestock trade and perceived the government's economic policies and attempts to regulate the market as an attack on the Isaaq business community. Furthermore, the control exercised over export and import licensing and letters of credit by the central bank in Mogadishu was a distinct disadvantage for northern merchants.

At the same time the north-west, which accounted for the largest share of export earnings, saw little return on this in development terms. Most state investment and foreign development aid were concentrated in the south and Mogadishu. In the 1987–1989 development budget, 41 per cent of planned investments were allocated for Mogadishu only and less than 7 per cent to the north-west (Watson 1990). Despite the importance of pastoralism to the economy, a much larger proportion of development spending in the 1980s went on large-scale commercial crop farming (Abdi Samatar 1989: 121). Some investment was made in economic infrastructure, but a cement factory in Berbera and an agricultural development project around Gabiley, west of Hargeysa, were the only large-scale development projects financed by the government in the north. Barre's reported reluctance to build a cement factory in Berbera is cited as further evidence of the regime's bias against the north.

Once the SNM insurgency got under way, government economic policies became more overtly discriminatory, aimed at curbing the influence of Isaaq business people. The state of emergency declared by the government in 1980 sealed off the north and prevented the free movement of civilians and goods. In 1982 the confiscation of a shipment of goods worth over US$50 million by the authorities at Berbera was interpreted as a direct attack on Isaaq businesses. After that the confiscation of Isaaq property became a common occurrence (WSP International 2005: 12). A ban on *qaad* cultivation in 1983 and the burning of *qaad* farms, while ostensibly carried out for health reasons, and to destroy a source of finance for the SNM, was also interpreted by Isaaqs as an attack on their livelihoods and communication links with Ethiopia. The subsequent involvement of the Somali army in the *qaad* trade was evidence of an emerging economy that was controlled through violence.

Another economic measure taken by the government was to end the *Franca valuta* exchange system, whereby Somali traders were permitted by the government to retain a proportion of their hard currency to purchase import goods. Restrictions were also selectively placed on livestock exports. This coincided in 1983 with the ban by Saudi Arabia on the import of Somali livestock to prevent the spread of rinderpest. While the implications of the ban were national, its impact was greatest in the north. If the economic policies of the government were intended to impose its authority and undermine the SNM insurgency, it had the opposite effect and simply served to increase the popularity of the SNM among Isaaqs.

A typical response of people who were politically and economically marginalised from Barre's patronage network was to migrate overseas to the Gulf States and elsewhere. Economic opportunities overseas attracted people from all over Somalia, but by 1987 the majority of the estimated 375,000 migrants in Gulf States were northerners (Ahmed 2000). Money was transferred to families in Somalia through an increasingly important informal remittance system. Lack of investment meant that people who might otherwise have obtained a livelihood from the state, particularly in urban settings, became more reliant on the informal economy. Therefore, while political discrimination left people in the north economically disadvantaged, it also encouraged greater autonomy from the state. The adoption of IMF policies in the 1980s further retrenched the role of the state in the delivery of services and encouraged greater local self-reliance, for example by supplementing educational costs through school fees.

National self-reliance had been a proclaimed aim of the 'bloodless revolution' in the 1970s. In the 1980s, the retrenchment of the state under IMF guidance meant that local self-reliance effectively became national policy. In this context, the only way the state was able to maintain its authority in the north was through coercion. In response to the SNM insurgency the government introduced identity cards and requirements for travel permission to move between towns, both of which restricted economic activity. Isaaqs faced discrimination in employment and access to services and the regime struck at the pastoral economy, considered the source of manpower and economic base of the SNM, with a scorched earth policy of asset stripping and killing. Water reservoirs were destroyed, farms were burned and rangelands were planted with landmines. The embargo on Somali livestock by Saudi Arabia and the disruption caused by the war increased distress sales of livestock and the terms of trade declined (Ahmed 1999: 245). In 1988 the escalation of the war led to a virtual closure of Berbera port for two years, which had a knock-on effect on rural communities. Thus a mutually reinforcing dynamic developed, whereby 'the more state policies restricted economic activities in the North, the more the SNM gained support within the north-western communities' (Brons 2001: 193).

The 1969 coup had established the military as the political elite throughout Somalia and as the insurgency in the north-west grew, it sustained its position and privileges through violence. Draconian emergency legislation gave the military and police extraordinary powers to counter the insurgency. A Regional Security Council and Mobile Military Court were established, with powers to arrest and impose the death penalty. Extrajudicial executions, rape, confiscation of private property and 'disappearances' became commonplace. The interests of the military were not solely political. After 1982 it is said that military transfers to the north were much sought after as an opportunity to make money. Arbitrary arrests were a common means of extracting money and Hargeysa police station became known as the 'meat market' (*saylada dadka*) (Africa Watch 1990). In the rural areas some of the most brutal attacks were reportedly carried out by forces known as the 'Isaaq exterminating wing' (*dabar-goynta Isaaqa*), who were allegedly recruited from amongst the Ogaden refugees (*ibid.*). The targeted nature of the repression gave rise to accusations that the government had embarked on a genocidal campaign against the Isaaq. These accusations appeared to have some foundation when a memorandum was found, dated January 1987, allegedly written by the military governor of Somaliland (and Siyad Barre's son-in-law) General Mohamed Said Hersi 'Morgan', which detailed policies to 'liquidate the Isaaq problem'. These allegations now form part of a human rights dossier compiled by the Somaliland Commission for War Crimes in Hargeysa, which seeks to hold former members of the Barre regime accountable for their actions against Isaaq civilians (UNDP 2001: 180). Memories of this period are strong in Somaliland and remain a real obstacle to restoring relations with Somalia.

The Somali National Movement

The absence of a popular political movement with the ability, capacity and interest to form an effective government has contributed to protracted collapse of the state in Somalia. In contrast, the restoration of stability in

Somaliland owes much to the existence of the SNM and the history of its struggle against the Siyad Barre regime. The SNM began, to use Clapham's typology (1998: 7), as a 'reform insurgency' with national objectives, intent on restructuring the government. It only began to develop into a 'separatist insurgency' after 1988. Although it was a clan-based response to the autocratic regime in Mogadishu and the consequences of the Ogaden war, its political objectives, internal organisation and source of financing distinguished it from the opportunistic and predatory armed factions that emerged in southern Somalia in the late 1980s. Furthermore, the practice of 'participatory democracy' in the SNM, as described by Ibrahim M. Samatar (1997), influenced the form of government that emerged in Somaliland. These characteristics also distinguished the SNM from most other military movements that emerged in Africa during and after the Cold War. Although divisions within the SNM threatened to drag Somaliland into civil war during its first two years of independence, the general stability that has prevailed since owes much to the fact that it avoided fracturing into a 'warlord insurgency', as happened with the southern armed factions in the early 1990s. An assessment of the SNM and its legacy is therefore important for understanding the evolution of Somaliland.[9]

Within a year of being formed, the SNM moved its headquarters from London to Ethiopia, emboldened by the growing opposition to the regime in the north. The SNM announced its military presence in the region in 1982 in a series of armed clashes with the WSLF and the Somali Armed Forces along the Ethiopia–Somalia border. Its first major military operation inside Somalia took place in January 1983, when it attacked Mandera prison and Adaadle armoury near Berbera, released several hundred detainees and escaped with arms and ammunition. The attack was supported by Isaaq officers within the Somali army, which indicated a growing support for the insurgency. However, between 1982 and May 1988, the SNM military campaign remained a small-scale revolt, comprising cross-border raids on government installations and convoys and political assassinations around Hargeysa and Burco. Although it consumed government resources, for much of the time it was little more than an irritant to the regime.

During this period several high-ranking government officials defected to the SNM and the movement took steps to extend the base of its support and its military operations. It failed to establish a working relationship with the Somali Salvation Democratic Front (SSDF), in part because of the authoritarian character of the Front's leader Colonel Abdullahi Yusuf, but briefly formed an alliance with the Hawiye leadership when it elected Ali Mohamed Ossobleh Wardhigley as Vice-Chairman and some of his

---

[9] I am grateful to Haroon Ahmed Yusuf for additional information provided for this section. For histories of the SNM see Compagnon (1991; 1998); Ibrahim M. Samatar (1997); Prunier (1991); Lewis (1994b); Adam (1994).

clansmen as members of the SNM central committee.[10] The government successfully engineered a rift between the SNM and Ossobleh, who went on to form the United Somali Congress (USC) (Lewis 1994),[11] but the appointment of General 'Morgan' as military governor in the north and his brutal counter-insurgency tactics failed to stem the insurgency. Eventually the threat of the SNM and the SSDF, combined with the internal pressures of the refugees and declining foreign assistance, led Barre to sign a peace accord with Ethiopia. But the formal ending of one regional war in April 1988 inaugurated an internal one.

In May 1988, faced with the loss of its sanctuaries in Ethiopia, the SNM mounted a daring assault on Burco and Hargeysa. In many respects the 1988 offensive was a military disaster for the SNM. Although it held parts of Hargeysa until August 1988, it lost almost half of its fighting forces. The government responded to the offensive with overwhelming force, sending planes piloted by Zimbabwean mercenaries from Hargeysa airport to bomb the city. The Somali Armed Forces made no effort to distinguish between civilians and armed combatants and between May 1988 and March 1989 as many as 500,000 civilians fled to Ethiopia and thousands of others southwards, and an estimated 50,000 civilians were killed (Africa Watch 1990: 3). In a detailed report on the refugee exodus, nearly 70 per cent of refugees interviewed in Ethiopia and Kenya described having witnessed violence against unarmed civilians (Gersony 1989). The government refused requests by the International Committee of the Red Cross for access to civilian casualties. Ogaden refugees were armed by the government in direct violation of their protected status. Humanitarian aid was diverted and the private property of civilians throughout the north-west was systematically looted. The SNM was also accused by human rights groups of summarily executing military officers and civilians associated with the regime.

The May 1988 offensive, despite being a military disaster and hugely costly in human lives, was a critical turning point for both the SNM and for Somalia. Up to this point, the SNM had failed to secure widespread support among civilians. The government's counter-offensive did as much to mobilise the Isaaq population as all the SNM's efforts over the previous eight years. The assault on the Isaaq population meant that civilians could not remain passive and overnight they became active participants in the 'struggle' and thus 'legitimate' targets for the government forces. This further boosted recruitment for the SNM and from the camps and the displaced populations a new movement emerged. In 1990 Prunier (1991) observed: 'In a way the SNM does not exist: it is simply the Isaaq people up in arms.'

Over the following three years the SNM progressively took control of

[10] As the Hawiye are genealogically related to the Isaaq, they were a more obvious partner than the Majeerteen. It was also a strategically important alliance because the Hawiye comprised the largest population in Mogadishu.
[11] Barre is alleged to have arranged the assassination of the popular SNM Colonel Abdulqaadir Kosar by a Hawiye.

the rural areas in the north-west that were traditionally Isaaq, but rarely ventured into non-Isaaq areas in Awdal Region in the west and Sool and eastern Sanaag regions in the east. Lacking a foreign sponsor, the SNM mostly relied on seizing vehicles and weaponry from the enemy. When the government began to arm the Gadabursi, Dhulbahante and Warsengeli as part of its counter-offensive, the SNM sought to widen the war by supporting other insurgencies in the south. Indeed, the SNM bears some responsibility for the emergence of 'clan militarism' in Somalia, by encouraging the formation of clan-based military factions such as the USC and SPM. On 6 August 1990 the SNM, USC and SPM met in Ethiopia and agreed to form a united front against the regime in Mogadishu. In January 1991, as the USC amid a popular uprising ousted the regime from Mogadishu, the SNM overran the remnants of the national army in the north-west.

The political vision

A major difference between the Somali politico-military factions that emerged in the late 1980s and 1990s and the SNM was the latter's political vision for post-Barre Somalia (Compagnon 1998: 74). This was first articulated in a political manifesto ('A Better Alternative') published in October 1981 (Lewis 1994b: 199). The manifesto called for a return to a representative form of democracy that would guarantee human rights and the freedom of speech, and proposed a devolved form of government based on five administrative regions within a unitary rather than federal structure. In addition, it espoused a mixed economy, a neutral foreign policy, and called for the dismantling of foreign military bases in the region. There was nothing new or radical in this. The SNM was not a revolutionary movement, and in no sense represented a class struggle. To the contrary, it was founded by a bourgeois émigré community. Its founders, however, were free from the demands of external backers and therefore able to develop their own model of government. What was radical about the manifesto was the way it acknowledged that the clan system lay at the root of political stability, social cohesion and economic activity, and argued that government in Somalia should blend 'traditional Somali egalitarianism and the requirements of good central government' (Ahmed Samatar 1988: 142). This challenged the political orthodoxy in Somalia which, since before independence, had viewed clanism as divisive and antithetical to unity and progress, and had advocated its elimination. It challenged the model of government inherited from the European colonialists by aspiring to a structure that was closer to the values of Somali society. The manifesto therefore proposed:

> a new political system built upon Somali cultural values of co-operation rather than coercion; a system which elevated the Somali concept of *Xeer* or inter-family social contract in which no man

exercised political power over another except according to established law and custom, to the national level. (*Ibid.*)

It proposed incorporating traditional institutions of governance into government in a bicameral legislature with an upper house of elders. The creation of a formal council of elders (the *Guurti*) became integral to the SNM's political and military strategy.

Beyond its reference to cultural values, the manifesto had no unifying ideology. Capitalism, Islam, democratic socialism, clanism and separatism all had their adherents in the SNM. The London-based founders were more secular and nationalist in their outlook than the Saudi-based group who favoured an Islamic and separatist-oriented movement. The former group initially prevailed under the chairmanship of Ahmed Gulaid, but within a year the Saudi-based group gained the upper hand and he was replaced by Sheikh Yusuf Ali Sheikh Madar, from the religious family that founded Hargeysa in the nineteenth century. Under Sheikh Yusuf the SNM committed itself to *shari'a* law and to instruct its fighters, who were renamed *mujahideen* (holy warriors), in Islamic teachings and practices.[12]

The influence of the religious leadership lasted little more than a year. Although it is reported that religious observance among its refugees in Ethiopia increased, religion was not a prominent factor in the SNM's campaign.[13] Liberals in the movement even accused the religious elements of undermining the armed struggle by preaching against the killing of fellow Muslims. Once the SNM became militarily active, its military leaders gained the ascendancy, backed by the Ethiopian Marxist regime – which itself objected to the ideological leanings of the previous civilian leaders (Simons 1995: 62). In 1983 Siyad Barre visited the north and attempted to discredit the SNM by lifting the state of emergency and offering an amnesty to Somali exiles. The SNM responded by scaling up its military activities and in November 1983, at a meeting of the SNM central committee, the military wing under Colonel Abdulqaadir Kosar Abdi assumed control. Professional soldiers were appointed to the position of Vice-Chairman (Colonel Aden Shine Mohamed) and General Secretary (Colonel Mohamed Kahin Ahmed). As many of the military officers had been trained in Eastern Bloc countries they used their links to solicit support from the socialist regimes in South Yemen, Libya and Ethiopia.

Their effort to run the SNM as a military organisation also lasted no longer than a year. Civilian politicians regained the leadership at the Fourth SNM Congress in 1984, at which Ahmed Mohamed 'Silanyo', a former Minister of Planning (1969–73) and of Commerce (1973–8, 1980–2) in the Barre government, was appointed chairman. Silanyo became the longest-serving chairman of the SNM. Holding the post until

---

[12] SNM Manifesto, p. 20.

[13] The SNM was supported for a time by al-Wahdat Shaabab al Islaami (Islamic Youth Unity, commonly referred to as Wahada) which was founded in Hargeysa in the late 1960s and opposed the Barre regime (Marchal 2004: 119). After the war it established educational institutions in Somaliland. See Chapter 7 for discussion of Islam in Somaliland.

1990, he presided over important changes in the organisation by opening membership to former officials of the Barre regime and to non-Isaaq. Several high-ranking government officials defected as a result, including Abdirahman Ahmed Ali 'Tuur' and Suleiman Mohamed Aden 'Gaal', and between 1984 and 1987 the SNM selected a Hawiye Vice-President. Silanyo was succeeded in 1990 by Abdirahman Ahmed Ali 'Tuur', who went on to become the first President of the new Somaliland.

The frequent changes of leadership reflected the dynamics of the war, changes within Somalia, the different ideological tendencies within the organisation and lineage politics. In relation to the last factor, the military takeover of the organisation is reported to have reflected tensions between the Habar Awal (the clan of Sheikh Yusuf Ali Sheikh Madar), key providers of financial support, and the Habar Yunis (the clan of Kosar), which reportedly provided the largest number of fighters (Simons 1995: 62). The military wing itself was said to be split between a group of radical colonels who had been trained in Eastern Bloc countries and gained the nickname *calan cas* ('red flag'), and another that became known as *shiish* ('snipers').[14] These factions were again broadly split along clan lines and tensions between them re-emerged in Somaliland after the war.

The acceptance of pluralism and dissent reflected a pragmatic and realistic approach to politics within the movement, but it also proceeded from a lack of organisational discipline that weakened operational effectiveness and strategic coherence (Prunier 1991). Critics of the SNM leadership have also argued that the divisions in the movement reflected the lack of a real commitment among its leadership to a political programme, or any forethought as to how the ideals expressed in its manifesto were to be implemented once victory was achieved. As one SNM commander explained:

> The primary objective of the movement was to overthrow Siyad Barre's dictatorship. We all agreed his government was oppressive and we concentrated on its removal. As for what came after that, everyone entertained his own dreams.[15]

Given that an independent Somaliland was not entertained in the SNM manifesto and its leadership anticipated the continuation of a unitary state, this criticism is perhaps unfair. However, it does help to explain the ineffectiveness of the first Somaliland administration, as will be seen in the next chapter. A more generous appraisal of the SNM by Adam

[14] The name *calan cas* has been used by Somalis to describe and disparage groups with left-wing tendencies and more generally anyone who opposes the existing authority. It was first applied to the socialist Somali Democratic Union party in the 1960s, which opposed the Somali National League and Somali Youth League. In the 1970s the label was applied to the exiled Socialist Workers Party. During the war the term was applied to SNM military officers trained in the Soviet Union and those critical of the leadership. After 1991 it was used to disparage SNM military officers who opposed the Tuur government, opponents of the Egal government in the 1990s, and members of the Kulmiye party in the 2003 elections.

[15] Abdirahman Ahmed 'Xuunsho', interviewed 2003.

(1994: 9) argues that the leadership rotation was an 'article of faith' rather than a consequence of power struggles and a demonstration of the movement's democratic principles. Between 1981 and 1990 the SNM held six popular Congresses to elect its leadership. It was during the SNM's insurgency that the clan-based system of power sharing (what has been called a consociational form of democracy; *ibid.*), which became the basis for government in Somaliland, took root.

Somalis disagree on whether the SNM ever represented a truly 'national' movement or sectarian Isaaq interests intent on secession. The SNM's stated objective was the removal of a tyrannical regime and the establishment of a devolved and democratic form of government. Constitutionally its membership was open to any Somali over the age of fifteen years who subscribed to its objectives (Somali National Movement constitution: 2). Indeed, one version of the constitution explicitly states that the SNM 'shall oppose any division of the country into regions or mini-states that are prejudicial to the unity of the country' (*ibid.*).

Nevertheless, the SNM was founded by Isaaq and remained an almost exclusively Isaaq organisation. The social base of the SNM shaped the nature and politics of the organisation, as with other Somali armed factions and other insurgencies elsewhere in Africa (Clapham 1998). It was a clan-based response to a growing sense of alienation among Isaaq people and during the years of insurgency little effort was made to broaden its clan membership. The early collaboration with the SSDF and the incorporation of non-Isaaq in the movement in the 1980s were pragmatic steps to increase the pressure on the regime.[16] But the SNM also rejected a proposal from a Dhulbahante leader to form a united front against the regime.[17] When the Hawiye withdrew from the SNM central committee in 1987, it became easier for the regime to portray it as a secessionist movement. By arming non-Isaaq clans, the regime was able to generate mistrust between clans and undermine any possibility of a united movement emerging.[18] Economic factors also affected the SNM's relations with non-Isaaq clans. Relations with the Gadabursi and 'Iise, for example, were affected by competition to control the lucrative trade through and from the port of Djibouti.[19]

Lewis (1994b: 208) maintains that the SNM's primary concern was to liberate the former Somaliland protectorate from domination by Barre, and that it had no more than a secondary interest in the south. While it

[16] In 1984 the Central Committee was composed of 8 Hawiye, 1 Dhulbahante, 1 Majeerteen, 1 Gadabursi, 1 Rahanweyn and 29 Isaaq (Gilkes 1992).

[17] Garaad Abdiqani Garaad Jama was sympathetic to the SNM aims and played an instrumental role in ending hostilities after the war.

[18] The Dhulbahante were armed against the Habar Ja'lo and the Gadabursi against the Sa'ad Muse, whose territories are contingent.

[19] In 1989, for example, the 'Iise-based United Somali Front attacked SNM forces in Zeyla and attempted to annex 'Iise areas in Somaliland to Djibouti. The SNM resisted and eventually defeated them in February 1991, which led to an improvement in relations with the Gadabursi (Gilkes 1992).

was based in Ethiopia the SNM could not openly pursue an independence agenda, because the Ethiopia government was not interested in supporting a secessionist movement. After 1988, however, when the SNM relocated to Somali territory, the sense that the Isaaq were fighting for control of their land increased. If independence had not been an overt aim of the movement's leadership, the idea began to take root among the *mujahideen* and civilian population, reeling from the government's response to the May 1988 offensive. The government's savage reaction turned what had been a relatively minor regional reformist movement into a separatist one (Adam 1994). Those who were laying down their lives for the struggle could now participate in shaping the political objectives of the movement, and the political objectives and *modus operandi* of the SNM changed as calls for liberation and secession increased. As a consequence, Bryden explains, independence became an aspiration among the 'grassroots' of the organisation: 'there is no doubt among the fighters about what they were fighting for: the end to southern domination of the north, and the liberation of their country under Somaliland or any other name' (1994b: 2). A former SNM cadre interviewed by Bryden explains why:

> The aerial bombings, the bombardment, strafing of refugees as they fled to the border, all helped to solidify our sentiment of separateness. Their looting of the cities, the systematic, indiscriminate shelling.... We realized we had nothing in common with these people from the south. (Bryden 1994a: 4)

Although the SNM included non-Isaaq among its leadership, its dependence on mobilising local support from the Isaaq inevitably reinforced its sectarian identity. However, reports that Isaaq elders met in February 1989 to discuss the formation of a provisional government in the north seem to have been unfounded (Simons 1995: 75). Even as the idea of secession gained grassroots support among some Isaaq, some leaders from other northern clans initiated dialogue with the SNM that would help to mitigate further inter-clan violence after the regime was overthrown.

A people's war

Its leadership, internal democracy and military organisation all distinguish the SNM from the other armed Somali factions. In contrast to the latter, the SNM was not associated with one particular leader.[20] During the decade-long insurgency the SNM had five chairmen who were selected at six popular congresses (see Table 3.1). The peaceful rotation of leadership demonstrated an adherence to democratic principles and consensus decision-making that are rooted in the traditions of governance in this pastoral society. To this extent the ethos of the movement reflected the society in which it was embedded. This was expressed not only at the

[20] For example, the SSDF was identified with its leader Abdullahi Yusuf and the United Somali Congress/Somali National Army with General Aideed.

Table 3.1 SNM Chairmen

Chairman	Period of Office
Ahmed Mohamed Gulaid	October 1981 – January 1982
Sheikh Yusuf Ali Sheikh Madar	January 1982 – November 1983
Colonel Abdilqaadir Kosar Abdi	November 1983 – August 1984
Ahmed Mohamed 'Silanyo'	August 1984 – April 1990
Abdirahman Ahmed Ali 'Tuur'	April 1990 – May 1991

level of the Chairman, Vice-Chairman and the Central Committee, who were selected at broadly representative congresses, but also at the level of the fighting units and SNM branches abroad, which selected their own leaders (Ibrahim M. Samatar 1997). The rotation of the leadership meant that the SNM avoided the type of autocratic leadership that characterised other Somali armed factions and that differences among its leadership and their constituencies were dealt with politically rather than militarily. As will be seen in later chapters, these democratic practices continued after the war in the peaceful transfer of power between governments.

Lewis (1994b: 177–220) has observed that this form of internal democracy inevitably meant that lineage politics influenced the organisation and its operations. Between 1981 and 1991 the posts of Chairman and Vice-Chairman revolved between the Habar Yunis, Habar Awal and Habar Ja'lo. Leadership rivalries expressed through their clans remained an undercurrent throughout the insurgency, but they were kept in check in the face of a common enemy.

In further contrast to most of the southern armed groups, the SNM was led by civilian politicians rather than military officers. Adam (1994: 10) suggests that because of this politics commanded arms in the SNM, rather than the other way around. Generally, military action had a political objective that contrasted with the wanton destruction of Hargeysa and Burco by government forces, and the clan violence, forced displacement and pillage that took place in the south. Up to the 1988 offensive, the SNM had an integrated force of some 3,500 fighters, from all Isaaq clans, organised on five fronts under the central command of trained army officers who were committed to having a professional force (Gilkes 1993: 10). The heavy loss of fighters in May 1988, including several military commanders, the mass of new recruits and the need to establish a presence in-country changed the way the SNM's forces were organised.

After the offensive, the SNM fighting units were organised along clan and sub-clan lines. Each major Isaaq clan had its own brigade[21] that operated territorially, and was supported from the refugee camps that

---

[21] The 1st brigade was Habar Ja'lo; 2nd brigade Habar Yunis; 3rd brigade 'Idagalle; and the 4th and 5th brigades Habar Awal (Sa'ad Muse and 'Iise Muse respectively). Later, the Arab had a brigade called San ani, the Arab and 'Idagalle had a joint brigade called Kood Buur; the Habar Yunis of Erigavo had the 9th brigade; and the Jibril Aboker the 99th brigade.

were also broadly organised along clan lines. The nature of the physical environment – one of scarce resources and large geographical distances – and the limited financial resources available to the SNM favoured a decentralised military organisation. Small, dispersed fighting units could survive better in their clan areas where they would be fed by their communities. The number of regular fighters was still small – estimated by Prunier (1991: 112–13) to be 4,000 by 1990 – but more could be mobilised rapidly if the need arose. However, few of the new recruits had any professional military training and they lacked the discipline of those they replaced. The command and control structures also changed. In response to the mass mobilisation that took place after May 1988, the SNM was obliged to incorporate the elders into the organisation by constituting a council of elders (a *Guurti*) to act as an advisory body to the SNM central committee. The creation of the *Guurti*, which reflected the objectives of the SNM's political manifesto to meld traditional and modern forms of political organisation, transferred social control of the SNM forces from the SNM political and military command to clan elders, effectively giving them a say in how the war was fought. After the war the *Guurti* was reconstituted as the Upper House of a bicameral Parliament.

The formal participation of the elders in the SNM was another critical difference from the southern factions, in which political entrepreneurs more so than elders mobilised fighters. During the war there were clear advantages for the SNM in organising its forces along clan lines. The social control exercised by the elders over the SNM fighters helped to mobilise resources and to minimise conflicts between Isaaq clans, and between Isaaq and other clans after the war. Although this form of mobilisation reinforced clan divisions and made it difficult to create a unitary army after the war, it did mean that demobilisation of the militia was largely in the hands of the clans, rather than politicians. This reduced the opportunities for individuals to mobilise SNM fighters in support of their own personal agendas.

This change in the nature of the organisation was reflected in the April 1990 SNM congress held in the border town of Baligubadleh. At the congress the central committee was enlarged to ninety-nine[22] to include members of all major Isaaq clans. The Baligubadleh congress is important historically, first because it involved a change of leadership from Ahmed Silanyo to Abdirahman 'Tuur', and second because a formula was agreed for the proportional representation of clans in the congress. Not everyone was satisfied with the new formula and, as will be seen in Chapter 5, it became a major source of contention in 1993 when it was also used for selecting representation in Somaliland's Parliament.

The SNM's reliance on the people it purported to be fighting for reflected the fact that the SNM insurgency attracted little international sponsorship. During the 1980s Ethiopia did support the SNM as a

---

[22] A symbolic number in Islam, which gives ninety-nine names to Allah.

counterweight to the WSLF by providing it with a secure base for its fighters and a sanctuary for refugees after 1988. However, it provided little material assistance. It also restricted the SNM's receipt of foreign aid out of a concern that it should not challenge Ethiopian authority over the Haud (Reno 2003: 32). The SNM's main source of military aid was the Peoples' Democratic Republic of Yemen. The evacuation of foreign aid organisations in May 1988 meant that very little aid was provided to the north-west that could have been plundered by the SNM fighters. The SNM, therefore, relied heavily on the support of the rural Isaaq communities in Ethiopia from whose territory it operated, Somali émigré communities in the Gulf states, East Africa and Western countries, Isaaq business people, rural communities in Somalia and, after 1988, the refugee camps in eastern Ethiopia.

The two largest sources of financial support were Isaaq diaspora communities in the Gulf states and Isaaq businesses. Although there was no systematic taxation of diaspora communities, as happened with Eritrean émigrés, SNM committees were organised abroad to raise funds. After 1988 the system for collecting and managing these funds changed. Rather than being managed by the central committee, fundraising was organised by the clans for their own militia. This system continued after the war and contributed to the divisions that occurred in Somaliland.

The SNM received substantial support from Isaaq business people who had fallen foul of the government's discriminatory trade practices. For some companies the informal economy that developed in the war proved very profitable. Somaliland's largest company – Dahabshiil – developed its money transfer business during this period, providing a conduit for money between Isaaq communities overseas and the refugee camps. The present owners of Daalloo Airlines similarly benefited in this period from their role as a conduit for SNM finances. At the same time, the SNM managed to shrink the government's own revenue, by curtailing the export of livestock through Berbera and humanitarian assistance to refugees in the north. While the business people had an influential role within the SNM as 'king makers', they did not harbour political ambitions as some business people did in southern Somalia.[23]

A third important source of support came from the refugee camps in Ethiopia. After 1988 the SNM became, as Gilkes has written, 'a political organisation, running a people's war' (1993: 22). The refugee camps in Ethiopia became a critical source of food, recruits and other essential supplies for the SNM. Organised by elders, the refugees donated a proportion of their food to the *mujahideen*, who during breaks in the fighting stayed in the camps where some had families. As the camps developed into business and social centres they became important political constituencies for the SNM. From 1988 the SNM also gradually extended its control in the rural north-west. In the 'liberated' areas it

[23] Business people have generally been more politically active in Somalia, a prime example being Ali Mahdi Mohamed, head of one faction of the United Somali Congress.

formed a rudimentary administration, a system of basic justice and established bush schools and dispensaries with support from Somali NGOs.[24]

The SNM's reliance on its people gave the movement an independence from foreign sponsors and obliged it to be accountable to its supporters. While Barre's soldiers had a free hand to extract resources by force from Isaaq communities, the SNM *mujahideen* relied on them for their survival. The relationship the SNM developed with civilians was therefore different from the predatory relationship between the Somali Army and other Somali factions and populations in southern Somalia. The SNM fighters were relatively disciplined compared to some militia in the south for whom plunder became a *raison d'être*. Its lack of independent finance and reliance on local communities limited the opportunities for political entrepreneurs to emerge from within SNM ranks (Reno 2003: 32). This relationship between the SNM and civilians might have been quite different had the SNM fought in non-Isaaq territories, but, with the exception of some contested areas in Awdal and Sanaag, it did not venture beyond traditional Isaaq lands.

Women played an important (and neglected) role in the 'struggle'. A small number of women fought alongside the men, although the SNM did not actively recruit female fighters, as happened in Eritrea and Tigray (Gardner and el Bushra 2004: 87). More commonly the role of women, prior to 1988, was to protect and provide for the family, assist jailed relatives and fundraise. In the rural areas held by the SNM, women provided food and resources for the *mujahideen*. Women's dual clan membership (of their fathers' and husbands' clans) gave them protection in different clan environments, and they were able to use this freedom to travel to gather intelligence and carry messages (*ibid.*: 89). After 1988, when the whole of the Isaaq population was mobilised, female teachers and health workers took a more active frontline role as nurses and paramedics. A founding member of the women's organisation *Alla-Aamin* (Faith in Allah) recalls:

> After we were uprooted from our homes by the military regime ... a group of women decided to contribute to the struggle ... by direct assistance. Every day we saw how the wounded fighters were brought back and laid down under makeshift shelters. There was a shortage of everything that the wounded needed.... We couldn't stand to see the suffering of the wounded so we women organised ourselves into different committees. Some women did the washing for the wounded, others cooked for them, some collected contributions and still other women took the responsibility of awareness raising so that people who did not know about the situation [the destruction of Hargeysa] could get information. The committee responsible for collecting contributions would walk to remote areas in the bush to collect milk

[24] These included the Somali Relief Association (SOMRA) and the Somali barefoot doctors.

from the pastoralists.... We even sent women to Mogadishu [over 1,000 km away] to buy medicines.... (Cited in Gardner and el Bushra 2004: 199)

In the refugee camps women nursed the wounded, provided food for the fighters and relatives who remained in Somalia, facilitated money transfers and held the family together. As the sole breadwinners for the family, they became active in business and made up the majority of petty traders in the camps. One common business involved taking ghee to sell in Djibouti for hard currency and then travelling to Mogadishu to purchase goods to sell in the refugee camps. These trade networks maintained lines of communication between the camps and relatives in Mogadishu and other parts of Somalia, and facilitated the transfer of money and other materials from the Gulf states to the camps and relatives in Somalia (*ibid.*: 124). Their indispensable contribution to the family and the struggle helped to alter social attitudes towards women. Involvement in business gave some women a new financial independence and since the war, some of the social support networks, cooperatives and business partnerships they formed have continued.

The legacies of insurgency

People in Somaliland today have mixed feelings towards the SNM. Many Isaaq respect the SNM's legacy as the front for a common struggle against the tyranny of the Barre regime and as the organisation that won Somaliland its independence. Its former leaders and supporters maintain that Somaliland's achievements after the war are due to the experience of the SNM and the people during the conflict and that the characteristics that differentiate Somaliland from Somalia – such as self-reliance, internal democracy, individual freedoms and the resolution of problems through dialogue and compromise – were not only principles articulated in the SNM manifesto, but qualities learned and practised by the SNM during its struggle (Ibrahim M. Samatar 1997). The civilian leadership, the democratic practices, the lack of external sponsors and the formal role of elders meant that no warlords emerged from the ranks of the SNM. In 1991, while the warlords in the south were battling over the spoils of the state, the SNM leaders had begun a process of reconciliation with those who had opposed them.

Other assessments are less positive. The Somali poet Mohamed Hadraawi, an ardent critic of the Barre regime and supporter of the SNM during the war, included the SNM in his criticism of the armed movements when he observed:

All the Somali armed movements reflected the failures of the previous thirty years of Somali politics. For thirty years mismanagement and injustice meant that a negative hatred was brewing. All those negative elements affected the struggles and the liberation movements. That is why they were all based on clan, hatred and revenge, with no plans, no visions, programmes or strategies.[25]

After the war the SNM had difficulty transforming itself into a government. As will be seen in the following chapter, the central committee failed to meet, the internal divisions that were apparent in the SNM during the war resurfaced, and the control that the leadership exercised dissipated. While the causes of civil strife in Somaliland after the war were diverse, the historical rivalries between the SNM's civilian and military leaders were an important factor (Farah 1999: 5–6). Ultimately, the organisation reflected the nature of political organisation in Somali society. It was embedded in that society and had no existence independent of the people who supported it. In 1993, when it no longer had that support, the SNM folded.

The refugee experience

The flight of some 500,000 civilians from northern Somalia to Ethiopia in 1988 was one of the fastest and largest forced movements of people recorded in Africa.[26] The vast majority of those who fled between 1988 and 1991 were Isaaq, mainly from the urban centres in northern Somalia. Their common experience of life as refugees, their self-organisation in the camps, and the common cause provided by the SNM, helped to mould a political community among the Isaaq that clearly influenced the decision to secede from Somalia in 1991 (Brons 2001: 204–7).

Somali clans are transnational, traversing the borders between Somalia, Ethiopia, Djibouti and Kenya, and the patterns of refugee flight illustrated the significance of familial ties and mutual cooperation. In 1988 civilians fleeing the war in the north-west spontaneously moved *en masse* to areas in eastern Harerghe in Ethiopia inhabited by their kin, often to where their own livestock were herded, and where the SNM had their bases. There they received protection and assistance from kin before the arrival of international relief assistance. The camps set up by the United Nations High Commissioner for Refugees (UNHCR) and the Ethiopian government to accommodate the refugees took their names from the sites of established villages located within the territory of a specific clan and hosted refugees from that clan. This ensured the safety of the refugees, the host populations and the aid workers (*ibid.*: 204). The Camp Abokor and Rabasso camps south of Jigjiga, for example, were located within 'Idagalle

---

[25] Mohamed Ibrahim Warsame 'Hadraawi', interviewed by the author in Burco, May 2003.

[26] There is no precise figure for the number of people who became refugees. UNHCR registered 381,369 Somali refugees in Ethiopia in 1990, rising to 473,170 in 1991 (Brons 2001: 202). Of these, 367,300 were Isaaq, mostly from urban areas. There are no figures for those refugees who settled outside the camps with their kinsmen, but in 1991, a Save the Children Fund (UK) survey of the Ogaden estimated there were 250,000 refugees living with their rural kinsmen (Holt and Lawrence 1992).

territory and the 'Idagalle formed the largest part of the population of these camps (Farah 1995).[27] Sub-clans tended to settle in distinct sections within the camps. The SNM did not manage the camps, but the Ethiopian government and UNHCR did not stop them from establishing relations with the refugees. The camps, therefore, became crucial for the SNM campaign, providing safe havens for civilians and recruitment and supply centres for the military.

For the largely urbanised population that had suddenly been dispossessed of their belongings, income and welfare services, life in the refugee camps was initially very harsh. Inadequate food and water, poor sanitation, cramped conditions, lack of healthcare and loss of income caused health problems and excessive child mortality. But with assistance from international aid agencies, and relatives in the rural areas providing livestock for milking, and for transporting water and charcoal, and with relatives overseas sending remittances, the refugees survived.

The Jigjiga region of Ethiopia, where the camps were situated, and Somaliland form part of a common economic and cultural zone where goods and people move freely. Over time, the camps located in the grazing lands of the Haud became incorporated into the seasonal migration patterns of pastoralists and an integral part of the regional economy (Farah 1995: 5). Women and children would stay year-round in the camps, where they had access to food, water, shelter, education and healthcare, and young males would join them in the dry season (Ryle 1992). As centres of food and commerce the camps developed into important regional markets. Hartisheikh, for example, developed into a livestock market and financial centre where the various Somali currencies could be exchanged with the Ethiopian birr and the US dollar. As the camps developed, they also became important centres of power for the clans in whose traditional territories they were located. Many wealthy Habar Awal traders from Hargeysa, for example, owned shops in Hartisheikh (Farah 1995: 6).

The camps also played a critical role in feeding and financing recovery in Somaliland after the war. After Siyad Barre's regime was defeated, more than half of the refugee population repatriated itself to Somaliland without UNHCR assistance. Food aid intended for the camps circulated freely throughout Somaliland, helping to avert the nutritional crisis that the south experienced in 1991–3. Although the war in Somaliland ended in 1991, the camps were not closed for another twelve years. Many people therefore continued to live in the camps and travel back and forth to

---

[27] Daroor camp, which was located between the 'Idagalle and Habar Yunis territory, accommodated Habar Yunis and 'Idagalle. South-east of Jigjiga, the Habar Awal were settled in Harshin and Hartisheikh A and B, with most Arab in Hartisheikh B. The Habar Ja'lo refugees were the only Isaaq clan with no camps in its territory. Some were located in Daroor, nearest to Burco, while most were located in Harshin and Hartisheikh A and B, probably due to an alliance at the time with the Habar Awal.

Somaliland for social and economic reasons. Their proximity to the Ethiopia–Somaliland border made them ideal centres for transborder commerce: food commodities, charcoal, *qaad* and consumer goods, as well as livestock and livestock products, were all freely exchanged. Goods reaching the camps from Somaliland were often cheaper than elsewhere in Ethiopia as they avoided customs and excise tariffs. In fact, the illicit market in goods became an important incentive for Ethiopia to hasten the closure of the camps.

If the refugee experience was important for shaping a political community in Somaliland, it also left a social and cultural legacy. Some former refugees suggest that the main legacy of the refugee experience was not political, but a shift in social and cultural norms, the repercussions of which continue to be felt in Somaliland (Cabdi 2005: 277–8). Women and children made up the majority of the camp populations. With able-bodied men involved in the fighting and after the war in wage labour, it fell to women to meet the basic needs of the family by engaging in business, trade and other forms of employment outside the home. Consequently, divisions of labour and forms of parental care within the family changed. Women gained a new financial independence, which affected their relationship with their spouses and gave them a greater decision-making role in the family. Some former refugees believe that the absence of men weakened parental authority and engendered a lack of respect for elders, particularly among boys, leading to delinquent behaviour, early marriages and high divorce rates. They also argue that family relations were affected by the way rations were distributed to individuals, because it weakened the interdependence of families and generated individualistic patterns of behaviour (*ibid.*). Regular relief assistance for over a decade, they suggest, created a dependence on handouts that has been perpetuated by remittances. Destitution, they believe, also led to a criminalisation of behaviour and a culture of corruption. Refugees seeking to emigrate to Europe would resort to illegal methods to obtain travel documents, even to the extent of a daughter acting as the wife of her father, or a brother as the husband of his sister.

Two other post-war trends are commonly linked to the refugee experience. First, is the increase in *qaad* consumption among men, women and youth, which has had a marked impact on the well-being of people in Somaliland. Second, because the services provided in the camps encouraged sedentarisation, many of the refugees who returned to Somaliland settled in urban centres rather than rural areas. This has brought changes to the economy and social relations, and pressure on urban infrastructure and services.

Despite the high social costs of the SNM insurgency and the life in refugee camps, one conclusion that can be taken from this period is that war does not only involve social breakdown, but can lead to new forms of social and political organisation. The 'struggle' of the people of northwest Somalia provided a shared experience of war and of cooperative living – in towns under siege, in refugee camps and on the battlefield – that was simultaneously harsh and positive. It created a political community of people with shared interests and shaped a common desire for a secure future: one that would involve a rejection of the former state.

4

A New ▌ Somaliland

Post-war recovery and the process of state-building in Somaliland began with a formal cessation of hostilities among northern clans in the port town of Berbera in February 1991, followed by the declaration of independence in May and the establishment of Somaliland's first government. The SNM's policy of peaceful coexistence among the northern clans and the decision to break with Somalia created an environment that was relatively stable: peaceful economic activity could begin, and international relief organisations could return after an absence of two years.

But Somaliland's immediate prospects were not promising. Public rejection of the union with Somalia should not have been entirely unexpected, given their experience of the previous ten years, yet the SNM leadership had made no preparations for the eventuality, anticipating instead that they would form a united government with the United Somali Congress (USC) and the Somali Patriotic Movement (SPM). The SNM interim government inherited a territory devastated by a decade of insurgency and war. It had no revenue, no financial institutions, no social services and no direct international support. The infrastructure was shattered, the country and towns were littered with landmines, and half of the population was displaced or living in refugee camps.

Post-war reconstruction and state-building was to bring many challenges: internal conflicts; the disruption of the livestock trade after Gulf states placed embargoes on Somali livestock; lack of diplomatic recognition; meagre levels of foreign assistance; limited human resources in government; a fragile infrastructure; and an environment under strain from sedentarisation and urban migration. But gradually since 1991 a modest state structure has been established that fulfils most international criteria of statehood. Why did a 'national movement' decide to break away from Somalia? How did a rebel movement, bereft of resources, set about rebuilding a government and a state? How and by what processes were security and law and order established?

The political and economic recovery and development of the new Somaliland state can be traced through four periods, coinciding with four different government administrations. The first, 1991–1993, covers the SNM post-war government. This period witnessed the spontaneous return of tens of thousands of refugees, the arrival of others displaced by war in the south and a destabilising conflict between political factions. Civil war was averted by a series of peace conferences, during which a framework for security and a power-sharing, clan-based system of governance were agreed and the political architecture of Somaliland began to take shape. The second period, 1993–1997, began with the installation of a new government under the presidency of Mohamed Ibrahim Egal. Between 1994 and 1996 progress towards a viable state was nearly derailed by civil war, which was formally ended in 1996 by another national conference. A third period, 1997–2002, covers the second administration of Mohamed Ibrahim Egal and ends with his death and the peaceful transfer of power to his successor Dahir Riyale Kahin. During this period, government bureaucracy expanded, the country enjoyed considerable economic development and a constitution was finalised and publicly approved. The fourth period, 2002–2005, covers the administration of President Kahin and the transition to a constitutional form of government and a multi-party democracy.

This chapter describes the declaration of independence and the process of stabilising Somaliland in its first three years and considers the role that customary institutions and elite interests played in restoring political order.

The cessation of hostilities

The SNM took no active part in the battle for Mogadishu and the final overthrow of Siyad Barre on 27 January 1991, or the bloody civil war that ensued. Regime change in north-west Somalia was of a very different nature. The SNM captured Berbera on 29 January and within a week had control of Hargeysa, Burco, Borama and Erigavo. The SNM's takeover was not entirely peaceful. Some government soldiers were subjected to summary trials and executions for alleged 'war crimes' (ICG 2003). The town of Dilla west of Hargeysa was destroyed in clashes with Gadabursi militia; an SNM force attacked the Warsengeli settlement of Hadaftimo in eastern Sanaag; and Dhulbahante families also evacuated Aynabo in Togdheer region. Fearing reprisals from the SNM, 125,000 people,[1] mostly from the Gadabursi, 'Iise and Darod clans, fled to Ethiopia, where they were settled in separate refugee camps.[2] In February SNM forces

[1] They comprised 105,170 Gadabursi and 19,362 'Iisa (Brons 2001: 202).
[2] The camps included Arabi, Teferiber and Darwanaje east of Jigjiga, and Kabari Byah and Aisha north-east of Diredawa. The Darod included former refugees from the camps in the north, and were associated with the Siyad Barre regime.

clashed with troops from Siyad Barre's army and fighters from the 'Iise-based United Somali Front when they tried to annex Zeyla to Djibouti (Drysdale 1992: 32). However, the military clashes were short-lived; most ex-soldiers were allowed to return to their regions of origin unharmed; and the SNM made no attempt to enforce its authority over the Harti regions in Sool and eastern Sanaag.

There are several reasons why the SNM decided against such action.[3] First, although Barre's government had armed the Harti and Gadabursi to combat the SNM, and several high-ranking members of his regime were from the Harti[4] and Gadabursi, these clans were not all united behind the government. Some sections and influential individuals aligned themselves with the SNM. The Dhulbahante *Garaad* Abdiqani Garaad Jama, for example, was sympathetic to the SNM insurgency and in 1989 held dialogue with its leadership in Ethiopia on the formation of a united front. Although the idea was rejected by the SNM, the *Garaad's* relationship with the SNM leadership helped to neutralise the potential for conflict between the Isaaq and Dhulbahante. In 1991 he secured a ceasefire with the SNM which prevented their forces from entering Las Anod and was supportive of the Burco conference. Second, once the Somali army was defeated, the SNM became the most powerful military force in the north-west, and could not be challenged by other northern clan-based political organisations.[5] Therefore the SNM had no need to project its force into non-Isaaq areas. Third, Isaaq and non-Isaaq clans are intermarried. The Habar Ja'lo, for example, were wary of antagonising their Dhulbahante neighbours in Sool, whose political support they might need. Fourth, there was a conviction in the SNM that one clan cannot 'liberate' another, or by extension subjugate it (Adam 1994:12). Finally, at this time the SNM policy still supported a united Somalia, so there was no reason to lay claim to the territory of other clans. It was only in historically contested areas, such as Dilla, eastern Sanaag or Aynabo, that clashes took place. The situation was very different, therefore, from parts of southern Somalia, where armed clan militia expelled residents from their land and property in a manner some people likened to the 'ethnic cleansing' taking place in the former Republic of Yugoslavia.

Instead of projecting the SNM's authority through force, which might have ignited a new war, the SNM leadership consented to a reconciliation process initiated by elders. In mid-February, less than two weeks after Barre was toppled, delegations from the Isaaq, 'Iise, Gadabursi, Dhulbahante and Warsengeli met in Berbera and agreed a formal cessation of hostilities and a date for a regional conference. A separate meeting also took place to reconcile the Isaaq and Gadabursi following the fighting in

[3] Author's interviews, Hargeysa, May 2003.
[4] Siyad Barre's son-in-law, Ahmed Suleiman 'Daffle', a Dhulbahante, was head of the notorious National Security Service.
[5] These included the Gadabursi Somali Democratic Association, the 'Iise United Somali Front, and the Dhulbahante and Warsengeli United Somali Party.

4.1 In this 'pastoral democracy' elders sit to deliberate (M. Bradbury)

Dilla. According to Drysdale (1992: 24), no mention was made in Berbera of secession, although talk of revising the 1960 act of union may have alluded to a future federal constitution.

The Grand Conference of the Northern Peoples

In May 1991, the senior elders of the Isaaq, Harti and Dir clans and the leadership of the SNM converged on the town of Burco for the 'Grand Conference of the Northern Peoples' (*Shirweynaha Beelaha Waqooyi*), and a meeting of the SNM central committee. They were joined by intellectuals, artists, militia commanders, religious leaders, delegates from the diaspora and business people who financed the event. The purpose of the conference was to consolidate the cessation of hostilities agreed at Berbera and to discuss the future of the north. Secession was not on the agenda of the SNM central committee. At the time, the SNM leadership had little interest in severing links with the south, believing such a decision would not secure international support (Drysdale 1992). Despite the formation of an interim government in Mogadishu by a faction of the USC in early February, the SNM leadership maintained its support for a unitary state with a devolved form of government. Shortly before the Burco conference, an SNM delegation to Mogadishu had stated its preference for a federal system with an Executive Prime Minister and a more equitable sharing of resources. Among the public, however, agitation to sever ties with Mogadishu was growing. Various factors contributed to this.

The widespread devastation uncovered by the SNM *mujahideen* and civilian refugees as they returned to the northern cities deepened Isaaq grievances against the south. The pre-emptive move by a faction of the USC to form an interim government in Mogadishu without consulting the SNM caused many Isaaq to fear that maintaining a relationship with Mogadishu would lead to a repeat of the persecution they had suffered under the military government. Stories told by people fleeing the violence in Mogadishu reinforced this fear.

The decision to secede has also been interpreted in terms of lineage politics. The unification of the Somali territories in 1960 had been predicated on nationalist aspirations to unite the Somali 'nation' within a 'Greater Somalia'. Subsequent events and the experience of alienation felt by many Isaaq meant that a united nation was no longer seen as an attractive or advantageous option.

The potential for a new relationship with Ethiopia, which was also undergoing 'regime change', may also have influenced the secessionist mood. Defeat in the Ogaden war had ended the dream of re-establishing access to the Haud grazing lands through a united Somalia. Years of conducting a guerrilla campaign from within Ethiopia, and the presence of Isaaq in refugee camps in the Haud in 1988, had healed relations with Ethiopia, and may have persuaded northerners that unhindered access to the Haud for pastoralists could better be achieved through cooperation with Ethiopia rather than through unity with the south.[6]

The declining relevance of the Somali state may also have been an impetus for secession. Pressure from armed movements, a reduction in foreign aid and the impact of structural adjustment programmes had greatly weakened state authority and its control over the economy. As the significance of the informal economy increased, the incentive for northern business people and the political elite to engage with the state of Somalia diminished. With the USC takeover of Mogadishu, opportunities to participate in the economy were unlikely to materialise. Potentially, independence could offer northern businessmen greater control or even monopoly over regional trade and economic assets. Some also believed that by restoring security in the north they could attract much-needed international aid.

By the time of the Burco conference a consensus was emerging among elders of the northern clans that the union with the south should be reviewed (Gilkes 1993: 8; ICG 2003: 9). On 15 May, an agitated crowd, including SNM fighters, surrounded the building where the SNM

---

[6] Interestingly the previous 'Grand Conference' of the northern clans occurred in 1954, when the British ceded the Haud to Ethiopia.

Congress was meeting after hearing from Radio Mogadishu that the SNM had agreed to hold negotiations with southern political leaders in Cairo. Witnesses describe how with chants of 'no more Mogadishu' they demanded the SNM central committee declare the 1960 Act of Union null and void (Drysdale 1992: 139–42). Lack of external sponsorship in the 1980s had obliged the SNM to develop a popular support base among the Isaaq. This now dictated the direction the SNM should take. With some reluctance, the SNM central committee acceded to popular demand and included in the conference conclusions a resolution establishing the Republic of Somaliland (see Box 4.1) (WSP 2005: 14). The name given to the new entity was chosen in preference to the 'State of Somaliland', as it had been known in 1960, and 'Puntland',[7] a name later adopted by the people in north-east Somalia. On 18 May 1991, having informed the USC in Mogadishu, the SNM chairman duly proclaimed the creation of the independent Republic of Somaliland and raised its flag for the first time.

Box 4.1 Resolutions of Burco Grand Conference of the Northern Peoples

• Reconciliation of the warring parties to the conflict.

• Declaration of the creation of the Republic of Somaliland.

• The establishment of an SNM government for two years and the accommodation of the non-Isaaq communities in the government.

• Initiation of a separate reconciliation process for Sanaag Region.

A provisional National Charter was hastily drafted, its first article proclaiming that the state formerly known as Somaliland was being 'reconstituted as a full Independent and Sovereign State' (ICG 2003: 9). The SNM was mandated to govern the country as the sole political party for two years, with its chairman Abdirahman Ahmed Ali 'Tuur' appointed as Somaliland's first interim President.

The Burco Declaration was agreed to by all the delegates assembled in Burco (Gilkes 1992), and in June 1992 a meeting of Dhulbahante elders reaffirmed their support for Somaliland (Gilkes 1993: 43). It is unclear, however, whether there was a common understanding among those assembled in Burco that what was being created was a new and fully independent state. Several representatives of the Dhulbahante, Warsengeli, Gadabursi and 'Iise who accepted the decision in Burco later retracted their support for Somaliland, as did several Isaaq leaders.[8] What is clear is that the Declaration was a response to a particular set of events and to public pressure, without benefit of planning or careful considera-

---

[7] Interview, Rashid Sheikh Abdillahi Ahmed, May 2003.
[8] Dr Ali Khalif Galayd, for example, who was part of the Dhulbahante delegation in Burco, was to become the first Prime Minister of the Transitional Federal Government in 2000 which claimed sovereignty over all Somalia including Somaliland.

tion of the possible consequences. Only after the fact did the Somaliland authorities develop their legal arguments in support of independence. This has two aspects: the existence of Somaliland as a geopolitical entity from 1897, when the British Protectorate was established, to 1960; and international recognition of Somaliland as an independent sovereign state between 26 June and 1 July 1960, when Somaliland gained independence from Britain and before it united with Italian Somalia to form the Somali Republic. According to Shinn, during these five days thirty-five governments recognised Somaliland, including the US (ICG 2003: 4fn9). The Somaliland authorities have asserted that the decision in Burco was not an act of secession *per se*, but a 'voluntary dissolution between sovereign states' based on the perception by one of the parties that the union had failed (Somaliland Ministry of Foreign Affairs 2002: 9).[9] The option of political association with Somalia in some form at some future date has never been ruled out totally. But successive Somaliland administrations have made recognition of Somaliland's independence status a precondition for their participation in Somalia-wide peace conferences.

The Burco conference did not end all hostilities, as will be seen, and it was followed by numerous local reconciliation conferences. Nevertheless, the immediate consequences of the decision to break with Somalia meant that Somaliland avoided being drawn into the protracted conflict in the south and could get on with rebuilding the shattered country.

The SNM administration 1991–3

In 1991 the SNM was the only organisation in Somaliland with sufficient authority to establish law and order and to oversee a process of recovery. Responsibility fell on Abdirahman 'Tuur' as the appointed President of the new republic to form the first interim administration. Its tasks were daunting: establishing security; accommodating non-Isaaq communities within the government; building institutions; drafting a constitution as a basis for the first democratic elections; reviving the economy; and restoring basic services. All this it had to accomplish within a brief two-year tenure. It was hardly surprising, given the condition of the territory and people, and the limited resources available, that this first administration failed to deliver on this.

A decade-long insurgency had devastated the country. Half of the population had been forcibly displaced to refugee camps in neighbouring countries, the south or further abroad. Mass graves in Hargeysa and Berbera were a testament to the criminal violence of the war. Between 70 and 90 per cent of buildings in Hargeysa and Burco had been damaged or

[9] For a detailed rehearsal of the historical and legal arguments for recognition see, for example, Rajagopal and Carroll 1992; ICG 2003, 2006a. For counter-arguments see Samatar and Samatar 2003.

4.2 Monument of Somaliland Unity, Hargeysa (M. Bradbury)

4.3 Monument to SNM's struggle, Hargeysa (M. Bradbury)

destroyed by military bombardment and the looting of public and private buildings (Coultan *et al.*, 1991: 52). In Hargeysa alone an estimated 60,000 houses were destroyed. Bryden (1994b: 4) records the trauma of a Hargeysa resident returning to the city after a decade in exile:

> Whatever anybody tells you, it's such a shock. You don't know what to do ... whether you should cry.... You can't imagine that kind of destruction. There was just one street left. The rest of the city was just garbage and unexploded bombs.

Other settlements had suffered similar fates. Water supplies had been contaminated or destroyed, along with sanitation and electricity systems, and the country was littered with upwards of two million landmines and unexploded ordinance (de Waal 1993). A handful of Somali and international agencies provided limited emergency health services, but there were no functioning schools. There was neither public administration nor public employment; commercial activity was limited; agricultural production was almost non-existent; road traffic was minimal; there was no commercial air traffic; and the main form of long-distance communication was via private VHF radios. Internationally Somaliland's declaration of independence was viewed initially as a regressive step that threatened to break up a sovereign state and with the Gulf War, the Balkans and southern Somalia consuming media and diplomatic attention there were no immediate promises of support. In 1991 only the ICRC and two other international relief organisations were operating in Somaliland.

Somaliland's first administration, formed on 4 June 1991, featured nineteen ministries, a civil service, a high court, security services and a central bank. A carefully chosen broad-based cabinet allocated six seats to non-Isaaq clans (Drysdale 1992: 8).[10] Police and custodial services were established in several towns and restrictions were placed on the carrying of weapons. But the transformation of a rebel movement into a government proved difficult. In contrast to the Eritrean People's Liberation Front in Eritrea, the SNM had not developed strong organisational structures that could be transferred to a new government and the leadership had no ready-made plan for a post-war administration. The SNM's organisational structure was therefore simply adopted by the provisional government, with the Chairman and Vice-Chairman transformed into President and Vice-President. The option of having a constitutional President and Prime Minister instead of an executive presidential system was discussed but rejected by the central committee (ibid.: 26). The intention was to transform the SNM central committee into a parliamentary-style national council, with the *Guurti* having a mediating and adjudicating function in the Upper House of a bicameral Parliament. But the administration proved to be little more than a chimera. Bereft of a revenue base, President Tuur failed to establish an authoritative administration capable

---

[10] Dhulbahante 2, Gadabursi 2, Warsengeli 1, 'Iise 1.

of addressing the country's needs. The central committee was legally bound to meet every six months but, due to disagreements over the clan allocation of seats, a lack of resources and concerns about a coup, it did not meet at all in 1992 (Gilkes 1993). This paralysed the government, because legislation could not be drafted or government appointments approved. Financial support for the SNM from the diaspora dried up. The unity that had existed in the face of a common enemy dissipated and the schisms that had existed within the SNM re-emerged. At this critical juncture the government and the central committee were both found lacking in leadership to steer the country forward.

During its two-year tenure the SNM government failed to create any local administrative structures. In their absence *ad hoc* councils of elders *(Guurti)* were formed that took on the functions of local quasi-administrations, managing militias, mediating disputes, administering justice, interacting with international agencies and raising local revenue (Bradbury 1994a: 75).[11] In July 1991, for example, the Gadabursi formed a *Guurti* to mediate with the SNM. As Gilkes (1993: 40) notes, this committee which controlled the Gadabursi militia, raised revenue and appointed a local governor, played a similar function to the council that used to advise the Gadabursi *Ugaas* during the colonial period.[12] A commercial tax was established to pay the militia, support the hospital and primary schools, and run the electricity supply. Similar councils were established in Burco and Erigavo in 1992. The Erigavo *Guurti* – created to replace the local SNM administration, which lacked cross-clan support in the region – set up various sub-committees, including an NGO Coordinating Committee to liaise with international NGOs working in the region (Bradbury 1994b). In February 1993 Dhulbahante elders from Sool, Sanaag and the Haud convened in Bo'ane near Las Canod and established an administrative council for Sool Region. Named *khussusi* after the advisory council of Sayyid Mahammed Abdalla Hassan, its task was to administer security, law and order, and to oversee social and economic development (Bradbury 1994a).

In the wake of the Barre regime, analysts were quick to point out that as civil war 'rolled back' the Somali state it produced a situation of extreme decentralisation rather than anarchy (Lewis and Mayall 1995; Menkhaus and Prendergast 1995). The councils of elders in Somaliland were an example of this. These councils differed from one district and region to another (Farah and Lewis 1993: 18), but they were all formed in response to a particular local crisis: in Borama the *Guurti* formed in the face of retaliation from the SNM; in Burco in response to conflict in the town; in Erigavo to prevent conflict spreading from Burco and to replace the local SNM administration; and, in Las Anod, in response to security incidents

---

[11] This also occured in different forms in southern Somalia, but the fluid military situation there prevented local councils from becoming well established (Menkhaus 1999a).

[12] There had been no Gadabursi *Ugaas* since a dispute over succession in the 1950s. The position was reinstated in 1992 (Farah and Lewis 1993: 23).

involving foreign aid (Bradbury 1994a: 75). Through these bodies elders resumed their traditional roles in conflict management, but in the absence of effective central authority they also provided the seeds of local government. Most elders recognised that government administration was not their responsibility, but they brought to the task a moral authority invested in them by communities. For the most part the government in Hargeysa, lacking both authority and resources to fulfil its administrative role throughout Somaliland, did nothing either to support or to challenge these local processes. When the government *did* attempt to intervene and establish central government authority – as part of the process of state building – it sparked conflict.

The 'sheep wars'
The peace established in May 1991 was shattered by fighting in Burco in January 1992 and Berbera in March 1992. The conflict, which lasted some ten months and killed over 1,000 people, was triggered by the government's first attempts to extend its authority by reorganising the SNM forces into a national army, and imposing control over revenue and aid coming into Somaliland through Berbera. These were both legitimate functions of government, but the manner in which they were done and the response to them revealed both the fragility of the political consensus behind the creation of Somaliland, and the challenge of demilitarising politics in a population that had been mobilised for war.

In 1991 Somaliland, like other post-war societies, was riven by political and social divisions. The advent of independence had been greeted with a mixture of celebration and trepidation, with opinion divided over Somaliland's withdrawal from the union. Publicly Tuur's administration was committed to seeking international recognition as an independent state, yet during its two years in office it did little to cultivate a sense of Somaliland nationalism. Tuur's personal commitment to Somaliland, and that of some of his colleagues, was later revealed to be transient: after losing the Presidency in 1993, he accepted a position in the equally unrecognised and short-lived government that Mohamed Farah 'Aideed' tried to create in Mogadishu. In contrast, some other prominent Isaaq politicians, such as Mohamed Ibrahim Egal and Omar Arteh, rejected the idea of independence in 1991 and participated in Somalia-wide reconciliation talks in Djibouti, but later stood as presidential candidates for Somaliland. Many Isaaq displaced from a cosmopolitan life in Mogadishu also felt alienated in the more conservative environment of the north (Gardner and el Bushra 2004: 137).

The shifting allegiances of politicians have sustained a view that Somaliland was and remains a vehicle for the ambitions of political elites. Yet in 1991 the faultlines in Somaliland's political consensus reflected real differences of interest and experience. This was recognised by Somalilanders who, in a neat play on words, divided the population into three groups: *mana-gaaho, mana-festo* and *mana-seer. Mana-gaaho* referred to a road in Ethiopia behind which the SNM had their bases, and denoted those who fought in the insurgency; *mana-festo* referred to those who stayed in Mogadishu until the fall of the regime and were associated with the Manifesto Group who sought to negotiate a political settlement in 1990; and *mana-seer* referred to those who lived abroad during the struggle and drank 'sweet drinks' (*aseer* being Arabic for a sweet drink).

The government's first challenge was to establish a secure environment. Prior to May 1988, the SNM were said to have 3,500 fighters, but when the war escalated there was a rapid militarisation of society.[13] In mid-1992 the government claimed there were 50,000 people with arms who needed to be demobilised (Nyathi 1995: 27). This may have been indicative of the number of weapons in private hands, but it hugely exaggerated the number of soldiers under SNM command in order to secure foreign aid. The mobilisation of SNM forces along clan lines had been advantageous during the war, but afterwards the difficulties of managing multiple clan militias with no central command became readily apparent. When the hostilities ended many *mujahideen* spontaneously demobilised and returned to civilian life, some remained together as SNM military units or as part of clan-based militia, but others turned to banditry and were joined by people who had never fought in the war. These gangs, who made a living through robbery and extortion, became known as *deydey* (meaning 'searching') (Bradbury 1994a: 79).[14] Public attitudes towards the *deydey* were ambiguous. In a conflict a group of *deydey*, who normally came from the same clan, could become the clan's main means of protection. Therefore one clan's militia could be another's *deydey*. At the same time, the whole clan was accountable for the activities of the *deydey* and, when they became a threat to the interests of their own clan, public pressure forced elders to take extraordinary measures – even killing their own kin, in some cases.

The administration's proposal for addressing the security problem was to put the multifarious clan militias into barracks and integrate them into a small national army (Drysdale 1992: 30). But, with limited resources available, its attempt to bring the militia under a central command and to remove the control of the elders provoked mutual suspicion among the Isaaq clans and between the civilian and military leaders. Some former SNM *mujahideen* fighters felt they were not adequately rewarded for their role in bringing down Siyad Barre. Others were suspicious that the government intended to use demobilisation to strengthen the forces of the President's own clan.

[13] Fighters who joined the SNM after the May 1988 offensive were given the nickname *jama rah* ('went on Friday'), referring to the Friday in May when the SNM attacked Burco.

[14] Referring to the looting and plundering of property. The origin of the term is unclear. One explanation is that the word is taken from a poem by Mohamed Ibrahim Warsame 'Hadraawi' that describes the looting and terror by soldiers in the last days of the Barre regime (Farah and Lewis 1993: 63). A common explanation was that the *deydey* were a 'disease born of poverty'. In southern Somalia armed gangs were known as *mooryaan* (after an intestinal worm; Marchal 1997) and in Puntland as *jiri* (after a parasitic bird).

These disputes were also fuelled by economic interests and in particular the control of public assets. Following the collapse of the Barre regime most public assets fell into private hands. In the absence of a government that could establish its authority, revenue-generating assets such as ports, roads, airports, land, water resources and former government property, as well as the organisation of trade and distribution of relief commodities, became a potential focus of competition between individual entrepreneurs and clans. In the early 1990s, roadblocks manned by gunmen and skirmishes over looted vehicles and other property were frequent, disrupting commerce and aid programmes. International aid agency compounds and aid resources were subjected to periodic looting, although aid workers themselves were rarely attacked. In 1991 and 1992 several UN food shipments through Berbera were looted and the first funds raised from the monetisation of food aid and banked with the government disappeared without trace.

Political disputes and economic competition eventually erupted into military confrontations. In January 1992 the government's attempt to bring heavy weapons under its control in Burco sparked a week of fighting between Habar Ja'lo and Habar Yunis militias which left over 300 people dead and many wounded. Burco, the second largest city in Somaliland, has long been a site of conflict between these clans (Lewis 2002: 285). The ferocity of the fighting damaged public confidence in the new Somaliland, highlighted the weakness of government, and brought to the fore the role of elders who eventually mediated in the conflict.

Fears for the future of Somaliland were renewed when fighting broke out in Berbera. The port is Somaliland's main economic asset and was the key potential source of revenue for the government. Animal exports through Berbera to the Gulf states resumed as soon as the war ended and the meeting of Somaliland's elders in Berbera in February 1991 had sensibly declared Berbera's port and Somaliland's airports to be national assets. In practical terms, however, the port was nominally under the control of the 'Iise Muse elders of Berbera, within whose traditional territory the town falls. The clan was accused by the government of withholding port revenues and using them to finance the upkeep of the 'Iise Muse militia under former SNM commander Colonel Ibrahim 'Dagaweyne'. The government's lack of control over Berbera challenged its authority and ability to raise revenue and to create an army. In January and March 1992 its attempt to impose control on Berbera through force provoked skirmishes. The fighting, which became known as the 'sheep wars',[15] pitched government forces, made up of the Garhajis (particularly the Habar Yunis clan of President Tuur) and Sa'ad Muse, against the 'Iise Muse militia of 'Dagaweyne', allied with the Habar Ja'lo. Although the government's forces were nominally a multi-clan national army, they were mostly drawn from the President's own clan. The clashes also

[15] The phrase came into use following a clash over a convoy of livestock destined for export through Berbera.

reopened historical fissures within the SNM, discussed in the previous chapter. The opposition were labelled *calan cas* ('red flag') alluding to the left-leaning tendencies of the former SNM commanders who opposed the government.

The fighting in Burco and Berbera had economic and political repercussions for Somaliland. The closure of the port hindered prospects for economic recovery and restricted the government's ability to build an administration, although Sanaag Region benefited because of increased trade through the port of Mait, and Awdal benefited from increased trade with Djibouti. The spectre of Isaaqs fighting amongst themselves weakened support for Somaliland among non-Isaaqs. With the closure of Berbera, the Dhulbahante began to look to the port of Bossaso in north-east Somalia for their commercial needs, and in 1991–2 Bossaso became the major outlet for much of eastern Ethiopia. Political parties representing the 'Iise (United Somali Front), Gadabursi (Somali Democratic Front) and the Harti (United Somali Party) publicly signalled their interest in reuniting with Somalia by participating in Somalia-wide peace conferences in Djibouti.

By August 1992 Colonel 'Dagaweyne' had control of Berbera and had moved to within thirty miles of Hargeysa. The Sa'ad Muse clan, who are related to the 'Iise Muse by descent from Habar Awal and live mainly in the Woqooyi Galbeed (Hargeysa Region), withdrew their support for the government. Livestock traders who were keen to reopen the port, the general public and a strong women's lobby petitioned the government and the national *Guurti* to sue for peace (Gardner and el Bushra 2004: 145–8). Facing military defeat and public opposition, President Tuur accepted the need to enter dialogue with the opposition. With the government at the centre of these conflicts and seemingly incapable of mediating them, Somaliland's elders stepped in to re-establish peace through two historic clan conferences held in the towns of Sheikh and Borama.

The stabilisation of Somaliland

In 1992 Somaliland was teetering on the edge of civil war. There are various reasons why Somaliland did not disintegrate into the protracted conflict and famine experienced in the south. Those alluded to so far include the sense of political community that existed in Somaliland as a consequence of its particular colonial history, the experience of north-west Somalia within the Somali Republic, and the experience of the Isaaq people within the Somali state and during the war. Other reasons include the particular political, social and economic conditions that existed in Somaliland in 1991, the particular form of international political and humanitarian engagement in Somalia in the 1990s, the ambitions of Somaliland's political and business classes, and the capacity of indigenous social institutions.

The SNM effectively won the war in north-west Somalia. Numerically the Isaaq are the most populous clan in Somaliland and in 1991 they were the most powerful militarily. As Lewis (1961) has written, in Somali pastoral society military strength can be a final sanction in any relationship. The SNM was not interested in imposing its authority, but was able to sue for peace from a position of strength. The SNM insurgency had been restricted mainly to Isaaq-inhabited areas and, therefore, while Hargeysa and Burco and other Isaaq settlements were devastated, non-Isaaq towns like Borama, Las Anod and Badhan escaped largely unscathed. The limited retribution by the SNM militia against non-Isaaq prevented a cycle of revenge between the clans.

The fact that the SNM was able to convene meetings in Berbera and Burco between clans who had been on opposing sides in the war also attests to the existence of some common values and trust between the northern clans. Somaliland does not have the same heterogeneity of clans and social organisations that prevails in southern Somalia. Clan territoriality is more clearly defined in the north and socio-cultural values and economic interests have historically been close among the northern pastoral clans.[16] The Isaaq, Gadabursi, Dhulbahante and Warsengeli have a long history of intermarriage and relations are therefore mediated by a common *xeer*. The northern pastoral clans share common interests in access to the Haud, and the Dhulbahante and Warsengeli also had investments in Berbera, Burco and Hargeysa. There were, therefore, economic incentives for peaceful cooperation. Elders assert that during the war certain prescriptions of *xeer* that governed the conduct of warfare, such as the protection of women and children, were adhered to, and that this minimised the potential for lingering hostility between the northern clans.[17] Furthermore, the SNM included people in its ranks who were not Isaaq and who were able to mediate between the SNM and other clans after the war. Colonel Abdirahman Aw Ali, whose mediation in 1991 prevented the SNM from sacking Borama, is one such figure. Another key player already mentioned is *Garaad* Abdiqani Garaad Jama, who led the Dhulbahante to ceasefire negotiations with the SNM in 1991. Meetings between Isaaq and Dhulbahante in Ethiopia as early as 1989 established a basis for constructive dialogue after the war.

Another factor that contributed to the political stabilisation was the resource-poor environment that existed in Somaliland in 1991. Economic and environmental scarcities are often identified as causal explanations of wars and their persistence (Berdal and Malone 2000). In Somaliland a lack of material resources reduced the potential for conflict. Industry,

---

[16] Author's interview with *Garaad* Abdiqani Garaad Jama, September 2003, Las Anod.

[17] Author's interview with *Garaad* Abdiqani Garaad Jama, September 2003, Las Anod. It is difficult to find evidence to confirm this, given the massacres that did occur in the north. The claim may reflect an attempt to project a feeling of moral superiority and a rejection of what occurred in southern Somalia, where these social codes were certainly broken (ICRC/SRC 1997).

agriculture and services had been more developed in southern Somalia than in the north and the resource base in the south was already highly contested before the war. In the 1980s the increasing value of real estate in the south, especially riverine farming land, had made it a target for violent appropriation (Besteman and Cassanelli 2000). Mogadishu, as the political capital and focal point of foreign investment, was a prize to fight over. In the north-west, disputes existed over rangeland use, but most real-estate disputes, which revolved around the presence of refugees from the Ogaden, were resolved once the SNM took control. Hargeysa had not been the national capital and therefore had not attracted the same level of investment as Mogadishu. During a decade of war much of the wealth of Hargeysa and Burco had been plundered or destroyed, and there was little of material worth to fight over – until the arrival of aid, that is. One spark for the conflict in Berbera was the resumption of relief aid to Somaliland, but the very limited international intervention in the early 1990s meant that this did not escalate.

Much has now been written on the way in which international humanitarian responses can become embroiled in wars, as a focus for violent appropriation, fuelling a war economy or sustaining predatory structures (see for example de Waal 1997). In the early 1990s Somalia provided a classic case study. UNOSOM's huge intervention in the south entrenched the predatory warlord structures, spawned a new class of entrepreneurs and perpetuated Mogadishu as a locus of conflict (UNDP 2001: 138–56). International assistance to Somaliland during this period was much more limited. The substantial international aid presence in the north-west that had serviced the refugees from the Ogaden war withdrew in 1988. Efforts by the UN and the Somali government to launch an emergency operation in government-held areas came to nothing, although some food assistance continued. In SNM-held territory a handful of international NGOs ran small-scale, clandestine humanitarian pro-grammes.[18] The main international humanitarian response to the war in the north therefore took place in Ethiopia in support of refugees. As we saw in Chapter 3, the SNM, which was supported by the refugees, benefited from this aid and after the war international aid to the refugee camps continued to sustain populations in Somaliland. Consequently, while conditions in Somaliland in 1991 were harsh, the region did not suffer the famine that affected the south. Following the cessation of hostilities a few international aid agencies returned to Somaliland to deliver some basic emergency services, provide livestock vaccinations, and undertake landmine clearance (Coultan *et al.* 1991). In 1991, the cost of longer-term rehabilitation assistance was estimated to be as high as US$270 million (Gilkes 1993). But, as an unrecognised government claiming sovereignty over an unrecognised territory, Somaliland was not eligible for development assistance, and humanitarian needs were greater

---

[18] These included MSF Holland, German Emergency Doctors and Partner Aid International.

in the south. Tuur's administration (1991-1993) coincided with the worst period of the civil war in southern Somalia, which consumed the attention of the international community.

People in Somaliland were themselves ambivalent about international assistance. While humanitarian needs existed, the public was wary of a plan to deploy UNOSOM troops to secure Berbera port for relief shipments, believing it to be part of an agenda to support reunification.[19] The government did eventually accede to the plan, but political developments in Somalia meant that it did not take place. Consequently, very little assistance reached Somaliland and virtually none was channelled through the government. The Tuur administration, therefore, lacked substantive international support to establish an effective public administration.[20] The government was quick to criticise the UN for this, but failed to develop a coherent recovery plan itself. Because of the disastrous military and humanitarian intervention in the south, an argument has been made that Somaliland benefited from being an 'aid-free zone' (de Waal 1997: 178). A counter-argument could be made that the international community missed the opportunity to build on the political consensus in Somaliland to reinforce principles of good governance. If limited international assistance to Somaliland did delay the physical, economic and political recovery of the country, then it had human costs. These are impossible to compute. Yet the lack of substantial foreign engagement did enable local political processes to take their course without being shaped by external resources and agendas.

If support for Somaliland from multilateral agencies and foreign governments was less than enthusiastic, the country did benefit from a cordial relationship with Ethiopia. This relationship had been forged during the war when Ethiopia had provided a base for the SNM forces and a safe haven for refugees. After the war Ethiopia's policy of maintaining open borders facilitated the free movement of people and trade. For Ethiopia a key incentive was to secure access to the port of Berbera. For Somaliland there were huge benefits. Diplomatically, Ethiopia shielded Somaliland from pressure to participate in national peace talks and supported its officials with international travel. The Somaliland government was later able to keep its foreign reserves in the Bank of Ethiopia. Refugees were able to maintain a secure base in the camps while they travelled to Somaliland to re-establish their homes or engage in business. This also ensured a pipeline for food aid to Somaliland. At the same time, the open border created a vast new market in Ethiopia for Somali traders, contributing to the recovery of Somaliland's economy and to stability.

Limited international assistance was offset, to some extent, by the

[19] Somalilanders were suspicious of the Egyptian UN Secretary-General Boutros Boutros-Ghali, because of Egypt's support for a united Somalia.

[20] Some ministries, such as the Ministry of Health, were supported by agencies such as Save the Children, but very limited assistance was given to building the capacities of government.

revival of the pastoral economy and livestock exports, and the investment in Somaliland by business people: both factors contributed to stabilisation. In southern Somalia, where people relied more on agriculture for their livelihoods, the destruction of infrastructure and the disruption to cropping cycles, combined with drought, rapidly rendered many people destitute. The northern pastoral economy is more mobile and proved less vulnerable to the ravages of war, as pastoralists can move their livestock away from areas of conflict and across borders. In the 1980s the export of livestock through Berbera had accounted for three-quarters of Somalia's foreign currency earnings. The Somalia government did penetrate the rural pastoral economy through rangeland development programmes, particularly in the central regions, but it was unsuccessful at capturing the export trade from Isaaq traders and their markets and finance systems therefore survived the war relatively intact. They were promptly re-established after 1991 and food imports and livelihoods were restored relatively quickly. With the collapse of the state, inter-clan conflicts over pastoral land also stabilised in some areas (the example of Sanaag Region is discussed below).

Exclusion from Siyad Barre's patronage networks helped to shape the organisation of the armed groups that opposed the regime in the 1980s. As described earlier, the regime's efforts to exert some control over the northern livestock trade had been interpreted as an attack on the Isaaq business community. A key factor behind the stability in Somaliland was the functional relationship that developed between the Somaliland government and Isaaq businessmen, the wealthiest of whom were based in Djibouti, where they had substantial capital and access to financial institutions. In the early 1990s, the economy of Djibouti experienced a downturn, in part due to the war between the government and the rebel Afar movement, Front pour la Restauration de la Démocratie. Somaliland, which provided a route into the Ethiopian market, became an attractive investment opportunity for these Djibouti-based traders. Concerned at the commercial consequences of the fighting in Berbera in 1992, they subsequently played an important role in restoring stability by funding peace conferences, providing resources for demobilisation and the new security services, and underwriting the state by providing loans to the administration.

In the early 1990s, Somalia became synonymous with the phenomenon of 'warlords', or political entrepreneurs who controlled territory, populations and economies through force. For various reasons this did not happen in Somaliland.[21] The democratic practices of the SNM and the lack of external sponsors prevented a single leader from building up a position of dominance within the movement. Somaliland did not have a large population of destitute and alienated urban youth, a key source of

---

[21] Somaliland's presidents have at times been inappropriately described as 'faction leaders' or 'warlords'. This neglects the democratic ways in which they have been appointed to office and the degree of consent that exists between the public and the government.

ready recruits for the southern warlords (Marchal 1997). Nor was there a great stockpile of weapons to sustain the fighting. As the major business people in Somaliland had a monopoly over the economy, there was no need to raise an army to protect their assets. Individuals who tried to do so in 1992 (and later in 1994) lost a great deal of money.

The presence abroad of a large Isaaq émigré population was another important stabilising factor for Somaliland. For historical reasons the Isaaq had a better-established diaspora than other clans when the state collapsed (Lindley 2006: 5). During the 1980s they supported the SNM's insurgency. Once the war was over in the north, Somaliland offered new business opportunities and for refugees seeking to return home there was an incentive to invest in stability in Somaliland. Isaaq diaspora communities have been particularly ardent supporters of Somaliland (Svedjemo 2002) – a theme returned to in later chapters.

Finally, a key stabiliser was the role played by informal political institutions – the *diya*-paying groups and elders – in reasserting social control. It has been argued that these indigenous social institutions were more entrenched, stronger and better endowed with moral authority in the northern pastoralist communities than in southern Somalia; and that this distinction reflects one strand in the region's colonial past – the British policy of indirect rule that reinforced the powers of lineage elders (Reno 2003). In the south, it is further argued, Italian colonial policy and the greater pace of urbanisation weakened these institutions. There may be some truth in this, but equally important was the formal role given to the elders by the SNM during the war, and the absence of warlords or charismatic leaders to provide an alternative source of authority. Indeed, while military factions and warlords increased in Somalia, in Somaliland there was a proliferation of councils of elders. In the absence of a state capable of managing social conflicts, these social institutions, despite all their complexities, were able to craft a new political order in Somaliland.

Nabad iyo Caano:[22]
grassroots reconciliation & state-building

In late 1992 the future of Somaliland did not look promising: the consensus that had compelled the SNM leadership to declare independence appeared to be dissipating into factionalism and conflict. The transitional SNM government of Abdirahman Ali 'Tuur' had, in the words of one commentator, presided over 'two wasted years' (Gilkes 1993). But while effective government was lacking, this was a crucial period of reconciliation during which the architecture of government and the direction of the new state was defined. This occurred in two ways: through Somaliland-

---

[22] The traditional saying, meaning 'peace and milk', became a popular slogan in the early 1990s in Somaliland.

wide, 'national' inter-clan peace conferences (*shir beeleed*) [23] and local grassroots reconciliation processes. These processes dealt with a range of 'constitutional' and 'civil' issues that existed in post-war Somaliland.[24] The Somaliland-wide conferences were concerned primarily with constitutional issues. That is, agreeing a framework for power sharing among Somaliland's clans, creating mechanisms for the participation of clan elders in government, structuring the institutions of government, and establishing acceptable systems for maintaining security. The first of these conferences had taken place in Berbera in February 1991 and established the SNM's policy of peaceful coexistence among the clans in Somaliland. It was followed by the May 1991 conference in Burco that established Somaliland's independence, a conference in Sheikh in December 1992 that ended the Berbera conflict, and the 1993 Borama conference that created a charter for governance in Somaliland. These conferences were key political events in the process of state formation in Somaliland.

In addition to and often in preparation for these large Somaliland-wide events, numerous other regional, district and village-level meetings took place between clans and sub-clans, variously organised by lineage elders, intellectuals, religious leaders and women's groups.[25] These locally managed and financed meetings were primarily concerned with 'civil' issues: that is, rebuilding social relations, reopening trade routes and pastoral rangelands, restoring property to its owners, formulating local agreements on the maintenance of security, and the restoration of law and order. In both the national and local processes people drew on the rich institutions and cultural practices of Somali pastoral society for conflict management, and the traditional leadership reverted to its classic role of mediating relations between conflicting parties.

The Tawfiq conference
The conflict over Berbera was brought to an end in October 1992 at a peace conference held in the town of Sheikh, also known by its propitious title *Tawfiq* (meaning 'understanding' or 'consensus'). Forty elders from the Gadabursi, Dhulbahante and Isaaq, along with religious leaders, gathered at Sheikh and brokered a ceasefire and political settlement between the Habar Yunis and 'Iise Muse. The conference was supported by business people and a vocal lobby of women (Cabdi 2005; Gardner and Bushra 2004).[26] In the process of reconciling the conflicting parties, several important political agreements were reached on the organisation of government and security.

[23] *Shir beeleed* is a clan conference, *shir* being a council of clan elders, while *beel* refers to a temporary settlement of nomadic pastoralists, a community and 'clan-family'.
[24] This useful distinction is made by African Rights (1993b) in South Sudan.
[25] Researchers at the Academy for Peace and Development in Hargeysa identify thirty-three clan peace conferences between February 1991 and 1996 (WSP 2005).
[26] Women also objected to the fact that the settlement involved a customary exchange of 50 women between the reconciling parties.

First, in resolving the conflict over the Berbera port, its status as a public asset was reaffirmed. This ensured that future governments of Somaliland had a source of revenue with which to build and sustain an administration. Significantly this rule was also extended to public facilities and state properties throughout Somaliland, thus preventing the capture of these facilities by private entrepreneurs as happened in Somalia. Second, the conference was a defining moment for the role of elders in Somaliland and their participation in governance. With the presence of titled and non-titled elders[27] from all the major clans except the Warsengeli,[28] the Sheikh conference represented the collective efforts of the Somaliland *Guurti* (Farah and Lewis 1993: 57). The intra-Isaaq nature of the Berbera conflict had given the Gadabursi elders a 'third party', mediation role (*ibid.*: 57). Their role at Sheikh indicated that the influence of the SNM was declining and that Somaliland needed the participation of non-Isaaq if it was to survive. The *Guurti* that had been created by the SNM to mobilise support during the war was therefore expanded to incorporate all of Somaliland's clans and formalise their role in the system of governance.

Third, the conference made progress in addressing the challenge of insecurity, by acknowledging the clans' responsibilities for controlling their militias, for preventing acts of aggression against other communities, and for defending Somaliland (*ibid.* 1993: 84–7). Reinforcing the moral authority of the elders in this way helped to prevent the emergence of 'warlords'. On 25 November 1992, 150 elders and thirty militia commanders took an oath of allegiance to the Somaliland state and pledged to maintain peace and public order (Gilkes 1993). After the conference Somaliland's first proper police forces were established in Hargeysa, Gabiley and Borama, with support from the diaspora. This formalisation of security arrangements was a critical step in what Brons (2001: 250) has described as a 'society-rooted process towards state formation', a process that was consolidated three months later in the Borama conference, in which representatives from all clans in Somaliland participated.

The Borama conference

The Sheikh conference achieved the main objective of halting the Berbera conflict. But it left many issues unresolved, including matters of power sharing, the structure of government, the weakness of the administration, and how to ensure a smooth transfer of power once the SNM's mandate ended in April 1993. President Tuur had proposed a six-month extension to his administration in order to prepare the constitution it had failed so far to produce. This was rejected by his political opponents, but when they also failed to mobilise adequate support for a meeting of the SNM central committee, a compromise was agreed: a national convention of

---

[27] A non-titled leader or elder is *oday*, while titled elders are *caaqil* and *Suldaan* among the Isaaq, or *Garaad* among the Darod.

[28] The Warsengeli were absent because of intra-clan negotiations.

the clans – a *shir beeleed* – would be held, chaired by the national *Guurti*.

The Borama conference – or Conference of Elders of the Communities of Somaliland (*Shirweynaha Guurtida Beelaha Soomaaliland*), also known by its propitious title *Allah mahad leh* ('tribute be to God') – opened in Borama on 24 January 1993, three months after the conclusion of the Sheikh conference. As a Gadabursi town, Borama provided a neutral and secure setting and gave non-Isaaqs a role in determining the future of Somaliland. The conference was scheduled to last a month, but in time-honoured Somali fashion time was elastic and it did not end until May 1993. This extended run ensured broad public participation and adequate time for contentious and substantive issues to be exhaustively debated in order to reach a consensus. It was chaired by Sheikh Ibrahim Sheikh Yusuf Sheikh Madar, of the prominent religious family of Hargeysa. The official voting delegates were 150 Somaliland elders – the Somaliland national *Guurti* – from all clans in Somaliland. They were accompanied by a further 150 official observers and advisers. During the five months an estimated 2,000 people attended, including many participants from the diaspora.[29] Women also attended the conference as observers and were strong peace advocates. An important feature of the conference is that it was wholly managed and almost entirely financed by the communities in Somaliland, who thus determined the agenda.[30]

The Borama conference was a watershed event in Somaliland. The agenda prioritised reconciliation, security and state formation, and three significant outcomes were achieved. First, Borama established a framework for managing security. Second, it advanced the vision of an independent Somaliland, by defining the political architecture for government. And third, it oversaw the peaceful transfer of power from the SNM government to a civilian government. Although the demise of the SNM was a consequence of the divisions that had long plagued the organisation, the peaceful transfer of power maintained its democratic traditions.

Conference deliberations on reconciliation and security produced the 'Somaliland Communities Security and Peace Charter' (*Axdiga Nabadga-lyada ee Beelaha Soomaaliland*). Its stated purpose was to 'rectify past mistakes' that had caused insecurity and to promote 'the strengthening of security and stability [and] peaceful coexistence among all the communities of Somaliland' (Somaliland Peace Charter 1993). It elaborated a code of conduct for the people of Somaliland, in accordance with their traditions and Islamic principles. It required every community to take 'a solemn oath not to attack another community', and gave elders the responsibility for settling disputes and mediating conflicts. The Peace Charter thus acted as a national *xeer* or social contract, restoring inter-

[29] Personal communication, Dr Adan Abokor, a conference participant.
[30] The UN provided very limited logistical support. Other contributions came from Somali communities abroad, Somaliland NGOs and business people, Community Aid Abroad, the Mennonites, the Life and Peace Institute, and the French and US embassies in Djibouti.

clan relationships and establishing the basis for law and order. It outlined a national security framework by detailing mechanisms for the registration and storage of weapons, demobilisation, the formation of local police forces and the securing of the roads. It reinforced the agreements reached at Sheikh by making clans and their elders responsible for controlling the militias, and for ensuring that all security arrangements were implemented. And it created judicial institutions that drew on customary and secular law.

Discussions on government and state-building produced a *Transitional National Charter*, which reaffirmed the sovereign independence of Somaliland and defined the political and institutional structures through which the country would be governed for two years, until a constitution could be drafted and ratified. A key challenge for those assembled at Borama was to fashion a form of government that accommodated the clan system within a modern structure of government, despite the divisive issues of political representation and power sharing arising from this. The solution was to establish what came to be referred to as a *beel* system of government, which incorporated clans and their leaderships in the system of governance.[31] This clan- or community-based system has been described as a 'dynamic hybrid of Western form and traditional substance' (Jimcaale 2005). The National Charter defined three branches of government: an executive (*Golaha Xukuumadda*) comprising a President, Vice-President and Council of Ministers; a bicameral Parliament consisting of an Upper House of Elders (*Golaha Guurtida*) and a Lower House of Representatives (*Golaha Wakiilada*); and an independent Judiciary (see Box 8.1, p. 186 below). The Charter also provided for an independent Auditor General, a Central Bank, and regional governors and mayors to be appointed by the government.

The *beel* system of government recognised kinship to be a fundamental principle of social organisation in Somali society. Government took the form of a consociational parliamentary democracy, in essence a power-sharing coalition of Somaliland's main clans, based on principles of proportional representation, pluralism and autonomy.[32] Seats in the Upper and Lower houses of the legislature were proportionally allocated to clans, according to a formula that had been devised at the 1990 Baligubadleh SNM Congress for allocating seats in the organisation's central committee, and expanded to include non-Isaaq and minority clans. In this way the Borama conference established a genuine multi-clan parliament. In fact, non-Isaaq members held a greater share of the seats than they had in the legislature under British rule. Similarly, ministerial appointments were made so as to ensure a clan balance. However, due to the 'traditional substance' of the system, there were no women in Parliament.

---

[31] *Beel* is a temporary settlement of nomadic pastoralists, and by extension also refers to a community and 'clan-family'. See Jimcaale 2005 for a fuller description.

[32] For a full description of this see the very useful *Menu of Options* (Lewis and Mayall 1995) commissioned by the EC for Somalia.

The National Charter gave lineage elders a formal role in government, by incorporating them into the Upper House of the new legislature, where they provided a check on the executive and the representatives. The Charter gave them responsibility for selecting the President and Vice-President, ensuring state security, demobilising the militia, and maintaining religious and moral values. Their role as peacemakers was institutionalised and defined in the Charter as being 'to encourage and safeguard peace [and] creating new or enforcing existing Codes of Conduct [*xeer*] among the clans' (Bradbury 1994a: 74). Their unique responsibilities were acknowledged by Sheikh Ibrahim, Chair of the *Guurti*, when he remarked: 'Our task is to ensure security and reconciliation. The government's responsibility is management, administration and development...' (Omaar 1994).

As discussed in Chapter 2, the inclusion of lineage elders in the state apparatus was not a new departure. The British colonial authorities had incorporated clan elders into the administration as salaried chiefs (*caaqilo*), as a means of extending control into rural areas, a practice continued by Somalia's independent governments. Under the Barre government the traditional leaders had been renamed peaceseekers (*nabad-doon*) and later integrated into the party structure. The SNM had integrated a *Guurti* into its organisation to mobilise support in the war, and, in line with its manifesto, to lay the basis for a more participatory form of democracy. Indeed, the National Charter reflected much of what was proposed in the SNM's manifesto for a post-Barre government: a government built on Somali cultural values; the elevation of *xeer* to the national level; and the incorporation of elders into a two-chamber legislature.

In June 1993, the 150-member *Guurti* selected Mohamed Ibrahim Egal as Somaliland's new President, with Colonel Abdirahman Aw Ali as his Vice-President. The high level of public participation in the conference and the responsibilities accorded to the clan elders for guaranteeing security and selecting a new President gave the new government a high degree of popular legitimacy; and the public thus had a stake in ensuring its success. The *beel* system of government was intended as a transitional arrangement for two years only, until a full constitution could be drafted and ratified. It lasted a decade.

The political arrangements agreed at Borama proved remarkably effective in creating a basis for government and addressing critical issues of security, reconciliation and reintegration. But it did not resolve all issues. In particular, the clan-based political arrangements generated new problems. At Borama non-Isaaq reaffirmed their support for Somaliland and increased their stake in the state. The Gadabursi, who had a prominent role in Sheikh and hosted the Borama conference, gained the position of Vice-President in the new government, while the post of Speaker of the Lower House went to the Harti. The perception of Dhulbahante and Warsengeli representatives at Borama, however, was that they had been treated unequally compared to the Gadabursi. This contributed to a sense of alienation from Somaliland, a situation that was to be exacerbated at another national conference in 1997. Of more immediate significance was the distribution of parliamentary seats among the Isaaq. Some Garhajis politicians (from the Habar Yunis and 'Idagalle clans) complained that they had received a disproportionately small share of seats, and later used this grievance to mobilise opposition to the government.

The Sanaag Grand Peace and Reconciliation Conference

If the Borama conference was concerned with constitutional issues, the Sanaag Grand Peace and Reconciliation Conference (*Shir Nabadeedka ee Sanaag*) held in Erigavo in north-east Somaliland is a classic example of a peace process that addressed civil issues.[33] Although there are overlaps with the national peace conferences, the agreements reached in Sanaag were specific to that region. Over a period of eighteen months of protracted negotiations, involving seven separate peace meetings, a regional peace agreement was endorsed by elders of the Isaaq, Warsengeli and Dhulbahante clans in October 1993.

Sanaag Region has historic relevance to Somali people as the place where many of the founding fathers of the clan-families are thought to have entered Somalia, lived and been buried. The tomb of Sheikh Isaaq in Mait is a site of pilgrimage. It is also a region where lineages of the Isaaq (Habar Yunis and Habar Ja'lo) and Harti/Darod (Warsengeli and Dhulbahante) closely reside, have intermarried and long established social and economic ties. Before the war the regional capital Erigavo accommodated a cosmopolitan mix of clans. With a mixture of pastoralism and agro-pastoralism forming the basis of people's livelihoods, the region has long experienced tensions over land use for grazing, water and agriculture (Prior 1994). These tensions were exacerbated by processes of land degradation, privatisation, state intervention and patronage. Spilling over into the war, the same tensions saw the Darod broadly supporting the government while the Isaaq backed the SNM.[34] The war displaced people out of and within the region. When the SNM won control of Erigavo in 1991 a ceasefire was agreed, and the Dhulbahante and Warsengeli withdrew to their traditional territories (*degaan*[35]). For twelve months, communication between the Isaaq and Darod was mostly via VHF radios, and through trading at markets along the territorial boundaries of the clans. Only women were able to cross these safely.

In 1992 elders of the Isaaq and Harti clans embarked on a lengthy

---

[33] Detailed descriptions of this conference can be found in studies by Farah and Lewis 1993; Yusuf 1996; Bradbury 1994a.

[34] As elsewhere during the war, fighting occurred within these alliances – between the Habar Yunis and Habar Ja'lo, for example.

[35] *Degaan* is territory controlled by a clan and includes the resources, such as wells, within that territory.

> **Box 4.2 Resolutions of the Special Conference between the Warsengeli and Eastern Habar Ja'lo at Shimbirale, 8–18 November 1992**
>
> • With effect from 18 August any property stolen or looted should be returned immediately.
>
> • Anybody who suffers injury cannot take revenge on the clan of the criminal, but will seek payment from the individual responsible or from his immediate sub-clan.
>
> • Those who suffer casualties should not take revenge themselves but inform the standing committee on peace. If they take revenge, they will be treated as bandits.
>
> • The standing committee on peace will use the services of the peace forces when needed.
>
> • Anyone killed or injured while involved in acts of banditry will be treated as a dead donkey, and will be denied any rights.
>
> • Any sub-clan engaging in acts of banditry which cause death or material loss should pay for whatever damages they have caused. In addition, they will pay a bond of one hundred female camels. This bond will be made over to the joint administration of the two sides, for common use.

---

process of reconciliation. This involved numerous bilateral meetings between the clans. In November 1992, for example, 400 delegates from the Habar Yunis and the Warsengeli assembled in the village of Jidili. The *shir* agreed that each clan would be responsible for maintaining law and order within its own territory. Any person wanting to enter the *degaan* of another clan to access pasture or water was to be responsible for protecting the lives and livestock of the host community, and vice versa. To reinforce the peace agreement, joint committees were to be established in the buffer zones between the reconciling communities to settle disputes or prevent disturbances that jeopardise the peace. These committees were known locally as *Guddida turxaan bixinta* (the 'committee which uproots unwanted plants from a field') (Farah and Lewis 1993: 20). It was also decreed that compensation for the actions of armed groups should be shouldered by the close families of persistent offenders, rather than extended to the whole *diya*-paying group, as is the normal practice. Similar meetings were held between the Isaaq and Warsengeli and Dhulbahante throughout the region. A meeting between the Habar Ja'lo and the Warsengeli at the village of Shimbirale produced a similar agreement (see Box 4.2).

The peace process in Sanaag utilised customary practices and institutions of peacemaking. Elders (*caaqilo*) of *diya*-paying groups met in assemblies (*shir*), together with religious leaders (*wadaado*) and paramount heads (*Suldaano*), and created new political treaties (*xeer*) between the clans. Following long-established practices, in small villages and rural settings these meetings took place in the shade of acacia trees. In the absence of formal legal institutions, there was a reversion to customary law, with decisions and judgements sanctioned by religious leaders. During these meetings poetry, the premier Somali art form, was commonly used to influence the mood of the participants in the negotiations.

This grassroots process of peacemaking was necessarily slow in order to be inclusive, and involved people at each level of clan segmentation resolving their disputes before convening as a larger body. Peace meetings were structured in a way that recognised the different relationships and grievances between the clans whose territories adjoin each other and share grazing lands, and those which do not. In Sanaag Region the Habar Yunis reside close to and are intermarried with the Warsengeli, while the Habar Ja'lo have closer ties with the Dhulbahante. Different rules (*xeer*) apply to the discrete relationships between the clans. These were broken during the war and the peace meetings involved constructing new treaties of cooperation. As the authority of the elders to negotiate new treaties is delegated to them by their clans, the meetings involved representatives chosen by the communities. In the perception of many Somalis the strength of these meetings lay in the presence of legitimate representatives chosen by the community, and the existence of common *xeer* between the parties. And for this reason, they proved more successful and their outcomes more enduring than the so-called 'national' Somalia peace conferences that were sponsored by foreign governments in foreign countries (Bradbury 1994a).

There were pragmatic reasons why such communities wanted to re-establish cooperative relations. This is alluded to in the Somali saying *nabad iyo caano* ('peace and milk' or 'peace and prosperity'), which stresses the relationship between peace and prosperity and stands in opposition to the phrase *'ol iyo abaar* ('conflict and drought'). Plentiful milk means healthy livestock and good grazing. Access to pasture and water is assured through peaceful cooperation. Access to land and its usage was an underlying issue in the civil war in Sanaag and a driving force behind the peace process there. In order for people to survive and resume their way of life there was a need to re-establish cooperative relations over pastoral resources and trade. Preserving economic livelihoods was dependent on the creation of new political and economic relations. The series of peace meetings that were concluded prior to the Erigavo conference set out the parameters for peaceful cooperation: freedom of movement; freedom of trade; access to common grazing areas; access to common water sources; and the return of private property.

It would be wrong to view such peacemaking endeavours as anachronistic or lacking relevance. On the contrary, they were dynamic and innovative. In response to the prevailing circumstances, social structures proved to be adaptable. In the absence of the state and other strong forms of association, the significance of kinship as a basis for social organisation increased. As clans fragmented the need for coordination and cooperation led to a proliferation of clan councils (*Guurti*) in Somaliland, which were given the responsibility for arbitrating on intra- and inter-clan disputes. Since 1991 many clans in Somaliland have anointed new Sultans as a way of enhancing their political weight (Farah and Lewis 1993: 22).[36] Elders delegated to talk peace included soldiers, businessmen and former civil servants. Educated professionals (so-called 'intellectuals') helped to organise and record the meetings. VHF radios enabled parties to negotiate with each other at a distance prior to the meetings, and video recordings were made of the meetings.

Women also played a significant role in peacemaking. This occurred in two ways: through their structural position in society, and as organised groups. A woman's dual kinship ties to her paternal clan and to affinal relatives in her husband's clan would enable her to act as an ambassador and channel of communication between warring parties and to cross from the territory of one to another. At the Erigavo conference, emphasis was placed on reinforcing the marriage ties between the clans. In addition, although women were excluded from formal peace negotiations, in many places they organised themselves to lobby the warring parties to sue for peace (Gardner and el Bushra 2004).

Numerous local meetings culminated in the Grand Peace and Reconciliation Conference held in Erigavo. The conference lasted three months and concluded in October 1993 with the adoption of the Sanaag Regional Peace Charter. Although the Sanaag conference ended after the Borama conference, the reconciliation process in the former contributed to the positive outcome of the latter. The Sanaag Charter borrowed some of the concepts and language of the National Charter. It guaranteed the right of individuals to move freely within the territories of all clans; the free movement of trade; the return of fixed assets, including land; the restoration of reciprocal access to grazing lands; the formation of a regional administration; and heavy sanctions against those who violated the peace agreement. A committee was also created to oversee the implementation of the agreement.

There is general acceptance that sorting out issues of property and land rights will be problematic in the resolution of the conflict in Somalia (African Rights 1993a). Foreign mediation has tended to assume that such issues will only be resolved once the state has been re-established.[37] The peace process in Sanaag suggests the opposite. In Sanaag Region, the absence of the state enabled negotiation over real estate to proceed. At the Erigavo conference a distinction was made between private and common

[36] In 2003 Sultan Rashid Sultan Ali Ducaale noted that there were forty-two titular heads of clans – Sultans and *Garaado*– in Somaliland, compared to nine in 1960. Interview with author, Hargeysa, 2003.

[37] The Somali National Reconciliation Conference (2002–4) sought to address the issue of land as part of the peace process, but although it was flagged and debated no solutions were offered, other than the need for a land commission.

property. Houses and movable property, such as animals and vehicles, were relatively easy to deal with. The owners were known, and once the principle was agreed that property should be returned, it was largely a matter of private negotiation. Land was more problematic, requiring a consensus among groups of users. The incentive for parties to resolve the conflict lay in renewed access to rangelands resources and the resumption of trade.

In August 1995, two years after the Sanaag Regional Peace Charter was signed, the elders in Sanaag embarked on a process of returning land to families displaced by the war. This mostly involved the Habar Yunis, Dhulbahante, Warsengeli and Gahayle. It was a complex process as the lands in question incorporated fourteen different areas of rangelands, former cooperative agricultural land and frankincense forests. Between August and October 1995, 500 families were resettled in homesteads on land that they had evacuated in 1991. This was accomplished with minimal external assistance.[38]

It has long been argued in regard to humanitarian disasters that the way in which people cope with and reduce their vulnerability can be a starting point for analysis and policy. In wars, social and political vulnerability caused by the violent break-up of communities and families, and the destruction of civil and civic institutions, can be as disastrous as economic vulnerability. The reconciliation process in Sanaag Region suggests that the restoration of such institutions is fundamental to the recovery of war-affected societies. Through such local peace processes in Sanaag people were addressing the source of their own vulnerability by reuniting families, restoring community relations and re-establishing assurance through cooperation and rules of collective behaviour and action.

Models of peace building

In the 1990s the institutions and mechanisms that had been designed to maintain international peace and security between states during the Cold War were challenged by a proliferation of civil wars, such as the one in Somalia. Alternative policy instruments were developed in response to these wars 'within' states. The concept of 'peace building' proposed in the United Nations publication *An Agenda for Peace* (Boutros-Ghali 1992), for example, signalled a shift from classic peacekeeping to multiple and multi-level forms of foreign intervention to end wars. The inability of many states (or their lack of interest) in mediating social conflict

---

[38] Information provided by Haroon Ahmed Yusuf and Sultan Rashid Sultan Ali Ducaale. The NGO ActionAid and the Australian organisation Community Aid Abroad provided some logistical support, but the government in Hargeysa was not involved and an embargo by the Nairobi-based Somalia Aid Coordination Body on aid to Sanaag meant that the redistribution of land took place outside the purview of international agencies.

also generated an interest in indigenous non-state approaches to conflict resolution, and a proliferation of non-state actors taking on tasks of conflict management.

The efficacy of indigenous processes of conflict resolution and the role of non-governmental organisations in conflict resolution have generated considerable debate.[39] Two conclusions can be drawn from the local peace processes in Somaliland that are relevant to these discussions. First, despite the efforts of the Barre regime and previous civilian governments to exorcise the clan system and 'modernise' Somali society, the traditional and indigenous system of governance remained strong. In the absence of effective government people placed their faith in their customary institutions to resolve and manage conflict. Second, the locally financed and managed peace processes in Somaliland proved to be more effective than externally sponsored 'national' conferences in Somalia.

The 1993 Borama conference was not only a defining political event in Somaliland, but also an example of an indigenous popular peacemaking process that has few parallels in contemporary Africa.[40] At the time it offered an alternative model to the formal peacemaking and state-building processes that were being supported by the international bodies in Somalia, such as the March 1993 National Reconciliation Conference in Addis Ababa (Bradbury 1994a). Some similarities existed between the Borama model and the process that led to the formation of the short-lived Digil-Mirifle Supreme Governing Council for Bay and Bakool regions in 1994, and the series of locally sponsored conferences of clan elders in north-east Somalia that led to the creation of the state of Puntland in 1998 (WSP 2001). In both these cases, however, the international community gave some support.

Since the beginning of the civil war in Somalia two schools of thought have tended to dominate approaches to conflict resolution and state building there. One has supported formal mediation between Somalia's *de facto* political leaders – the warlords or faction leaders – to secure a ceasefire and a power-sharing deal. The other, so-called 'bottom-up' or 'grassroots' approach has advocated support for local reconciliation and peacemaking to build cross-clan cooperative relations, which would marginalise and disempower the warlords. In the early 1990s, UNOSOM pursued two 'tracks'[41] in southern Somalia. It engaged with the warlords and their factions through internationally brokered peace conferences, while simultaneously opening dialogue with what was intended to be a broader, grassroots constituency through the formation of district

[39] For example, see the papers of the All-Africa Conference on African Principles of Conflict Resolution and Reconciliation, held in Addis Ababa, November 1999. For Somalia see, for example, Farah and Lewis 1993; African Rights 1994; Helander 1995; Menkhaus 1999a.

[40] Another example of grassroots peacemaking in Africa is the 1999 Wunlit Peace Conference in South Sudan and the wider people-to-people peace process (New Sudan Council of Churches 2002; Bradbury *et al.* 2006).

[41] In diplomatic parlance these two approaches are also referred to as Track I and Track II diplomacy.

councils. Both approaches proved to be problematic. UNOSOM was a bureaucratic, state-centric body constituted by governments, with a mandate to re-establish a central government, albeit one with some decentralised structures. International diplomacy did nothing to rein in the predatory forces which unleashed the violence. On the contrary, the internationally sponsored peace conferences shored up the authority of the faction leaders, who were paid to attend, and prevented alternative leaders from surfacing. There was little incentive for these leaders and their militias, who were profiting from plunder and extortion, to implement any peace accord. And as long as the peace conferences were held outside Somalia there was little social pressure on the factional leaders to adhere to the agreements. On the other 'track', the formation of district councils was poorly managed and implemented.[42] In places they legitimised the capture of territory by clans and exacerbated violent competition. Elsewhere they did provide a vehicle for improved inter-clan relations, but their impact was highly localised (Bradbury 1994a; Human Rights Watch 1995).

The contrast with Somaliland was very striking. In Somaliland there was a synergy between the Somaliland-wide peace conferences and the local peacemaking processes, which succeeded in containing violence while crafting a political consensus and power-sharing arrangements that provided the foundations for new state structures. Again, to understand the different functions of local and Somaliland-wide peace conferences, the distinction between 'constitutional' and 'civil' issues is helpful. In Somaliland the defeat of Barre's forces effectively resolved the constitutional conflict by leaving the SNM as the only real power in the north-west. This enabled local and regional peace processes, like that in Sanaag, to focus on civil issues. These included the restoration of cooperative relations to facilitate commerce; the opening of roads and access to grazing lands; the restoration of stolen property; the reduction of livestock raiding; and the attraction of investment, including support from international aid agencies. When these local processes tried to deal with 'constitutional issues', it usually proved detrimental. This was apparent at a peace meeting between the Warsengeli and Habar Yunis in Sanaag Region in November 1992. The Warsengeli refused to recognise the presence of SNM representatives in the Habar Yunis delegation. The only way they were able to proceed with peace negotiations was as clans (Bradbury 1994b). By removing the state as a primary object of conflict, social relations could be addressed through customary institutions.

Key differences between the peace processes in Somaliland and the external peacemaking efforts in Somalia were that the former were locally designed, managed and financed; that they generally involved the participation of locally selected leadership; that they accepted the need for a long time-frame; and that they involved broad public participation.

---

[42] The UN insisted on token women representatives, and officials were helicoptered into villages for meetings and to approve councils.

Critically, they were also rooted in a popular desire for peace and stability that was linked to the aspiration for international recognition of an independent Somaliland. This did not exist among the warlords and 'spoilers' in Somalia, who had interests in perpetuating state collapse (Menkhaus 2004). Moreover, in Somalia the peace meetings were designed to meet external agendas, were externally financed, and were primarily oriented to re-establishing central government.

In Somalia, over time, the need to restore cooperative and predictable community relations to ensure livelihoods, facilitate trade and economic recovery has generated a variety of localised governance structures, including municipal administrations, business consortiums, committees of elders, religious communities – and, since the mid-1990s, Islamic courts. These have brought modest levels of security and lawfulness to some places. The internationally sponsored Somalia national peace talks in Djibouti in 2000 and Kenya in 2002–4 sought to apply some lessons from past experiences, taking a longer-term, more holistic approach to conflict resolution, and engaging both political leaders and civic actors. To call them peace conferences or 'peace processes', however, is perhaps a misnomer. They were exercises in politics and power, in which political elites manoeuvred for a share of government and its anticipated spoils. Thus, to date, external efforts to reconstitute a state have served to exacerbate armed conflict (ibid. 2004). In Somaliland the series of peace conferences in the early 1990s were critical events in the formation of a new state, but it was the absence of effective government that allowed these local processes to succeed. Whereas externally funded processes in Somalia came to nothing, the Somaliland conferences created a system of government that lasted for a decade and provided the basis for a state that, at the time of writing, has endured for sixteen years – a third of the territory's eventful journey since it first gained independence in 1960.

5
State & the Long Building Transition

The declaration of Somaliland's independence in May 1991 created an opportunity for people to break with the corrupt and unrepresentative form of government that Somalis had experienced in the past and to build systems of legitimate and accountable governance. But in the catastrophic post-war environment of Somaliland the interim SNM government, bereft of revenue and external support, could make little progress. The new President, Mohamed Haji Ibrahim Egal, selected by the *Guurti* at the Borama conference, was given two years (later extended by eighteen months to October 1996) to complete a task that was hardly less daunting than the one President Tuur faced in 1991. His transitional government initially made rapid progress on two critical fronts: improving security and creating state institutions. But the political consensus crafted at Borama was damaged by two years of civil war between 1994 and 1996. Egal gained a second chance when he was reselected as President in 1997. From then until his death in 2002 Somaliland advanced steadily: government authority and bureaucracy was expanded; a constitution was finalised and approved by plebiscite, opening the way for multi-party politics; and the country experienced considerable economic development. The two 'transitional' administrations of Mohamed Ibrahim Egal, lasting some nine years, were therefore critically important in consolidating and shaping the Somaliland state as it exists today. This chapter describes the dynamics of state-building during this period.

Egal's First Government 1993–7

The new President
Mohamed Haji Ibrahim Egal took office amid the euphoria that followed the successful conclusion of the Borama conference. Born in Odweyne, midway between Berbera and the rangelands of the Haud, the son of a wealthy merchant and property owner, Egal was educated in former

British Somaliland, Sudan and England. He entered politics in the 1950s when he joined the Somali National League, then agitating for independence from Britain. In 1956 he was elected head of the Berbera branch and two years later had risen to be the party's General Secretary. In a long political career spanning fifty years, he held posts in all Somali governments. In 1959 he was appointed First Minister in the advisory council set up by the British colonial administration to prepare the colony for self-governance. It was he who led Somaliland to independence on 26 June 1960 and into the union with the newly independent Italian Somalia. In the 1960s he was Defence Minister in Somalia's first cabinet (1960–2) and later Minister of Education (1962–3). Then, in 1967, he was selected as Prime Minister by President Abdirashid Ali Sharmarke. Under Egal's premiership, government dissolved into a morass of corruption and clan nepotism, before he was removed from power by the 1969 military coup, arrested, and detained until 1975. On release he was appointed ambassador to India, but rearrested after only six months, accused of conspiracy and held in solitary confinement in the notorious Labaatan Jirow jail for seven years. After his release in 1982, he returned to government as Chair of the Chamber of Commerce, Industry and Agriculture until the outbreak of the civil war. In 1991, he was selected as one of the co-chairmen of the 1991 Somali reconciliation conferences in Djibouti.

In many respects Egal was a strange choice for President of Somaliland. His political career was blighted by the failures of his premiership in the 1960s; his relationship with the Barre regime had been ambiguous; he had not been a member of the SNM; and he had co-chaired the Somalia national peace conference in Djibouti which rejected Somaliland's independence. In his favour was the fact that senior elders had worked with him in the past and remembered his contributions to the country's struggle for independence from colonialism. Being outside the SNM meant that he was not party to the feuds within the organisation. The fact that his paternal clan was 'Iise Muse (of the Habar Awal) and maternal clan was Habar Yunis, encouraged public optimism that he could reunite the Isaaq. He also received the backing of some of Somaliland's wealthiest merchants, who had interests in keeping Berbera free of conflict. The fact that he had once been the leader of an independent Somaliland, if only for a few days, also struck a chord with the public. As did being a seasoned politician and an internationally recognised statesman of the generation of African leaders who led their countries to independence from colonialism. The public hoped that he could again win international recognition for an independent Somaliland.

The seeds of recovery

The public's trust in Egal soon appeared well placed. Agreement on a political system and institutions of governance, a mechanism for demobilisation, the creation of a revenue system and the provision of a secure environment for economic recovery were early and substantial achievements.

During the first two years of Egal's premiership, government ministries were revitalised, offices were refurbished, morning and afternoon work hours were instituted, and a Civil Service Commission was created. Ministerial and civil service staff (which numbered about 2,500 in 1995) received regular salaries, as did MPs, the police and the army. The government even introduced a minimum wage. A government-controlled Central Bank was created and a new Somaliland currency introduced. Professional police officers were organised and equipped in Hargeysa, Borama and Berbera, and a judicial system of regional and district courts was put in place, utilising the 1960 penal code. Customs offices were established and revenue collected. In November 1994 Somaliland's first annual budget was agreed: some 50 per cent was allocated to the security services, with education and health combined receiving 17 per cent (Gilkes 1995). Regular coordination meetings were established between the Ministry of Planning and international NGOs and UN agencies. Although the government's writ rarely reached beyond Hargeysa, Berbera, Burco and Borama, it began to develop a functional relationship with the regions. Regional health and education plans were authorised by the Ministry of Health and regional health workers and some education officials received incentives through the government, often funded by international agencies. Hargeysa municipality, supported by UN-Habitat, embarked on a programme of town planning and civil engineering, including repairs to government offices and hotels.

The previous government had failed to establish a revenue base on which to build and sustain an administration. Egal rectified this. The government's main source of revenue would come from import and export tariffs levied at the port of Berbera and customs and excise facilities at the border crossing to Djibouti. One of Egal's first moves on taking office was to create the Berbera Port Authority as an autonomous body directly under the President's office to manage the port and its revenue. He was able to do this without opposition because the Sheikh and Borama conferences had reaffirmed Berbera's status as a national asset and because Berbera lies within the territory of Egal's own 'Iise Muse clan. The manner in which the Port Authority was established also provided the President with a source of revenue over which the legislature had no political control and this would eventually lead to accusations of corruption and impeachment hearings. On taking office, however, it provided an immediate revenue source for government, which by September 1995 was estimated to be between US$10–15 million per year.[1]

The government benefited particularly from the revival of the livestock export trade when the Saudi Arabian market was reopened to Somali

---

[1] John Drysdale, personal communication, September 1995.

meat. The presence of large camps of Somaliland refugees in eastern Ethiopia, the political changes within Ethiopia following the fall of the Derg, the open Somaliland–Ethiopia border and the regular movement of refugees across that border had created a new market in Ethiopia for Somaliland's traders. In the early 1990s some 60 per cent of livestock exported through Berbera originated in Ethiopia and central Somalia – from as far south as Belet Weyne – and some 65 per cent of imports through Berbera were destined for Ethiopia. With the port of Djibouti in decline, Berbera, like Assab in Eritrea, began to challenge Djibouti as the main port for eastern Ethiopia in terms of volume of trade. In addition to lower customs duties, Berbera provided a non-bureaucratic and well-run facility. Berbera also benefited from the closure of the southern ports of Kismayo and Mogadishu due to the conflict there and its superior capacity to Bossaso. Returns from exports financed the lucrative import business and assisted with the recovery of the rural economy.

The revival of trade through Berbera benefited Somaliland's wealthiest merchant families, and Egal's relationship with them was crucial to his ability to re-establish government institutions. In the early 1990s some of the wealthiest Isaaq merchants and wholesalers were from the Habar Awal clan, which includes Egal's 'Iise Muse clan. Based in Djibouti, they had global trading networks, importing commodities such as sugar to the Horn from as far away as South America. In Somaliland they monopolised the trade between Berbera, Hargeysa, Ethiopia and Djibouti. As already described, these business people provided finance for the Sheikh and Borama conferences and supported Egal's appointment at Borama. In the early days of his presidency they provided food for the army and police. In 1993, crucially, they provided the government with a loan of US$7 million, which was to be repaid through tax exemptions, and financed the printing of Somaliland's new currency, the Somaliland shilling. The introduction of the currency in October 1994 produced a considerable financial windfall for the government. Another important source of government tax revenue was the *qaad* trade, which generated about 10 per cent of the government's income. In the early 1990s, this was estimated to be worth US$137 million in Hargeysa alone and US$250 million for Somaliland as a whole (Gilkes 1995).

The new political consensus made Somaliland an attractive investment environment and Somalilanders from the diaspora began to open new businesses. A critical development was the establishment of Somaliland's first international telecommunications system in Hargeysa in June 1995. This was quickly extended to Berbera and Borama and facilitated the flow of overseas remittances, which has since become the mainstay of Somaliland's economy.

Disarmament and demobilisation
Economic recovery was assisted by a greatly improved security situation. The failure to bring the SNM forces and disparate militias under a central

command and to deal with armed banditry contributed to the demise of President Tuur's administration. The Borama conference had made demobilisation and disarmament a priority for the new government and had sought to address the problem through a security framework that gave the communities, through their elders, responsibility for security. An elder from Burco explains how this was achieved:[2]

> After the collapse of Barre's army, and after the Burco conference, the real SNM fighters demobilised. Once there was an agreement here, every clan was asked to bring their fighters for the national army. But the clans selected the worst. When they were collected together the SNM government could not pay and control them, so they started looting and fighting. Because of the collapse of the government anyone would carry a gun, especially those from the rural areas. The problem was solved through the clan structures. Because of need the young people began selling their guns. At the family level, fathers and uncles took guns away from their sons by force sometimes. The worst ones were dealt with through the family and *diya*-paying group, because the *diya*-paying group did not want to continue paying *diya*.

Through the actions of communities and with assistance from business people the government was able to remove unofficial checkpoints from the main roads and bring banditry under control. As the establishment of police forces and a judicial system began to restore a semblance of law and order, the public display of guns was no longer tolerated. During the Tuur administration the lack of law and order and banditry had meant that international aid organisations spent excessive resources on protecting their compounds and on hiring local vehicles. The improvements in the security environment meant that foreign organisations were able to reduce the amount they spent on their security and the UN was able to import its own vehicles.[3]

On taking office, the Egal government announced that it did not intend to form a national army. Efforts by Tuur to create such a force had been strongly opposed and the new government had no immediate resources to support one. Within a few months, however, the policy changed and Egal reached an agreement with militia commanders and elders to assemble their forces in cantonment sites where they would be retrained and absorbed into Somaliland's new security forces or given skills for civilian life. A key element of the agreement that Egal struck with the militia commanders was for the government to pay off the owners of the *technicals* (the armoured Landcruisers), the most prized weapon in the militia's armoury. Businessmen were prevailed upon to provide food for the encamped militias. The cantonment of forces moved faster than anticipated as

---

[2] Author's interview with Jama Farah Abdi, elder from Togdheer. Burco, 2003.

[3] The need for private security never reached the level experienced in southern Somalia, and attacks on aid agencies were rare. To this day aid agencies operating in southern Somalia hire vehicles and pay heavily for armed protection.

militias sought to reap the benefits of retraining and employment in the new security forces. In September 1993 there were 3,000 militia members encamped in Mandera; by October this figure had doubled. Assistance was expected from UNOSOM, which had a mandate and a substantial budget to support demobilisation in Somalia (Bradbury 1994a: 82). This did not materialise. The most significant input, from the United Nations Development Programme (UNDP), was its assignment of two Zimbabwean consultants to advise the government on demobilisation. With the exception of short-term assistance for the encamped militias from a few international NGOs, international support for demobilisation was very limited. Somaliland, therefore, was left largely to its own devices in orchestrating the demobilisation and reintegration of ex-combatants.

Yet this lack of assistance helped to avoid the pitfalls of many externally funded demobilisation, disarmament and reintegration programmes that commonly become a source of revenue for military leaders, and to strengthen local management of the process. Two organisations were established: the National Demobilisation Commission (NDC) and a veterans' association, SOOYAAL, to support ex-SNM combatants and their widows. In 1994, at a ceremony in Hargeysa football stadium, clans publicly handed their heavy weapons to the government. By February, the NDC claimed it had acquired three-quarters of the weapons from five brigades in Hargeysa and western Somaliland, and that as many as 5,000 militia members had been disarmed (Nyathi 1995: 27).

The demobilisation of the SNM in 1993 succeeded in improving security and the ceremony to hand over heavy weapons to the government was an important symbolic event in the process of consolidating the Somaliland state. As an elder explains:[4]

> Because there were no international peacekeepers, when we made peace and trust increased we pooled our military resources and gave them to the government. We set them up to be a national army. Although technically the weapons belong to us, it is not possible to withdraw them.

The demobilisation process built on the renewed political consensus achieved at Borama. It established a central command over the military, enhanced the authority of the police, removed the gun from the streets and signalled a commitment to the idea of government having a monopoly over security. However, demobilisation fell short of being a total success for two reasons.

First, the process was uneven across the country. It was less successful around Burco and did not take place at all in Sool and eastern Sanaag regions. Without foreign aid the reintegration programmes were inadequate to meet the needs of the militia. Several hundred of those encamped in 1993 were recruited into the police and customs forces, but the remainder

---

[4] Author's interview with Jama Farah Abdi, elder from Togdheer. Burco, 2003.

were sent home unemployed. In early 1995 an informed estimate suggested that some 10,000 militia members remained to be demobilised (Gilkes 1995).

Second, efforts at reintegration were set back by the outbreak of war in 1994, which led to a temporary remobilisation of forces along clan lines. The government was accused of going against the spirit of the Peace Charter when it recruited militia members into its ranks. The 1st brigade of the new National Army became operative by March 1994 and by September 1995 there were estimated to be as many as 15,000 uniformed soldiers. Although the government stated that it would demobilise them once the war was over, the positive environment that existed in 1993 had dissipated. Many thousands of fighters have therefore never formally been demobilised. In 2003 the working figure agreed by the government and the UN for the number of people employed in the army, police and custodial corps was 17,000 and these forces were consuming up to 70 per cent of the national budget. Arguably, this has been money well spent on preventing the military from becoming a predatory force. In the words of the government, in the early 1990s there was no alternative but to 'hold the lion by the ears' until major development assistance could be secured for a full-scale demobilisation. However, this also meant that resources were not available to be spent on other development needs and, as will be described in later chapters, government security spending over time became a focus for allegations of corruption and patronage.

A return to war

Despite the progress made in establishing the institutions of government and creating a secure environment for economic recovery, the new state remained politically fragile and vulnerable to the ambitions of politicians and international interference. Egal commanded greater authority than Tuur due to his recognised statesmanship and charisma, but the effectiveness of his administration relied on the revenues generated by Berbera port and the political support of the Habar Awal, the most urbanised Isaaq clan and a dominant force in trade and commerce in Somaliland. With Abdulrahman Aw Ali, a Gadabursi and former SNM commander, as his Vice President, Egal could count on some support from Awdal Region and from the wing of the SNM that opposed Tuur. Beyond western Somaliland, however, the political consensus was fragile. The geographical and political extent of the state was only clear on paper. The Harti in eastern Somaliland were disappointed not to have been given the position of Vice-President in the new government and, despite their participation in the Borama conference, their support for Somaliland began to wane. The continuing fragility of the new state was exposed only eighteen months after Egal became President when violent conflict erupted in Hargeysa in November 1994, spreading to Burco by March 1995.

The war, which broadly pitched government forces against the Garhajis militias (formed of 'Idagalle and Habar Yunis) involved the heaviest fighting since the war against Siyad Barre. Up to 180,000 people fled the fighting to Ethiopia, from where many had only recently returned, and as many as 4,000 are estimated to have been killed in Burco alone. Property that had been rehabilitated after 1991 was again destroyed and both sides rearmed, bringing new weapons into the region. The war damaged the economy, causing currency devaluation, inflation and a retraction of international assistance programmes. Trade in the east of the country was greatly curtailed and the government's budget was drained by allegedly spending US$4.5 million on re-equipping the army. But perhaps the most damaging effect was the loss of public confidence in the political leadership and the viability of Somaliland.

The factors that precipitated a return to war in November 1994 were similar to those that had triggered the conflict in Berbera. Control of port revenues had been a catalyst in 1992; in 1994 control of Hargeysa airport and its revenue was the spark. But both disputes were a manifestation of other tensions related to the process of state-building (Bryden 1994a). These now concerned the government's attempt to extend its authority beyond Hargeysa, unresolved issues of power-sharing, historical divisions within the SNM, competition over Somaliland's resources (particularly trade and currency), the ambitions of the political elite, the influence of external parties in the south, and the international community's diplomatic engagement in Somalia. Although the conflict was largely confined within the Isaaq confederation and predictably was projected along clan lines, the concentration of fighting around the main urban and commercial centres indicated that this was a struggle between sections of the urban political elite rather than an inter-clan war. The involvement of parties from southern Somalia also gave it a broader political dimension, as did insecurity in Awdal Region. In the case of Awdal, the government's attempt to establish its authority over the border with Djibouti and control of the Djibouti–Hargeysa trade and Zeyla port, led to sporadic clashes with 'Iise militia backed by Djibouti and Gadabursi from Ethiopia's Somali Region. By August 1995, the government had reasserted its authority in the west.

The political consensus achieved in Borama began to unravel when Egal announced his first cabinet. Habar Yunis and Warsengeli leaders refused the two ministerial posts offered them. In July 1993, only a month after the conclusion of the Borama conference, Habar Yunis leaders gathered in Burco and, at a meeting known as the 'Liiban Congress', declared that they would neither take up their seats in Parliament nor be bound by its laws. The Garhajis listed several grievances. They asserted that the election of Egal had been unfair; that the Garhajis were under-represented in Parliament and the Habar Awal too dominant; that the government included representatives of the *calan cas*; and that the National Charter had been violated.

For the Garhajis the *beel* system adopted at Borama had not resolved the issue of power-sharing, and their objections to it highlighted the complexities of a system of proportional representation based upon lineages. Their leaders complained that the formula for allocating parliamentary seats – which was the same formula used to allocate seats on the SNM central committee – did not adequately reflect the size and geographical spread of the Garhajis.[5] This had been tolerable while Abdirahman 'Tuur' (Habar Yunis) was chairman of the SNM and President of Somaliland. But once Egal (Habar Awal) became President the balance of power changed. Egal rejected calls for another national conference to resolve the issue, arguing that it should be settled by a constitutional committee. Egal was also accused of demonstrating anti-Garhajis sentiments by forming a government that was dominated by the Habar Awal and that accommodated as allies the so-called *calan cas* faction of the SNM, who had opposed Tuur during the Berbera conflict and supported Egal's presidential candidacy (Bradbury 1994a). This was perceived as undermining the spirit of reconciliation achieved at Sheikh.

These political disputes were played out in the conflict over Hargeysa airport which like Berbera port was a public asset, and a potentially important revenue stream for the government. The 'Idagalle now claimed the airport as their asset because it lies within their traditional territory and sought to justify this by reference to the National Charter, which stipulated local security arrangements. However, the militia forces that controlled the airport had a reputation for harassing and extorting taxes from commercial flights and international aid agencies. The dispute was used by former President Tuur and General Jama Mohamed Qalib 'Yare'[6] to challenge the government's authority. Matters came to a head in November 1994 when the government lost patience with the pace of negotiations and took control of the airport by force. Having secured this objective, however, government forces proceeded to attack the 'Idagalle village of Toon, an act of aggression that served to rally the Garhajis against the government.

After Hargeysa was secured, the government sought to assert its authority in the east of the country. In March 1995 fighting broke out in Burco when government forces moved to take control of the checkpoints. The historical conflicts between the Habar Yunis and the Habar Ja'lo in Burco lent the war there a different character. As soon as the fighting started, most of the population of Burco evacuated the town.

[5] This formula allocated parliamentary seats proportionately among the Isaaq on the basis of their genealogical descent from the ancestor Sheikh Isaaq. The Habar Ja'lo claimed more seats in the Central Committee, on the grounds that the Habar Ja'lo clan incorporates the lineages of four sons of Sheikh Isaaq. The Habar Yunis, for their part, staked their claim to seats on their reported size and geographical distribution within Somaliland.

[6] General Jama Mohamed Qalib 'Yare' is a prominent 'Idagalle politician. A former police commander and Commissioner for Refugees in the Barre government, he opposes Somaliland's independence and has participated in several governments formed in Mogadishu, including that of General Aideed, the TNG and the TFG.

Efforts to mediate the conflict were impeded by government and opposition disagreement about its genesis. The government tried to claim the high moral ground by portraying the war as a conflict between proponents and opponents of independence – 'nationalists' versus 'federalists'. This presentation gained some credence when Tuur accepted the position of Vice-President in General Aideed's government in Mogadishu, where he was joined by his former Minister of Finance Ismail Hurre 'Buba' and General Jama 'Yare'. Aideed's material support for the opposition and his public pronouncements that he was fighting Egal's administration further strengthened the government's position. Tuur's apparent *volte face* was influenced by inducements from UNOSOM. Desperate to clinch a peace deal prior to the withdrawal of US forces in March 1994, it invited him to participate in a UN-sponsored reconciliation conference (Bryden 1994a). After renouncing Somaliland's independence, Tuur sought to rally local support by resurrecting the SNM, a strategy that failed because Egal's first cabinet included several colonels who could as credibly claim to represent the SNM.

Despite the imbalance within his administration, Egal could claim legitimately that his government represented a broad coalition of Somaliland's clans. He therefore rejected overtures from elders for inter-clan dialogue on the grounds that this was a 'political' rather than 'clan' conflict. Among the opposition, however, the 'federalist' position was limited to the clique of political figures such as Tuur and Yare. The Habar Yunis Liiban Congress of July 1993 had reaffirmed the clan's commitment to Somaliland, and it was not until July 1994, at the second Liiban Congress, that Tuur received any support for his position from Habar Yunis elders.

The economic dimensions of the war

Economic recovery was crucial for Somaliland's survival and Egal's ability to re-establish government institutions. The clash over Hargeysa airport was one element in an increasingly complex economic environment that involved shifting monopolies in the livestock and *qaad* trades and control of the Somaliland currency. As the war persisted without an obvious resolution in sight, its economic dimensions came under scrutiny, with both sides accusing each other of profiting from instability. In August 1995 Egal complained in interviews on Hargeysa Radio and the BBC Somali Service that the war had become a 'project' for some people, and tasked the Vice-President to investigate allegations that individuals on the government's side were enriching themselves from resources intended for the war effort. For many – particularly the opposition – it was the first indication that Egal was not happy with the hardliners (the *calan cas*) in his camp.[7]

There is a clan dimension to Somaliland's political economy. Historically, the Habar Awal has been the most urbanised Isaaq clan, with

---

[7] Information provided by Haroon Ahmed Yusuf.

prominent businessmen in the commodity trade long established in Djibouti. Since colonial times the Habar Yunis have been more prominent in government and the civil service, while the Garhajis and Habar Ja'lo were both dominant in the livestock trade. By taxing and harassing commercial and aid flights the 'Idagalle militia affected the economy of Hargeysa and therefore Habar Awal businessmen, who were crucial to Egal's ability to re-establish government institutions. They not only provided food for the army and police, but, as we have seen, also underwrote the government with loans. The airport therefore became a focus for a range of competing economic interests.

Control of the new Somaliland shilling was also an economic and political issue in the war.[8] The printing of the Somaliland shilling had been ordered by Tuur's finance minister, but the new currency was not introduced until 20 October 1994, a month before war broke out. It was exchanged for the old Somali shilling at the preferential rate of fifty-four Somaliland shillings to one US dollar, immediately making large profits for the government. The opposition, which lost out on this opportunity, accused the government of 'the greatest robbery in Africa'.[9] The lack of a banking system throughout Somaliland, however, meant that circulation of the new currency was confined to the west of the country. In fact, money sent from Hargeysa to the army in Burco had to be sent in dollars or converted into old Somali shillings. Within two years, the currency had devalued massively to a market rate of 4,500 shillings to the dollar. Constant devaluations, coupled with spiralling inflation, eroded government salaries and caused food insecurity among Hargeysa's poor, but having introduced the currency, it was politically impossible for the government to withdraw it.

The war brought changes to the social organisation of Hargeysa's market. Much of the initial fighting in Hargeysa took place around the central market where the Garhajis owned many buildings. As part of the rehabilitation of the city, Hargeysa municipality broke up the central market and created smaller markets around the city, with the intention of spreading the economic benefits. The livestock market, which historically had been located in a Garhajis area, was also moved. Increasingly, in the east of the country, the livestock trade came to be dominated by a single Habar Ja'lo trader. All of these changes to the organisation of trade reinforced Garhajis suspicions that the Egal administration was intent on strengthening the economic standing of the Habar Awal. Hargeysa certainly prospered during Egal's tenure, even during the two years of war. In contrast, areas outside Hargeysa, particularly in the east, suffered economic hardship. This had a long-term impact on post-war recovery and wealth distribution, and accelerated urban migration. Areas outside Hargeysa and in the east have taken much longer to recover. A legacy of

[8] Control of the printing of currency and the money supply has also been a source of conflict in southern Somalia.
[9] Interview, Hargeysa, October 1996.

this period has been evident in economic and social imbalances, not only in 'opposition' areas, but also in rural as opposed to urban areas.

Decentralisation and governance

Despite the progress that had been made at Borama in designing an architecture for the new state, the civil war highlighted a continuing tension over the system of governance that was being created and the limits of government authority. The centralisation of state authority in Somalia had peaked under the regime of Siyad Barre. But, even then, the reach of the state beyond the main urban centres had been limited. Apocryphal stories persisted that in remote rural areas there were Somalis who had never heard of Siyad Barre.[10] State collapse revealed the superficiality of state institutions and resulted in a radical decentralisation and localisation of authority. While the creation of Somaliland reflected a broad public consensus on the need for some form of government to manage internal political competition, provide security and handle external relations, self-governance was also guarded jealously.

To guard against a return to centralised authoritarian government, the principle of decentralised governance was enshrined in the provisional National Charter. Article 21 of the Charter stated that the decentralised government would be established through the creation of regional and district councils. However, this statement of intent did not elaborate on the precise remit of local authority structures, the mechanism for selecting them or their fiscal powers – an issue that was at the heart of the conflict over Hargeysa airport. A constitution was required to do this. In its absence, the approach of government was to develop functional local government structures, with responsibilities for revenue collection and municipal administration. In early 1995 the government attempted to redraft Article 21 of the National Charter, to establish the legal basis for a relationship between the centre and the regions, but negotiations with Parliament broke down.[11] The key points of contention were political representation and finance. Local councils were happy to receive financial support from central government for services such as the police or education, but also wanted the right to make local government appointments without central government involvement. Egal eventually chose the route taken by Tuur and made appointments centrally; he also belatedly began work on a constitution in 1995.

Another governance issue highlighted by the war was the role of the national *Guurti*. The incorporation of the *Guurti* in the bicameral legislature had recognised the indispensable role played by elders in restoring stability to Somaliland in the absence of government. This institutionalisation of their role in central government, however, compromised their perceived neutrality, moral authority and ability to intervene in national

---

[10] A story the author heard in Sanaag Region.
[11] John Drysdale, personal communication, October 1995.

politics. One consequence of the war was to split both Parliament and the House of Elders. The members of the *Guurti* who remained in Hargeysa were seen to be allied to the government, earning a salary and thus having a vested interest in the survival of its source. Consequently, the House of Elders did not try to intervene in the conflict and bring it to an early conclusion.

Surviving the civil war

The civil war could easily have ended people's support for an independent Somaliland. If anything, it served to strengthen it. After a year and a half of low-level conflict, 'federalists' within the opposition had not been able to convince their clansmen to reunite with the south, nor had they garnered support from non-Isaaq clans. The human and economic costs of the war were felt most keenly in opposition areas, from where most people were displaced. If the war had been intended to unseat Egal, it also failed to do this. In April 1995, when Egal's two-year mandate ended, his tenure and that of the legislature were extended by the House of Elders for a further eighteen months to enable him to end the war, finalise a constitution and prepare the country for elections.

In June 1995 concerned individuals in Hargeysa organised a meeting between 'Idagalle elders and members of the National *Guurti* in Harshin, on the border with Ethiopia. Although these initiatives were undermined by the main protagonists, by September 1995 there were signs of compromise. Egal reshuffled his cabinet to reduce the influence of the *calan cas* within the government, while the Garhajis also changed their military leadership. By the end of 1995, the war had reached a stalemate, but there were no signs that the two sides were ready to talk. It was this situation that concerned Somalilanders in-country and outside sought to rectify through the Peace Committee for Somaliland.

The Peace Committee for Somaliland was an initiative of Somalilanders overseas. In April 1995, a conference of Somalilanders in London concluded that, in the absence of any genuine moves towards reconciliation between the government and opposition and the apparent failure of the Somaliland elders to intervene, an independent mission should be convened to broker dialogue between the warring parties (Peace Committee for Somaliland 1995). A committee composed of professionals from the diaspora was therefore formed and convened for the first time in Addis Ababa in September 1995.

The goals of the Peace Committee were threefold: to achieve an immediate ceasefire; to prepare a framework and venue for dialogue; and to prepare a report on lessons learned that could be used to prevent similar conflicts from arising (*ibid.*). The committee also stated that it would disband once a ceasefire had been achieved and the parties had agreed to resolve their differences through dialogue. Its objectives were later revised to promote substantive discussions on the causes of the conflict; on what could constitute a 'viable government' in Somaliland;

and on the relevance of 'traditional systems of governance'.[12] With finance from the diaspora and its individual members, and some limited external funding, the committee was able to be independent and flexible.

The strategy of the Peace Committee was to harness the lineage-based political structures which had proved so effective in 1993, rather than encourage dialogue between the 'government' and 'opposition'. It treated the Burco and Hargeysa conflicts separately and encouraged parallel dialogue between the Habar Yunis and Habar Ja'lo to resolve the conflict in the east, and between the 'Idagalle and other Hargeysa clans to address the conflict in the west. It hoped this would create conditions for dialogue between the government and the opposition, to be followed by a constitutional conference (Peace Committee for Somaliland 1996). The overall impact of the Peace Committee is contested, but, in the words of one Somali, 'The Peace Committee for Somaliland introduced the word "peace" at a time when no-one was talking about peace and that helped.'[13]

From May 1996 a peace process began to unfold through a series of intra- and inter-clan peace meetings (see Table 5.1). This evolved along two axes: in the west between the 'Idagalle and the Hargeysa clans (Habar Awal, Arab, Ishaaq, Tol Ja'lo and Ayuub) to resolve the conflict around Hargeysa; and in the east between the Habar Ja'lo and Habar Yunis to resolve the conflict in Burco.

Table 5.1 Inter-Clan Peace Conferences in 1996

Reconciling clans	Date	Venue
Habar Ja'lo and Habar Yunis	June 1996	Gaashaamo
Habar Ja'lo and Habar Yunis	July 1996	Duruqsi
Habar Ja'lo, Habar Yunis, and 'Iise Muse	July 1996	Warabeye
Sa'ad Muse, 'Idagalle and Hargeysa clans	June 1996	Camp Abokor
Habar Ja'lo and Habar Yunis	Sept. 1996	Beer

In July 1996, representatives of the 'Idagalle and Hargeysa clans met in Camp Abokor refugee camp in Ethiopia. The Camp Abokor conference, known as *Geedi-Socadka Nabadda ee Beelaha Hargeysa* (Progressive Peace Process Initiated by the Clans in Hargeysa), was considered by many as a breakthrough, being the first substantive talks between the 'Iidagalla and representatives of the Hargeysa clans of the Sa'ad Muse/Habar Awal (Farah 1996). The Peace Committee for Somaliland which helped to organise and facilitate the conference also won the backing of the Ethiopian regional authorities. The meeting resolved that local groups in the Hargeysa area should live together 'harmoniously' and collaborate in restoring stability and peaceful coexistence; it also proposed a follow-up meeting inside Somaliland to continue the peace dialogue. This was prevented by the government,

[12] Draft agenda for a 'Forum of Somaliland Intellectuals' (October 1996).
[13] Interview, Hargeysa, October 1996.

which viewed the meeting as a threat to its authority and influence.

The peace process in the east proved more successful. Burco had twice been affected by conflict since 1991 and a sustained peace settlement there was considered to be of great significance for Somaliland. The key protagonists were the Habar Yunis and Habar Ja'lo, with the Arab and 'Iise Muse less directly involved. Although this conflict was considered more intractable, once the Habar Yunis agreed to negotiate within the framework of an independent Somaliland the peace process evolved faster than that in the west (Farah 1996). The intervention of Ethiopia also proved to be an important catalyst. The first peace meeting between the Habar Ja'lo and Habar Yunis occurred because of pressure from the Ethiopian authorities, who were concerned to prevent fighting from spreading to Ethiopia. This meeting took place in Gaashaamo in Ethiopia in May 1996, followed by meetings in Baali Dhaaye and Duruqsi in June and July. These meetings, accompanied by a withdrawal of Somaliland government soldiers from around Burco, created a momentum for reconciliation. The death of General Aideed in Mogadishu in August assisted the process because it meant that external support for the 'federalists' diminished. A peace agreement was finalised in the village of Beer in October 1996, which established procedures for the disengagement of forces, the safe return of properties to their rightful owners, and mechanisms to prevent future conflicts between the two clans.

The rapprochement between the Habar Yunis and Habar Ja'lo at Beer, and the participation of other eastern clans, was interpreted by some in Hargeysa as a challenge to Egal's government.[14] But both the Habar Yunis and the Habar Ja'lo were themselves divided and the fact that the Habar Yunis agreed to negotiate within the framework of an independent Somaliland also strengthened the government's hand. Although the war had threatened to foreshorten Somaliland's existence, in the end it served to consolidate public support for the territory's independence and to strengthen central government. The challenge to the Somaliland state had been defeated. The revelation that the war had become a 'project' for politicians and factions within the SNM weakened their capacity to mobilise further support. The destruction and the repeated experience of displacement impressed upon people the futility of conflict. And, some argued, the deaths of militia members during the war helped to solve the problem of uncontrollable militias.[15] The Somaliland state was further consolidated through a fourth national conference, held in Hargeysa.

There were interesting similarities and differences between the peace process that ended the civil war in 1996 and the reconciliation processes in 1992 and 1993 that culminated in the Borama conference. In both 1993 and 1996 the conflicts were ended through the efforts of Somalis themselves and the international diplomatic community was notable by its absence. With the UNOSOM mission due to end in early 1995, the UN

---

[14] Author's interviews, Hargeysa, October 1996.

[15] Author's interviews, Hargeysa, 2003.

was preoccupied with trying to strike a peace deal between factions in Somalia and showed no inclination to support reconciliation in Somaliland. The only foreign country to intercede was Ethiopia, which brought some pressure to bear on the Isaaq clans living in Somaliland and Ethiopia to be reconciled. A difference between 1993 and 1996 was the mediation of the Somaliland Peace Committee, which demonstrated the growing political and economic importance of Somaliland's diaspora. The substantive difference in the two periods was the existence in 1996 of a government that had resources and carried authority. Although the importance of grassroots dialogue was demonstrated again in the inter-clan meetings in the east, the presence of government altered the terms of the dialogue. This became apparent in the Hargeysa conference that formally ended the civil war.

The Hargeysa national conference
The war was formally ended by another national reconciliation con-ference, held in Hargeysa between October 1996 and February 1997. By mid-1996, with his extended term of office due to end in November, Egal had failed to complete the tasks with which he had been charged: ending the war, finalising a constitution and preparing the country for elections. The preparation of a constitution had been delayed by a disagreement between Parliament and the executive over responsibilities for drafting it. This resulted in two drafts, one written by a parliamentary committee and a second by a Sudanese lawyer commissioned by the office of the President. Heated debates over the respective drafts resulted in a vote of no confidence in the Chair followed by a boycott of Parliament by thirty of its members, who were critical of the President's interference.[16] As elections could not be held without a constitution, a compromise was agreed: to hold a national conference as the only viable mechanism for selecting the head of state. In early October, therefore, the House of Elders announced that a national conference would be held in Hargeysa from the 15th day of that month.

Prior to the conference Somaliland appeared to be more divided and fragmented than at any time since independence was declared. Isaaq unity was damaged by the war and even sub-clan and *diya*-paying group unity was no longer a given. The paramount *Suldaan* of the Habar Yunis, for example, had accepted a rapprochement with the government, while a second Habar Yunis *Suldaan* gave his support to the Beer conference. The government's appointment of new *caaqilo* (elders) and *Suldaano* contributed to the fragmentation. The potential financial benefits accruing from government patronage created competition within clans and led one Somali to observe: 'Now there are no more Isaaq, only *beel*. The clans do not work collectively together any more.'[17] There was therefore a pressing need for dialogue to renew a national consensus.

---

[16] Interview with parliamentarian, October 1996.
[17] Interview, Hargeysa, December 1996

However, the short notice given by the *Guurti* about the conference, its location, the proposed procedures for selecting conference delegates, and the role of the *Guurti* all proved controversial. The eastern clans proposed that Sheikh would be a more neutral venue than Hargeysa. Some people argued that a conference should not take place until a cessation of hostilities had been agreed. As the conference was due to open before the meeting in Beer was concluded, it raised the possibility that Somaliland could end up with two presidents. A petition signed by seventy-nine prominent people called on the government to establish a neutral *Guurti* and preparatory committee to ensure a conference based on the equitable representation of the whole population.[18] The petition was rejected by the *Guurti,* the government refused to countenance any debate, and ministers suspected of questioning the government's actions were dismissed. Under such pressure, the elders of clans meeting in Beer decided to join the Hargeysa conference rather than risk the consequences of a parallel one.

The Hargeysa conference was the fifth Somaliland-wide conference held since 1991, and it proved to be the last. Like the previous ones in Berbera, Burco, Sheikh and Borama, the Hargeysa conference was managed and largely financed without foreign support.[19] But it differed from the previous ones in several respects. The conference was mostly financed by the government, which allowed the President to have a direct influence over its outcome. In Egal's view, the existence of a government meant that the political ground in Somaliland had shifted since the 1993 Borama conference. In recognition of this, the conference was called a 'national conference' (*shir qarameed*) rather than a 'clan conference' (*shir beeleed*) (ICG 2003: 11). The number of voting delegates was doubled to 300. Half came from Parliament and half were newly selected clan representatives. There were also one hundred invited observers, including several women.

The conference proved to be another watershed political event in Somaliland. Nearly five months of deliberations produced a formal cessation of hostilities. Opposition grievances were partially addressed by increasing their share of seats in the two Houses of Parliament. To address grievances in the east, a special government fund (*aafada*) was created for the reconstruction of Burco, to be paid for by a supplementary tax. Consideration was given to the rights of minority communities in Somaliland, who gained representation in Parliament for the first time.[20] An interim constitution was adopted by amalgamating the two drafts drawn up by the Executive and Parliament. Superseding the Borama charters, it set Somaliland on the road to constitutional government, laying out the steps for the legalisation of political parties and the holding of multi-party elections.

On 14 October 1996 a new flag was adopted, symbolising the Somali-

---

[18] Notice of the 'Forum for Peace and National Reconciliation', August 1996.

[19] The World Food Programme contributed some food for the conference.

[20] Despite strong lobbying it took another eight years for women to win seats in Parliament.

land people's aspirations for independence. The new flag was based on the red, white and green striped flag of the SNM in recognition of its past, but with the stripes inverted and inscribed with the *shahada* and a five-pointed black star. Green is for prosperity, white for peace, red for the fallen heroes and the *shahada* is for Islam.[21]

In early 1996 Egal had stated that he would not stand for re-election, but once the conference got under way, it became clear that it was being organised to favour exactly that possibility. By December twelve people had announced their candidatures for President. Rules for eligibility passed by the conference immediately ruled out several of them. Although many people were critical of Egal's presidential record, a concern among people in western Somaliland at losing the benefits accrued during the previous five years assured him of considerable support, and his deft use of a political slush fund secured him the victory. On 23 February 1997 Egal was duly re-elected by a landslide of 223 votes as President of Somaliland for a further five years. His new Vice-President was another Gadabursi, Dahir Riyale Kahin. Egal's closest rival for the presidential seat, Suleiman Mohamed Aden 'Gaal', was magnanimous in his defeat and pledged to work with the new administration.

Egal's reselection was not welcomed in all quarters, but the peaceful conclusion of the conference was greeted with great relief. Displaced families could return to their homes, people could invest in rebuilding their livelihoods with a sense of certainty about the future, and the business of building a state could resume. But the Hargeysa conference also had certain long-term political consequences. Egal's influence over the conference damaged the credibility of a national *shir* as a mechanism for political change in the future and re-affirmed patronage as a central element of politics. The conference also had a negative effect on relations with Harti clans in the east. The selection of a Gadabursi Vice-President at the 1993 Borama conference had left the Dhulbahante feeling marginalised in Somaliland. When this was repeated at the Hargeysa conference, it gave the impression of a state dominated by Somaliland's western clans (Isaaq, Gadabursi and 'Iise). The relationship between the Harti and Somaliland deteriorated further when Egal rejected a list of ministerial and parliamentary candidates proposed by the influential Dhulbahante *Garaad* Abdiqani. The loss of influence within Egal's government and equivocation over independence led the *Garaad* and other Dhulbahante leaders, including the speaker of Somaliland's Parliament Mohamed Habsade, to withdraw their support from Somaliland and give their backing to the formation, in the north-east in 1998, of Puntland State of Somalia. In 2001 Ali Khalif Galaydh, who had been a member of the Dhulbahante delegation at the Burco conference in 1991, was appointed Prime Minister in the Transitional National Government of Somalia. This

---

[21] See note on p. i about the cover photograph of the paperback edition.

gave the Dhulbahante a political stake in a united Somalia and guaranteed that at least part of Sool would be loyal to the south. Consequently, while the Gadabursi became politically integrated into Somaliland, the Dhulbahante and Warsengeli felt more marginalised, even though the important ministerial portfolios of Foreign Affairs and Finance were held by their clansmen. Ironically, although the Hargeysa national conference helped to consolidate the state of Somaliland in one direction, it also opened fissures within the polity. These problems would come to fruition in time, but in early 1997 the ending of the civil war inaugurated an unprecedented period of security and development.

Peace and prosperity: Egal's second term, 1997–2002

In many respects Egal's first term in office had been a failure. The political consensus that had been crafted at Borama in 1993 was damaged by the two years of internecine war. His government failed to introduce a constitution, to move towards the democratic form of government envisaged in 1991 and to achieve international recognition. Nevertheless, despite the social and physical damage caused by the civil war, this period ended, by and large, with a stronger government and a more integrated country than had existed in 1993. With a new peace deal and power-sharing formula agreed, Egal's second term was to prove more productive.

The agreements reached at the 1997 Hargeysa conference ushered in six years of uninterrupted stability, during which time Somaliland experienced high levels of economic growth and reconstruction. The stability and the law and order that went with it were symbolised by the erection of Somaliland's first traffic lights in Hargeysa. In 1997 the export of livestock through Berbera exceeded all previous records, and overseas remittances steadily increased, facilitated by the introduction of new telecommunications systems. The Somaliland diaspora, encouraged by the political settlement, began to invest in Somaliland again, particularly in housing construction. The government capitalised on its new mandate by reforming the revenue system and cutting public expenditure through civil service reforms. By 2000 the government had repaid the loan it had taken from the businessmen in 1993, thus freeing surplus revenue for investment in development projects and the extension of the administration to the east of the territory. As had been agreed at the Hargeysa conference, the government also created a special fund for the rehabilitation of war-damaged Burco by placing an additional 2 per cent on customs tariffs. Foreign companies also began to show an interest in Somaliland. In May 1996, for example, the government signed an agreement with the oil company Total Mer Rouge to rehabilitate and manage the oil storage depot in Berbera.

With security restored, refugees began to return to Somaliland in large numbers, international aid increased and rehabilitation and reconstruction accelerated. In the late 1990s, after peacekeeping forces had withdrawn from Somalia, the international aid donors adopted what they called a 'peace dividend' approach to providing assistance. The intention was to use aid as a political tool for conflict resolution, by making its provision conditional on a secure environment and good governance (Bradbury and Coultan 1998: 6–21). Thus, the UN Somalia Country Team stated that 'the most important work of the UN is to invest in the rehabilitation and development of the social and economic fabric of relatively peaceful areas' (UNCT 1998). In theory this policy favoured the more politically stable areas of Somaliland and Puntland State.

Internationally, Somaliland's star appeared to be on the rise. The manner in which Somaliland had ended its own war contrasted with the continuing failure of international efforts to facilitate a political resolution in Somalia. In 1996 and 1997 initiatives by Ethiopia and Egypt both failed to engineer a lasting political accord that could restore a government to the south. The resolution of the war in Somaliland meant that international agencies could engage more directly with the administration without fear of being accused of taking sides. Although this did not release funds directly to the government, there was a growing pragmatic acceptance of Somaliland. The difficulties of operating in the south and the northward drift of resources encouraged more international aid agencies to move their operations to Somaliland. The largest proportion of the aid for Somaliland was to assist with the return and resettlement of refugees from Ethiopia, and landmine clearance. The particular interests of the international donors meant that certain ministries benefited more than others: the Ministry for Rehabilitation, Resettlement and Reintegration, for example, received substantial resources from UNHCR.

These developments were marred by the sudden ban on the importation of Somali livestock by the Gulf states in 1998 and again in 2000, in response to an outbreak of Rift Valley Fever (RVF) detected in southern Somalia in the wake of severe flooding in 1997 (Bradbury and Coultan 1998). Although RVF was not found in Somaliland, the Gulf countries applied the embargo to livestock from all the Somali-inhabited regions of the Horn. The loss of the country's biggest export market led to a slowdown in the Somaliland economy, which had a detrimental impact on rural livelihoods, the environment and government revenue. The reduction in revenue forced the government to cut back on its development plans, as we shall see in the next chapter. For individual families, particularly urbanised ones, this economic downturn was cushioned by the increasing flow of remittances.

While there were many progressive developments during this period, people's trust and confidence in the system of governance was gradually undermined by Egal's increasingly autocratic style of leadership, the stalled process for drafting the constitution, the lack of progress on international recognition, and concerns about corruption in government.

Somaliland also faced new challenges to its sovereignty from political developments in Somalia.

Puntland State of Somalia and the Transitional National Government

By the end of the 1990s, the fragmentation and localisation of political authority that had characterised state collapse in Somalia in the early part of the 1990s had given way to broader political alliances. At the same time, the country was undergoing economic revival. As a centre for expanding global trading networks, telecommunications systems and private financial institutions, Mogadishu was becoming a significant regional economic hub (UNDP 2001). In 1998 Puntland State of Somalia was established in north-east Somalia as a non-secessionist, 'autonomous self-governing state' with veteran SSDF leader Colonel Abdullahi Yusuf as its head of state (WSP 2001). In 1999 the Rahanweyn Resistance Army established an administration in Bay and Bakool regions of southern Somalia. And in September 2000 the Transitional National Government (TNG) of Somalia was formed at the conclusion of the Somalia National Peace Conference, held in the Djiboutian resort of Arta. The creation of Puntland and the TNG presented the most serious challenge to the political and territorial integrity of Somaliland since 1991.

The Puntland government and the TNG, like the government of Somaliland, derived their legitimacy from consultative conferences. North-east Somalia emerged from the civil war in the early 1990s relatively unscathed and under the fragile administration of a reconstituted SSDF.[22] The impetus to establish an autonomous entity in the north-east arose from the failure of a dozen national reconciliation conferences to restore a government in Somalia. The failure of the Ethiopian-backed Sodere Conference of 1996, which was undermined by the 1997 Cairo Accord sponsored by Egypt, finally persuaded political leaders in the north-east to consider an alternative, federated approach to state reconstruction. In a manner not dissimilar to Somaliland, a series of locally sponsored and inclusive regional meetings formulated a political Charter for the governance of the regions, which was adopted at the Garowe Constitutional Conference of August 1998. Unlike the Somaliland Charter, however, the Puntland Charter affirms the unity of Somalia. As a non-secessionist state, Puntland came to epitomise a potential 'building block' for a federal Somali state. It received external support for this political experiment from the international community which, having failed to re-establish a central authority through national reconciliation, began to encourage the development of regional and transregional political authorities as precursors to a reconstituted state.

Puntland is founded upon a notion of Harti/Darod unity, which includes the Majeerteen of Mudug, Nugal and Bari regions of north-east

---

[22] Very little fighting occurred in the north-east. The exception was along its southern borders, between the SSDF and the forces of General Mohamed Farah 'Aideed', and military clashes between the SSDF and the militant Islamic organisation Al Itihad al Islamiya in 1992.

Somalia,[23] the Dhulbahante of Sool Region and the Warsengeli of eastern Sanaag Region. The correspondence between territory and clan identity established Puntland as a form of 'ethno-state'. This distinguishes it from Somaliland which claims greater pluralism by incorporating Isaaq, Dir and Harti territories, although it is considered by many Somalis an 'Isaaq project'. Prior to the war, the Harti was not a politically significant grouping, but became so during fighting between Harti clans and Hawiye for control of the southern port of Kismayo in the early 1990s. Abdullahi Yusuf appealed to Harti unity and drew support from the Dhulbahante and Warsengeli to overcome rival Majeerteen candidates for the Presidency of Puntland. Puntland's clan-based approach to federalism in Somalia was later used by Abdullahi Yusuf in his bid to become President of the Transitional Federal Government of Somalia in 2004. This neatly illustrates both the dynamic nature of the kinship system and the way in which it can be politicised.

In 1998 the immediate challenge to the government of Somaliland was Puntland's claim to sovereignty over parts of Sool and eastern Sanaag regions inhabited by the Dhulbahante and Warsengeli. As noted already, the loss of influence within Egal's government by key Dhulbahante and Warsengeli leaders and equivocation over independence led them to back the formation of Puntland in 1998, in which the Dhulbahante gained the post of Vice-President and a proportion of parliamentary seats.

The creation of the TNG in 2000 further challenged the authority of the government in Hargeysa over the territory of Somaliland. The thirteenth internationally sponsored Somalia national reconciliation conference, held in Arta, Djibouti, was the initiative of Djiboutian President Ismail Omar Guelleh, who succeeded first President, Hassan Gouled Aptidon, in 1999. Guelleh used his inaugural speech at the UN to propose a political initiative for Somalia that would be hosted by a Somali-speaking country and draw on Somali cultural traditions. Supported by the regional Inter-Governmental Agency on Development (IGAD) and the UN, and endorsed by the US and Italy, the Arta conference was novel in the way that it involved elders, business people, religious scholars, artists and women – and sought to marginalise the warlords. It produced a Transitional Charter and a 245-member Transitional National Assembly based on clan representation. This Assembly selected Abdulqassim Salad Hassan[24] as the interim President of Somalia. The President in turn selected Ali Khalif Galaydh, a Dhulbahante, as his Prime Minister. The TNG moved to Mogadishu in September 2000, with a three-year mandate. The presence at its inauguration of IGAD member states and the UN, the EU, the Arab League, the Organisation of African Unity, France, Italy, Kuwait, and Libya gave the TNG a considerable degree of international recognition.

---

[23] Other Darod clans, such as the Leylkasse and Awrtable, also live in Puntland.
[24] Abdulqassim Salad Hassan was a former Minister of the Interior under Siyad Barre; during the civil war he had supported General Aideed.

The UN also invited the TNG to take up Somalia's seat at the UN General Assembly, which had been vacant for nearly a decade.

The existence of Puntland, which claimed sovereignty over large parts of eastern Somaliland, and the establishment of the TNG, which claimed sovereignty over the whole territory of Somalia, presented a clear challenge to the authorities in Hargeysa. The appointment of a Prime Minister from Sool Region – Ali Khalif Galaydh – was viewed as a provocative move in Somaliland, as well as in Puntland. It left the Dhulbahante split three ways between Somalia, Puntland and Somaliland. Whereas regional and international bodies neither sought to intervene in Somaliland's civil war nor provided support for the war's resolution at the Hargeysa conference, the TNG received foreign political and financial support.[25]

But the challenge to Somaliland passed. Despite gaining acceptance in the UN, the African Union, IGAD and the League of Arab States, the TNG failed to establish any meaningful authority in Somalia. A coalition of warlords, who called themselves the Somali Reconciliation and Restoration Council, formed an armed opposition to the TNG with backing from Ethiopia. Puntland had become embroiled in its own conflict and constitutional crisis when Abdullahi Yusuf refused to step down from the office of President. By October 2002, when IGAD launched the fourteenth Somali national peace conference in Kenya to pave the way for a successor institution to the TNG, violent conflict in Somalia was more widespread than at any time since the mid-1990s. While Somaliland survived these challenges, they nevertheless spurred a process of further political change in the fledgling state.

Constitutional developments
The Hargeysa conference had set Somaliland on the road to constitutional government by adopting a draft interim constitution. Disagreement over the powers it ascribed to Parliament and the executive, however, meant that it took another four years to produce a mutually acceptable draft. The public suspected that Egal was stalling, but on 30 August 1999 he brought some urgency to the task by publicly declaring that international recognition for Somaliland depended upon it adopting a multi-party system of democracy. The impetus for this came from political pressure within Somaliland and the changes in the external political environment.

In Somaliland the *beel* system of power-sharing government established at Borama, while essential for establishing peace, had come to be viewed as an impediment to effective government. The manipulation of the Hargeysa conference had underlined the weaknesses of the *shir beeleed* as a mechanism for political change. At the same time Somaliland and its political elite were challenged by the formation of Puntland in 1998 and the TNG in 2000. It was speculated by some that Egal still harboured ambitions to become President of a reunited 'Greater

---

[25] The UN requested US$5 million as immediate support for the TNG (UNRC 2000).

Somalia'.[26] Although Somaliland continued to absent itself from national reconciliation conferences, Egal maintained relationships with political figures in the south.[27] After the failures of the Ethiopian-sponsored Sodere conference between Somali factions in 1996 and the Egyptian-sponsored Cairo talks in 1997, Egal had offered to host peace talks on Somalia in Hargeysa, but failed to win international backing for this. He was no doubt galled when President Ismail Omar Guelleh's proposal to host talks in Djibouti was accepted instead. The degree to which Egal and his government felt threatened by the Arta conference became apparent in the introduction of new public order laws. In August 2000 the adminis-tration decreed the creation of a National Security Committee, with emergency powers to suspend *habeas corpus*, ban public rallies, restrict the movement of people considered detrimental to public order and detain people without charge for up to ninety days. The emergency laws were used to detain several Somaliland citizens for attending and voicing opinion in support of the Arta conference, as well as for questioning the government's contracts with foreign commercial companies (UNDP 2001: 177). With only a year of his five-year mandate left, Egal's other response to counter the perceived threats of Puntland and the TNG was to hold a referendum on the draft constitution that would reinforce the local legitimacy of Somaliland and inaugurate a process to establish a consti-tutionally based and popularly elected government.

The process that evolved in developing a constitution is a further example of the locally constructed nature of Somaliland's political system. Egal had been tasked on taking office in 1993 with drawing up a constitution to replace the interim National Charter, but it was not until 1997 that agreement was reached on an interim constitution, amalga-mating two versions drafted separately by the President and Parliament. The slow process of constitutional drafting arose, in part, from a protracted debate over the respective powers of the executive and the legislature. It went through a further revision in 2000 before being submitted to a plebiscite. The finalised version gave the executive most of the powers demanded by Egal, but Parliament successfully resisted his attempt to remove certain human rights articles. Parliament also gained additional powers of financial oversight and a role in the approval of ministerial appointments, and the role of the *Guurti* was strengthened. The lengthy process of developing a constitution meant that it was subjected to a degree of public debate and underwent several revisions. Members of the Somaliland diaspora also contributed their comments on the constitution.[28] There was no broad public consultation,

---

[26] With a political career that spanned colonial and independent Somalia, close associates suggest that he was keen to be recognised as an African elder statesman. Author's interviews, Hargeysa 2003.

[27] For example, the Hawiye businessman and warlord, Osman Ali Atto, visited Somaliland on several occasions and had business interests there.

[28] Interview with Ibrahim Hashi Jama, July, 2003, Liverpool. See the website of the Somaliland Forum for commentary on the constitution (www.somalilandforum.com).

however, so public knowledge of its contents was limited.

The constitutional referendum took place on 31 May 2001. The Somaliland government reported that 1.18 million people voted in the plebiscite, with 97.9 per cent approving the constitution. Although the constitution was clearly endorsed by the majority of the public,[29] the official figure for the turn-out is very dubious, especially in the light of the subsequent general elections and because the plebiscite was boycotted in parts of eastern Sanaag, Sool and Awdal regions. Yet, even if the manipulation of the voting figures marred the exercise, the referendum remained significant.

The constitution provides a legal framework for the political system of Somaliland based on a plural democracy. The first article establishes Somaliland's independent and sovereign status – and its approval by the majority of the electorate provided a clear statement of the population's collective aspiration to protect this sovereignty. As Egal remarked, 'Once you have accepted that constitution, you have accepted Somaliland' (IRIN 2001, 28 May). A reversal of that policy could only be effected through another referendum. Not surprisingly, the TNG condemned the exercise as 'illegal' (IRIN 2001, 10 July). The referendum was the first opportunity for people to exercise a democratic vote in Somalia for thirty years. It took place, almost to the day, ten years after the SNM had reclaimed Somaliland's sovereignty and tasked the first government with drawing up a constitution. Through the referendum, the public endorsed a proposal to change the political system from a single-party, power-sharing system of government to a restricted form of multi-party democracy in which the head of state, the legislature and district councils were to be elected by a secret public ballot, rather than selected by an electoral college of elders. The referendum legalised the formation of political parties. It also secured for women the right to vote and to hold political office, even though no women had been consulted in drafting the constitution. Finally, and ironically, while the referendum demonstrated majority support for an independent state, it also deepened divisions between the Isaaq and those Harti of eastern Sanaag and Sool who rejected it.

In accordance with the new constitution, on 6 August 2001 the Somaliland Parliament legalised the formation of 'political organisations' which, as will be described in Chapter 8, would become 'political parties' by contesting district council elections. Once political organisations were legalised, Egal immediately announced the formation of Somaliland's first political organisation: UDUB (*Ururka Dimoqraadiyadda Ummadaha Bahoobay* – the United Democratic Peoples' Party). A further six organisations had registered by the end of September 2001.

Progress towards the elections was dogged by political clashes between the President, Parliament, opposition politicians and traditional

---

[29] According to observers from the Initiative and Referendum Institute of South Africa.

leaders. Egal's opponents accused him of becoming autocratic and corrupt. UDUB was widely perceived to be the 'government party', financed by government resources. The demarcation of constituency boundaries, the process of voter registration and citizenship all became contentious issues. Government critics expressed concern that a free and fair election would not be feasible and that the move to reshape the political system, after years of procrastination over the constitution, was simply a ruse by Egal to engineer his own political survival because, they argued, another *shir beeleed* would not have reselected him as President. In August 2001 Egal narrowly survived a motion of impeachment in Parliament, when the management of revenue by Berbera Port Authority and the government's handling of a contract given to Total Mer Rouge for handling the fuel storage depot in Berbera came under parliamentary scrutiny (IRIN 2001, 22 August). The same month a group of powerful sultans with strong backing in the east of the country challenged his authority, demanding that UDUB be dismantled and that a *shir beeleed* be held to decide on the future of the country. When several of the sultans were arrested while visiting Hargeysa, Somaliland was taken to the brink of another civil conflict. It was only averted through the mediation of political, religious and business leaders and civic activists.

On 18 December an independent Somaliland National Electoral Commission (NEC) was inaugurated to oversee the electoral process. As the original timetable for elections could not be met, the NEC's first task was to postpone the district elections. In another compromise move, the Upper House extended the term of the administration for a further year to enable more political organisations to register, and for the elections to be properly organised.

On one level, the dispute between President Egal and the opposition at this time can be read simply as a power struggle between old political rivals, reflecting ongoing divisions within the Isaaq. Egal's most ardent opponents came from what was perceived as a revived *calan cas*, who had opposed Tuur's government and whose exit from government had been engineered by Egal during the civil war. This group received political support in the east of the country, particularly amongst the Habar Ja'lo, who felt marginalised from a government they perceived as dominated by the Habar Awal and Habar Yunis. Egal's presidential rival in 1997, Suleiman 'Gaal', had emerged as one of the opposition leaders and in May 2001 had been arrested under emergency laws on suspicion of plotting to sabotage the constitutional referendum (afrol News 2001). At another level, however, the dispute reflected genuine public unease over the consequences of the transition from a clan-based political system to a multi-party system of government. Although the constitution had been overwhelmingly endorsed by the public, many people were circumspect about the need to change a system of government that had fostered reconciliation and recovery and maintained the peace for a decade – a period longer than Somalia's previous experience of democratic government. Many people were convinced that the stability enjoyed during this period had provided the bedrock for recovery. Given the lack of civic education, the low level of literacy and undeveloped civic organisations, some questioned whether Somaliland was really ready for a Western form of multi-party democracy. They were circumspect, too, about the implications of changing from a system based on consensus decision-making to one involving hierarchical authority and majoritarian rule. Somalia's previous experience with parliamentary democracy in the 1960s did not augur well for Somaliland.

On the other hand, modernisers criticised the *beel* system for prioritising clan balance over meritocratic appointments to government, for entrenching nepotism and corruption, for stifling issue-based politics, for hampering the development of a functional bureaucracy and, therefore, for being unequal to the task of modern government (Jimcaale 2005: 86). The *beel* system discriminated against women's participation in politics – an anachronism in a modern state, they argued – whereas the principle of universal suffrage enshrined in the constitution gave women the right to vote and to hold public office. Since 1991 Somaliland had had only two women ministers and there were no women parliamentarians. Consequently, women were forced to express their political views and advocate for their rights through independent women's organisations (Gardner and el Bushra 2004).

The *beel* system offered one solution to the thorny issue of representation in politics, by ensuring the proportional representation of clans in Parliament. In practice, however, few were satisfied with their allocation of seats (Jimcaale 2005: 85–6). The proliferation of titled clan elders has made the exercise more complex. Since colonial times successive Somali governments had created titled leaders as a way of eliciting support from clans and organising rural populations. However, the growth in elders has been particularly prolific since 1991, with some 267 new titled elders (*caaqilo*) recognised, along with many new sultans and *Garaads*. In the *beel* system minority groups such as the Gabooye felt under-represented, rural people (*reer miyi*) felt dominated by urban people (*reer magaal*), and women were excluded from politics. Multi-party elections based on one person one vote seemed to offer an alternative way of handling competitive politics and changes in power from one regime to another. A constitutionally based multi-party democracy, it was asserted, could resolve the thorny issues of representation, equity and decentralisation. The actions of the sultans were therefore perceived by modernisers as a reactionary attempt to retain their authority and power within society.

The President did not live to contest the elections. On 3 May 2002 Mohamed Haji Ibrahim Egal died unexpectedly while undergoing surgery in South Africa. Egal's sudden death generated an outpouring of nationalist sentiment. Respected as an elder statesman and for having steered Somaliland through several difficult years, his funeral in Berbera was attended by his opponents as well as his supporters. The hope of people in Borama in 1993 that Egal would win Somaliland international recognition had not been fulfilled. Although in his latter years he was frequently accused by opponents of economic mismanagement and corruption, and of being insincere about independence, even his most ardent critics concede that under his presidency security was restored, clan militias were demobilised, government institutions were established, the economy recovered and a political entity with most of the attributes of a self-governing state emerged. He was given a hero's funeral in his hometown of Berbera. The eulogy of the Ethiopian Minister of State for Foreign Affairs, Mr. Tekede Alemu, who attended his funeral recognised Egal's achievements and status as an elder statesman:

> The peace and stability that have been achieved in Somaliland over the last twelve years has been extremely critical for us, for Ethiopia and as far as I am concerned for the sub-region as a whole. This is the legacy that Egal has left behind.... He has been active in Somali and African politics for fifty years. He was one of the greatest statesmen in Africa without any doubt. He has been the leading statesman in our sub-region without any doubt. And his achievements we see today here in Somaliland. (*Somaliland Times*, 11 May 2002).

For people in Somaliland, Egal's death was a severe test of the robustness of the constitution and political system that he left behind. In line with that constitution, both houses of Parliament approved Vice-President Dahir Riyale Kahin as his successor. The peaceful manner in which power was transferred proved that the state was now stronger than one individual. Egal's death also served to level the political 'playing field' and to create an environment in which former opposition groups could rejoin the electoral process for district elections in December 2002.

6

Rising
from the Ashes

Economic
Rebuilding
& Development

Visiting Somaliland for the first time today it is hard to imagine what the country looked like in 1991 when Somaliland announced its independence. The main cities of Hargeysa and Burco had been reduced to rubble by a decade and a half of war, aerial bombing and the systematic looting of public and private properties. The cities and the countryside were strewn with landmines and unexploded ordinance. Road bridges, water pumps and electricity generators had been destroyed and there was no telephone system or banks. Gunmen without uniforms manned checkpoints along the roads from ports and airports, demanding money in return for access.

Over the past fifteen years the cities, small towns and villages have been substantially rebuilt and expanded. Commercial activity is vibrant. Utilities have been restored, telephone systems have been established linking Somaliland into the world-wide web, where numerous Somaliland webpages can now be accessed, and Somali companies have established services throughout the country that facilitate financial transfers from anywhere in the world to the smallest village in Somaliland.

Somaliland's international critics have never ceased to doubt that such a 'sub-national' polity could be organised to manage a local economy, engage in international trade, provide basic services, enforce law and order and provide protection for its civilians. But this is what people in Somaliland have done – and in a manner largely free from the violence that has plagued southern Somalia during the same period. The revival and development of the economy has been critical to the survival of Somaliland as a political entity. The end of the civil war in Somaliland and the agreements reached at the Hargeysa conference inaugurated an unprecedented six years (1997–2002) in which the country experienced neither internal nor external security problems. Refugees in Ethiopia and Djibouti repatriated to Somaliland, the economy grew, infrastructure and services were rehabilitated and international aid increased. While the absence of diplomatic recognition has constrained forms of international economic support, it has not prevented Somaliland from participating in the regional and global economy. And although Somaliland remains a poor and, for some, an impoverished country, the economic and infra-structural developments that have taken place challenge the typical image of social regression with which the Somali region and other countries in the throes of conflict are associated. This chapter describes some key post-war economic developments in Somaliland.

Economic revival

During the 1980s, the command-style economy fashioned under Scien-tific Socialism was eroded after Somalia, under IMF guidance, adopted free-market liberal economic policies. By the end of the decade Somalia was in most respects a free-market economy. A local, largely pastoral economy and an informal economy of remittances and trade provided the bulk of economic activity, operating outside and in competition with the formal state economy (Jamal 1988; Little 2003: 9). While government persisted, the private sector was constrained by state monopolies and regulations. Once the state collapsed, the monopolies and economic controls disappeared, facilitating the growth of the private sector. In this respect the Somali economy after state collapse was a natural progression of the 'unconventional' economy described by Jamal (1988) before this event. The collapse of financial institutions, for example, had little impact on the majority of Somalis; indeed, it enabled the emergence of money transfer companies which, in facilitating remittances, provide financial services that are of much greater relevance to most people than formal banking institutions (Little 2003: 9).

In Somaliland – with over half the population obtaining their liveli-hoods from nomadic pastoralism, informal trade, an unrecorded remittance economy and unreliable population figures – measurements of the economy are problematic. Between 1991 and 2000 it appears that Somaliland experienced sustained economic growth, albeit starting from a very low base. During this period the government played a role in the management of the economy: it set exchange rates, for example, con-trolled the money supply and allocated procurement contracts (UNDP 2001). The creation of a public administration, a revenue system and tax laws restored a degree of regulation and the government exercised control over certain assets. The decision by the SNM and Somaliland elders to retain the port of Berbera as a public asset kept Somaliland's main economic resource largely free from conflict, and in the mid-1990s trade through the port surpassed pre-war levels. The desire of government to retain some control over the economy has also been apparent in the reluctance to allow the opening of a commercial bank. Some of the new service-oriented companies in Somaliland that have been established since the war complain that government bureaucracy and patronage

6.1 New construction,
Hargeysa (Nick Sireau/Progressio)

6.2 The telecommunications
sector has flourished in the
absence of government
regulations (M. Bradbury)

hinder free enterprise.[1] But generally Somaliland businesses, and in particular the larger established trading enterprises, have been supportive of the government, at times ensuring its survival by underwriting its costs. The government has made some effort to promote inward investment from Somalis and foreign companies by offering tax relief on raw materials and on capital investments. But the lack of international legitimacy has made foreign companies nervous to invest and the Somaliland government has been very slow to formulate foreign investment laws. By 2000 the only foreign company to have made a substantial investment in Somaliland was Total Mer Rouge, which won the contract to rehabilitate and manage the fuel storage depot at Berbera.

The highly privatised nature of the economy is evident from employment patterns, with public sector employment only marginal and self-employment providing the main source of income (World Bank and UNDP 2003). The biggest structural change in the economy has been the privatisation of services. Prior to the war most service-based and industrial output was provided by the public sector. The weakness of government has led to the *de facto* deregulation of the service sector, stimulating rapid growth. There have been significant private investments in transport, telecommunications, money transfer services, airlines, hotels, utilities, education, health, trade and marketing. Consequently, many services are more widely available than before the war. The Dahabshiil money transfer company and Daallo Airlines have developed into two of the largest Somali companies, with international operations. This economic restructuring has been shaped by global economic changes, including mass migration to richer countries, which has stimulated the remittance economy; the technological revolution, which has made telecommunications systems more accessible; and the liberalisation of some sectors, such as airlines.

Somaliland's political separation from Somalia has not severed economic links. Trade flows by road, sea and air between Somaliland and Somalia. As in other aspects of life, the kinship system is integral to economic activity. Central to most people's livelihoods, it provides a structure for organising trade by mobilising social relations across internal and international borders. In an informal economy the kinship system also provides a form of regulation, one based on trust rather than contract.

From the mid-1990s, political stability in Somaliland also facilitated an increase in international aid in support of local efforts to restore essential services and infrastructure, clear landmines, reintegrate displaced populations, demobilise militia and build the capacity of new civil society organisations. Stability and economic growth also facilitated an expansion of the population, with refugees returning from neighbouring countries and the diaspora, and economic migrants from

---

[1] Interviews, Hargeysa, 2003.

some of the poorest regions in southern Somalia[2] and from Ethiopia.

At the beginning of the millennium Somaliland's economy began to falter, slowed by external factors. The imposition of two successive embargoes by Gulf states on the importation of Somali livestock meant the rate of growth could not be sustained. The events of 11 September 2001, the Iraq war and the murders of foreign aid workers in 2003 prompted a fall in foreign aid. Another unexpected blow to the economy was Ethiopia's closure of its border with Somaliland in 2003, in an attempt to prevent Somali traders from avoiding the payment of custom duties. Furthermore, while the vibrancy of the private sector was critical to Somaliland's recovery the benefits of economic growth were not evenly redistributed. Instead, differences in the living conditions and incomes of socio-economic groups became more marked (King 2003).

Somaliland's economy, then, has been rebuilt on four main pillars: livestock production and export; foreign remittances; transit trade; and an expanding service sector. In addition, foreign aid has been an important fillip to the economy and there is a growing but still modest manu-facturing sector. We shall consider each of these elements in turn.

The pastoral economy & livestock trade

Historically, nomadic pastoralism has been the dominant economic activity in Somaliland. Exchange and trade have always been essential to pastoralists' livelihoods, but with the advent of colonialism the commercial export of livestock to foreign markets became a critical part of the pastoral economy. Sheep and goats have formed the bulk of exports, with cattle and camels exported in smaller numbers. Isaaq traders have long been dominant in livestock exporting, and as we saw in Chapter 3, the Barre government's effort to exert control over the trade was one of the grievances that fuelled the SNM uprising. For some time analysts have argued that pastoralism as a way of life in the Horn of Africa has been in decline, weakened by the change from semi-sub-sistence to market orientation, the impact of state policies, demographic and climatic change, an altered international environment and, finally, war (Markakis 1993). Nevertheless, it has proved a remarkably robust and adaptable economy. Pastoralists were generally better able to survive the war than sedentary farmers, being able to move with their assets away from violence, often across international borders such as with Ethiopia. And, as the armed factions recruited young fighters from nomadic communities, wealth accumulated in the war may have trickled back into the rural communities. The livestock export trade recovered quickly after the war and flourished in Somaliland and parts of Somalia (Little 2003).

[2] Many are Elay/Rahanweyn, from families said to be related by kinship to Isaaq clans.

The pastoral economy was critical to the survival of people in north-west Somalia during the war. Although pastoralists sustained losses to their herds due to restrictions on mobility and the reduction in veterinary services, the government never entirely controlled the rural areas. Some exports of livestock continued through tertiary ports such as Mait in Sanaag Region. Herd sizes recovered fairly quickly after the war, assisted by emergency veterinary programmes provided by the ICRC and other international agencies. The financial infrastructure of traders based in Djibouti was largely unaffected and exports through Berbera and tertiary ports resumed immediately once the war ended, assisted by European Union support for animal health inspection services. Exports exceeded pre-war levels to reach a peak of 2.8 million head of sheep and goats in 1997, generating US$120 million per year in income (UNDP 2001: 61). The numerous peace meetings that took place in Somaliland from 1991 opened up grazing lands and facilitated the movement of herds – a fundamental requirement of transhumant pastoralists (Bradbury 1996). This stimulated the recovery of rural livelihoods, while exports stimulated economic growth and provided an important revenue stream to finance a public administration, security and demobilisation.

Livestock production continues to be an important pillar of the Somaliland economy, providing livelihoods to an estimated 60–65 per cent of the population, according to the Somaliland Ministry of National Planning and Coordination (MNPC 2004: 19). In normal years livestock exports are estimated to account for up to 80 per cent of export earnings, 60–65 per cent of the domestic economy and some 30 per cent of government revenues (Holleman 2002: ii–iii). As 50–60 per cent of all livestock exported through Berbera originates in Ethiopia or central Somalia, Somaliland's economy is also closely tied to the health of the economy in Somalia and Somali-inhabited regions of Ethiopia (*ibid.*: 3).

In 1998 and 2000, as noted in the previous chapter,embargoes by Saudi Arabia and other Gulf states[3] on the import of livestock from Somali regions in the Horn of Africa following a Rift Valley Fever outbreak[4] had a major impact on Somaliland's economy, individual livelihoods and government revenue. For Somaliland, the loss of the Saudi market, which accounted for some 95 per cent of its livestock exports, was critical. One study conducted twenty-eight months after the second ban estimated that Somaliland had lost up to US$435 million in export revenues from the two bans (*ibid:.* 23). This translated into a loss of income to producers of up to US$233 million. Somaliland pastoralists alone, who it is estimated provide some 40 per cent of livestock exports, lost US$93 million in

---

[3] During the first ban livestock continued to be exported through Yemen. The second ban, imposed by Saudi Arabia, Bahrain, Oman, Qatar, Yemen, and the United Arab Emirates, was more comprehensive.

[4] Rift Valley Fever, which is carried by mosquitoes and can cause haemorrhaging and death, was detected in Somali livestock after the major flooding in southern Somalia in 1997, associated with the El Niño weather phenomenon.

income. Thousands of other people involved in livestock marketing and secondary jobs and services were also affected; a third of the port workers at Berbera were laid off and more than 70 per cent of an estimated 7,500 people involved in the trade in Burco lost their incomes (*ibid*.: 42). The embargoes also affected the structure of the trade. The number of livestock traders dropped from seventy in 1997 to just three in 2003. Of these, one trader controlled 80 per cent of all exports and 70 per cent of imports. Such monopolies reduce market competitiveness and increase opportunities for price manipulation (Gaani 2005).

The first first ban is estimated to have led to a 45 per cent fall in government revenue and a budgetary shortfall of US$7.5 million (UNDOS 1998). Within twenty-eight months of the second ban, it is estimated that the government lost US$22.5 million in foreign-exchange earnings plus an additional US$6.6 million in exchange-rate earnings, and the economy as a whole suffered from the loss of hard currency (Holleman 2002). The government sought to limit the impact on its revenue by amending the exchange rate and increasing tariffs on imports and exports. But this short-term solution persuaded some traders to move their businesses to Bossaso in Puntland, where the tax regime was lighter.

The cessation of exports also impacted on the environment. The dominance of pastoralism as a mode of production and way of life means that Somaliland's rangelands are a key resource requiring proper management. Concerns have been voiced ever since colonial times about the management of this resource, although long-term degradation is difficult to verify and the causes, extent and nature of environmental change are a topic of continuing debate (Gaani 2005). There is some evidence that the enclosure of rangelands, the development of private water resources, sedentarisation, the embargoes on livestock export, economic hardship, the breakdown, during the war, in reciprocal relations between clans and environmental practices may all have damaged the rangelands (Ahmed *et al.* 2001). Organisations working with pastoralists point to changes in the vegetative cover and species diversity in the Haud as evidence of ecological change. There is also evidence that the use of rangelands for purposes such as charcoal or fodder production is forcing pastoralists onto less productive rangeland. Charcoal production increased after the livestock export bans as rural producers sought alternative incomes. Coupled with reduced off-take and overgrazing, this exacerbated the serious drought conditions that affected the eastern regions of Sool and Sanaag in 2003, precipitating the first serious humanitarian emergency in Somaliland since 1996 (United Nations 2003). Given the huge losses of income to producers and revenue to the government, it seems curious that the import bans on Somali livestock did not precipitate a broader economic and livelihoods crisis. The likely reason is that the negative effects were offset by remittances, which increased during this period, as we shall see.

The Gulf market for livestock from the Horn of Africa has slowly reopened. By 2004 the volume of live exports from Somaliland to the

United Arab Emirates (UAE), Oman and Yemen, with onward sale to Saudi Arabia, had almost reached pre-embargo levels, although it was still less than half of what it was at their peak in the mid-1990s. This was in part a consequence of competition from Bossaso in Puntland, which is closer to the alternative markets in the UAE and Oman. The ban by Saudi Arabia depressed prices and created unfavourable terms of trade for pastoralists, although these appear to be improving (World Bank 2006: 80). In upholding the embargo, the Saudi government has legitimate concerns about the lack of a credible system of health surveillance and certification of Somali livestock and livestock products. But the fact that Rift Valley Fever has never been detected in Somaliland leads many Somalis to conclude that the embargo is sustained by political and economic interests in Saudi Arabia.[5] They allege that senior members of the Saudi royal family have personal financial interests that oppose lifting the ban.

Even if the export ban was lifted, it is unlikely that livestock exports through Berbera would reach the same level as in the mid-1990s, as it faces competition from Bossaso and a resurgent port in Djibouti, where the US government, in support of the Red Sea Livestock Trade Commission and the Djibouti Chamber of Commerce, is financing the construction of a livestock export facility. The timing of this project coincides with the stationing of the US Combined Joint Task Force for the Horn of Africa at Camp Lemonier in Djibouti for monitoring and disrupting 'transnational terrorist' groups in the region. The reopening of the Mogadishu port by the Islamic Courts in 2006 for the first time in over a decade – if sustained – would provide another alternative outlet to Berbera. Meanwhile, the monopolisation of the export trade in Somaliland by a smaller number of traders could also reduce exports by discouraging competition.

The Somaliland government has reaped the benefits of the livestock trade in terms of revenue and its special relationship with the traders. However, the government has put little back into the sector, other than by maintaining law and order. Most services previously provided by the Somali state – animal health services, laboratories for inspection and disease control, quarantine holding grounds – have been privatised. The government has neither the resources nor the political authority to regulate the sector or enforce policy on issues such as land tenure, range management or environmental preservation. Its efforts to manage the impact of the livestock bans were ineffectual. It responded to the 1998 ban by appealing for international assistance to offset the budgetary shortfall and to support income-generating projects (UNDOS 1998). As we have seen, the increase it imposed on import duties in response to the ban of 2000 led to a decline in imports and a loss of trade to Bossaso. The government's lack of international legitimacy also means that it has very little leverage when it comes to lifting the embargo on Somaliland's livestock.

[5] Interviews by author, Hargeysa, July 2005.

Structural alterations in the wider economy and in the overseas markets, the sedentarisation of rural populations and environmental change all present a challenge to the once-dominant pastoral economy. The impact is apparent in changes in the structure of internal markets, in herding strategies, herd compositions, labour patterns and levels of poverty. Poor pastoralists are considered by aid agencies to be amongst the most vulnerable sections of Somali society, while mainly male urban migration is causing rural labour shortages and giving women (and children, who look after livestock) greater responsibilities for animal husbandry (UNDP 2001). Weak government and the absence of an enforceable framework for rangeland management have enabled wealthier livestock owners to privatise land and water sources. In so doing they are disrupting patterns of grazing and watering and the traditionally flexible regime of land rights that has enabled nomadic pastoralists to manage rangelands as a common property resource.

Some adaptation is taking place in response to these pressures. Economic diversification is occurring gradually. The loss of markets for livestock exports and the monopolisation of the trade have led to investment in abattoirs and the export of chilled meat and hides and skins,[6] and in light industries producing detergents, bottled water and foam mattresses. Another spin-off from the embargo has been an increase in milk marketing, and the airfreighting of livestock to the UAE.

Changes in pastoralism are not just an economic issue but a political, social and cultural one. The political constitution of Somali society is intricately linked to the pastoral economy and there is a close relationship between this semi-subsistent mode of production and socio-political organisation, culture, identity, rights and economic security. Fundamental changes in the economy could therefore have an irrevocable impact on politics and culture. The poet Mohamed 'Hadraawi' laments the changes in the rural way of life and links it to a lack of progress in Somaliland:[7]

> In the last five years, against our expectations, there have not been any major achievements in Somaliland, because the conditions have not been there that would allow us to progress. The first reason is economic. Our people are mostly pastoralists, and the rural economy is the most productive part of our economy. But people are leaving that way of life. Rural people, especially young people, are being attracted to the urban way of life, by advertisements and all the material things that are available in the urban areas. When young people come to the urban centres with no skills and no employment opportunities the towns become like refugee centres. When people come to the urban centres their needs increase. They see the services available and also

---

[6] This new industry is better developed in Puntland and southern Somalia.

[7] Interviewed by author, September 2003, Burco.

want them. The livestock we export cannot satisfy those needs. People have left economically productive areas and have come to urban centres where there is little work. So we see people seeking ways of getting rich quick, searching mountains for riches to fulfil their needs.

Other productive sector activities
Other productive sector activities contribute only marginally to the economy. Only 3 per cent of land in Somaliland is under cultivation – mostly rain-fed farming in the higher rainfall areas to the west of Hargeysa and on the northern escarpment of the Gollis mountains (Somaliland MNPC 2004). The main agricultural areas were severely disrupted by the war, with most farming families fleeing to Ethiopia. Cultivation resumed with the assistance of foreign aid agencies, but on a reduced scale. There has been an expansion in the irrigated cultivation of vegetables and fruit along the banks of seasonal streams and water courses, but the scale is limited, with the produce grown for home consumption and local markets. A significant expansion of agriculture is constrained by rainfall, soil and topography. The harvesting of frankincense and myrrh for export from the Boswellia forests of the northern escarpment has resumed, but on a much smaller scale than pre-war, when Somalia claimed to be the world's largest exporter of these gums.

The most undeveloped sector with high potential is fishing off Somaliland's 850 kilometres of coastline. Fishing communities supply the internal market in Hargeysa and Burco, and in 2002 local businessmen rehabilitated the Soviet-built fish cannery in Las Qoray, where they now produce tinned tuna for the market. However, there has been little other investment in this sector.

Remittances

Given the absence of direct foreign investment, and the instability in the livestock export sector examined above, another input has been crucial to the growth and relative buoyancy of the economy in Somaliland: the phenomenon of remittances. In terms of value, money transferred to Somaliland by Somalis living in foreign countries has overtaken livestock exports as the main source of income. The remittance economy is also a vital catalytic element. It is a key source of hard currency, it supports family livelihoods, it is used for investments, it generates employment, and it is an instrument of trade and commerce.

Money earned abroad and remitted home has long been a significant element in the Somali economy and a source of household income. The origins of the Somali remittance or *xawilaad*[8] system have been traced

[8] This is the Somali transliteration of the Arabic *Hawala,* which means bill of exchange, promissory note, or transfer. It is also a common Hindi and Urdu term and this form of money transfer system is well known in the Middle East and South Asia. The term *xawilaad* may have

back to the 1960s, when Somalis migrated to southern Africa to work on the construction of the Tanzania–Zambia railway (Omar 2002: 5), although the existence of Somali immigrant communities in Britain during the colonial period predates this (Harris 2004: 22) (see Chapter 7). The importance of this informal system of money transfer grew significantly in the 1970s and 1980s as the oil boom in the Gulf states and political oppression in Somalia encouraged labour migration to the Middle East, North America and Western Europe. During this period the most common form of transfer was the *franco valuta* system, whereby migrant workers in the Gulf purchased high-value goods for duty-free sale in Somalia (Jamal 1988). Others simply remitted money or goods to relatives through traders. By the 1980s remittances to Somalia were estimated to be worth US$370 million annually (UNICEF 1991), equal to thirteen times the Somali-based national wage bill. This partly explains how households at the time were able to survive on basic government salaries that covered only a meagre 8 per cent of household expenditure (Mubarak 1996). Having a value several times larger than Somalia's export earnings, remittances were a significant part of the 'shadow economy' in the 1980s, over which the state had no control and which therefore weakened people's reliance on the state.

The civil war stimulated a further development of the system, as migration of Somalis to the Gulf, Western Europe, the Americas and other parts of the world increased. Currently it is assumed that over one million Somalis live outside Somalia (UNDP 2001: 61). For the refugees from north-west Somalia in Ethiopia, remittances became a crucial source of support. It is from this period also that Somaliland's main money transfer company Dahabshiil developed its dominance in the market. In the immediate post-war period VHF radios were used to facilitate trade and money transfers, but the major development of the remittance economy occurred alongside the development of telecommunications companies in the mid-1990s. The advent of telecommunications, with the recent addition of email, greatly increased the speed and efficiency of the remittance system.

Today money transfer and telecommunications enterprises are the largest companies operating in Somaliland, and in Somalia. After 2001, Dahabshiil, based in Hargeysa, became the largest of all Somali money transfer companies, after the US government forced the closure of the Mogadishu-based Al Barakat company, because of suspected links with Al Qaeda (Marchal 2001). There are numerous remittance companies (*xawaala*) in addition to Dahabshiil in Somaliland which also operate in Somalia. Dahabshiil, which reports having twenty-eight agents in Mogadishu alone, has also developed an impressive international reach with 400 branches in nineteen countries – mostly serving Somali diaspora communities, but increasingly other migrant communities as

[8] (cont.) come into use among Somali speakers only recently.

well.[9] Over time, Dahabshiil and the other large companies have expanded to offer the services normally associated with banks, including customer accounts and cheque books. Since 11 September 2001 they have had to comply with international financial regulations in order to continue operating (UNDP 2001; Lindley 2004). Thus they have migrated from the informal to the formal financial services sector. However, the *xawilaad* system also has various advantages over formal banking systems. Being built around a relationship of trust (*amaano*), it is highly suited to the Somali kinship system. As the transaction costs are less than moving funds through the formal banking system, it better meets the needs of poor people. As remittance companies have an extensive network of agents servicing most towns and villages, access to finance is also easier and more efficient. The system operates twenty-four hours a day and seven days a week. It requires limited paperwork and flourishes in environments where there is no regulatory oversight.

The total volume of remittances received in Somaliland and the value of the remittance economy are unknown. Estimates range from a low of US$200 million to a high of US$500 million per annum (Ahmed 2000).[10] Money transactions are of three main types: regular monthly transfers to families to meet livelihood needs; larger-scale transfers for investment in property or businesses; and remittances linked to international trade. But remittances can also take the form of material goods. The economic impact of remittances is apparent in trade, in the financial services sector, in household livelihoods and in the 'dollarisation' of the economy, with the dollar commonly used in transactions, particularly in the urban centres.

Roughly 50 per cent of the money handled by remittance companies is reported to be received as household income. Taking the most conservative estimates of annual remittances, they may account for between 22.5 and 25 per cent of total household income (World Bank/UNDP 2003; Lindley 2006: 5). As in the 1980s, remittances are therefore a crucial part of people's livelihoods. One study in Hargeysa found that remittances to families averaged US$200 per month, compared to the average annual income of US$491 per annum (Lindley 2006: 11). In other words, the average monthly remittance was more than sufficient to lift people out of poverty. Remittances to families are mainly used to meet consumption needs, both food and social services and play a particularly important role in meeting emergency survival needs in times of stress, such as periodic droughts or currency depreciations. During the livestock export bans, remittances were crucial in supplementing the loss of incomes and financing food imports (Gaani 2005). But they are also important in sustaining 'social capital', through the financing of marriages and payment of *diya*.

[9] Author's interview with Dahabshiil, London, June 2004.
[10] For Somalia as a whole estimates range from US$375 million to US$1 billion annually (Lindley 2006: 5).

Somaliland has been viewed by the diaspora as a 'country of opportunity' and somewhere to invest (Forster 2002) and one of the major uses of remittances has been investment in property and land. For Somalilanders in the UK, their home country has certainly been a more feasible investment environment than their host country's overheated property market. Indeed some Somalilanders who had the opportunity to purchase property in the UK years earlier made a windfall on their sales, which they invested in property in Somaliland.[11] One study suggests that remittances to Somaliland peaked between 2000 and 2003, when refugees and migrants from the early 1990s had become settled and economically active in their new countries of residence (Lindley 2006:16). But from 1997 the increasing scale of investment was also indicative of a growing confidence people had in Somaliland's political stability and security. Given the relationship between shelter and well-being, the importance of housing to social recovery should not be underestimated. The rehabilitation and reconstruction of housing in Somaliland (and elsewhere in Somalia) by Somalis is a stark and telling contrast to the post-war shelter reconstruction programmes financed by the international community in the Balkans. The lack of international support for similar housing programmes in Somaliland highlights, perhaps, a certain prejudice in the way international aid is prioritised in African countries.

Diaspora remittances, it was suggested above, also have an important economic multiplier effect. They pay for education and health; they spawn businesses and developments in the service sector, such as telecommunications, hotels and transport; and in the productive sector, too, they generate new sources of income. This has been occurring on a growing scale. The Ambassador Hotel in Hargeysa, the rehabilitated tuna canning factory in Las Qoray and Amoud University are all examples of developments supported through remittances from the diaspora. Another example is the Somali diaspora-based association, SomScan and UK Cooperative Associations, with members in different European countries, which pooled resources to build a new settlement of 330 houses outside Burco (Kleist 2004).

Remittances have other important socio-economic effects, which are viewed less positively. Whilst readily acknowledging this vital source of finance for Somaliland's recovery, some Somalis express concern that a substantial proportion of remittances is being spent on *qaad* imports, and that remittances encourage a 'culture of dependency' rather than stimulating economic productivity.[12] One study suggests, however, that households receiving remittances are as likely to be economically active, if not more so, than those without (Lindley 2006: 14). Nevertheless, there is evidence that remittances can serve to increase economic differentiation in society. The main beneficiaries of remittances tend to be urban

---

[11] Interviews by author, Hargeysa, August 2003.
[12] Interviews by author, Hargeysa, August 2003.

households with educated and skilled members in the diaspora, while the rural poor, minorities such as the Gabooye, and the internally displaced from poorer groups tend to have fewer relatives abroad and less access to remittances (Medani 2000). By enabling recipient families to educate their children, construct better housing and invest in other forms of income generation, remittances can reinforce existing socio-economic divisions – although there is always some redistribution of wealth through kinship and other social networks.

Remittances can serve to reinforce clan as well as class divisions. Remittance patterns vary depending on the socio-economic position of migrants in their host country. The poor education of many Somali migrants means they are often living on the margins in those host societies and it can take time for families to settle, find incomes and begin to remit significant amounts of money. Somaliland's colonial past, its proximity to the Gulf, the flight from war and repression in the 1980s, and easier immigration conditions in the late 1980s were all factors that helped Isaaq families to become established in the UK earlier than members of other clans. Isaaq refugees in Ethiopia were already receiving remittances; Isaaq families in Somaliland are therefore likely to have benefited from remittances before members of other clans, and this may have contributed to socio-economic divisions between Isaaq and non-Isaaq clans in Somaliland.

Remittances have also had an impact on the role of women. As women are the primary recipients of family remittances in Somaliland, this has reinforced their economic role in society (Lindley 2006). It appears that women in the diaspora are more likely than men to support their families back home through remittances. This has led Somali men to remark that they would prefer to have a daughter, rather than a son, as the daughter can be relied upon to support the family economically.

Remittances being such a dominant feature of the economy, it has been suggested that Somaliland's main export commodity in the 1990s was labour (UNDP 2001). Stability in Somaliland, coupled with tougher immigration policies in Britain and other European countries have slowed the pace of migration overseas. Some Somalis express concern that, as immigration falls, refugee returns increase, or that, as diaspora populations become more integrated in their host countries, the remittance economy will decline with nothing to replace it. It remains to be seen whether children of migrants will continue to remit money to relatives they have not met in a country that they may never have visited. Dahabshiil anticipates that there may be only one more 'surge' in overseas remittances,[13] and that the next generation of Somalis born overseas will be less motivated to maintain a relationship with their extended families in Somaliland. Dahabshiil is planning to expand its client base to other nationalities and diversify its business in anticipation of this. Others argue that the

[13] Interview with Dahabshiil, London, August 2001.

remittance system will remain a significant part of the Somali economy for the foreseeable future (Omar 2002). As most people who fled Somaliland in the 1980s and early 1990s were quite young, the links are likely to remain strong for two to three decades. This provides a relatively long-term planning horizon for the economy.

Remittances, therefore, have been fundamentally important to socio-economic and political recovery in Somaliland. As will be discussed further in the next chapter, the diaspora has played a key role in building Somaliland. However, remittances are not directly taxed, although customs tariffs are a form of indirect tax on the remittances that pay for imports. Such an economy can produce a different relationship between citizens and the state, compared to one where income or production is taxed directly. Furthermore, when remittances are used to pay for services or to offset economic crises, government is relieved of its usual responsibilities. An economy based on remittances rather than local production thus shapes the trajectory of development and the nature of the state.

Trade

Trade is the third pillar of the Somaliland economy. Trade has always been an integral part of the economy of the Somali-populated regions of the Horn. In ancient times international networks traversed the Somali region, linking eastern Africa to North Africa, the Middle East, Persia and Asia. Early trading institutions employed Somali middlemen or *abbaan* ('protectors') to secure the passage of caravans through Somali-inhabited territory (Ahmed Samatar 1988). The creation of states placed certain constraints on the development of trade networks by interposing national borders and establishing protective controls and tariffs. With the collapse of government, Somalia's 'national' economy was suddenly inter-nationalised as these state-imposed barriers disappeared, and trade has subsequently re-emerged as an increasingly vital part of the economy of the Somali region. The trade economy is particularly vibrant in southern Somalia, where Mogadishu's Bakara market has developed into an important commercial centre for the entire Horn and East Africa region (Marchal 1996; Little 2003). However, dispersal of the population during the war and political fragmentation have been accompanied by economic decentralisation. While Bakara market remains the biggest commercial centre, others have flourished, among them Hargeysa in Somaliland and Bossaso and Galkaiyo in Puntland.

In Somaliland, commerce – together with the transportation, financial, telecommunications, port and security services that support commercial activities – is a source of employment and income for households second only to livestock production. Many households are involved in some form of commerce that is linked to the import-export trade, ranging from petty trade in imported *bagaash* (non-food items), to selling *qaad*, to the sale of a few head of livestock for export, all the way to wealthy traders buying and selling on the international market. Commerce has developed differently in Somaliland than in Somalia, shaped by a different trading structure, a different resource base, proximity to different regional markets, the differential impact of the war, the different experiences of émigré communities, and the presence of a government. Many businesses in Mogadishu profited from the huge injection of resources made by UNOSOM in the early 1990s, something that bypassed Somaliland (UNDP 2001: 138–58), and are linked into the flourishing commercial environment of Dubai, which has developed into a kind of commercial emporium for the Horn and East Africa. In Somaliland, the domination of the Djibouti-based Isaaq merchants in the 1990s, together with government, constrained the development of the kind of entrepreneurial economy that has flourished in southern Somalia and Puntland.

A major economic development in the Somali region over the past decade has been the growth of transshipment and transborder trade and the emergence of an entrepôt economy (UNDP 2001). Somalis have exploited the region's location as a sea, land and air link between Africa and the Persian Gulf, Asia and Europe, replicating some of the ancient trading networks. Indeed, in southern Somalia the notion of *abbaan* has been resuscitated, with armed militias providing protection to convoys traversing the insecure lands. The port of Berbera is positioned advantageously for this trade, as it had been historically. Its location on the southern coast of the Gulf of Aden, with a natural harbour protected by a sandspit, has made it an alternative to Djibouti for goods in transit to Ethiopia, Somalia and other parts of the Horn of Africa. When Ethiopia lost access to Assab and Massawa following its war with Eritrea in 1998, the light tax and non-bureaucratic regime at Berbera made it a credible alternative to Djibouti. The closure of Mogadishu's main seaport for over a decade and insecurity surrounding Kismayo, as we noted in the previous chapter, also helped Berbera to grow as a commercial centre, and from 1991 until the first livestock embargo in 1998 it experienced a steady rise in port traffic and imports.

The downturn in Berbera's fortunes that accompanied the livestock embargoes, the loss of trade to Bossaso and the rejuvenation of Djibouti, as described above, were compounded by the deteriorating road infrastructure along the 'Berbera Corridor' between Somaliland and Ethiopia. However, while the number of vessels calling at Berbera annually fell from 595 to 233 following the ban, there has been an increase in the number of containers handled by Berbera as traders have diversified their businesses (Louis Berger *et al.* 2003). In recognition of the importance of the Corridor as a route for trade and humanitarian supplies, the EU and the Ethiopian road authority have assisted in upgrading the road network. As one of the four main ports on the Europe-Far East maritime trade route and having Africa's longest runway, Berbera has also attracted international interest as a commercial transport hub for the region.[14] Although the decision by the elders and SNM to maintain the port as a national asset avoided the protracted conflict experienced over Mogadishu's port, and generated government revenue, its management by the state has become problematic. During Egal's presidency the role and legal status of Berbera Port Authority became an increasingly controversial issue between the President and Parliament, with revenue unaccounted for and very little reinvested in the rehabilitation and maintenance of the port. One solution under consideration by the Somaliland authorities is to establish a free trade zone in Berbera, possibly to be managed by a foreign company.

Saudi Arabia, Yemen, Oman, the UAE and Egypt are Somaliland's top markets for its livestock-dominated exports. Most vehicles, construction materials, consumer items and perishables are imported from Dubai. Somaliland's other main sources of imports are the UAE, Saudi Arabia, Kenya, Italy, Thailand, Brazil, the Netherlands, Britain, Japan, South Korea and France. Somalia is also an important trading partner: ironically, the economies of southern Somalia and Somaliland are probably better integrated now than they were before the war. A significant volume of livestock exported through Berbera originates in central Somalia. The Somali shilling is still used in eastern Somaliland. Currency exchange rates in Somaliland are still influenced by Bakara market in Mogadishu. Somaliland companies like Dahabshiil and Daallo operate in Somalia, while Somalia businesses have been investing in real estate, services and commerce in Somaliland. This has generated some local resentment, voiced through the media, but neither the government, the Chamber of Commerce nor the Somaliland business community have tried to prevent the development.

Somaliland's main trading partner, however, is its giant neighbour Ethiopia. A high percentage of livestock exported from Berbera originates there, as does most of the *qaad* entering Somaliland (probably the fastest-growing trade since the war). In return, Ethiopia provides a huge market for Somaliland's re-exported imports. Ethiopia acknowledged the importance of this relationship by the posting of a Trade Delegate to Hargeysa, and in 2000 secured an agreement over the use of the port of Berbera. By the following year Ethiopian traffic through Berbera was estimated to constitute 30–50 per cent of the total port traffic (IRIN 2001 April).[15] The port is also used by the EU to ship food aid to Ethiopia. Trade relations were further strengthened when Ethiopian Airlines began scheduled flights between Addis Ababa and Hargeysa in April 2001.

State deregulation as a consequence of an under-resourced and un-recognised government has been liberating for commercial activity. Somaliland businesses have been creative in overcoming some of the constraints imposed by the lack of financial services in Somaliland and

[14] The runway was built by the Soviet Union in the 1970s and was later considered as a potential landing site for the Space Shuttle by the US in the 1980s.
[15] Author's interview with the port manager, September 2003.

the absence of recognised legal and commercial institutions. They have resorted to off-shore offices in neighbouring Djibouti, Dubai and elsewhere. Indeed, as several of the prominent Isaaq merchants are Djiboutian nationals, they have borrowed that country's sovereignty in order to do business in a state whose sovereignty is not recognised (Reno 2003: 32). The Somaliland government also holds its foreign reserves in Ethiopia. The presence of foreign companies like Total and Ethiopian Airlines has helped to 'formalise' aspects of the economy and provided Somaliland with an element of 'legitimacy' (Little 2003: 166). Nevertheless, non-recognition of Somaliland does place some constraints on business development. Lack of full diplomatic relations with Ethiopia makes it difficult to set up transit agreements between the two countries, for example. Foreign vessels wanting to use Berbera have to pay higher insurance premiums, and Somaliland is unable to offer any financial facilities in-country, or issue letters of credit. Foreign companies will be reluctant to invest in managing the port of Berbera, as is proposed by the government, until formal financial institutions exist and Somaliland's status is resolved.

Services & manufacturing

The privatised nature of Somaliland's economy is perhaps most evident in the development of services and industries that were previously publicly owned and managed. In an environment free of government regulation, Somaliland's service sector has experienced rapid growth in the post-war period, fuelled by remittances and trade. Telecommunications, financial transfer and postal services, electricity generation and air transport have been some of the main growth areas. Telecommunications, largely financed by people in the diaspora, has been one of the most critical economic developments, being the main conduit for transferring money from the diaspora to Somaliland. The open competition means that telephone companies in Somaliland, as in Somalia, provide mobile and landline services that are amongst the cheapest in Africa, so that calls can be made, even in remote villages, at a lower cost than in neighbouring countries (World Bank 2006). Seven private Somali-owned airlines fly regularly to Hargeysa and other airstrips in Somaliland (Somaliland MNPC 2004). Data from the Somaliland Ministry of Civil Aviation and Air Transport show a steady rise in passenger and cargo traffic. In 1997, 419 flights to Hargeysa were recorded. By 2003 this number had risen to 3,103 international and domestic flights in Somaliland. The number of incoming passengers rose correspondingly from 14,000 in 1998 to 50,000 in 2003 (*ibid.*). Daallo Airlines, Somaliland's second largest company after Dahabshiil, began with a small twin-engine plane and a US$30,000 investment.[16] A decade later it has become an international carrier, with

[16] As noted, the owners of Daallo were a conduit for diaspora funds for the SNM during the war.

flights between Somaliland, Somalia, Dubai, Kenya, Paris and Amsterdam. The expansion of these services has created a new labour market employing skilled professionals as well as semi-skilled and unskilled workers. However, none of these businesses are labour-intensive. Dahabshiil, for example, has branches throughout the country, but they employ just one or two people at each.

Manufacturing was never a significant part of Somalia's economy, and was mostly concentrated in Mogadishu and the south. The tuna canning factory in Las Qoray and a cement factory in Berbera were the two exceptions in the north. In 2003, the Somaliland government signed a memorandum of understanding with an Emir from Qatar to rebuild the cement factory and to develop another fish cannery, shrimp fishing, a small boat-building plant and a salt-processing plant in Berbera. If successful, it will utilise Somaliland's considerable marine resources and tap into a potentially large market for fish in Ethiopia.

The business class & government

The role played by the Somaliland business community – first in support of the SNM insurgency, then in the stabilisation of Somaliland and finally in the formation of government – has been remarked on in earlier chapters. Since 1991, with a limited revenue base and no access to international loans or budgetary support, the government has relied on the business community for financial assistance. Business leaders therefore believe they have played an important and constructive role in restoring law and order and in building government institutions.[17] At the 1993 Borama conference, Egal was the favoured candidate of the dominant Isaaq businessmen and on becoming President he negotiated a loan of US$7 million from them. Financial support for the re-establishment of security and government in Somaliland was beneficial to their own business interests. By sponsoring the state they established a monopoly over regional resources and markets, particularly in the livestock trade. In the mid-1990s, this relationship of co-dependency between the business class and the government was described by one analyst as 'a profit-sharing agreement among the dominant livestock traders, with a constitution appended' (de Waal 1996: 7).

By 2000 the government had repaid the loan with interest through tax exemptions and reduced tariffs. Since then the government has continued to borrow from the private sector. This arrangement with the business community has not always been smooth and carries a cost. Loans have to be repaid through tax breaks which constrain the government's ability to raise revenue. Indebtedness to the business community leaves it vulnerable to pressure from interest groups that can compromise

[17] Author's interviews with business people, Hargeysa, October 2003.

policy and decision-making. The relationship has been managed without parliamentary oversight, and as the loans do not always pass through the state ledgers, it has left the administration open to the charge of lacking transparency. As the business community has expanded, relationships between business people, and between them and government, have been strained. The wealthiest, mostly Isaaq, merchants are accused by smaller, middle-level traders of monopolistic practices and pushing them out of the market. This has encouraged some smaller non-Isaaq traders to look outside Somaliland to Bossaso and Mogadishu for business opportunities. At the same time, businesses accuse the government of denying them a role in some sectors through lack of appropriate legislation, such as commercial banking. The line between what is 'public' and 'private' is ambiguous, and the government's relationship with the business community has been strained when the government has tried to participate in the market, particularly in the areas of foreign company investment and currency control.

In addition to direct support to government, another developing area has been public-private partnerships. These take various forms, such as the management of municipal water supplies, or contracting out of services such as electricity or baggage handling at Hargeysa airport. Other examples are the Universities of Amoud, Hargeysa and Burco, and Edna Adan Maternity Hospital,[18] which are funded through a mixture of donations from the diaspora, fees, government subsidies and corporate sponsorship. Corporate sponsorship, or more broadly 'corporate social responsibility', is another development. Companies have always been obliged to pay *zakaat* (alms),[19] but some of the newer, larger companies are contributing additional resources to community reconstruction and development projects. For example, one of Somaliland's leading telecommunications companies, Telesom, reportedly spends some US$18,000 a year on 'community projects'. These have included contributions to rehabilitating the Borama–Hargeysa road, a bridge in Burco, a wall around Hargeysa airport, school buildings, the universities of Hargeysa and Amoud, and the rehabilitation of the orthopaedic ward at Hargeysa Hospital.[20] Telesom considers it part of the company's social responsibility to support such projects, and it is good for public relations. Dahabshiil has plans to establish a charitable foundation for similar purposes. The opportunities for developing public-private partnerships and corporate social responsibility are far from exhausted, as the scale of these

---

[18] Edna Adan, a former wife of the late President Egal, was a pioneering campaigner against female genital mutilation; she built the first private maternity hospital in Somaliland and became the first female Foreign Minister in 2002.

[19] The payment of *zakaat* is one of the five pillars of Islam (along with faith, prayer, fasting and pilgrimage), whereby every Muslim is obliged to donate annually a fortieth of their assets to a designated category of citizens, including the poor, destitute, religiously devoted or people in need.

[20] Interview by author with the Managing Director of Telesom, Hargeysa, July 2004.

ventures is relatively small. But while a limited tax base continues to constrain the development of publicly run services, it is an area in which further experimentation is likely.

Foreign aid

In terms of direct contributions to the Somaliland economy, foreign aid comes a poor fourth after the livestock trade, remittances and trade. In the early 1990s, foreign aid virtually bypassed Somaliland as the international community committed billions of dollars to humanitarian and peacekeeping operations in southern Somalia. When US forces withdrew from their UNOSOM mission in 1994 – followed in 1995 by the rest of UNOSOM – multilateral aid organisations and Western NGOs lost their security umbrella and moved their headquarters to neighbouring Kenya. For aid agencies in Somaliland who ran their operations out of neighbouring Djibouti, improvements in security and infrastructure after 1993 enabled them to establish permanent offices in-country. As aid programmes in southern Somalia contracted, there was a northwards drift of resources and aid agencies. As described in the previous chapter, this was encouraged by a change in donor aid policy which made assistance conditional on a secure environment and a demonstrated commitment to peace – the so-called 'peace dividend' approach (Bradbury and Coultan 1998). The UN Secretary-General reflected these sentiments when he urged the international community to provide development assistance to areas that have established relative peace and a certain level of regional authority (United Nations 1999).

After the 1997 Hargeysa conference, aid to Somaliland gradually increased relative to other areas of Somalia. According to the Somalia Aid Coordination Body, by 2002 some 44 per cent of the annual aid programme for Somalia was being allocated to Somaliland (SACB 2002).[21] This amounted to US$43 million in 2002[22] – approximately twice the government's reported annual expenditure of US$20 million (see Chapter 9) Given that three-quarters of the population of former Somalia live in the south, this reflected a stark shift in donor priorities. However, lack of diplomatic recognition limits the type of aid available to Somaliland.

The growth in aid to Somaliland was not predicated only on a more secure operating environment, but also on the presence of local authorities with whom agencies could engage. However, aid strategies are handicapped by international conventions that privilege only 'legitimate' states

[21] The Somalia Aid Coordination Body was a donor led forum for the coordination of international aid to Somalia, based in Nairobi, established in February 1994 to address the problems arising from UNOSOM.

[22] Accurate figures on aid disbursed to Somaliland are not available. This is an estimate of the aid actually spent in Somaliland, based on figures for 2002 collated by the Somalia Aid Coordination Body.

with development assistance, and are highly ambivalent about how to work with 'quasi-state' polities (Macrae and Shepherd *et al.* 2003). Lack of diplomatic recognition limited the type of aid available to short-term assistance, and it was only after 2003, that the World Bank began to re-engage in Somalia through the LICUS (Low-Income Countries Under Stress) initiative, constrained until then both by significant arrears on past debt-servicing obligations and the lack of a functioning national government. Despite the presence of an authority being a prerequisite for a peace dividend, international political sensitivities over Somaliland's status have meant that very little assistance has been directed to support the building of government institutions. Select ministries, such as education, health and the Ministry of Rehabilitation, Resettlement and Reintegration, have benefited from donors' priority interests in basic services and refugees. There has been some support for district and municipal-level authorities from UN-Habitat and some training for Somaliland's legislative institutions and security services. But, in contrast to the situation before the war, when international aid was directed through government, aid to Somaliland largely bypasses government. This is why international aid has never been incorporated into Somaliland's national budgets.

Rather than engaging in state-building, aid agencies have tended to work around local authorities. In pursuing a goal of 'local ownership', the policy choice of donors and agencies has been to build the organisational capacity of 'communities' through the formation of various kinds of committees, 'civil society' organisations and private service authorities for the private management of public goods. This accounts for the large number of international NGOs operating in Somaliland and the even larger number of Somaliland NGOs. In 2003, forty international NGOs and 543 Somali NGOs were registered with the Ministry of National Planning and Cooperation in Hargeysa (Somaliland MNPC 2004). Such a strategy not only neglects the opportunity for influencing the development of accountable and legitimate public institutions, but also places a burden on already impoverished communities.

With as little as 8 per cent of the government's budget allocated to social spending, Somaliland has substantially relied on foreign aid to support the restoration of social services such as health and education and the rehabilitation of water supplies and other essential infrastructure. Donor-funded landmine clearance by international agencies, coordinated through the National Demining Agency in Hargeysa and the Somaliland Mine Action Centre, has also greatly reduced the risks to life and health. The achievements in landmine clearance are illustrative of the impact that a change in donor policy priorities can have. Landmine clearance in Somaliland began in the early 1990s with one private security firm, but made slow progress. As a result of the global anti-landmine campaign more donor funds became available for this type of activity in the late 1990s, which resulted in several landmine agencies working in Somaliland. By 2010– 2012 Somaliland is likely to be declared safe from land-mines and unexploded ordinance (UNDP 2001: 64).

A significant amount of aid money feeds into the economy through salaries, property rent and other expenditures. But there is no danger of Somalilanders being wholly dependent on foreign aid. Meagre levels of social spending by the government and limited aid mean that responsibilities for meeting the costs of welfare services and utilities such as water, electricity or veterinary care have fallen on individual households through so-called 'cost sharing' and a range of self-help schemes. Donor policies have encouraged this trend further by making aid conditional on the privatisation of services such as water provision or road maintenance. In doing so, government has been relieved of responsibility for the management and implementation of social services, and its developmental role has been restricted to policy formulation and regulation. But international aid has only played a complementary role in reconstruction. The real engine of recovery has been the private sector, with income from livestock exports, remittances and trade dwarfing international aid. Remittances, as described, have been crucial for social spending on education, health and shelter. The rehabilitation and expansion of housing has been an important social and economic development which impacts on health and other aspects of well-being, and is remarkable for being entirely financed by remittances. This is very important for Somaliland because international aid is a notoriously unstable form of finance, vulnerable to changes in political agendas and fashion. If a functional national government does emerge in Somalia, international attention will refocus there and Somaliland is likely to experience a decline in aid. Without alternative sources of government or donor funding, social services will become wholly reliant on private financing or collapse.

7
Social ▌ Developments

In Chapter 3 we saw that a strong sense of inequitable development in Somalia – a perception that the bulk of state resources and foreign aid were consumed in the south, or in support of refugees from the Ogaden – was one underlying grievance that precipitated the SNM uprising. Somaliland's break with Somalia provided an opportunity to rectify this, and rather than simply rehabilitate and reconstruct a state as it has been, to craft something different and establish a new trajectory for development. Since 1991 the people of Somaliland have not only had to negotiate the delicate process of building a functional state, but have done so against a background of a society undergoing complex social change. This chapter considers some of the key social developments that have occurred in Somaliland.

Socio-economic developments

Estimating the population of Somaliland with any accuracy is difficult, given its recent history of wars, displacement and urban migration, as well as the traditionally nomadic nature of the population. The Ministry of National Planning and Coordination put the population at three million people in 1997 (Somaliland MNPC 2004). Other estimates place the population as low as 1.1 million.[1] Some 55 per cent of Somalilanders are thought to be nomadic (*ibid.*).

[1] Prior to 1988 the population of north-west Somalia was estimated to be between 1.78 and 2.05 million, excluding Ethiopian refugees. Several hundred thousand people fled abroad and to the south in 1988 (Africa Watch 1990). In 1992 one survey estimated there were 1.35 million people in Somaliland (Holt and Lawrence 1992). In 1997 a study by the United Nations Population Fund projected a population for Somaliland of 1.09 million in 2000 (Vaidyanathan 1997). In 1997 the Ministry of National Planning and Coordination estimated the population to be three million (Somaliland MNPC 2004). The voter turn-out in the 2005 presidential elections indicated the population may be closer to 1.9 million in the areas that voted, suggesting a total population of between 2 and 3 million.

Following the declaration of independence in 1991, thousands of refugees in Ethiopia and Djibouti returned spontaneously and unassisted to Somaliland, but as many as 150,000 people again fled the hostilities that erupted in Hargeysa and Burco in 1994, mostly to Ethiopia (Bryden 1994a). By 1997, however, with the country enjoying stability and economic growth, Somaliland had ceased being a refugee-producing area. A combination of spontaneous and assisted repatriation has brought the majority of refugees home from Ethiopia and the camps there have been closed. There is also evidence that more people are returning to Somaliland from overseas than are leaving,[2] while physical security and economic prosperity in Somaliland have also attracted as many as 60,000 people from some of the poorest communities in southern Somalia and Ethiopia.[3]

Another clear post-war trend in Somaliland has been sedentarisation and urban drift, reflected in the rapid growth of urban centres like Hargeysa. Over half of the refugees returning to Somaliland, and most migrants from the south and Ethiopia, have chosen to settle in Hargeysa district, attracted by the concentration of services, employment opportunities, aid programmes and access to remittances from the diaspora (UNDP 2001). Sedentarisation and urban drift also indicate the increasing immiseration of rural areas. The urban population of Somaliland was estimated to be between 748,000 and 1.2 million in 2002 (Woods and Mutero 2002) and the population of Hargeysa has risen from a few thousand in 1991 to over 300,000, according to the Somaliland government (Somaliland MNPC 2004). Most towns in Somaliland have experienced a similar growth in their populations. Rapid urban drift is placing a strain on the infrastructure and the environment and creating tensions over the ownership and management of resources. In Hargeysa, for example, there is an urgent need to find new water sources for the expanding population. More people and a real-estate boom have also driven up the price of land.[4]

The informalisation and deregulation of the economy and the obstacles to collecting viable and reliable data make the task of assessing human development with any accuracy very difficult. Disaggregated social data on Somaliland are hard to find because Somalia's existing territorial borders remain the reference area for international aid policy. Indices for Somalia point to very low levels of human development: an average life expectancy of forty-seven years; an infant mortality rate of 224 (per 1,000 live births); a maternal mortality rate of 1,600 (per 100,000); just over 19 per cent literacy among adults and as low as 7 per cent among rural women; and an average annual *per capita* income equivalent, in 2003, to

---

[2] Personal communication, Peter Hansen, Hargeysa, August 2003.

[3] This leads to the popular belief that many of the poor are not from Somaliland.

[4] For example, between 1992 and 2003 a plot of land of 18 x 24 metres near the Mansoor Hotel had risen from US$300 to $9,000. In other parts of the city the value of land increased at least ten times over the same period. Interviews by author with property agents, Hargeysa, 2003.

Table 7.1 Selected Disaggregated Social Development Indicators

Indicator	Somaliland
Health	
Maternal mortality (# of deaths per 100,000 live births)	1,600
Infant mortality rate (# of deaths per 1,000 live births)	113
Under-five mortality (# of deaths per 1,000 live births)	188
% of under-fives underweight (moderately and severely malnourished)	21
% of under-fives with acute malnutrition	10
% of population with access to safe drinking water	38
% of population with access to safe sanitation	47
Education	
% of children attending primary school	88
% of male population above 15 years that is literate	55
% of female population above 15 years that is literate	25
% of population above 15 years that is literate	27

Sources: UNICEF (2000); UNDP (2001); World Bank/UNDP (2003).

only US$226 (UNDP 2001; World Bank/UNDP 2003). Over 73 per cent of the population of Somalia is estimated to live in general poverty and 43 per cent in conditions of extreme poverty.[5] Unemployment is high at 47 per cent of the economically active members of the population.

Somaliland-specific indices would probably give a brighter picture than the Somalia-wide ones. The few data that do exist point to better levels of human development – with infant mortality at 113 (per 1,000 live births), and under-five mortality at 188 (per 1,000), for example (see Table 7.1) – and to higher levels of *per capita* income in most regions of Somaliland compared to most parts of Somalia with the exception of Mogadishu (UNICEF 2000). People in Woqooyi Galbeed (Hargeysa region) have the highest average *per capita* income in Somaliland of US$350. Studies of the remittance transfers discussed in the previous chapter and Jamal's (1998) description of the informal economy would suggest that *per capita* income is actually higher. There have also been some impressive developments in education services. The number of primary schools more than doubled between 1995 and 2003, enrolment has increased more than tenfold, and the percentage of children attending primary school may be as high as 88 per cent, according to one set of data (UNICEF 2000).

Health indicators, however, are more sobering. A maternal mortality rate of 1,600 per 100,000 shows expectant mothers in Somaliland to be at higher risk than most women in the world. Food security in Somaliland may have been better than in southern Somalia over the past decade, but malnutrition remains a chronic problem in places and can quickly

---

[5] Extreme poverty is defined as the proportion of population living on less than US$1 per day and general poverty at less than US$2 per day, measured at purchasing power parity.

become acute in areas of drought or socio-economic hardship. A nutritional survey in Hargeysa in June 2001 found about a sixth (16.3 per cent) of the whole population to be acutely malnourished and found 6.4 per cent severe acute malnutrition amongst returned refugees and displaced populations. A similar figure for global acute malnutrition of 17 per cent was recorded in 2002 among children in the Sool plateau and the Gebi Valley, where four years of failed rains, environmental degradation and progressive asset depletion had taken their toll on livelihoods.

The persistence of poverty is linked to structural factors such as dependence on a single export, the vulnerability of livestock production to market changes, and a lack of labour opportunities. Poverty studies in Hargeysa suggest that benefits of growth are not trickling down to the poor, as there is evidence of disparities in wealth between social groups, between genders, between the east and the west of the country, and between urban and rural populations. The asymmetry between east and west is apparent in better educational access in the west and a higher concentration of Somaliland NGOs there. A higher level of school enrolment in western Somaliland not only reflects the greater density of population, but also the growing dominance of the capital, Hargeysa. That government and aid organisations lack a policy to address better distribution of resources by decentralising development programmes to other regions is reminiscent of pre-war Somalia, when Mogadishu was so dominant. Development policies have changed very little since then, it seems.

A comparative study of wealth groups in Hargeysa between 1998 and 2003 concluded that the wealth gap was increasing and that in dollar terms the poor had become poorer (King 2003). In 2003 it was estimated that between 3 and 7 per cent of Hargeysa's population were 'poor': that is, living on US$3 per day or less (*ibid.*). Since 1998 the percentage had increased and the percentage of households earning less than this – the 'very poor' – had also increased. This was in a period when remittances generally were increasing, indicating that the 'very poor' and 'poor' had no direct access to remittances and relied instead on begging and on gifts from members of their immediate and extended families. The increase in the numbers of poor may have been due to an influx of people from the Ethiopian refugee camps and poor rural households who had lost their livestock. Over the same period, the percentage of households in the 'middle' wealth group remained roughly constant.

The revival of social services

The re-establishment of basic welfare services illustrates some of the transformations that have occurred in Somaliland as a result of the war and the challenges and choices that face the country. Prior to the war, basic services were managed by central government and heavily subsidised by foreign aid. War and state collapse have resulted in the

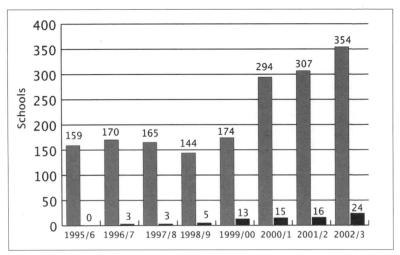

Figure 7.1 Growth of Primary and Secondary Schools in Somaliland
Source: Somaliland in Figures, 2004

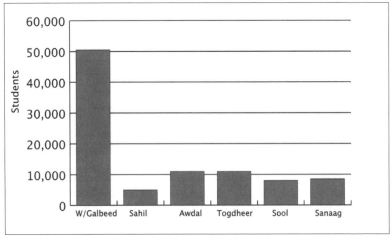

Figure 7.2 Primary School Enrolment by Region
Source: Somaliland in Figures, 2004

deregulation, privatisation and decentralisation of all basic services. In Somaliland the administration provides very modest support to social services, mainly in the form of salaries. Some municipalities or district councils do likewise. In the absence of a well-resourced government, the task of reviving these services has fallen to a mixture of communities, international aid agencies, Islamic charities, diaspora organisations and Somali businesses.

In 1991 there were no educational institutions operating in Somaliland. A modest public education system has since been established supported by communities, foreign donors and the government. The public system exists in parallel with a traditional system of Qur'anic schools and a large number of private educational establishments offering vocational training. By 2003 there were 354 primary schools, 24 secondary schools, and two universities (see Figures 7.1–7.2). The number of primary schools now exceeds the number in the late 1980s. Enrolment has increased steadily from as few as 8,600 primary school students in 1995 to 96,200 in 2003. That year there were also 9,266 secondary school students, while 497 university students enrolled in 2003 (MNPC 2004).

There are, however, marked disparities in educational access. The cost of education is prohibitive for some poorer families, female enrolment is disproportionately low, there is an urban bias in education provision, and more children go to primary schools in Woqooyi Galbeed than in all the other regions of Somaliland combined. The growth in private educational establishments reflects the difficulties of establishing a sustainable system of public financing for education. The government's budgetary allocation for education covers only a fraction of recurrent costs. Aid donors have therefore promoted the community management and financing of schools through community-based committees and parent associations and school fees. Given the *per capita* income of families, however, establishing a fully self-financing system is an unrealistic expectation. The educational system therefore relies on support from the diaspora.

Somaliland's diaspora has been making substantial investments in education, from Qur'anic schools to secondary schools and universities (Kent, von Hippel and Bradbury 2004). Such support tends to be on a clan or sub-clan basis, and is part of the set of kinship obligations. Universities attract broader public support. The assistance given to primary schools can be considerable and long-term, and includes the construction and maintenance of school buildings, the payment of teachers' fees and food to keep children in rural areas in school. The diaspora can also fund university fees. Beneficiary communities are becoming increasingly sophisticated, using the internet to raise funds for schools and to provide progress reports to sponsors.[6]

Healthcare has been better funded by international aid agencies than other services (SACB 2003). But, as with education, the policy of international health agencies, in the absence of a well-resourced government, has been to decentralise the management of the health sector and to promote community financing of minimal public health services through so-called 'cost sharing', whereby patients pay fees that cover a portion of the costs. Consequently health care is not a free public service. The decentralisation of health management has brought improvements in some public health facilities where personnel demonstrate exemplary commitment. The regional health board of Woqooyi Galbeed, for example,

[6] Interviews by author in Hargeysa, July 2004.

7.1 Educational services have been restored (Nick Sireau/Progressio)

7.2 Amoud University computer lab (Nick Sireau/Progressio)

7.3 Some health services have been restored, Hargeysa hospital (Nick Sireau/ Progressio)

7.4 *Qaad* sellers, Hargeysa (Nick Sireau/Progressio)

has made improvements to Hargeysa Group Hospital by attracting a mixture of public and private funding.[7] However, scaling up such successes in the absence of a funded national health system is difficult. The efficacy of cost sharing is also questionable. There is no evidence that it will be sufficient to sustain services and some that it may exclude poor people from access to healthcare. Despite the greater donor investments in health services, there has been little improvement in overall health indicators. Some of the underlying reasons for this are a lack of qualified health professionals, weak management of health services, an urban bias in health provision, a decline in referral services because international assistance has focused on primary health care, a weak drug certification regime, and poor public sanitation.

Public health facilities like Hargeysa Hospital are being challenged by a growth in private hospitals. These are financed in various ways, by benefactors in the Gulf states or through a mixture of fees, assistance from businesses and support from the diaspora. The private hospitals are generally better equipped than public ones but, as with other aspects of privatisation, there are problems of coordination and planning, a lack of oversight and regulation, and a lack of access for those who cannot pay (although the facilities normally provide some free services for those identified as 'poor').

The water sector provides a further illustration of the changes that have occurred in the management and provision of previously publicly-run services. Donor policy promotes the private management of water systems. In most municipalities, therefore, piped systems have been outsourced to local business consortiums with a modicum of public overview. Many rural boreholes that previously were government-managed have been taken over by private individuals. Despite extensive work on rehabilitating water resources, over 60 per cent of households in Somaliland still do not have access to safe drinking water. Even in Hargeysa the average daily household consumption of 40 litres of water is well below the minimum World Health Organisation standard of 140 litres per day for urban populations.

Another sector of critical importance, of course, is shelter. The rehabilitation and expansion of housing has been an important social and economic phenomenon which impacts on health and other aspects of well-being and is remarkable for the fact that it has been entirely financed by remittances.

Amoud University

Amoud University in Borama is a good example of a Somaliland institution substantially supported by the diaspora and developed through a

---

[7] Author's interview with Woqooyi Galbeed RHB, July 2004.

mixture of private and public finance.[8] Before the war the absence of a university in the north-west was further proof for northerners of the uneven development in the state and the regime's neglect of the north. Somalilanders have set about rectifying this. Three universities have been established since 1991 in Amoud, Hargeysa and Burco.

The idea of establishing a university in the British-built former secondary school in Amoud Valley outside Borama originated in 1996 among Somali professionals in Somaliland and the diaspora. It was opened in November 1998 through the combined efforts of the diaspora and the Borama community, with little foreign assistance. Initially it was conceived as a community-run institution and the Borama community continues to be an important source of support. Described by its founders as 'a vehicle for peace and development', they believe the university has made its contribution to both, by building confidence and restoring hope after years of war.[9] It strives to be inclusive and is open to students from all parts of Somaliland and Somalia. It is respected throughout Somaliland and its success has inspired confidence in self-help projects elsewhere.

In its first five years the student intake has risen from 60 to 420 and the number of lecturers from three to 33. The university offers faculties in Business and Public Administration, Education and Medicine. Student fees help to finance the university and the diaspora has helped to equip it and fundraise for it. The university's buses were supplied by Somalis working in the Gulf; its computers were a gift from the President of Djibouti; the mosque was financed from Kuwait; medical books came from Saudi Arabia; but the lion's share – around 70,000 books, furniture, equipment – was donated by Somali communities in the United States. Some international NGOs have also provided expatriate teachers and librarians, and UN agencies have assisted with the rehabilitation of buildings and equipment. Significantly, the Somaliland government's backing for the university has grown steadily from twenty million Somaliland shillings in 1998 to fifty million in 2001 and one hundred million in 2003.

Before Amoud opened, opportunities for higher education in Somaliland were non-existent. To pursue a higher education abroad was only an option for families with resources. One of the main challenges faced by the university is whether there will be sufficient opportunities for graduate employment in Somaliland. Many of Amoud's graduates are playing an active role in the local community, forming NGOs or in business, but for the majority of graduates finding paid employment is difficult. The university itself struggles with financial sustainability. It is always easier to get donations of materials and temporary human

[8] This author is grateful for additional information provided by Mary Enright, a former development worker with Progressio who worked as a librarian at Amoud.

[9] Interview with the University founder and President, Professor Suleiman Ahmed Gulaid, August 2003.

resources than money. Providing relevant courses is also difficult. The number of donated books is impressive, but lack of choice means that the curriculum can be decided by what textbooks are available rather than books being ordered on demand to back new curriculum choices. Similarly, short courses offered by visiting researchers or teachers are not always an ideal fit with the needs that exist. The needs of the medical faculty are particularly demanding, but in the absence of any other source of medical training, Amoud is at least a start and a foundation that can be built on.

The experience of Amoud mirrors in several respects the reconstruction of the state of Somaliland. Like Somaliland, it lacks a core and consistent revenue. It relies on remittances to cover many costs: for the running of the buses and electricity generators; for paying the salaries of staff; or, in the case of students who sometimes miss the first weeks of their courses while waiting for money from abroad, for the payment of academic fees. It is also dependent on donors whose priorities and goals may be different, and whose projects may be short-term and unsustainable. It is not recognised abroad. Equally, however, it reflects a spirit found elsewhere in Somaliland – a wish to see the new state right the wrongs of previous neglect; a spirit of self-help, optimism, self-reliance, and absolute determination not to be defeated.

Qaad & poverty

A major social change that has taken place in Somaliland over the past fifteen years has been the growth in *qaad* consumption, which has serious social and economic impacts on families and the state. *Qaad*,[10] a shrub (*catha edulis*) whose leaves are chewed for their mild narcotic effect, similar to amphetamine, is cultivated in the highlands of Ethiopia, Kenya and Yemen. Historically, *qaad* was used for medicinal, recreational and religious purposes in eastern Africa and the Middle East (Gebissa 2004). In Ethiopia and Djibouti it continues to be used in some Muslim ceremonies, but its main use throughout the Somali-inhabited regions of the Horn of Africa is as a recreational drug, as it is among non-Somali populations in Ethiopia and in Kenya (where it is known by its Swahili name *myrrha*), and by Somali immigrants in countries where it is not banned.[11]

Qaad was probably introduced into Somali society by Muslim sheikhs who used it to recite the Qur'an for long periods without tiring. From the 1940s its consumption was mostly associated with the urbanised salaried class who could afford to indulge in the habit. In the late 1960s peasant farmers west of Hargeysa began to cultivate *qaad* as a way of overcoming

[10] Various other spellings are *qaat*, *khat* and *chat*.
[11] The World Health Organisation classifies *qaad* as a substance of abuse, but it is not controlled under UN treaties and its sale and consumption is legal in many countries, including Britain and Canada.

deteriorating conditions in the agricultural sector (Abdi Samatar 1989). The government of Siyad Barre banned its consumption in 1983 on health grounds, in part to attract foreign health sector support, but the subsequent destruction of *qaad* farms in the north-west was perceived by the Isaaq as politically motivated. With the outbreak of war the chewing of *qaad* expanded hugely. Once the habit of wealthier urbanites, it is now consumed by people of all classes in urban and rural areas. Some estimate that up to 90 per cent of the adult male population of Somaliland chew daily, and its consumption has increased among women and youth. Lack of state regulation, changes in social mores, its use by combatants to ward off fatigue and to allay fear, remittance money and lack of employment are all contributory factors to the spread of the habit (Cabdi 2005). In Somaliland the growth of the habit is also linked to its use in Ethiopian refugee camps, from where practices such as chewing in public at tea stalls have been introduced. Commonly consumed in company, chewing *qaad* has become an accepted element in social gatherings. *Qaad*-chewing sessions are occasions for networking, talking politics, transmitting and gathering information, negotiations, mediations, or striking business deals. Indeed, one study suggests that the *mefrish*[12] has become 'the most important forum for communication among urban males' (Ducaale 2005: 149). As such, *qaad*-chewing sessions are generally the domain of men. Women are excluded from these opportunities for networking, doing business and participating in political debates.

The economic impact of *qaad* is huge. One study suggests that in Somaliland some US$70 million per year may be spent on importing *qaad* (Cabdi 2005). This is more than three times the government's annual revenue, but 12 per cent of that revenue is raised from taxing the trade. In 1998 an estimated 1,500 persons were involved in *qaad* distribution as pilots, drivers, sales agents, retailers and porters. Selling *qaad* is an important source of subsistence for women, although their profits are often marginal and their involvement in the trade can have negative consequences for the family (*ibid.*).

Many Somalis now believe the habit is a source of major economic and social problems in Somaliland. It is a major drain on hard currency and it is conjectured that a large percentage of remittances are spent on *qaad* consumption. Studies indicate that it contributes to the persistence of poverty and to the break-up of families (*ibid.*). In a country where a significant proportion of the population is thought to live on less than US$2 a day, $3 dollars per day spent on *qaad* and its *mefrish* accoutrements (cigarettes and soft drinks) diverts household resources from spending on food, medicine, education and economic investments. As chewing normally begins at midday, the working day is short and the hangover (*qaadiro*) induced by the stimulant impacts on productivity and

---

[12] *Mefrish* refers to a venue for chewing *qaad* and a circle of acquaintances who routinely meet for this purpose.

efficiency. In rural areas *qaad* chewing is blamed for men abandoning their livestock and farms, increased debtedness, and urban migration. Although its addictive qualities are debated, continual consumption can have an adverse effect on a person's physical and mental health, and chewing at close quarters indoors is linked to high transmission rates of tuberculosis. Disputes over the trade have in the past been a source of violence, but are now rather less frequent.[13] However, it is associated with petty criminality as people look to feed the habit. In spite of these problems, the value of the trade to the government and those who work in it is such that there is little incentive to regulate or stop it.[14]

Civil society developments

Under the military regime of Siyad Barre all forms of civic organisation that were not controlled by the governing party were proscribed, although in the latter years of the regime, in response to the influx of refugees and as a condition of Western political and fiscal support, the formation of a few non-governmental welfare organisations was permitted (Abdullahi 1996). In Somaliland, with no such state restrictions, numerous informal structures of governance and forms of voluntary association have developed outside of the extended family or clan and the state. These types of voluntary associations that mediate relations between the extended family and the state are commonly described in Africa and elsewhere as 'civil society' (Thompson 2004: 5). The term 'civil society' is ubiquitous in development and has been criticised on a number of levels: for being linked to Western neo-liberal ideas of the state; for falsely creating a division between society and the state; or for being ethnocentric by amalgamating different types of social organisations. International development organisations often simplistically associate 'civil society' with non-governmental (NGO) welfare or issue-based organisations, whose 'capacities' are 'built' to model the foreign organisations whose ideas of human development they propagate. In Somaliland a broader definition is required that includes 'traditional' institutions such as elders' committees, welfare organisations, community-based organisations, professional associations, Islamic charities, religious organisations, milk-marketing and transport cooperatives, political parties, and organisations formed around issues such as the rights of women, children, the disabled and minorities.

In Somaliland, the limited resource base available to the government limits its ability to deliver services and govern across the territory. Although many civic organisations may have a narrow geographical focus and represent parochial lineage interests, some do perform functions that

[13] This continues to be the case in southern Somalia, where the trade generates large incomes for the warlords who control its access and distribution in the country. See UNSC 2003.
[14] In 2006 the Islamic Courts managed to temporarily ban the consumption of *qaad* in Mogadishu.

would normally be considered the preserve of local or national government. As such, they 'mediate' relations between local communities and interest groups and the state (Menkhaus 2005). As the model of governance in Somaliland has developed and adapted, a division of labour has been negotiated between these organisations and the government. This is articulated in government legislation on NGOs and in the organisations' own charters. While capable of being critical of the authorities, they are in many respects an extension of government, working with it to re-establish and provide basic services.

Chapter 4 described how in the early 1990s, in the absence of a functional government authority, community-based organisations of elders and religious leaders emerged to address problems of law and order and to mediate in conflicts – roles that in other settings would have been performed by government. In a manner that is probably unique in Africa, these elders and religious leaders have taken on both state and civic functions, providing national-level leadership in the Upper House of the legislature, while continuing to manage conflict, crime and security at a local community level. In the absence of strong public institutions, numerous other organisations have been formed to provide welfare services and act as channels for international aid. Many have been short-lived, created to attract foreign aid, but several have developed into organisations with a cadre of experienced professionals who are active on a range of socio-economic issues in development, education, human rights, livelihoods and the environment. Organisations pressing for women's rights have attracted particularly strong funding from Western donors. For some women, these organisations provide an opportunity for participation in civic life that is denied by existing political institutions, and they have become important forums through which women have been able to lobby on political and social issues and for participation in government. Many of these organisations have been active in the peace and reconciliation conferences in Somaliland and in support of the multi-party elections. International agencies have been much slower to engage with associations and networks of skilled and semi-skilled professionals – doctors, lawyers, journalists, stevedores, truck and bus drivers, and women's marketing cooperatives – that also bring together people from different clans and tend not to be overtly political in their orientation.

International agencies have encouraged local welfare NGOs to form 'umbrella' bodies in order to pool resources, regulate their activities, protect their interests and simplify relations with the donor agencies. In some cases this has worked well. Indeed, efforts at self-regulation and coordination have in many respects been more fruitful than similar moves among international aid agencies. But often initiatives by international organisations to encourage Somaliland and Somalia NGOs to collaborate, on the assumption that they are all 'civil society' actors with the same concerns, have backfired acrimoniously. Through associations with international agencies some of these organisations have been linked into global networks with positive spin-offs in terms of knowledge development and access to funding. The EU has also encouraged the creation of 'non-state actor forums' as a representative mechanism through which it can engage with Somali society and disburse resources. The assumption has been that these organisations are representatives of society. In fact, many lack legitimacy and durability, being externally introduced models of social organisation reliant for their survival on external funding and largely representative of urban-based, elite interests rather than the interests of rural and 'grassroots', or poor and illiterate people. They can also reinforce the divisions within society. There is, for example, a disparity in the capacity of civil society organisations in different regions of Somaliland that reflects other inter-regional socio-economic differences. Of the 542 local NGOs registered with the Ministry of National Planning and Co-ordination in 2003, 66 per cent were located in Woqooyi Galbeed region.

Another post-war development has also been the growth of independent media in Somaliland. After years of tight state control under the Barre regime, there are several independent newspapers in Somali and English and two TV stations. The government has, however, sought to bring the other media under its influence through legislation and the intimidation and arrest of journalists. It allows only only one public radio – Radio Hargeysa – and that is government-managed. But another important change over which the government has no control has been the internet and the development of websites. Though mostly hosted abroad, these can still be very parochial – but they do provide an outlet for critical commentary on the performance of the government and other matters.

We have seen that, in a context in which the legitimacy of government is contested, international agencies aspiring to goals of 'local ownership' have bypassed government institutions and sought instead to strengthen the organisational capacity of 'community-based organisations', welfare organisations and private service authorities. Several of the larger civic organisations receive substantially more resources than local and national government ministries. This can create tensions when the organisation becomes more influential than the government, or when government demands its 'share'. It is a moot question as to whether such a policy is supporting the development of a form of government that relies on non-governmental actors to govern, or creating an obstacle to state-building by diverting resources away from government. However, these civic organisations will have an important function in articulating and addressing social needs – a role that the creation of popularly elected political parties may yet challenge.

The transnational state: diaspora & development

Diaspora communities have played a crucial economic and political role in the formation of Somaliland and have been an important pillar of the

Somaliland state-building project. Somalis have a long history of migration, whether travelling overseas to trade or in search of employment and education. As early as the beginning of the twentieth century small communities of northern Somali men who had been recruited into the British merchant fleet and the Royal Navy were established in the dockland enclaves of several British cities – Cardiff, Liverpool, London, Bristol, Hull and South Shields (Harris 2004: 22). Others travelled to the Gulf states and even to America. Somali immigration to Britain increased during the two World Wars, when more Somalis were recruited into the navy and army. The 1950s post-war economic boom attracted a further wave of Somali migrants to Britain, and this is when the first Somali communities in the East End of London were established. In the 1960s many Somalis migrated to Tanzania to work on the construction of the railway, and to the newly oil-rich Gulf states. Political oppression and economic hardships at home in the 1970s and 1980s encouraged a further wave of economic and political migrants, from among whom the SNM was formed. The largest wave of overseas migration, however, took place over a decade in the 1980s and 1990s, following the outbreak of civil war in the north and the massive displacements of populations that took place as the war spread (Hansen 2004).

The number of Somalis living outside Somalia is not known, but a commonly quoted estimate is over one million (Nair and Abdulla 1998). The locations of Somali diaspora communities have changed over the past two decades. Whereas the Gulf states hosted the largest number of Somalis up to the 1980s, since the outbreak of war Somalis seeking asylum have headed for Europe and America and exploited opportunities elsewhere around the world in Europe, the Gulf, Asia and Australia. Changes in immigration regimes in Europe and the ebb and flow of business opportunities have also led to migration between host countries. Britain, which is reported to host the largest number of Somalis outside Somalia (Harris 2004: 24), has experienced an influx of Somalis holding European passports from other EU countries in recent years. In 2002 there were estimated to be 250,000 Somalis in Britain and Somalis were second to Pakistanis in terms of numbers granted settlement in the UK (*ibid.*: 32-3).

British colonial connections and the outbreak of war in the north in the 1980s meant that Somalis – particularly Isaaq – from Somaliland were better established in the UK than other Somali groups, and probably constitute the largest number of UK Somalis, although again their exact numbers are unknown. Large immigrant communities from Somaliland exist elsewhere in Europe, as well as in Canada and America (Farah 2000). These communities have been and continue to be important 'drivers' for political, economic and social change in Somaliland. Indeed, the participation of the diaspora in Somaliland is sufficiently influential to challenge traditional definitions of a state as a sovereign system of government within a delimited territory. In many respects Somaliland resembles a 'transnational state', with its capital in Hargeysa but many of its citizens outside Somaliland or in transit, and much of its economy generated from outside the country (Glick Schiller and Fouron 2002: 358). This is acknowledged in Somaliland's citizenship law, which recognises people's right to hold more than one passport. For example, there are reported to be 1,500 passport-holding Canadian citizens living in Hargeysa alone.[15] The globalised nature of Somaliland is apparent in the number of businesses that imbed the word 'international' in their names – and so today, suited by an international tailor and coiffured by an international hairdresser, the Somaliland businessman flits in and out by way of Egal international airport. And it is neatly captured in the mission of Somaliland's private carrier Daallo Airlines, that is: 'Proudly Connecting the Horn of Africa to the Global Village'.[16]

Diaspora engagement in Somaliland's development takes various organised forms – through the nuclear family, extended family networks, non-governmental charitable associations, transnational business partnerships and, since 2002, political parties (Cassanelli 2004). It is also important to recognise that the Somaliland diaspora is not homogeneous, but divided along lineage lines. Glick Schiller and Fouron (2002: 360) distinguish between diaspora communities who identify with an existing state and 'long-distance nationalists' who desire to construct a new state. While 'long-distance nationalists' probably best describes most Isaaq from Somaliland overseas, the more commonly used description 'diaspora' is preferred here, as many non-Isaaq migrants from Somaliland are Somalia nationalists rather than Somaliland nationalists, but nevertheless have contributed to its development.

The diaspora has contributed to the creation and development of Somaliland in several ways. The SNM was founded by Isaaq émigrés and it depended on diaspora communities to fund the insurgency. The notion of a 'homeland' is often important for the construction of a diaspora identity. The Somalilanders (particularly Isaaq who migrated from the late 1980s) have done much since 1991 to develop a sense of long-distance nationalism and promote the concept of an independent Somaliland in foreign capitals (Griffiths 2002; Svedjemo 2002). The former colonial connections with Britain have been a particular advocacy platform among Isaaq communities in the UK. They have also actively engaged in inter-communal politics within Somaliland, supporting their communities during periods of conflict or acting as mediators and peace advocates through forums such as the Somaliland Peace Committee. They have supported the development of Somaliland's political institutions. The Somaliland Forum in the UK, for example, sent observers to the constitutional referendum and has provided critical comment to Parliament on the constitution and various pieces of legislation including the Media Bill.[17] The diaspora has also been influential in the emergence

---

[15] Interview by author, Hargeysa, September 2003.

[16] www.daallo.com

[17] See www.Somalilandforum.com

of the multi-party system and in supporting the campaigns of the political parties, as we shall see in the next chapter.

The economic role of the diaspora has been crucial in the remittance economy, described in the previous chapter. This has taken a number of forms: economic support for the livelihoods of extended family networks, finance for public services and infrastructure, real-estate development, investment in multi-million dollar businesses such as telecommunications and hotels and petty trade, and income-generating activities. Some of the larger business ventures, such as telecommunications, often involve transnational partnerships, and diaspora business people have served as an important link to international markets. The opportunity to make a quick return on investments has given rise to a number of 'mobile businessmen' who travel between Somaliland, Europe and America. The tens of thousands of people from the diaspora visiting Somaliland every year, particularly in the European school holidays, have also generated a tourism economy, with seasonal peaks and troughs. In many regions, the 'season of diaspora' (June–September) injects a significant amount of capital into the 'home' economy.

Diaspora entrepreneurs have been key innovators, bringing in new technologies like telecommunications. Some are experimenting with animal ranching (reported around Hargeysa) which, if successful, could initiate new forms of animal husbandry.[18] There is also a transfer of skills and knowledge from the diaspora – through returning professionals, particularly in business and new technologies, and to a more limited extent in other professions, such as teaching and health care. But poor levels of remuneration make a return to Somaliland less attractive for skilled professionals.

The diaspora has also contributed through the establishment of social welfare organisations. Some Somalis returning from abroad establish NGOs in-country, which retain support from the diaspora. This is helping to exploit new sources of capital outside Somalia, such as foundations and grant-making bodies in both Western and Islamic countries. The social impact of the diaspora is also apparent in the adoption of new religious practices, social mores and cultural habits.

The Somaliland government has recognised the importance of the diaspora and has sought to encourage diaspora-led investment in the country by offering tax breaks on certain types of imports like construction materials. The Mayor of Hargeysa, for example, has sought to encourage investment by 'fast tracking' the procedures for purchasing real-estate, and has lobbied the government to reduce airport taxes on Somalilanders returning from abroad.[19] The Hargeysa municipality website promotes the home business environment, and the Woqooyi Galbeed Regional Health Board also raises funds in the diaspora.

---

[18] Author's interviews, Hargeysa, July 2004.
[18] Interview by author with Mayor of Hargeysa, July 2004.

Some Somalilanders, nevertheless, express concern at the impact of the diaspora: that remittances are creating a false economy and new forms of dependency; that by financing imports remittances discourage efforts at local production, do little to generate employment, support unsustainable social services and help to sustain the *qaad* trade. The diaspora's largely unplanned investments in Somalia have resulted in some duplication and wasted investments. The interest and sometimes obligation to support the community of their kin may lead to two schools being constructed in an area that only requires one. In Somaliland such developments are often not coordinated with the existing public system. And the 'pull' of the diaspora can sometimes produce effects as unwelcome as the 'push' of ill-advised returning investment. The desperate efforts of some Somalis to migrate abroad, for example, has reportedly led to cases of children being smuggled out of Somaliland (Hannan 2003).

As previously noted, studies of remittances and wealth groups in Somaliland indicate that the rural and urban poor, internally displaced and economic migrants from the south, are likely to have fewer relatives abroad and therefore less access to remittances than other wealthier groups (Medani 2000; King 2003).

The diaspora also has a differential impact in different regions of the country (UNDP 2001). Warsengeli in the diaspora, for example, are reportedly less active in supporting their kin than other clans because they are smaller in number, more integrated overseas and therefore less attached to the homeland.[20] The Dhulbahante, on the other hand, have made significant investments in the Sool Region and are more involved in the politics of Somaliland, Puntland and Somalia – partly because many of their diaspora leaders are ex-politicians. Historically, migration has been one of several economic strategies open to Somali families and it is claimed that the Dhulbahante strategically created a diaspora by exploiting immigration loopholes into the US in the late 1990s.[21] This has resulted in increased remittance flows to Dhulbahante areas of the Sool and Sanaag regions and stimulated reconstruction in urban centres like Las Canod. This strategy may have been precipitated by their perceived marginalisation within Somaliland and has enabled them to establish a degree of economic and political autonomy from both Hargeysa and Garowe.

Information on the social impact of the returning diaspora is very limited. There is anecdotal evidence that more men than women are returning to Somaliland. Most are older men who are unable to find employment overseas, but also find it difficult to access employment in Somaliland or cope with a more conservative environment than the one they have become accustomed to abroad. Some people return distressed by their experience of asylum, where, for example, families experience

---

[20] Interview by author, Horn Relief, Nairobi, September 2003.
[21] Interview by author, Las Anod, September 2003.

high levels of divorce. People in Somaliland express concern that families overseas send 'difficult' children back to Somaliland, where they form gangs and are equally difficult to control.[22] Returnees import other aspects of their experience in the diaspora. An interesting social phenomenon is the emergence of Scandinavian, Canadian and British associations and clubs based on the aquired citizenship of the host country. Many people return with assets and skills and assume leadership roles in business, in politics, and in welfare, religious or international organisations. Sometimes such high-flyers create local tensions, especially if they are perceived not to have suffered as much as those who stayed in the country.

Currently the diaspora experience seems to encompass both assimilation and transnationalism. While assimilation within host countries is likely to increase with time, many in the diaspora are establishing and deepening transnational linkages between Somaliland and their host countries through dual citizenships and trade. Although many in the diaspora express a desire to return to Somalia, there are currently few inducements to do so. Studies of the Somaliland diaspora in the UK show that people will be reluctant to return until there is confidence in the political situation in the Somali region, adequate health care and educational services, and employment opportunities (Forster 2002). Families with dual citizenship therefore move backwards and forwards between Somaliland and other countries, depending on the particular needs of the family and the opportunities that arise (Hansen 2003). European asylum laws, which are becoming increasingly strict, may eventually force many more Somalilanders to return to Somaliland. However, given the importance of a national identity to the diaspora and the average age of those who left in the 1990s, the link between the diaspora and Somaliland is likely to remain strong for several decades. Forms of engagement may change over time. The elections that took place after 2002 indicate that political engagement remains strong. Reports of the involvement of UK passport holders in the Islamic Courts movement in Somalia emphasise that the relationship continues to be a dynamic one (*The Guardian*, 12 January 2007).

Islamic revivalism

After two decades of secular-leaning socialism, the past fifteen years have witnessed a revival of Islamic learning and practice in Somaliland and Somalia that is influenced both by local events and developments elsewhere in the world. Islam in Somaliland has long been associated with the *sufi* orders, of which the Qaadiriya, Ahmadiya and Saalahiya are the most prominent. In the *shafi'i* version of the faith followed by most

---

[22] Interviews by author, Hargeysa, August–September, 2003.

Somalis, the ancestors of Somali clans are venerated as saints and the tombs of ancestors like Sheikh Isaaq in Mait are places of pilgrimage. Islam informs most aspects of people's lives, but while militant forms of Islam have arisen in Somali history – famously in the anti-colonial and religious struggle of Sayyid Mahammed Abdalla Hassan – in the independent era Somali society has generally been known for its religious tolerance.

Prior to the war, religious practice was reportedly more conservative in northern Somali society, more influenced by the proximity to the Gulf states than modern Western developments in the south (Marchal 2004). In the early 1970s there was a brief resurgence of Islamic organisations in reaction to the ideas of Scientific Socialism propagated by the military government. Al-Wahdat al-Shabaab al-Islaami (Unity of Muslim Brotherhood), inspired by the Muslim brotherhood of Egypt, found adherents in the northern regions, especially among the Isaaq. Suppressed by the regime, al-Wahdat lent its support to the SNM.

Since the outbreak of war, reformist Islamist movements have proliferated more in southern Somalia than in Somaliland for a number of reasons.[23] In the absence of a central authority, people turned to religion for security and the moral and physical reconstruction of their communities. Support for this has been forthcoming from Islamic charitable foundations and benefactors outside Somalia, who have financed welfare organisations, educational establishments and the building of mosques. In the early 1990s political leaders, like General Aideed and Ali Mahdi, opportunistically promoted the growth of some groups as part of their political strategies. Some Somali businessmen attached themselves to religious groups to gain access to markets in the Gulf countries, while in Somalia they invested in *shari'a* courts as a way of improving security in the absence of a police force. Islamist organisations have also emerged to try and fill the political vacuum of the collapsed state influenced by wider political developments in Islam. The most prominent of these, the Salafist-Jihadist organisation Al Itihad al Islamiya was thought to have had links with Al Qaeda. The organisation attracted adherents from all Somali clans – its Chairman Sheik Ali Warsame being from Burco in Somaliland – and gained prominence in the early 1990s in southern and north-east Somalia, when it took over and held territory by force. Defeated by Abdullahi Yusuf in Puntland and by Ethiopian military in southern Somalia, the organisation dissolved, but several of its leadership remained politically active. The influence of political Islam in southern Somalia increased with the formation of the TNG in 2000, whose leadership were aligned to the moderate and progressive Al Islah. When the events of 11 September 2001 and the 'war against terrorism' reignited Western interest in Somalia as a potential source and haven for transnational terrorism, the TNG's opponents accused it of harbouring Islamists.

---

[23] For analyses of the rise and influence of Islamist movements in Somalia and Somaliland see ICG 2002, 2005a, 2005b; Marchal 2004; Le Sage 2004; Menkhaus 2004.

In 2004 some of these opponents, supported by Ethiopia and Western countries, went on to replace the TNG with the TFG formed through the medium of the national reconciliation and peace talks in Kenya.

In response to this, Islamist groups through the network of Islamic courts formed a political alliance that, in 2006, became the Union of Islamic Courts (UIC). As factional leaders continued to demonstrate an inability and unwillingness to govern, public support for the UIC grew. In 2006, with the TFG weakened by internal divisions, the UIC, with popular support, defeated a US government-sponsored alliance of warlords in four months of heavy fighting in Mogadishu. They brought the capital under a single authority for the first time in sixteen years and temporarily held sway over large areas of southern Somalia. Within a year the UIC was in turn removed from power when Ethiopia and the US government intervened in support of the beleaguered TFG.

In Somaliland the influence of political Islam and reformist Islamist groups has, to date, been very limited. In part this is due to the strength of the traditional leadership and the presence of a government since 1991 which, despite its relative weakness, averted the development of a power vacuum. The presence of a judicial system, however flawed, and government security forces reduced the need for *shari'a* courts which have not gained any real influence in Somaliland. In late 1991 the stoning to death of a woman in Hargeysa deeply shocked Somalilanders and the incident became a catalyst for a women's peace movement in the country (Gardner and el Bushra 2003).

Nevertheless, in Somaliland an Islamic revival is apparent in the growth in the number of mosques, the disappearance of some old traditions, and the growing influence of the puritanical *Wahaabi* school of Islamic thought emanating from central Arabia. The proselytising Jama'at al-Tabliq sect has found a growing following and owns the largest number of mosques and religious educational establishments in Somaliland. In 2002 the sect held a conference in Hargeysa attended by some 7,000 Somalis and several hundred foreigners (ICG 2005b). Al Islah has only a small presence in Somaliland. Supporters of the militant Islamic group Al Itihad al Islamiya have had a presence within Somaliland since the early 1990s in areas where the influence of the government in Hargeysa has been weakest – in Las Qoray in eastern Sanaag and Las Anod, and also around Burco where Sheikh Ali Warsame is from. In 1998 Egal alleged that members of this group were being sheltered in Yerowe (near Burco) and in Borama. Supported by Ethiopia, he confronted Islamic leaders and made it clear that Somaliland would not tolerate Islamic militancy: the suspects were handed over to the Ethiopian authorities. Since then the influence of militant Islam in Somaliland politics has been limited, although its profile was elevated again following the killings of foreign aid workers in 2003 and 2004, and during the UIC's tenure in Mogadishu when Sheikh Ali and several other Somalilanders joined the courts' governing council.

Some of the most vocal critics of the new movements have come from followers of the established *sufi* orders, to which many of the older generation of politicians are affiliated. The Timaweyn, a section of the Qaadiriya, have been openly critical of the new movements and will not enter mosques managed by militant Islamist groups. Egal used to appoint only Qaadiriya-affiliated sheikhs to head his Ministry of Religious Affairs and shunned the new orders. The new political parties curried the support of these Islamist groups for the elections, but were unwilling to give key positions to their members, concerned that accommodating such groups could undermine efforts to gain international recognition for Somaliland.

Nevertheless, there are indications that the social influence of Islamists is growing in business and in education. Since the war ended there has been an increase in mosques and Qur'anic schools throughout Somaliland. For the youth, the religious schools have filled a gap in educational institutions, and the movements offer an outlet for those who see limited prospects in Somaliland. As elsewhere in the Muslim world, the confrontation between secular Western powers and *jihadist* groups is also influencing people to join the reformist movements. The construction of mosques is supported by wealthy individuals in the Arabian Gulf countries. Historically, the established *sufi* orders have not had strong business interests. Members of the new Islamist sects, however, are engaged in medium-sized shareholding businesses in the import/export and small-scale manufacturing sectors. Furthermore, members of these sects do not chew *qaad* or smoke, which makes them the preferred employees of the telecommunications and money transfer companies.

The influence of the new orders is also apparent in changes in religious and cultural practices and social mores. The wearing of the *hijab* (headscarf) by women has become much more common, for example. The new sects are accused of simplifying marriage customs by reducing the dowry and wedding expenses, with some Somalis complaining that this is leading to increased polygamy and divorce. They have also discouraged the veneration of saints and pilgrimages to tombs of the saints, like Sheikh Isaaq in Mait and the tomb of Sheikh Yusuf Al-Kawnien in Aw-Barkhadleh[24] between Hargeysa and Berbera. Before the war the pilgrimage to Sheikh Al-Kawnien's tomb had been an annual holiday for people in and around Hargeysa. Today there is no public holiday and the pilgrimage takes places on a much smaller scale.

Finally, as will be discussed further in the next chapter, the murder of four expatriate aid workers in Somaliland in 2003 and 2004 has highlighted the vulnerability of Somaliland to religious extremists seeking an opportunity to target Westerners. Somaliland representatives have sought to highlight this danger as a reason to support recognition,

---

[24] Sheikh Al-Kawnien is revered for translating Arabic into Somali to ease people's understanding of the Qur'an.

arguing that a strong government is needed to fight terrorism.[25] However, the authorities have also used the terrorism threat to legitimise the expulsion of southern Somalis seeking refuge in Somaliland.

[25] Author's interview with Dr Omar Duhod, August 2003.

8
Democratic Transitions

Mohamed Ibrahim Egal had been selected in 1993 to head a two-year transitional government. By the time of his death in early 2002 he had been Somaliland's head of state for nine years and the country appeared stuck in a seemingly endless political 'transition'. Political developments in Somalia, meanwhile, were beginning to pose a serious challenge to Somaliland's proclaimed sovereignty. Anyone in Somaliland wishing to challenge the performance of the government publicly, or question the country's future, risked falling foul of emergency laws and being denounced for endangering the country's hard-won stability. This led some people in Somaliland to observe that they had become 'hostages to peace'. The public approval of the constitution in 2001 and the scheduling of multi-party elections offered a way forward.

The timing of the constitutional plebiscite and Somaliland's first elections may have been influenced by the inauguration of Somalia-wide peace talks in Djibouti and Egal's interest in securing his own political survival. Nevertheless, it also fulfilled a commitment originally articulated in the SNM manifesto two decades earlier and repeated in May 1991: to establish Somaliland as a democratic state. The large numbers of men and women who turned out to vote in the referendum and the subsequent elections indicated popular support for this political transition. Lack of international recognition was no impediment to creating a democratic, elected and constitutionally based government. In fact, the democratisation of Somaliland's political institutions was considered a necessary step towards achieving recognition and a bulwark against reunification.

The transformation of Somaliland's political institutions from a system of selected representation to elected representation occurred over three years, with district council elections in December 2002, presidential and vice-presidental elections in April 2003, and parliamentary elections two years later in September 2005. Although it had been intended to hold presidential and parliamentary elections concurrently, in hindsight the staged process enabled the organisers, the parties and the public to become familiar with the system and to learn from each election. Election days were huge political events in which the whole country was engaged. The large public and private resources invested in the elections by government, parties and candidates stimulated a mini economic boom. These were the first multi-party democratic elections in Somaliland and the first for Somalis in thirty years. Although they adopted international electoral norms they also reflected the unique social and political context. This chapter describes this exercise in democracy and its implications.[1]

The district election

In line with the constitution, the democratisation of Somaliland's political system began with the election of district and municipal councils. The constitutional rationale for holding district elections first was to determine which political organisations could contest the presidential and parliamentary elections. While the constitution guarantees the right of all citizens to participate in political life and to be elected to political office, Article 9 restricts the political parties to just three and proscribes any party based on religion, regionalism or kinship. Six political organisations contested the election for twenty-three district councils, but to become an accredited national political party, an organisation had to win 20 per cent of the votes in four of Somaliland's six regions. If this threshold was not achieved the three organisations with the largest popular vote would qualify to become parties. This system, which drew on the experience of Nigeria, is intended to ensure that the political parties have national constituencies and to prevent the emergence of religious or clan-dominated parties, as happened in 1969 when over sixty parties contested the election. The district election would also test Somaliland's technical ability to hold parliamentary and presidential elections.

The six political organisations that contested the district election – ASAD, Hormood, Kulmiye, SAHAN, UCID and UDUB – were the first legally recognised political organisations in Somaliland since the demise of the SNM (see Box 8.1).[2] The requirement to demonstrate support in all regions forced them to construct cross-clan alliances. In practice, it also ruled out the possibility of the Harti or Gadabursi or 'Iise forming a party. Not surprisingly, all the founders of the organisations were Isaaq, although they included non-Isaaq vice-chairs and after Egal's death President Riyale, a Gadabursi, became the leader of UDUB. In 2002 only UDUB

---

[1] For other descriptions of the elections see Bradbury *et al.* (2003); ICG (2003); Lindeman and Hansen (2003); Abokor *et al.* (2003); Abokor *et al.* (2005); APD (2006).
[2] Eight organisations were registered, but two amalgamated with others. English translations of the organisations' names vary according to different sources.

Box 8.1 Somaliland's Political Organisations in 2002

ASAD (Alliance for Salvation and Democracy) was headed by Suleiman Mohamed Aden 'Gaal', with former Vice President Abdulrahman Aw Ali (Gadabursi) as deputy Chairperson. Several of its prominent members were associated with the radical elements of the SNM, and the organisation competed with Kulmiye for the votes of Suleiman Gaal's Habar Ja'lo clan.

Hormood (Champions for Peace and Prosperity) was founded by civil activists and initially attracted support among civic organisations, including former members of the Hargeysa Group. The late appointment of the politician Omar Arte Qalib, Siyad Barre's last Prime Minister, as its chairperson was intended to raise its profile and attract funding. Instead Hormood became closely associated with one particular Isaaq sub-clan (Sa'ad Muse/Habar Awal), which lost it support outside Hargeysa. It also lost support when it reneged on a pledge to appoint a woman as a deputy chairperson and to ensure that 50 per cent of its candidates were women.

Kulmiye (the Unity Party) was founded by Ahmed Mohamed Mohamoud 'Silanyo' in 2002 after Egal's death. Silanyo had served in Barre's government before becoming the longest-serving chairman of the SNM in 1984, and he served in President Egal's administration in Somaliland. During the district elections Mohamed 'Fagadhe' (Dhulbahante) served as his Deputy, but he gave way to Abdulrahman Aw Ali in the presidential elections. Kulmiye initially drew much of its support from Sanaag and Togdheer regions in eastern Somaliland, the home of Silanyo's Habar Ja'lo clan, but it was also able to attract support from diverse constituencies by creating a quota system in its executive and central committee. It received strong support from women in the district and presidential elections and from some Islamic leaders, even though Kulmiye's leadership is mostly secular. In the presidential election Kulmiye demonstrated a capacity for professional campaigning and an ability to raise resources, particularly from the diaspora.

SAHAN (Somaliland Alliance for Islamic Democracy) was led by Dr Mohamed Abdi Gaboose, a member of the SNM and a former Interior Minister in Egal's government. Its main source of support was Gaboose's Habar Yunis clan. The party also advertised its Islamic leanings by using a Qur'an in its logo.

UCID (Justice and Welfare Party) was founded by its Chairperson Faisal Ali Farah 'Waraabe', who returned from Finland to found the party. UCID campaigned on a set of centre-left welfarist policies. In the district council elections UCID drew most of its support from the 'Idagalle population in Woqooyi Galbeed region. After winning third place in the district elections it has developed a broader support base for the presidential and parliamentary elections.

UDUB (United Democratic People's Party) was founded in July 2001 by the late President Mohamed Ibrahim Egal. Following his death, the Vice-President, Dahir Riyale Kahin, became the party's Chairman and presidential candidate. UDUB draws support from across Somaliland and has received the majority vote in each election. Its electoral successes have been based on its ruling-party status, the public desire for stability and continuity, and the resources at its disposal.

and Kulmiye could claim realistically to represent a broad cross-section of all clans in Somaliland.

The road to Somaliland's first election was full of risks. The National Electoral Commission (NEC) consisted of seven commissioners nominated by the President, the Upper House and political organisations for terms of five years.[3] None had experience of managing an election; the political organisations had no experience of running election campaigns; the public was uninformed about electoral practices; and the media lacked experience in covering elections. None of the parties were pro-active in selecting women candidates. There was little trust between the parties, or between the parties and the NEC. UDUB was criticised for using government resources to support its campaign, and a lack of clarity over the demarcation of districts led to accusations of government gerrymandering.[4] The ambivalence of some people in Sool and eastern Sanaag towards Somaliland and the opposition of Puntland's authorities to the poll challenged Somaliland's ability to hold a country-wide election. Ten days prior to the election forces loyal to Puntland attacked President Riyale while he was visiting Las Anod, forcing the NEC to 'postpone' the poll in parts of these contested regions.

Another challenge to implementing the election was the absence of an electoral register, which could not be drawn up without a census. The Somaliland constitution gives all its citizens over sixteen years of age the legal right to vote. Citizenship is defined in the constitution (Article 4.1.1) as open to anyone who is the descendant of a person resident in the territory of Somaliland before the union with Somalia in 1960. This potentially enfranchises many people in Ethiopia and Djibouti and in the diaspora, and disenfranchises migrants from elsewhere in Somalia (Jama 2000). It also effectively gives citizenship rights to people born abroad who have never been to Somaliland. The registration of voters and distribution of polling cards proved impossible to administer in the time available,[5] so the government statistic that 1.18 million people had voted in the constitutional referendum was used as a planning figure (Gers and Valentine-Selsey 2002). Voter eligibility was to be corroborated on polling day by a local elder, and indelible ink was used to prevent double voting.

The NEC's strategy for dealing with these contentious issues was to engage the political organisations and other stakeholders in defining the process, and to appeal for external support. Each aspect of the process, such as the use of indelible ink, was discussed at length. The political organisations placed observers in every polling station and each vote was counted in front of them. Civic organisations took on educational and

---

[3] Two of the commissioners were prominent members of local NGOs and one of them was a woman.
[4] Since 1991, twenty new districts and one new region (Sahil) have been created by the government in Somaliland. Many of these have not been accepted formally by Parliament (see Chapter 9).
[5] The NEC, government and municipal authorities experimented with registration cards before the elections, but they proved impossible to administer without identity cards.

monitoring roles. Given the high levels of illiteracy, there was a need to ensure voters were educated about the importance of the election and the voting procedures. NAGAAD, an umbrella body for women's organisations, and COSONGO, an umbrella body for Somaliland NGOs, undertook the tasks of voter education and training of domestic observers. NAGAAD and the Women's Political Forum lobbied the political organisations to select women candidates. A code of conduct drawn up with the political organisations and the NEC by the Somaliland Academy for Peace and Development (APD) recognised the primacy of the law; established acceptable campaigning practices and procedures for resolving disputes; and committed the organisations to accepting the decisions of the NEC. A committee of community activists, religious leaders and business people formed the Integrity Watch Committee to monitor adherence to the code. Other organisations, including religious groups, campaigned for the election to be conducted peacefully. The government, for its part, contributed funding and human resources, including 2,283 police; and on election day, government vehicles were put at the disposal of the NEC. This collective effort at times hampered the efficiency of the electoral process, but ensured that it was admirably transparent.

The elections attracted the first substantive support from international donors for political activities in Somaliland. Through the European Commission (EC), international donors co-financed the election with the government, assigned foreign consultants to the NEC and funded both voter education and the training of over 3,000 election workers and domestic observers.[6] The US International Republican Institute provided training to the political organisations. The readiness of international donors to assist with the district elections contrasted with their lack of support for previous peace conferences in Somaliland and the 2001 referendum. While the election was initiated, managed and substantially funded by Somaliland, external support did leave it open to foreign agendas. The EC's support for the district elections, for example, was part of a wider programme to promote democracy and good governance in 'Somalia', and was intended to support what the EC declared was an essential step towards a 'more democratic' system of governance than a clan-based system (EU 2002). The UN again maintained a distance from the whole electoral process to avoid a potential conflict of policy with its support for the TNG – in spite of its declared support for governance and the fact that it had previously supported the formation of district councils in Somalia. Foreign monitors were also present at each of the elections, mostly from non-governmental organisations. Their numbers increased and their participation became more formalised with each election.

---

[6] The contributing governments were Denmark, Finland, the Netherlands, Switzerland and Britain.

On 15 December 2002, Somalilanders went to the polls for the first time in over thirty years to elect local councils. Some 440,067 voters elected 332 councillors (out of a possible 339) in nineteen districts (out of twenty-three) in Somaliland's six regions (Gers and Valentine-Selsey 2002). There was no vote in four districts in Sool and eastern Sanaag and in parts of Buhoodle District in Togdheer Region following threats by supporters of Puntland to disrupt the election. Polling day passed without any major security incidents.[7] Foreign election observers concluded that the election was carried out in a manner that was transparent, free from intimidation and, by and large, in line with internationally recognised electoral norms. They also noted the high participation of women voters.[8] Some procedural problems that were identified were attributed to a lack of experience among electoral officials and voters. For example, adherence to a secret ballot was compromised in some cases when illiterate voters publicly named the organisation they intended to support.[9] Allegations of ballot stuffing in one region were unsubstantiated, and even if true would not have altered the outcome substantially.

On 23 December the NEC declared that UDUB, Kulmiye and UCID had won the right to form political parties and to contest presidential and parliamentary elections. UDUB was the clear winner, receiving 41 per cent of all the votes cast and exceeding the required threshold of 20 per cent of votes in five regions. Exit interviews with voters on election day indicated that support for UDUB was based on name recognition; a desire to maintain the *status quo* in Somaliland; and the strong local candidates that UDUB's greater financial resources and its status as ruling party enabled it to attract. Kulmiye picked up the second largest number of votes, and although it gained more than 20 per cent of votes cast only in Sanaag and Togdheer regions, it demonstrated a capacity to attract support in all regions. The decision to award the third place to UCID was controversial as the organisation failed to obtain 20 per cent of the vote in any region and only beat SAHAN to third place by a small margin of 1,500 votes. Some 60 per cent of its votes came from Hargeysa Region, home of the sub-clan of its chairperson Faisal Ali 'Waraabe'. By winning control of the local councils UDUB increased its monopoly over Somaliland's political institutions. After the councillors from losing organisations joined the accredited parties, its share of council seats increased to over 55 per cent (Bradbury *et al.* 2003). Consequently, the majority of mayors elected by the councils were also UDUB candidates.

---

[7] One person was injured in Awdal Region when police fired over the heads of a crowd of youths who were trying to force entry into a polling station.

[8] See Abokor *et al.* (2005). Foreign observers were present from the EC, the British Embassy in Ethiopia, the Royal Danish Embassy in Kenya, Sweden, South Africa and Britain.

[9] The literacy rate in Somalia is amongst the lowest in the world, with only 22 per cent of men and 17 per cent of women able to read and write (UNDP 2001).

The presidential election

Presidential and parliamentary elections should have followed in January, a month before the end of the government's term in February 2003. The delay in holding the district council elections, the need for additional electoral legislation and lack of preparedness among the parties meant the elections were rescheduled for April and the government's tenure extended for a second time by three months. The plan to hold presidential and parliamentary elections simultaneously was abandoned when lack of agreement over the regional allocation of parliamentary seats and the demarcation of parliamentary constituencies meant the appropriate legislation could not be passed in time. It was therefore agreed to delay the parliamentary election in order to resolve the impasse. Parliament's tenure was extended for a further two years and, in line with the constitution, the term of the House of Elders had to be extended for a further three years.

The task of organising the presidential election again fell to the NEC. The government committed US$1 million to the election (IRIN 2003), but political sensitivities made the EC unwilling to finance the presidential election.[10] Some European governments, including the United Kingdom and Denmark, independently supported some of the costs of technical assistance and voter education, but a lack of donor coordination affected the preparations.

Drawing on the experience of the district council election, the NEC increased the polling stations to 900; tightened control procedures, with a mandatory one-year prison sentence introduced for people caught double voting; stationed senior polling station staff away from their home areas to reduce opportunities for vote rigging; and gave additional training to political party representatives. Civic organisations again engaged in training election staff, domestic observers and party representatives, while the Integrity Watch Committee was reconstituted and worked with the parties to recommit themselves to a code of conduct. The NEC intervened in the campaign to try and ensure a fair election, admonishing the government for appointing regional ministers of state without portfolio to curry votes – dubbed 'ballot box ministers' – and UDUB's use of government vehicles for campaigning. However, it had no real power to control the parties' campaigns. When new Somaliland shillings were released just prior to the election, the government was accused of buying votes for UDUB. It is estimated, however, that Kulmiye spent as much if not more on its campaign, with money raised from the business community and the diaspora.

Members of the organisations that had lost out in the district elections scrambled for posts in the three national parties. The new alliances of

[10] At the time the EC was funding the fourteenth Somalia National Reconciliation Conference in Kenya, facilitated by IGAD.

convenience that were formed highlighted the opportunistic nature of politics and created a degree of cynicism among voters, who had difficulty identifying any substantive policy differences between the parties. For each party Somaliland's independence was a central tenet, and they all espoused a liberal economy. The parties by and large represented the urban population and for the most part it was the personality of the leaders, their ability to field key supporters, and clan loyalties which influenced voter choices. There were, however, differences between the parties that were highlighted in their campaigns.

UDUB campaigned on a platform of continuity and peace that was symbolised in its name and party symbol – *udub*, the central wooden pole of a traditional Somali dwelling – and reflected in its slogan *nabad iyo caano* ('peace and milk'). Although UDUB has not espoused any clear ideology or political programme, its emphasis on experience and continuity of the establishment suggests a conservative leaning. Riyale's appointment of the widely respected Edna Adan as Foreign Minister and first woman member of the Somaliland cabinet won him support.[11] UDUB's prospects were also strengthened when Suleiman 'Gaal' joined the party from ASAD. Previously a vocal critic of Egal and associated with the radical wing of the SNM, he split the Habar Ja'lo vote for Kulmiye by joining UDUB.

Kulmiye campaigned on a platform of 'change', promising a cleaner and leaner administration and a greater role for women in government. Kulmiye is a complex alliance of interest groups, with a core of former SNM socialist officers, including its vice-chair Abdulrahman Aw Ali; a religious group; former members of the Hargeysa Group; and civil activists, particularly women. The collaboration of different interest groups that transcend clan loyalties distinguishes Kulmiye from the other parties. The presence of former SNM officers within Kulmiye attracted some supporters, but also lost it support among the more conservative voters and Habar Yunis, who held them partially responsible for Somaliland's war in 1994–1996.

UCID had the clearest political programme of all. Its party leader and other senior members had lived in Scandinavia and were influenced by Scandinavian-style social democracy. It promised a more welfarist state with investment in health and education and enhanced participation of women, all of which appealed to youthful voters. UCID also sought to distinguish itself from the other parties with a leader who was new to Somaliland politics and therefore not associated with the established political elite.

Voting took place on 14 April 2003 throughout Somaliland, with the exception of two districts in eastern Sanaag and three in Sool where voting was again postponed.[11] As in the district elections, the poll passed off peacefully. Some 488,543 valid votes were counted, an increase of just

---

[11] One polling station in Awdal Region also did not open.

8.1 Registering voters for the 2002 district elections, Burco (M. Bradbury)

8.2 Ballot papers being counted in 2003 presidential elections (M. Bradbury)

8.3 Women and men vote in large numbers in the 2003 presidential elections
(M. Bradbury)

8.4 Voting in the 2005 parliamentary elections
(M. Bradbury)

over 10 per cent on the district elections. International and domestic observers again gave a generally favourable report on the manner in which polling was conducted.[12] Various irregularities were noted, however: the management of different polling stations varied greatly; the ban on the transportation of voters was ignored in some locations; the screening of voters by age was not always enforced; and multiple voting by individuals was observed in Hargeysa and Burco. Inconsistent regional voting patterns between the district and presidential elections indicated more serious irregularities. The NEC was subsequently criticised for weak control measures and for issuing voting ink that was easily removed. However, the parties were more culpable in circumventing procedures, transporting supporters from one station to another, and offering incentives to people to vote more than once.

The result of the election was a harsh test for this aspiring democracy. The preliminary results, announced by the NEC on 19 April, gave UDUB a narrow victory over Kulmiye by a margin of only eighty votes. The result confounded the popular expectation of a Kulmiye victory and triggered small protests in Burco and Gabiley among its supporters, raising concerns that the situation could turn violent. Further opportunities for public expressions of dissatisfaction were prevented by the government, which invoked emergency laws and banned peaceful protests and opposition rallies.[13] Given UDUB's marginal lead, Kulmiye had every right to question the result. The personal wealth invested by Kulmiye supporters in the campaign also made defeat difficult to accept. Kulmiye's chairman, Ahmed 'Silanyo', demonstrated considerable political responsibility and judgement by refraining from publicly accusing the NEC or the government of malpractice, and by resisting pressure from within his party to form an alternative government. He stated that he had no intention of taking Somaliland down the path of Mogadishu, where two rival presidents – Ali Mahdi and General Aideed – had been the cause of so much death and destruction. He committed Kulmiye to the constitutional process by contesting the results through the Supreme Court.

As stipulated in Somaliland's electoral laws, the Supreme Court was responsible for reviewing the conduct of the elections and making a final ruling on the results. The manner in which this was done was a crucial test for Somaliland's fledgling democracy and the legitimacy of the government (Jama 2003). On 11 May, after three days of listening to submissions by the parties and the NEC, the Supreme Court pronounced in favour of UDUB, confirming its victory by a marginally higher 214

---

[12] The largest delegation came from South Africa, with observers from Ethiopia, Sweden, Norway, Holland, Canada and Britain. The presence of foreign correspondents also gave the election some coverage in the international media.

[13] The emergency laws had been introduced without parliamentary approval by former President Egal at a time when several of the Kulmiye supporters held positions in the government.

votes. Kulmiye questioned a verdict that did nothing to clarify matters because it was based on a new set of figures (African Rights 2003b). Kulmiye's questioning of the court's competence was not without foundation, because Somaliland's judicial system had been a subject of public criticism, as an editorial in the English-language weekly *The Somaliland Times* illustrates:

> Chronically corrupt and grossly under-qualified Judges, coupled with frequent interventions by the Executive Branch in the Judiciary process, have effectively reduced Somaliland courts to an open market where Justice is sold to the highest bidder. (6 July 2002)

One of Riyale's first acts as interim President had been to make extensive changes to the Supreme Court. Although this was welcomed by the public, his appointment of the Chair of the Supreme Court and all six new judges served to highlight the judiciary's lack of independence from the government. Furthermore, among the sitting judges there was little knowledge of constitutional matters. But Kulmiye's stand had an insecure foundation: it had fought the elections without questioning the Court's competence.

On 16 May Riyale was sworn in as the first directly elected President of Somaliland, with a five-year term of office. It took another three weeks and the mediation of clan leaders to persuade Kulmiye to concede defeat. UDUB's electoral successes gave the ruling party sweeping control over Somaliland's political institutions, a situation that could only be changed through parliamentary elections. Although the government's actions to manage the post-election tensions that followed the presidential elections should not be exaggerated, the invocation of emergency laws, censorship of the media, and harassment of opposition sympathisers – backed by the activities of the National Security Committee and the alleged expansion of Somaliland's internal security apparatus – were troubling developments (African Rights 2003b). For the multi-party system to survive and to prevent a slide into one-party rule, it was important that strong opposition parties existed and that a parliamentary election was conducted without delay. This would not occur for another two years.

New security threats

For a period of six years, from the cessation of Somaliland's civil war in 1996 until December 2002, when Puntland forces attempted to assassinate President Riyale, Somaliland had experienced a long period of security undisturbed by armed conflict. Even the UN, which operates under very tight security regulations, downgraded its risk assessment in Somaliland. The attacks on the US of 11 September 2001 caused the UN and the EC to withdraw foreign aid workers as a precaution and for reasons of insurance,[14] but they returned within a couple of weeks. The peaceful conduct of the district and presidential elections in 2002 appeared to augur well for the future. However, in the two years between the presidential elections and the parliamentary elections, several events occurred that eroded the image of Somaliland as an oasis of security.

Terrorism

The events of 9/11 and the US and international response to it reignited Western security interests in the region, with Somalia identified as a potential source and haven for transnational terrorism. In late 2001, there was speculation that Somalia might follow Afghanistan as the next military theatre in the US-led international 'war on terror', due to alleged links between the Somali Islamist movement Al Itihad al Islamiya, the Somali-owned money-transfer business Al Barakat, and Osama bin Laden's Al Qaeda network. In late September 2001, Western newspapers reported that there were several thousand members of Al Qaeda and Al Itihad operating in Somalia, and that bin Laden was setting up new operational bases there (*Daily Telegraph*, 28 September 2001). The absence of clear targets meant that no military action took place, but as part of a 'financial war' against terrorism measures were taken by the US administration to close the operations of Al Barakat, while several Western countries established an air and maritime surveillance regime over the country.[15]

Although the rise of militant Islamist movements in southern Somalia with links to Al Qaeda had been documented, there was little evidence of an active presence in Somaliland, Sheikh Ali Warsame, former Chairman of Al Itihad, returned to Burco after the movement dissolved but stayed politically inactive. The social influence of reformist Islamist movements like Tabliq was expanding through educational institutes and business, but their political influence was less apparent than in Puntland or southern Somalia. People in Somaliland were therefore deeply shocked in October 2003 by the murders, in close succession, of three foreign aid workers. In Borama, a respected Italian nurse who had worked for several decades in Somalia and Somaliland was killed in the clinic she ran for TB and HIV/AIDS patients. In Sheikh, two elderly British teachers who were managing the recently refurbished secondary school were shot and killed. In April 2004 a fourth aid worker from Kenya was killed, along with her Somali driver, in an ambush on the Hargeysa-Berbera road. As the assassins sought to flee into Ethiopia, villagers in Dhoqoshi, who had been alerted over the attacks, apprehended them and handed them over to the Somaliland authorities. It subsequently emerged that they were part of a network of *jihadists* based in Mogadishu thought to be linked to

---

[14] The UN had to renegotiate insurance cover for its chartered planes.

[15] The US and UK governments also carried out reconnaissance missions to the country.

Al Qaeda (ICG 2005a). The suspects were put on trial along with two others already in the custody of the Somaliland police. Before the verdict was announced, and a few days before the presidential elections, several other members of the network, who were allegedly planning a raid to release their colleagues, were arrested in Hargeysa. In November 2005, eight of the prisoners were found guilty of involvement in the murders of the foreign aid workers and sentenced to death, while seven others accused of abetting the assassins were given life sentences (IRIN 2005).

The targeting of foreigners raised a concern that Somaliland was being used by militant groups sympathetic to Al Qaeda as a 'soft target' against Western governments. There was a fear that the actions of a few would scare away foreign aid agencies and the government appealed to the international community for assistance to 'enhance the country's counter-terrorism capabilities' (*Somaliland Times*, 27 March 2004). The UN increased security restrictions on its staff following the murders and supported a special Somaliland police force – the Special Protection Unit – to provide security for foreign agencies in Somaliland. For the first time since the early 1990s foreign aid workers in Somaliland had to become accustomed to travelling with armed escorts, although the formation of this security service was indicative of how far the Somaliland state had developed since that time. In Somaliland there was a concern that the murders were an attempt to destabilise the country (*ibid.*). More troubling, perhaps, was the fact that several of those involved in the killings were from Somaliland, revealing the previously unmarked presence in the country of adherents to a more politically militant form of Islam. Their presence introduced a new threat to Somaliland's security and there was a call by some Somalilanders to 'rise up to meet the challenges posed by the threat of terrorism' (*ibid.*). Somaliland authorities used the potential terrorist threat to press their case for international recognition.

Sool & eastern Sanaag

The more immediate threat to Somaliland's security and territorial integrity came from Puntland and the regions of Sool and eastern Sanaag. The dispute over these regions, where the political affiliations of the Harti clans are divided three ways between Somaliland, Puntland and Somalia, has been described as 'one of the deepest fault lines in contemporary Somali politics' (ICG 2003: 30).

A decade earlier senior Dhulbahante and Warsengeli elders had acceded to the declaration of independence and the political arrangements put together at Borama in 1993. Members of these clans have held senior posts in all of Somaliland's administrations. Nevertheless the authorities in Hargeysa failed to establish an effective administration in these regions and many of those who previously supported Somaliland have reneged on it. Although the Somaliland government provided some economic support to the regions, such as salaries for teachers and police, the political and commercial dominance of the Isaaq in Somaliland left many Harti feeling marginalised. The vigorous trade through Bossaso has also encouraged them to look east for their economic livelihoods, with Harti in the diaspora assisting through investment. The creation in 1998 of Puntland State, which asserts territorial claims to these regions on the basis of Harti unity, and the formation of the TNG in 2000 with a Dhulbahante Prime Minister, exacerbated the latent tensions.

Somaliland's constitutional referendum and district and presidential elections reinforced the fissure. The fact that the people of eastern Sanaag and most people of Sool Region (with the exception of Aynabo) did not vote in the referendum or the elections, meant there were no elected councils in these regions which respected the government in Hargeysa. Following the attack on Riyale in Las Anod, Abdullahi Yusuf, then President of Puntland, extended his administration to Sool Region and as far as Dhulbahante areas of Buhoodle in Togdheer, which were claimed as part of a new region called 'Ayn'. Riyale was criticised in the Somaliland press and by the opposition for not responding to Puntland's provocation. Riyale defended his policy on the grounds that he did not want to damage the positive image of peace and stability that was the basis for Somaliland's bid for international recognition. It also avoided exacerbating the humanitarian crisis caused by a prolonged drought. In October 2003 the UN Office for the Coordination of Humanitarian Affairs (UNOCHA) had declared that 90,000 people in the Sool Plateau were facing critical food shortages (FEWS Net and FSAU 2003 November). Livestock herds had been depleted and many pastoralists had moved to the urban centres for water and food relief.

Following the presidential election Somaliland's political parties jointly identified the dispute over the eastern regions as their first priority for resolution through dialogue. Simmering tensions led to military clashes between Somaliland and Puntland at the end of 2003. Puntland's assumption of control in Las Canod undoubtedly formed part of Abdullahi Yusuf's political manoeuvrings at the Somali reconciliation conference in Kenya, where he was vying for the presidency of Somalia. His selection as President of a new Transitional Federal Government (TFG) of Somalia in October 2004 rendered the issue more complex. The vulnerability felt among Somalilanders was forcefully expressed in statements by the Somaliland government that they were determined to defend Somaliland's independence at all costs (IRIN 2004 October 15). In October 2004, just two weeks after Abdullahi Yusuf's selection, there was a brief and bloody clash between Puntland and Somaliland forces in the village of Adi-Addeye north of Las Canod, in which a hundred people were killed (IRIN 2004 November 1). The clash brought a swift diplomatic response from regional bodies and the UN urged the two sides to withdraw. Clan elders from the region intervened to calm the situation. In December 2005 negotiations led to a final exchange of prisoners through the offices of the International Committee of the Red Cross and UNOCHA.

Sool and eastern Sanaag are of critical political and economic importance to Somaliland, Puntland and Somalia. The limited authority that the Hargeysa administration exercises in these regions undermines the sovereignty and territorial integrity of Somaliland. The rejection of Somaliland by the people in these regions challenges the country's self-image as a pluralistic multi-clan entity. By the same token, the limited control that Puntland exercises in these regions weakens its claim to be a regional state based on a notion of Harti unity. Somaliland's claims over the regions also challenge the sovereignty of Somalia. The possibility that there may be commercial oil reserves in Sool Region increases its significance as a potential site of conflict (*Somaliland Times* 2005, October 18). Access to any such resources would strengthen Somaliland's ability to become a sustainable entity. Likewise, for Puntland or a united Somalia the economic benefits of oil reserves in this region could be huge.

The dispute is not necessarily amenable to straightforward negotiations. Relations between the Harti and the Isaaq are complex and vary between sub-clans. The relationship between some Dhulbahante and the Barre regime has left a legacy of unresolved grievances among the Isaaq. But many Dhulbahante feel aggrieved at what they see as their economic and political marginalisation within Somaliland, and because they have not benefited from the international aid that Somaliland receives. For the Harti who have invested in the expanding commercial centre in Bossaso, Puntland is a more attractive option than Somaliland. But some Dhulbahante have closer ties to the Isaaq than the Majeerteen. Some Dhulbahante believe the solution would be to establish Sool itself as a federal entity. Within Somaliland there are numerous views on how the dispute can be resolved, ranging from allowing the Harti to vote on where they wish to be, to retaining the regions through force of arms. Others believe the best way to keep them within Somaliland is to create a just society.

The Transitional Federal Government

A further challenge to Somaliland during this period arose from the Somalia National Reconciliation Conference (SNRC), the fourteenth internationally sponsored peace talks on Somalia, which began in Kenya in October 2002. The talks, which were again facilitated by IGAD, were intended to establish a body to take over from the TNG, whose mandate was due to end in 2003. Tainted by corruption scandals and opposed militarily by the Ethiopian-backed Somali Reconciliation and Restoration Council (SRRC), the TNG had failed to establish meaningful authority further than a few kilometres around Mogadishu.

In contrast to the Arta talks, which had excluded the warlords, the SNRC aimed to incorporate them in a comprehensive political deal. Two years of lengthy and often acrimonious negotiations, external pressure and a great deal of money produced a provisional Federal National Charter and a Transitional National Assembly which selected the President of Puntland, Colonel Abdullahi Yusuf Ahmed, as Interim President of Somalia in October 2004, with a five-year term of office.

Despite a litany of problems with the peace talks and the process of setting up a government (ICG 2004; Terlinden and Hagmann 2005; Menkhaus *et al.* 2005), the TFG was granted a high degree of international recognition, taking Somalia's seat in the UN, the African Union, IGAD and the Arab League. In 2005 the World Bank and the UN embarked on an ambitious Joint Needs Assessment with the new government to prepare a national reconstruction and development plan to release donor funds. In contrast, amongst Somalis, Abdullahi Yusuf and his Prime Minister struggled to gain acceptance (ICG 2006b). The Transitional National Assembly split acrimoniously, soon after it was formed, over President Yusuf's demands for the deployment of foreign peacekeepers. Unwilling to move to Mogadishu without the protection of foreign peacekeepers, the government was temporarily established first in Jowhar and later Baidoa, from where it struggled to project any meaningful authority. Only diplomatic and financial support and pressure from the UN and foreign governments kept the TFG afloat. For most of 2006 its presence and authority was overshadowed by the Union of Islamic Courts, which temporarily controlled much of southern Somalia. It was only at the close of 2006, with military backing from Ethiopia, that the TFG was able to enter Mogadishu.

Somaliland had again refused to participate in the SNRC. The policy of the mediators was to focus on achieving a political deal in Somalia without upsetting the stability and economic recovery that had been achieved in Somaliland. The TFG was advised to refrain from provocative statements about Somaliland and sovereignty. Nevertheless, the creation of the TFG, which was accorded conditional recognition, was a clear threat to aspirations for independence in Somaliland. Not only did it challenge its sovereignty and territorial claims, but as the formal representative of the country at international fora the TFG was in a position to divert diplomatic and financial resources intended for it. Furthermore, Somalis from Somaliland who participated in the IGAD talks and held posts in the TFG could weaken the unity of purpose in Somaliland by creating internal tensions. The government in Hargeysa felt especially threatened by developments in public discussion of its future in the Kenya conference. In July 2004 the Minister of the Interior reverted to Egal's tactics during the Arta conference and issued a decree banning all organised debates on the potential impact of the SNRC on Somaliland. The brief detention of the pro-unionist politician Jama Mohamed Qalib 'Yare' in Hargeysa in August 2003 resulted in an exchange of gunfire at the airport, illustrating a continuing fragility in the political consensus in Somaliland.

Social tensions & civil liberties

Other external factors were having an impact on living conditions in Somaliland. The onset of the war in Iraq in April 2004 had negative consequences for the economy, already affected by the prolonged embargo on livestock sales to Gulf states. At the outset of the Iraq war the international staff of aid agencies withdrew from Somaliland. Although aid projects continued with local staff, foreign income declined and the funding of some of the projects was jeopardised. The value of the Somaliland shilling halved against the US dollar. The price of fuel and other imported commodities rose beyond the reach of many people, particularly the nomadic pastoralists, who were suffering from the loss of markets for their livestock. Worst hit were the populations in Sool, eastern Sanaag and eastern Togdheer, regions that were experiencing a prolonged drought.

Economic pressures on people exacerbated other resource tensions. As a result of demographic pressures, structural changes in the economy and changing political relations between clans, systems for the management and distribution of productive assets such as land and water were becoming strained. Sedentarisation and urban drift have increased the value of land in and around settlements. Consequently, land has become a common cause of neighbourhood and inter-clan violence and homicide. In September 2003, for example, riots occurred in Burco over public land and property that was being 'squatted', during which one person was killed. Interventions by local and central government prevented the issue from escalating, but, unmanaged, such tensions could escalate into broader inter-clan conflicts.

Elite competition was another source of friction in Somaliland. The presidential elections revealed an unresolved tension between former SNM military officers who backed Kulmiye and some members of UDUB, who were former officers of the despised National Security Service (NSS), including President Riyale.[16] Questions raised about Riyale's past in the NSS highlighted continuing grievances and issues of impunity for alleged past crimes, fomenting a debate on whether the SNM 'struggle' had brought real political change or just the perpetuation of the old system (African Rights 2003b).

Human rights violations against the Isaaq people had been one of the underlying causes of the war against the Barre regime, and were a factor in persuading the public to call for a withdrawal from the union with Somalia. In contrast to the former regime, Somaliland has been virtually free of systematic human rights abuse. The National Charter of 1993 proclaimed Somaliland's adherence to the Universal Declaration of Human

---

[16] The division was not clear-cut, as some SNM leaders supported UDUB.

Rights, a course which President Egal publicly pledged to maintain in 1998. In the latter years of Egal's tenure Somaliland's reputation was tarnished by the way the government arrested and detained its critics, the limitations it placed on the media, and the institution of emergency laws (UNDP 2001: 176). In advance of the presidential elections, the opposition parties and human rights groups had questioned the legality of the National Security Committee, while government critics pointed to the growing influence of former NSS officers in an internal security service[17] which was not governed by legislation and was accountable only to the President (ICG 2003: 33). In the wake of the presidential elections concern grew about the government's actions against its critics, including restrictions on public demonstrations and the harassment, arrest and detention of political activists (African Rights 2003b). Civic activists also objected to the government's ban on public debates on the SNRC in Kenya, as an infringement of civil liberties. The controversial arrest and trial of a young woman in August 2004 on charges of espionage brought criticism by Somali and international human rights organisations of Somaliland's judicial system and the government's commitment to human rights (Amnesty International 2004). With a weak judiciary and in the absence of an elected parliament to hold the executive to account, the public was troubled that human rights and civil liberties in Somaliland were unprotected.

Parliamentary elections

In the period before parliamentary elections there was a risk that the opposition parties would collapse and disappear. This did not happen. Riyale's decision not to form a coalition government helped to sustain the semblance of a multi-party system.[18] After the presidential elections the three parties engaged in some constructive dialogue and produced an agreement on how to deal with eastern Sanaag and Sool, on the non-participation of Somaliland in the IGAD peace talks in Kenya, the pursuit of foreign recognition, freedom of the media, the release of political prisoners, financial support for political parties, and a timetable for parliamentary elections with recommendations on the distribution of parliamentary seats.[19] However, the parties had little leverage to turn recommendations into practice, and in the two years prior to the parliamentary elections there was little evidence of party activity. Lack of finance was certainly a severe constraint. The presidential candidates and their supporters had spent considerable personal resources during the elections, and although the principle of public funding for parties had

[17] Called *mukhabaraat* by Somalilanders after the Egyptian intelligence services.
[18] Riyale was encouraged by Ethiopia and public opinion to form a coalition, but may have been advised against this by other donor governments.
[19] Joint position paper by the three national parties, 4 July 2003.

been accepted, they failed to agree an amount with the government. In the absence of an elected parliament, there was no institution through which the parties could participate formally in politics until parliamentary elections were held. Parliamentary elections, of course, promised power as well as survival to the parties: control of the Lower House would give them the opportunity to institute political change.

In July 2003 the parties and the NEC had agreed that parliamentary elections should take place within a year, and that the necessary legislation should be completed within six months, a timetable the President appeared to accept.[20] However, disagreement by the sitting parliamentarians and the cabinet over the distribution of parliamentary seats to Somaliland's six regions, the delineation of constituency boundaries, and the lack of a census and register of voters hindered production of the necessary electoral law. A key concern was the change that direct elections would bring to the representation of the smaller clans in Parliament. Under the *beel* system smaller clans were guaranteed representation, whereas a majoritarian electoral system favoured the larger clans, as the district council elections had already demonstrated. Gadabursi elders and parliamentarians had refused a draft bill in 2003 on the grounds that it would reduce their number of parliamentary seats. Reaching agreement on the distribution of parliamentary seats was extremely difficult in the absence of a population count against which to measure the claims of the competing clan constituencies. Similarly, the delineation of administrative boundaries was contentious, as it impacted on traditional clan territories. While the Parliament and the President drew public criticism for procrastinating, the opposition parties and civic organisations offered few constructive proposals on ways forward. The lawmakers were also faced with the problem of dealing with areas of Sool and Sanaag that had not participated in the district elections, and which by late 2004 had become a military flashpoint between Somaliland and Puntland. In addition, Parliament had to consider the representation of women and the marginalised Gabooye (occupational castes). In October 2004 sufficient consensus was found in Parliament to reject a proposal – on constitutional grounds – to amend the electoral law and grant women a quota of seats.

Eventually, 29 March 2005 was agreed as the date for parliamentary elections, thus enabling parliamentarians to complete their two-year extension. It was not until January 2005, however, that the requisite legislation was tabled and passed by Parliament. Controversially, the legislation, which was endorsed by the Upper House a week later, set preconditions for elections that were impossible to meet in the time remaining, including a population census, voter registration and the demarcation of constituencies. Parliament's actions were widely denounced. The first Deputy Chairman admonished the House for 'gambling with the future of

[20] Author's interview with President Dahir Riyale Kahin, Hargeysa, September 2003.

the nation' because a census and voter registration could not be undertaken in the time available. The MPs, many of whom had been in Parliament for ten years, were accused by the media of being reluctant to vacate their seats and of placing their own interests above those of the country (*Somaliland Times*, 29 January 2005). It was perhaps no coincidence that MPs' salaries were increased the day before the election law was brought to the floor of the House. But the problem had less to do with individual interests than with the pressure on MPs to defend the clan interests they represented (APD 2006: 23). After reviewing the bill, the NEC declared that the preconditions meant that the elections could not be held as rescheduled. In a joint communiqué with the three political parties it proposed that the preconditions should be suspended and the elections rescheduled for the end of April. The NEC also proposed a formula for the regional distribution of parliamentary seats which, pending a census, could be revised for subsequent elections.

The executive was slower to react. The public suspected that the President was stalling on an election that might produce an opposition-controlled Parliament. The President was also under pressure from his Gadabursi clan, still concerned about the loss of seats in Parliament. However, with the opposition threatening civil unrest if the elections were not forthcoming, holding them became vital to the stability of Somaliland. The Somaliland NGO, APD, maintained the pressure for an election by hosting a series of public forums on the electoral law (APD 2006: 19). Foreign governments, who had supported the previous elections, also intervened constructively to ease tensions between the parties, and the British government through its embassy in Addis Ababa funded a consultant to assist in revising the electoral law (*ibid.*: 17). The impasse was overcome when the President passed the legislation to the Supreme Court (acting as the Constitutional Court), which ruled that the contentious articles in the law requiring voter registration and a population census were unconstitutional because they would prevent elections from being held. The President returned the proposed amendments to Parliament, which passed the bill, creating a law that paved the way for parliamentary elections to take place on 15 September 2005.

Some 246 candidates competed for the eighty-two parliamentary seats. These were allocated on a regional basis according to a formula used for selecting members in Somaliland's last Assembly in 1960, when Somaliland briefly received international recognition as an independent state. According to this Woqooyi Galbeed (Hargeysa Region) was given twenty seats, Awdal thirteen, Sahil ten, Togdheer fifteen, Sanaag twelve and Sool ten.[21] Nine of these were 'reserved seats' for the contested regions of Sool and eastern Sanaag and Buhoodle district in Togdheer, where elections would again be postponed, and which were to be apportioned to parties on the basis of their regional vote. An electoral system was also agreed

[21] The number of seats were multiplied by 2.5 to take account of population growth.

that combined a system of open party lists and proportional representation, in which voters were expected to vote for the candidate rather than the party.

After two elections the NEC had gained considerable knowledge and experience in the organisation and management of elections.[22] Still – with 1.3 million ballot papers to be printed, 1,500 ballot bags to be distributed, 985 polling stations to be identified and equipped, seventy-five international observers to be coordinated, and 4,000 polling station staff, 6,000 party agents, 3,000 police and 700 domestic observers to be trained – the parliamentary election was a major undertaking. Additional external assistance was channelled through the APD, which assembled an international and Somali team to provide legal, technical and logistical support (APD 2006). The government again contributed to the cost of the elections but, having financed two elections and with declining revenues and increased military expenditure on the territorial dispute with Puntland, it was only able to provide 30 per cent of the projected costs (*ibid.*: 11). The balance was borne by donor governments, who financed the costs of the NEC and training needs and voter education. Donors this time included the EC: having declined to support the presidential elections, it was now ready to support the parliamentary elections as part of a broader democratisation project in the Somali region.

Following the practice of the previous elections, the parties signed a new code of conduct prepared in discussion with the NEC. It covered the conduct of the campaign, the use of public finance, compliance with electoral law and measures to deal with existing gaps in the law, and a timetable for public rallies. An Election Monitoring Board was established under the NEC in place of the Integrity Watch Committee to monitor the election, mediate disputes and provide a formal public assessment of the elections. After some cajoling the media similarly signed a voluntary code of conduct for their coverage of the elections. As in the previous elections, the NEC made a point of engaging the parties in many aspects of electoral management, such as the selection of electoral officers, in order to ensure transparency.

The election campaign

These measures ensured that the elections passed off peacefully, like the previous two. As before, the government was criticised for using public funds to support UDUB, for monopolising the use of state-run television and radio, and for appointing new ministers of state to curry favour with clans. Ministers were criticised for using government vehicles and other resources in support of their preferred candidates. The government in turn accused privately owned newspapers and TV stations of being

---

[22] The commissioners also visited South Africa to learn about election management.

biased towards the opposition parties. The Election Monitoring Board issued several press releases critical of the government. The NEC pressed the government to allow equal access to the state-run radio and television and as a result media coverage became more equitable, although it proved difficult to control the use of government funds. The most serious incident involved a police raid on the headquarters of Kulmiye, which UDUB was accused of orchestrating. This led to a critical breach in relations between Kulmiye and the President. The international team that monitored the election campaign nevertheless concluded that, despite these obvious problems, conditions were such as to allow for a reasonably free and fair election process (Abokor *et al.* 2005).

As in previous elections there were few substantive policy differences between the parties, although the opposition parties had a list of reforms that they wanted to introduce in Parliament (see Chapter 9). The absence of clear party platforms and messages meant that individual candidates were left to run their own campaigns. These focused on convincing their constituencies of their leadership qualities and ability to deliver social and economic benefits to them. In contrast to the presidential election, which was about the party leaders and the party, the parliamentary elections were more about establishing clan representation in government, for which the parties were the vehicle. The substantive focus of the election campaign, therefore, was on the dynamics between the parties, clans and individual candidates.

The parties are required by election law to submit their list of candidates to the NEC, who scrutinised their qualifications according to established criteria of age, citizenship and education. However, as it was in the interests of the parties to have candidates who could deliver the votes of their constituencies, the clan leadership played a key role in selecting the candidates for the parties and in financing their campaigns. The motivations for this were various. Better access to government resources, jobs, and better services were all incentives to ensure the success of their candidates, but as government resources are limited, increasing the prestige and political relevance of the clan was an equally important motivation.[23] Within clans certain lineages have historically been more politically powerful than others. Due to the war, changes in the economy and urbanisation, this balance of power has changed. Certain lineages were therefore vying for influence within the larger lineage. Some felt that they gained nothing from having supported UDUB, for example, and so switched allegiance. There was also tactical selection of candidates and voting. In some cases the parties sought to undermine support for opposition candidates by selecting a close relative to run against them. Ministers promoted candidates from within their own clans and one minister is even alleged to have supported three candidates from the three parties from within his clan. In nominating candidates, clan

---

[23] Interviews by author, Hargeysa and Gabiley, September and October 2005.

leaders had to be able to assess the numbers of votes they could muster. It happened that some sub-clans did not gain any seats because they had several candidates in different parties which spread the vote too thinly.

The ambition of the candidates themselves was also important in the nomination process. Nominees had to consider both party and clan affiliation, with the latter normally being the deciding factor. However, some candidates refused to join the party that their clan supported, which split the clan. Others switched parties during the campaign, making light of party loyalty. While some relied on their clans to finance their campaigns, others invested significant resources of their own. Some candidates reportedly ran up bills as high as US$200,000 on advertising, renting premises where their supporters could meet, providing *qaad*, or paying off the debts of voters.[24] Several of the candidates were recent returnees from the diaspora, bringing money and support from abroad.

Their reliance on clans for finance and votes meant that most candidates stood for election in the regions where their clans are populous and campaigned in the districts where they are a majority. There were a few, however, who stood on a so-called 'national ticket'. One example was the owner of the Ambassador Hotel, one of Hargeysa's new luxury hotels, who could draw on his personal wealth to do this. Prior to the election the candidates and their parties moved large numbers of people to vote in the region of their clan, particularly out of Hargeysa. Consequently, the vote in Woqooyi Galbeed declined as a percentage of the overall vote (see Table 8.1). As clan territories extend across the border to Ethiopia, the candidates and parties also campaigned there and organised for people living there to vote in Somaliland. The movement of voters, which occurred peacefully, required considerable organisation by the candidates, their clans and the parties. There is evidence that some candidates with sufficient resources to transport large numbers of voters to their constituencies were able in this way to tip the vote in their favour (APD 2006: 41).

The candidates and their clans were therefore the driving forces in the campaigns, rather than the parties from whom they received very little financial support. As a campaign required personal wealth or resources within the clan, this discriminated against aspiring candidates who were less well off or from 'minority' clans. Inevitably, women candidates were one of the casualties of this system. Women in Somaliland have been making gradual inroads into formal politics since 2002, with three women appointed to the cabinet and two elected as district councillors. But after the proposal to grant women a quota of parliamentary seats failed to win Parliament's approval, women were left with no alternative but to compete with men for election. Unlike male candidates the women were selected by the parties rather than proposed by the clan. But as women could not guarantee clan support there was no incentive for the

---

[24] Interviews by author, Hargeysa and Gabiley, September and October 2005.

parties to select female candidates and only seven of 246 candidates in the parliamentary elections were women.[25]

Clan politics may have overridden issue-based politics. Nevertheless, the large number of candidates and the active participation of the clans did give a sense of broad public participation in the election. The nature of political debate linked local district and regional politics to national politics. Rather than Hargeysa dominating the national debate, local politics had an influence on national-level politics in a way not dissimilar to the clan conferences in the 1990s.

The election results

On 29 September 2005 people in Somaliland voted in the first parliamentary election since the election for the National Assembly of the Somali Republic in 1969. A total of 670,320 valid votes were counted. This was less than half the 1.3 million ballot papers that were printed for the election, but considerably higher than in the previous two elections, with over 182,000 more votes counted than in the presidential election (see Table 8.1). The higher turn-out can be accounted for partly by the increase in polling stations (from 900 in the presidential elections to 985 in the parliamentary elections), and the timing of the poll, which meant that pastoralists were grazing their herds in Somaliland during the parliamentary elections. A substantial number of people from Ethiopia and Djibouti may also have participated, which could account for regional variations in voting, although there is no hard evidence for this.

Table 8.1 Regional Votes in Somaliland's Three Elections

Region	District 2002	%	Presidential 2003	%	Parliamentary 2005	%
W/Galbeed	186,383	42	208,864	43	253,229	38
Awdal	100,495	23	65,934	13	133,026	20
Sahil	27,234	6	30,537	6	52,479	7
Togdheer	66,598	15	115,064	24	121,751	17
Sanaag	53,096	12	57,938	12	89,286	15
Sool	6,261	2	9,702	2	20,557	3
Total	440,067		488,039		670,328	

Sources: Bradbury *et al.* 2003; National Electoral Commission 2005

When the results were announced by the NEC on 14 October and confirmed by the Supreme Court on 1 November,[26] all the parties could claim some success. The ruling UDUB party repeated its successes of the

---

[25] UCID three, UDUB two, Kulmiye two.

[26] The Somaliland constitution allows for a grace period before the final confirmation, during which parties can raise objections.

Table 8.2 Parliamentary Election Results 2005

Party	Total Votes	% of vote	Parliamentary Seats
UDUB	261,449	39	33
Kulmiye	228,328	34	28
UCID	180,551	27	21
Total	670,328	100	82

Source: National Electoral Commission 2005

previous elections by winning the popular vote and returning the largest number of MPs – thirty-three. Kulmiye came second with twenty-eight and UCID third with twenty-one (see Table 8.2). This made UDUB the largest party in Parliament, but with a combined opposition of forty-nine seats it did not command a majority. This ended UDUB's monopoly over Somaliland's political institutions and, uniquely in Africa, means that the ruling party in Somaliland does not control the legislature.[27]

While all three parties saw their total vote increase, UCID made the most gains, winning parliamentary seats in all regions and beating Kulmiye into third place in Sahil. This was a significant development for UCID, which had come a poor third in the district elections, positioning the party as a potential power broker. Kulmiye lost ground in terms of the popular vote in Sahil, Togdheer, Sanaag and Sool regions, but it picked up a majority of the parliamentary seats from Togdheer and, perhaps more importantly, the majority in Woqooyi Galbeed, including Hargeysa. The relative fall in the popular vote for Kulmiye probably reflects the strength of the Habar Yunis vote: this clan increased its representation in parliament. Compared to the presidential elections, UDUB lost support in Woqooyi Galbeed and Togdheer, but gained votes in Awdal, where its vote increased by more than 70 per cent from the presidential election. The high vote in Awdal, Riyale's region, has added significance because it was the only region where UDUB won a majority of votes.

Table 8.3 Seats Won by the Political Parties by Region

	UDUB	Kulmiye	UCID	*Total All Parties*
W/Galbeed	6	8	6	20
Awdal	7	3	3	13
Sahil	4	2	4	10
Togdheer	5	6	4	15
Sanaag	5	5	2	12
Sool	6	4	2	12
Total Seats	33	28	21	82

Source: National Electoral Commission 2005.

[27] This is always a possibility in some democratic systems, such as the US.

Choosing politics over violence

It has been argued that the main reason for adopting an electoral system in Somaliland was to create a mechanism for peacefully changing the country's leadership, since the *shir beeleed* could no longer serve that purpose.[28] In early 2003, the UN regional information service predicted that the presidential elections would 'either demonstrate Somaliland's political maturity, or lead to fighting' (IRIN 2003, 17 January). Fears of violence proved to be unfounded. The peaceful manner in which the elections were conducted and the legal resolution of the tightly fought presidential contest demonstrated again the readiness of people in Somaliland to negotiate political change without resort to violence. When the presidential results were contested, the public made clear its opposition to violence as a way of dealing with the issue. Elders, businessmen, religious leaders and civic activists, through forums such as the Integrity Watch Committee, stepped in to mediate and advise the parties to settle the matter peacefully. Although the government's actions to manage the situation by invoking emergency laws and harassing opposition sympathisers were troubling (African Rights 2003), the lack of public support for mass protests illustrated the limited power of political parties to mobilise public opinion. In a country where the government, of whatever hue, can offer little in terms of public services, this is perhaps not surprising. And, given the marginal difference in the vote, no party could claim a moral victory. The decision by Kulmiye to contest the presidential election results through the courts showed a determination to settle political differences through constitutional means and illustrated how the political system had matured since the 1994–6 civil war. This contrasted with Puntland, where a constitutional crisis in 2001 led to two years of internal strife, and southern Somalia, where the TNG was being opposed militarily by the Ethiopian-backed SRRC.

As with previous political events in Somaliland, the three elections were financed substantially from local resources. The government spent US$2.4 million on the district council and presidential elections, and a smaller amount on the parliamentary elections (APD 2006: 45). The funds, which amounted to roughly 10 per cent of the annual budget, had been collected for this purpose over a number of years from municipal revenues, demonstrating a long-term commitment by the political elite to a form of constitutionally based democracy. Constructive engagement by international donors illustrated the benefits of limited technical support and financial assistance to such processes where a local commitment exists, and again contrasts with the millions of dollars spent on peace conferences for Somalia, with no such commitment.

---

[28] Interview with Mohamed Hassan Gaani, APD, August 2003.

The conduct of the elections

After thirty years in which people had no right to choose their government freely, people in Somaliland exercised their democratic rights by voting in large numbers. All of the elections were deemed to be reasonably free and fair by international observers (Abokor *et al.* 2003; 2005). Indeed some observers considered them to be amongst the freest and most transparent democratic exercises ever staged in the Horn of Africa (ICG 2003). The NEC demonstrated a great capacity to manage such a complex task and asserted its independence and neutrality with increasing confidence. Despite accusations of foul play in the presidential elections, a report by the International Crisis Group on the election noted that there was no evidence 'to substantiate claims that the outcome was rigged or that the commission bowed to political pressure' (*ibid.*: 25)

The elections were not faultless. Despite the efforts put into voter education, the government, the parties and the public clearly had difficulty in adhering to international electoral norms. From its foundation, UDUB was accused of using the prerogatives of its incumbency as the ruling party to take advantage of its access to government resources and the media. The government's appointment of 'ballot box ministers' prior to the elections established a negative precedent and expanded an already bloated bureaucracy. Ministers' use of government resources to support their candidates, and the openness with which candidates courted supporters by providing *qaad* or paying off debts was tantamount to vote buying. Attempts at double voting, underage voting and the transportation of people by the parties were all observed in places on polling day and revived memories among older citizens of election campaigns in the 1960s.[29] The process of counting votes was very open, but the delay this caused in announcing the results provided opportunities for disputes to develop between the parties, with calls for recounts and the disqualification of ballots in some areas.[30] This left lingering doubts over the final results. While technical and procedural problems can be overcome with more experience, training and supervision, the inculcation of internationally accepted democratic practices among politicians and voters will require changes in attitude among the parties and their leaders.

The lack of a census and voter registration makes it difficult to ascertain the impact of such practices on the results. However, marked variations in regional voting between the three elections raises some difficult questions, particularly in Awdal and Togdheer, which were politically important regions for the two main parties. In the President's home region, Awdal, the vote swung from 23 per cent of the national vote

---

[29] Interviews by author, 2003, Hargeysa.

[30] After polling day, two full weeks elapsed before the parliamentary results were announced.

down to 13 per cent and back up to 20 per cent in the three elections (see Table 8.1). The turn-out increased across Somaliland in the parliamentary elections, but was greatest by far in Awdal Region. The increase was linked to the high number of votes in the remote districts of Baki, Lughaya and Zeyla. The commission queried the results, after allegations of vote rigging, but stopped short of annulling the vote (APD 2006: 40). Togdheer was almost the mirror opposite (Bradbury *et al.* 2003). There, the vote swung from 15 per cent of the total vote in the district election to 24 per cent in the presidential election and back to 17 per cent in the parliamentary election. In Salahley District, a UCID stronghold, the vote fell by 10,000 between district and presidential elections. Given that UCID was awarded third place in the local elections over SAHAN by a small margin, clearly such disparities could have affected the contest to become the third party. Such large swings in votes could not be accounted for by seasonal variations in the timing of the elections, changes in polling station supervision or the movement of people within Somaliland or from Ethiopia. At the very least, it reinforced the need for voter registration.

Winners and losers

Developing a system of political representation that satisfies all has been a key governance challenge in post-war Somaliland. Political representation is amongst the most contentious issues in Somali society, with claims to representation variously based on different interpretations of genealogical position, or the relative size or geographical distribution of the clans. The *beel* system provided one solution, establishing a form of consociational arrangement that gave all communities a stake in the state, although not everyone was satisfied with the allocation of parliamentary seats and this was a factor in Somaliland's civil war. The constitution established an alternative system for managing political competition and popular representation, moving responsibility for selecting a government from an electoral college of elders to individual citizens. Given the relatively small number of invalid votes (around 2 per cent) in the elections, the results can be considered a fair representation of voter opinion and preference.[31] A key issue is whether this system will give the communities a sufficient stake in the state and sustain a balance of power that has provided the basis for Somaliland's stability.

Over 60 per cent of all the votes in the elections were cast in Somaliland's three western regions, and most of these were in Woqooyi Galbeed, which incorporates Hargeysa. Better transport and infrastructure, shorter

[31] The NEC's turn-out figures are based on validated voting forms. If cases of under-age voting, ballot stuffing and double voting are considered, they probably give us only an approximation of the actual turn-out. Interestingly the turn-out in the elections was much lower than the 1.18 million figure the government claimed in the constitutional referendum.

Table 8.4 Distribution of Seats by Clan and Party

Clans	UDUB	Kulmiye	UCID	Total Seats
Sa'ad Muse	2	5	2	9
'Iise Muse	3	1	3	7
Habar Yunis	8	1	8	17
'Idagalle			2	2
Habar Ja'lo	5	9	2	16
Arab	2	3		5
Ayuub		1		1
Gadabursi	7	3	3	13
'Iise	1			1
Warsengeli	2	2		4
Dhulbahante	2	3	1	6
Hawiye-Fiqishini	1			1
Total Seats	33	28	21	82

Source: Haroon Ahmed Yusuf, Hargeysa 2005.

distances for voters to travel, better media coverage, more intense campaigning and voter education, a more sedentary population – all these factors facilitated a higher turn-out in the west. But it also reflected the larger population in the west and the growth of the capital Hargeysa since the war. In part, the smaller number of votes in the three eastern regions of Togdheer, Sanaag and Sool can be accounted for by the non-participation of parts of eastern Sanaag and Sool regions (with Sool accounting for only 2 to 3 per cent of the total vote: see Table 8.1), and the smaller, more nomadic population in the east. It also indicates that the elections were largely urban events. While efforts were made to extend the election coverage to rural areas, a large percentage of the nomadic rural population (*reer miyi*), estimated to represent up to 50 per cent of the country's total population, did not participate in the elections.

Non-Isaaq clans had been represented in both the executive and legislative wings of government since 1991, and after 1997 minority clans and the Gabooye gained seats in the legislature. The change from the *beel* system to a majoritarian electoral system produced 'winners' and 'losers' and changed the nature of representation in Somaliland's political institutions. The limitation set on the number of parties is intended to reduce the influence of the clan in politics, but not surprisingly voters were influenced by clan loyalty. Consequently, the composition of elected district councils reflected the main clans in the district. There is evidence that candidates of major lineages (*laan-dheere*) were favoured in the party lists over those from smaller lineages (*laan-gaab*). The Gabooye won only one seat in one council. In the presidential elections party votes corresponded closely with the regional and clan origins of the party leaders. In the parliamentary elections this was less clear, as the parties received support in all regions and across all clans. Nevertheless, the

Table 8.5 Change in Clan-Family Composition in Parliament

Clan-families	Old Parliament	New Parliament
Isaaq	48	57
Gadabursi	11	13
'Iise	5	1
Dhulbahante	9	6
Warsengeli	5	4
Hawiye/Fiqishini	1	1
Minorities	4	0

Source: Haroon Ahmed Yusuf, Hargeysa 2005

parliamentary results pointed to a bedrock of support for UDUB among the Habar Yunis and Gadabursi, for Kulmiye among the Habar Ja'lo and Habar Awal (mostly Sa'ad Muse) and for UCID among the Habar Yunis (see Table 8.4).

The shift to a majoritarian electoral system changed the clan composition of the Parliament (see Table 8.5). The most obvious change was that Isaaq representation increased by nine seats to fifty-seven. The Gadabursi gained two seats. However, the Dhulbahante and Warsengeli of Sool and eastern Sanaag regions lost four seats. The results left Parliament dominated by the Isaaq and Gadabursi, which will exacerbate the Harti sense of marginalisation within Somaliland. The 'Iise saw their seats reduced from five to one, partly because 'Iise candidates withdrew from the elections shortly before polling day. It also reflects a gradual withdrawal of 'Iise people from Somaliland to Djibouti, where they predominate (APD 2006). The biggest losers were the 'minorities' (including the Gabooye, Somali-Arabs, Jibrahil and Gugure) who lost all of their seats in the legislature (see Table 8.5).

Changes also occurred in the representation of the Isaaq clan-family. The number of seats held by the three largest clans increased, with the Habar Awal (Sa'ad Muse and 'Iise Muse), Garhajis (Habar Yunis and 'Idagalle) and Habar Ja'lo together winning fifty-one seats, while the smaller Arab and Ayuub clans saw theirs reduced. Within the Isaaq the most significant change was in the increased representation of the Habar Yunis in Parliament (see Table 8.4). Together with the 'Idagalle, the Garhajis won over 20 per cent of the seats; they have representation from across Somaliland and, with the exception of Awdal Region, are potentially the single largest 'clan block' of votes in Parliament.[32] A shift in Habar Yunis allegiance from UDUB to UCID also made UCID into a serious third party contender. In 1993 the Habar Yunis perception that they were under-represented in Parliament was one of the grievances behind Somaliland's civil war. The equitable representation of the three major Isaaq clans should mitigate such clan-based conflicts. It is notable,

[32] Even in Hargeysa three Habar Yunis candidates were elected, which is surprising given that they are more populous in Togdheer.

however, that only one of the seventeen Habar Yunis MPs elected to Parliament is in Kulmiye (APD 2006: 42), which points to a lingering political cleavage. Other changes were apparent at the level of sub-clans. Some of the larger (*laan-dheere*) and politically stronger lineages lost ground to smaller (*laan-gaab*) lineages, partly because they fielded too many candidates. The impact of these changes will only become apparent over time, but while clan politics continues to influence the political system, the representative nature of that system will continue to be judged by people in lineage terms, rather than in terms of government policies.

Women were again at the mercy of patriarchal clan politics. In all three elections they exercised their constitutional right to vote by doing so in large numbers. They also participated in the organisation, management and monitoring of the elections, and as activists in the political parties. But women candidates had little chance of being elected. In the district elections, no women candidates were ranked higher than seven on the party lists and only two women from over 2,000 candidates were elected onto a council. Accordingly, women – although they constitute a majority of the voting public, and contribute significantly to local government revenues through their small businesses – have no direct voice in these councils. The parties became conscious that women are a large constituency that could not be ignored and, following his electoral success, President Riyale appointed three women to senior positions in his government, as Minister of Foreign Affairs, Minister of the Family, and Director General in the Ministry of the Family.

Women had everything to gain from the parliamentary elections, there being no women MPs. But only two of the seven women that stood in the elections became MPs; one was elected, and the other got in on a reserved seat. The lack of wider success convinced those pressing for women's participation in politics that as long as the kinship system remains so influential women will not be elected to Parliament. They thus conclude that more can be obtained from a quota system, which has given women in Puntland and Somalia a larger representation in their respective parliaments. In their assessment of the elections civic groups stated:

> [In] a clan-based society struggling to transform itself into a multi-party democracy a quota for women is the only solution to advance the participation of women who essentially contributed to peace building and economic reconstruction and rehabilitation of this country. (NAGAAD et al. 2005)

The biggest challenge to the legitimacy of the Somaliland elections and the representative nature of the political system came from the Warsengeli and the Dhulbahante areas of eastern Sanaag and Sool. Threats from the Puntland authorities and their supporters to disrupt the polls left the NEC with no option but to 'postpone' elections in several districts in Sool and eastern Sanaag.[33] A significant proportion of the population living within the borders claimed by Somaliland therefore did not vote. This has important implications for the territory. The democratisation process was seen by many voters as strengthening Somaliland's chances of recognition. The district election was an important step towards institutionalising the state of Somaliland by creating popular councils that recognised the authority of the government in Hargeysa and paid taxes to it, and by practically defining the limits of the state. The election of a non-Isaaq president gave credence to the claim that Somaliland is a multi-clan polity. The parliamentary election changed this. The non-participation of most of the population of Sool and eastern Sanaag regions, and the decline in parliamentary seats in these areas, served to shrink the size of the polity and make Somaliland politics more exclusive. Some Harti simply dismissed the elections as 'Dir elections'.[34] It appears that the parties insisted on holding the poll in some parts of Sool Region against the judgement of the NEC, so as to bolster the number of their own seats (APD 2006: 27–9). In those areas where polling occurred the results were clearly not representative of the local population. In the parliamentary elections all six of the seats allocated to Sool were won by Isaaq candidates. The non-participation of the populations in these regions cannot be addressed satisfactorily by appointing Warsengeli and Dhulbahante to positions in the administration. Undeniably, the lack of local representative political structures that are loyal to Somaliland weakens the government's claim to represent people in these regions.[35] The domination of the elected institutions by certain groups reinforces the perception of a political system that has 'winners' and 'losers'. Ironically, the elections, which were supposed to enhance Somaliland's recognition claims, made it more difficult for Somaliland to present itself as a multi-clan polity. Furthermore, the denial of representation to minor clans and women does not augur well for the future of representative democracy.

The political parties

The elections restored party politics as a legitimate way for managing society's varied concerns. However, kinship has historically been the

---

[33] In the district elections the Hormood party claimed success in Dahar District in eastern Sanaag with an unopposed list of candidates, but no voting took place in Badhan or Las Qoray. In Sool polling took place in Aynabo, and ASAD claimed success in Hudun District, but no voting took place in Las Anod or Taleh. As district councils have not been formed in Dahar or Hudun, it is doubtful whether elections took place there at all.

[34] Meaning they were elections for the Isaaq and Gadabursi only. The Dir include the Gadabursi and 'Iise, and, depending on perspective, can include Isaaq. Interviews by author, Las Anod, 2002.

[35] At the last minute five 'Iise candidates from Zeyla area withdrew from the elections after they were refused a quota of seats in Parliament.

basis for political organisation and Somalis have little experience of organising along political party lines. The first Somali parties, like the Somali Youth League, were driven by Somali nationalism, but after independence this dissipated into more parochial clan concerns. Under the military regime political parties were proscribed. Somaliland's parties are weak institutions that have shown little life outside of the election campaigns and largely appear to be vehicles for the ambitions of their leaders. The scramble by politicians after the district elections for posts in the new national parties, and the alliances of convenience that were formed, illustrated the absence of loyalty to the parties and their policies. The parties' links with and control over members elected in their name to the district councils have been tenuous. Unless party organisation and practices change, it is likely that the same leaders will continue to contest the presidential elections and prevent other candidates from competing. Now that they are the lawmakers, there will be little incentive for the parties to change.

Although the elections established political parties as an alternative form of political association to the clan, the influence of clan loyalty on voting was clear. It will be instructive to see whether MPs vote in Parliament along party or clan lines. Because the parties did not bring their candidates together to formulate policy during the campaigns, it will be hard for them to enforce discipline over them. As the party leaders did not stand in the parliamentary elections they may find it difficult to enforce adherence among their MPs to party policies from outside Parliament. Limited party resources will also make it difficult to ensure party loyalty. For the candidates, the parties were a legal mechanism for entering parliament. One of the few forms of leverage that the parties have over their MPs is to refuse to re-nominate those who do not follow the party line. At the beginning of the first session of the new Parliament UCID removed one MP from their party for voting with UDUB (Jama 2006). After the presidential elections it was unclear whether the President and his administration governed in the name of UDUB and in accordance with its manifesto. The Head of Mobilisation for UDUB implied that this was not the case when he commented after the presidential election that 'UDUB has a manifesto, but it is not applicable now'.[36] It is not surprising, therefore, that the political parties elicited a degree of public cynicism. Comparing the current parties with those of the past, one Somali political analyst noted:

> With the SYL [Somali Youth League] and SNM people were paying membership and contributing to the formation of those parties. Now it appears the other way around. Votes are purchased by the parties.[37]

The parties are also likely to come under public pressure for reform. Women and civic organisations will urge them to review their policies on

[36] Interviewed by author in Hargeysa, August 2003.
[37] Author's interview with Abdi Yusuf Duale, APD, Hargeysa, August 2003.

women candidates and make changes to their structures, policies and political agendas that will ensure the participation of women and minorities in politics (NAGAAD et al. 2005). A debate continues in Somaliland on the validity of a three-party system in a plural democracy. While the parties themselves are unlikely to push for a change, there is likely to be popular pressure for the system to be reviewed (see Chapter 9).

Democratisation & state-building

The road to a popularly elected government in Somaliland has been long. By the end of 2005, Somaliland could boast that it had most of the attributes of a democratic state: a constitution that enabled a peaceful transfer of power following the death of the head of state and guards civil liberties; democratically elected institutions; a government in which the executive and legislative branches of government are controlled by different political parties; and active civic organisations. But elections are a means to an end and Somaliland faces many challenges when putting democracy into practice. A measure of its democracy will be the way in which Somaliland's elected institutions function and are utilised by the parties and the public. The future of the *Guurti*, its role and the mechanism for selecting its membership remain to be settled; to date, only half of the legislature has been elected. Democracy in Somaliland will also hinge upon the manner in which the political parties develop and the relationship they negotiate with the government and the public at large.

In 1999, President Egal argued that democratisation would facilitate international recognition of Somaliland. Although the parties campaigned on a pro-independence platform and many Somalilanders saw voting as a patriotic act, the elections were not solely put on for an external audience or for advancing aspirations to independence. They were also intended to effect a change in the internal balance of power. Having staged three elections, the commitment of the Somaliland people and the political elite to a democratic form of politics cannot easily be questioned or ignored. Foreign donors supported the elections, contributing up to 70 per cent of the costs of the parliamentary elections, but Somalilanders themselves invested substantially in all three elections, which were locally managed and adapted to local culture. The elections were also part of the ongoing process of building state institutions and were another expression of people's desire and ability to manage their own affairs. This has implications for the status of Somaliland and its relationship with Somalia.

The elections further institutionalised Somaliland's separation from Somalia and highlighted the gap between Somaliland's elected government and the non-elected TFG, which at the time of the parliamentary election was failing to sustain a semblance of parliamentary consensus.

The international community supported the elections and, following the parliamentary elections, Somaliland's achievements were recognised by the Arab League, the US and (through the Secretary-General's Special Representative for Somalia) the UN. After all its circumspection, the UN commended people in Somaliland 'for the progress they have made towards security and true democracy' (UNPOS 2005). Internally, Somaliland's biggest challenge lies in the eastern regions, where a sizeable section of the population lacks the commitment to Somaliland. It will also be important for people in Somaliland to see the benefits of democracy through foreign investment in the country's infrastructure and services. A lack of such support for a democratic Somaliland would not go unnoticed in neighbouring countries, or other Islamic countries in the region. There is also an expectation that the democratic institutions now established should stand the country in good stead when building bilateral relations. Lack of progress in this regard may reduce appetite in Somaliland for further democratic reform.

The Practice **9** of Government

The protracted nature of state collapse in Somalia is commonly described as being rooted in a 'crisis of government'. The declaration of independence in 1991 provided people in Somaliland with an opportunity to break with the repressive form of government that Somalis had experienced over the previous two decades. With the holding of three multi-party elections between 2002 and 2005, people in Somaliland have demonstrated a capacity for self-government and non-violent politics. But elections are a means to an end – the end being a functioning democratic state. Democratisation of the political system is an ongoing process. Having successfully held three elections there is still a need to reform and refine the electoral laws; to reform the judicial system; to empower local government; and to enhance the role of civic organisations in shaping policy and holding government to account. The gradual institutionalisation of government not only reinforces Somaliland's political separation from Somalia but also strengthens its claim to be treated as a *de facto* state. This chapter examines the evolving practices of government in Somaliland and some of the governance reforms that have occurred in the process of state formation.

The structure of government

Somaliland's structure of government fuses a US-style executive President with a British-style bicameral Parliament. The decision to have an executive President rather than Prime Minister was made at the 1991 Burco conference, and broke with the model of government adopted by Somalia in 1960.[1] The structure was further elaborated in the Transitional National Charter adopted at the 1993 Borama conference and accommodated clan-based representation within Western-style political

---

[1] It also differs from that elaborated in the Transitional Federal Charter agreed to by parties in the Somalia National Reconciliation Process in 2004.

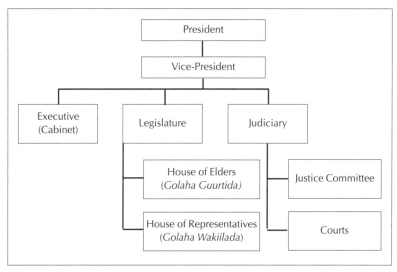

Figure 9.1 Structure of Somaliland's Government

institutions. This structure of government, which was confirmed in the constitution, comprises three branches: an executive President who nominates a cabinet of ministers, subject to parliamentary approval; a legislature with a bicameral Parliament consisting of an upper House of Elders and a lower House of Representatives; and a judiciary (see Figure 9.1). In the *beel* system, clan representation was explicit in the composition of both houses of the legislature and in the executive.[2] The key change introduced by the constitution was the method of selection, subjecting the President and members of the legislature to election by secret ballot in a 'free general election' (Article 40). It is implicit, but not spelt out in the constitution, that the President and members of the House of Representatives should be members of one of the three accredited national political parties. By late 2005 all of Somaliland's political institutions, with the exception of the *Guurti*, had been publicly elected.

Somaliland's US-style constitution provides a legal framework for governance, but leaves plenty of room for interpretation. Ambiguity remains over the roles of different branches of government and the division of responsibilities between the government and both Houses of Parliament. Many by-laws are required to clarify its articles, and until this happens some of the gaps in the law will be filled by customary practices. The experience of the elections has given rise to calls for a constitutional review to address a number of issues, such as the ceiling on political

[2] The constitution also makes provision for the creation of a committee of religious scholars (*Ulema*) who are responsible for clarifying and issuing guidelines on matters of religion. To date this committee has not been active in the affairs of the state.

parties and a quota for women MPs. Nevertheless, the constitution has been used increasingly to provide guidance and rules for governing and to resolve political disputes, even in the absence of a constitutional court. In 2002, it was used to facilitate the smooth transfer of power from the late President Egal to his Vice-President Riyale, and in resolving the contested presidential election results.

The executive

As defined in the constitution, the President is the head of state, directly elected every five years, for a maximum of two terms. The next presidential election is due in 2008. One issue that has to be resolved is whether incumbent President Dahir Riyale Kahin will be eligible to stand again. He has only been elected once, but some interpret his one-year 'caretaker presidency' as his first term.

The President is the head of the Council of Ministers whose membership, duties and functions are described in the constitution (Articles 80–96). They include drafting legislation, setting budgets, managing national security and appointing cabinet ministers and senior officers of the state. In 1993, designating Parliament as the forum for clan representation should have relieved pressure on the President to prioritise the clan balance of the cabinet, permitting instead the meritocratic selection of ministers. This did not happen. Both Egal and Riyale have fallen back on clan patronage to shore up support. Since 1993, the number of ministers has risen from nineteen to over thirty. Riyale's appointment of two women to his first post-election cabinet, including Edna Adan to the Ministry of Foreign Affairs, was widely welcomed as an astute move, but has been criticised from within and outside government for failing to fulfil his pledge to create a lean government.[3] In his defence, he has argued that he inherited his ministers from his predecessor.[4] But, as we saw in Chapter 8, for example, the practice of appointing regional 'ballot box' ministers to raise support during elections only serves to expand an administration that is a heavy burden on the state budget. Riyale has also been publicly accused of nepotism in his choice of ministers; while Egal had been a master of dispensing political patronage, he was not accused of favouring his own family or clan.

The choice of ministers is not entirely the responsibility of the President, however, as appointments are in theory subject to parliamentary approval. So there is a degree of bargaining over key cabinet positions between clans, ministers and Parliament. Criticism of Riyale's administration arose partly because the channels of patronage changed. Conse-

---

[3] Author's interviews with the Ministry of Foreign Affairs, Ministry of Commerce and UDUB, Hargeysa, August 2003.
[4] Interview by author with President Riyale, Hargeysa, September 2003.

quently certain individuals, and their clans, who had enjoyed benefits under Egal lost out under Riyale. Clan is not the only vehicle for patronage; common membership of a religious sect or shared experience in school or workplace can also be significant. Riyale has appointed former colleagues in the NSS to positions of authority in his government, including the Head of Internal Security. This form of patronage can affect the legislative process. After the presidential and parliamentary elections, for example, relations between the President and Parliament became strained when Parliament failed to confirm several ministerial appointments (Jama 2006: 5–6). Lack of confirmation did not prevent the ministers from holding office, but it raised questions over the legality of their positions and policies emanating from their office. The responsibility of Parliament in confirming presidential appointments is therefore one area that requires clarification.

A key responsibility of ministers and Parliament, according to the constitution (Article 77), is to initiate legislation, which is subjected to scrutiny and parliamentary approval. The President should present an annual legislative programme and budget to Parliament in a 'state of the nation' speech at the start of each calendar year, but up to 2005 this had not happened. With the oversight of an elected legislature, the government will be under pressure to do so in the future. Policy formulation and decision-making within government is often *ad hoc* and based on the personal initiative of a minister. It is not unusual for the President, or one of his ministers, to issue a decree without cabinet consultation and sometimes in contradiction to policy elsewhere in government. With an opposition majority in Parliament, it will be more difficult for the President or his cabinet colleagues to govern by decree, and they will be under pressure to follow proper procedures and channels for drafting and approving legislation. In 2006, for example, a presidential decree extending the tenure of the *Guurti* created a constitutional crisis.

The legislature

The original membership of Somaliland's two legislative houses was derived from the 150 voting delegates at the 1993 Borama conference. The membership of each house was increased to 82 at the 1997 Hargeysa conference, to accommodate the concerns of the opposition and to incorporate representatives of minority clans. Membership of the Lower House was substantially changed through the elections, while membership of the Upper remains much the same, except for members who have replaced those who have died.

The Upper House of Elders (Golaha Guurtida)
Somaliland's Upper House of Elders is a unique government institution in Africa. Comprising elders of Somali clans, it blends modern political

institutions with traditional forms of political organisation. Its origins lie in the SNM's war against Siyad Barre, when a *Guurti* was established to mobilise the Isaaq people for the struggle. Its mediation in 1992 brought Somaliland back from the brink of civil war and since it was formalised in the 1993 Borama Charter as a legislative Upper House, it has emerged as the supreme moral authority in Somaliland, providing a check on the power of the Executive and the Lower House. The integration of traditional authorities in the post-war administration of the state was intended to guard against the re-emergence of authoritarian rule. In the 1993 Charter its responsibilities were to protect the traditions of Somaliland and to maintain peace and security. These roles were formalised further in the Constitution (Article 61), and expanded to include initiating legislation on religion and culture and reviewing legislation initiated by the Council of Ministers and the Lower House.

Members of the *Guurti* believe that it was they who brought peace to Somaliland and that they continue to play this role around the country. They mediate relations not only between the President and the Lower House, but between society and government.[5] The public recognises the role that the *Guurti* played in mobilising the population in the war against Siyad Barre and in shepherding Somaliland through the minefields of post-war politics and state-building. However, as we saw in Chapter 5, this public reputation was tarnished by its failure to mediate in the 1994–6 civil war, while its metamorphosis into a permanent institution of government has led to accusations that it is too close to the executive.[6] The first chair of the *Guurti*, Sheikh Ibrahim Sheikh Yusuf Sheikh Madar, held considerable moral authority in the country, because he hailed from the historic religious family that founded Hargeysa. Following his death in July 2004, the veteran politician Suleiman Mohamed Aden 'Gaal' was appointed as the new chair. In the view of some, this has further politicised the *Guurti* and undermined its neutrality (APD 2006: 14). A controversial politician, who both served in Egal's government and was his vocal critic, Suleiman 'Gaal', as noted in Chapter 8, came to the *Guurti* after supporting UDUB in the presidential election. In the parliamentary election his support of UDUB is said to have split the vote of his own Habar Ja'lo clan.

The members of the Upper House were nominated by their clans at the 1993 and 1997 clan conferences,[7] and after the elections to the Lower House it remained the only unelected legislative institution. The constitution leaves open for debate and legislation the question of the

---

[5] Interview by author with Secretary to the *Guurti*, Hargeysa, August 2003.

[6] In 2001, opposition to Egal's government found expression in an *ad hoc* Council of Sultans, which challenged the authority of the Egal administration to hold elections. But while Sultans have played a role in nominating clan representatives to the legislature and mediating between clans, they do not have a constitutional role.

[7] The *Guurti* also has honorary members, such as the former Vice-President Abdulrahman Aw Ali, and before his death the former President Abdulrahman 'Tuur'.

basis and method by which the *Guurti* should be selected in future.[8] The constitutional responsibilities of the *Guurti* also need clarification. In the decade since it was created the Upper House has commented on legislation, but only initiated one bill. Among the public there is a view that its members lack the capacity to fulfil their legislative responsibilities and that these should therefore be restricted.

The approaching expiry date of its mandate – October 2006 – brought urgency to the debate on how the *Guurti* should be formed: whether it should be elected, nominated, or reconstituted, with a different make-up and responsibilities. In the immediate aftermath of the parliamentary elections, there appeared to be a consensus emerging among the parties, the NEC and the public that the *Guurti* should remain a nominated body, although the selection process needed to be agreed.[9] It was felt that the country could not afford another election immediately and that the *Guurti* should be retained in its existing form as a place where smaller clans and minorities with no representation in Parliament – including women, some thought – could be represented. During the first year of the new Parliament, the *Guurti* was expected to play an important role in helping it to settle in. Indeed, *Guurti* mediation skills were called upon immediately when Parliament opened on 28 November, after a dispute erupted between the government and opposition parties over the election of the Speaker and his two deputies (Abokor *et al.* 2005: 24). The *Guurti* interceded and the opposition's candidates were duly elected.

Hopes of reaching quick consensus on the matter were upset in May 2006 when a presidential decree, issued without consultation, extended the tenure of the *Guurti* for a further four years. The justification was that the country did not have the resources or capacity to hold another election, and that the extension would allow time for the requisite legislation to be drawn up (APD 2006: 49). The *Guurti* concurred and voted to extend its own mandate. The episode polarised opinion in Parliament and provoked a constitutional crisis (Jama 2006: 7–8). For the opposition, the key concern was the length of the extension and the manner in which it was granted without reference to the Lower House. The President's actions not only challenged the authority of Parliament but also aligned the *Guurti* with the government. This displeased the parties, because the *Guurti* has constitutional power to extend the term of the President without an election if conditions do not allow for one to be held. The opposition in Parliament threatened not to recognise the authority of the *Guurti* after its mandate expired in October 2006. By the end of 2006, the external threat from the rise of the Islamic Courts appeared to be pushing the parties towards some compromise agreement on an extension, although agreement on a selection process for the *Guurti* was still to be settled.

As people in Somaliland experiment with democratic multi-party

---

[8] Nominations at the clan conferences were managed by a *shir-gudoon* (a 'chairing committee'), whose impartiality was questioned during the Hargeysa conference.

[9] Interviews by author with the chairmen of UCID, Kulmiye and NEC, Hargeysa, October 2003.

politics, they will be challenged to maintain and incorporate the positive attributes of a pastoral democracy – consensus building, mediation, arbitration – within the system of government. The *Guurti* has been at the heart of the clan-based power-sharing and consensual politics that has sustained stability in Somaliland. Although the conservative nature of the *Guurti* may rankle with modernisers, the way it fuses modern political institutions with traditional political organisation reflects, to some extent, the original vision of the SNM for governance in Somali society. There are many sources of legitimacy and authority in societies, and while the authority of the *Guurti* is not based on a popular vote, its authority is no less legitimate for that.

The House of Representatives (Golaha Wakiilada)
The House of Representatives was established at the 1993 Borama conference as a temporary non-party legislature, in which seats were apportioned on a clan basis, awaiting the establishment of political parties and elections. It continued as such with numerous extensions for twelve years, but with little change in membership until it became a directly elected chamber in October 2005. In the old, unelected Parliament most members were able to satisfy the minimum criterion of a secondary education, but the process of nomination lacked transparency (Jimcaale 2005). Clan leaders did not always consult broadly on nominations. Representatives were often sponsored by a small elite and were not necessarily representative of the consensus view of their clan. Individuals from the larger *laan-dheere* lineages tended to be favoured over those from smaller *laan-gaab* lineages.

The Somaliland constitution identifies the Lower House of Representatives as the main legislative chamber, similar to the British House of Commons, with the authority to initiate, amend, reject and approve legislation submitted by the Council of Ministers; to approve or reject ministerial appointments and the national budget; to impeach the President; and to propose a vote of no confidence in the Council of Ministers. One of its main functions is to act as a check on the power of the executive. The ability and confidence of Parliament to do this developed over time as the representatives gained experience, and was enhanced through the constitution. On occasions it has demonstrated real independence in the exercise of its mandate: during the drafting of the constitution; in defending the independence of the media and the judiciary; in the impeachment proceedings against President Egal in 2001; and in rejecting Riyale's first budget in 2003. In the absence of parties and policies, however, its approach tended to be one of compromise in its dealings with the Executive. Its approach to the preparation of the government's budget, for example, over which it had formal oversight, was to influence the preparatory process in order to generate a consensus that would secure the approval of the House.[10]

[10] Author's interview with the First Deputy Speaker of Parliament, August 2003.

During its first twelve years the unelected Parliament did not draft legislation itself, in part due to the lack of resources to initiate research on legislation and to publish it. The poor state of parliamentary resources was illustrated by the fact that during impeachment proceedings against Egal, the First Deputy Speaker took guidance on managing the process from internet sites that documented the impeachment of US President Richard Nixon. [11] Bills initiated by Parliament, therefore, were mostly restricted to parliamentary by-laws. One of Parliament's main achievements was to win certain concessions from the government in the constitution. However, decisions taken by the Lower House were not always perceived to be exercised in the interests of the public, and a lack of public hearings on prospective legislation meant that the legislative process itself was less than transparent. The public came to believe that the parliamentarians were easily swayed by financial incentives, and as a result they earned the derogatory name *dhaameel*.[12]

As the main legislative chamber, the Lower House potentially has considerable authority, but its ability to exercise that authority independently of the government was limited prior to the election. By producing a Parliament that is not controlled by a single party, the election of 2005 enhanced its authority and independence. It also brought about a wholesale change in its composition, with only fourteen of the old representatives re-elected. The new members were generally younger and better educated, with more professionals, members of civic organisations, members from the diaspora and, for the first time, two women. The new representatives lacked experience and were unfamiliar with the functions of Parliament, while the government faced the challenge of working with a legislature in which, for the first time, it did not hold a majority. During the elections the opposition outlined the political reforms they wanted to see (Box 9.1), changes which would bode well for Somaliland's parliamentary democracy if they could be carried out. The extent to which the political parties are able to work together to bring about these reforms will be one test of Somaliland's democracy.

The honeymoon period of the new Parliament was always likely to be turbulent as the new members and the parties negotiated their relationships with each other and with the executive. The opening of Parliament in November 2005 gave a hint of the rocky road ahead when the parties clashed over who was to control the legislature through the election of the Speaker and Deputy Speakers. Although the *Guurti* intervened to resolve the issue in favour of the opposition, the incident established an acrimonious relationship between the government and the House that peppered parliamentary business over the following twelve months. Subsequent to this, Parliament rejected several ministers, the government proved reluctant to cooperate with a review of the annual budget, and a

---

[11] Author's interview with the First Deputy Speaker of Parliament, August 2003.
[12] This is the name of the seed of an acacia tree that pastoralists feed to goats. It implies that they are persuaded by powerful interests.

Box 9.1   The Opposition Parties' Reform Agenda for Parliament[13]

• Revoking emergency laws.

• A constitution aimed at curbing the powers of the executive and reviewing the size of Parliament, the restrictions on political parties and the need for a Prime Minister.

• Impeachment of the President, openly discussed during the elections, though opposition party leaders relented when the voting was over.

• A reduction in the size of the cabinet from fifty to a maximum of eighteen ministers, with greater parliamentary oversight of appointments and the removal of unpopular ministers.

• Increased fiscal accountability and transparency in government, through greater oversight of the national budget and reviews of foreign investment contracts, fishing concessions and Berbera port management, and the establishment of a commission to tackle corruption.

• Measures to open up and stimulate the economy, including plans for the leasing of Berbera port facility.

• A review of the media law.

• An open debate on Somaliland's relationship with Somalia, and the status of the contested eastern regions.

• A review of the security sector budget, with the aim of cutting it and investing more in social services.

• Voter registration and a census – seen as essential, not only for holding elections but as part of a state-building process of defining and counting the citizens of the country.

• A review of electoral law, to consolidate and iron out contradictions in the existing legislation.

• Strengthening of local government laws for the decentralisation of government.

• A review of the role of the *Guurti*, and its appointment.

• Renewal of the mandate of the NEC.

---

crisis developed over the extension of the *Guurti*'s term of office (Jama 2006). With no party holding a monopoly of power in Parliament, negotiation, consensus and compromise will be a necessary part of parliamentary business. However, the acrimony between government and Parliament arises partly from misunderstandings of the constitutional powers and responsibilities of both parties, which will require a further elaboration of the constitution and rulings by the judiciary to resolve.

The relationship between the Lower House and civic organisations that are active in such areas as gender equality, human rights and social welfare provision will also be important in institutionalising democracy. As organisations that attract international funding, they have become

[13] Interviews, Hargeysa, October 2005.

important players in Somaliland, taking on functions that were previously the assumed responsibility of the state and mediating between society and the state. Parliament includes several MPs who were formerly active in civil society organisations. It remains to be seen whether the new Parliament proves to be more amenable to external advocacy than in the past, and whether it will actively seek opinion from these groups and defend civil liberties. In the eyes of foreign organisations and donors the significance of Parliament as a representative forum has grown as a result of the elections. During 2006, for example, Parliament persuaded the government not to reject a UN and World Bank Joint Needs Assessment in Somaliland because of its associations with the TFG,[14] and took upon itself an oversight role. In the diplomatic community, Parliament is also perceived as a potential forum through which dialogue with Somalia could be opened.

The experience of the elections has given rise to calls for a constitutional review to address a number of issues. One that will affect Parliament and test its commitment to open debate is the three-party political system. Some Somalilanders favour the restriction on parties, judging it to be a sensible approach in a society where lineage ties shape political competition. Others argue that the restriction on the number of parties contradicts the right to free association and effectively gives the three parties eternal life. Possible options of opening up the system would be to deregister any party which cannot demonstrate popular support, lifting the restriction on the number of parties contesting district elections or reducing the threshold for qualification to become an accredited party, currently 20 per cent of the vote in four regions. Another proposed constitutional amendment that is likely to be considered is a quota system for women to increase their participation in Parliament. A constitutional review process that tackles these issues in an inclusive manner would do much to enhance legitimacy of the political system.

The judiciary

Establishing the public institutions of law has been important in the process of state-building in Somaliland. The creation of a secular legal system in Somaliland, not withstanding its problems, highlights again the different trajectory of developments compared to Somalia, where Islamic courts have emerged as a dominant source of law and order. In Somaliland, alongside the formal judicial system, traditional law and the arbitration of elders continue to provide the basis of day-to-day law and order in many aspects of life in many communities. But having an effective and independent judiciary is crucial to developing a political system

---

[14] The Joint Needs Assessment (JNA) was formally initiated at the request of the TFG, which has a seat on the JNA steering committee and would potentially have an executive role in the disbursement of funds. For these reasons the Somaliland government initially refused to participate.

in which the exercise of power can be checked. The imperative for this increases with a shift to competitive multi-party politics.

Somaliland's legal system is based on the civil system inherited from pre-war Somalia,[15] and its structure and functions are defined in the Law on the Organisation of the Judiciary, adopted by Parliament in 1993. This provides for three levels of courts, with a Supreme Court in Hargeysa having jurisdiction over the whole of Somaliland and acting as the Constitutional Court. The law defines the functions of the Office of the Attorney General, and those of a ten-member Judicial Commission appointed to oversee the whole system. A review of the Somaliland judiciary in 2002 highlighted a catalogue of problems (APD 2002). The legal system needs clarification, being a hybrid of secular and religious laws derived from different and often contradictory legal traditions. This confusing legal system, combined with allegations of corruption, incompetence and interference by the President, have undermined public confidence in the judiciary. The system lacks experienced and qualified individuals, with some judges trained in civil law and others in Islamic *shari'a* law. Remuneration is poor and corruption is reportedly endemic. Budgetary allocations to the judiciary were doubled in the fiscal year 2000 but still accounted for less than 1.5 per cent of the total government budget. In 2003 judges received the equivalent of US$115 per month, which compared to monthly salaries of US$154 and US$256 respectively for a parliamentarian and a minister. In addition, basic training and refresher courses were unavailable in-country, there was no association or regulatory body for the legal community, the courts lacked basic equipment and facilities, and there were no legal libraries or journals.

The constitution stresses the independence of the judiciary, and the fact that its independence has been one of the most hotly contested aspects of government indicates a public awareness of the importance of this principle. However, judicial independence has been functionally constrained by the fact that it is the Ministry of Justice, which administers the courts, salaries and budgets, and the President who has the constitutional authority to appoint judges to the Supreme Court and to dismiss them. This is supposed to occur in consultation with the Judicial Commission and Parliament, but in practice the President has had unchecked influence. Consequently the judiciary has been unable to offer a just recourse to those whose legal rights have been infringed, whether by government or the private sector. A judiciary that provides little legal protection of opposition and minority views, or legal safeguards for economic investments, can be an impediment to political pluralism and economic activity. Furthermore, the lack of a competent Constitutional Court that can provide clear rulings means that constitutional disputes remain unresolved and open to interpretation.

On taking over the reins of government in 2002, President Riyale ordered a shake up of the judicial system and replaced thirty-five sitting

[15] Interview by author with Dr Tahlil Haji Ahmed, UNDP, Hargeysa, August 2003.

judges, including judges of the Supreme Court. This was a popular move, but it left the judiciary lacking trained and experienced personnel, and with judges who were mostly trained in *shari'a* rather than civil law. The ease with which the President ordered a wholesale change in the judiciary also highlighted its lack of independence from the executive. The changes made to the Supreme Court in advance of the elections raised questions about the Court's impartiality in judging the outcome of the elections. Since 2002, Somaliland's reputation for liberal government has been called into question by some high-profile legal cases, creeping corruption, and an increasing investment in internal security (African Rights 2003b). The existence of an elected Parliament which can hold the executive to account can be an important mechanism for protecting civil liberties. Having committed itself to constitutional rule, the government will need to demonstrate its respect for civil liberties, human rights standards and the rule of law by supporting the development of a competent and independent judicial system.

Local government

The formation of popularly elected district councils in 2002 was, as described in Chapter 8, an important step in the institutionalisation of the Somaliland state. The 1993 Borama Charters and the Somaliland constitution produced a framework for a decentralised system of government that would strengthen popular participation in government and prevent a return to authoritarian rule. In practice, as the state has developed there has been an ongoing tension between central and local government bodies. As the centre has sought to extend its authority and expand its revenue base, so the regions and districts have guarded their independence, while seeking support from the central government.

In 1991 the writ of the first Somaliland administration hardly held beyond Hargeysa. At a regional and district level an *ad hoc* mixture of councils of elders and self-appointed SNM commanders were the main source of local authority. Under Egal, the government's writ was gradually extended across the territory through the creation of regional and district-level councils, the appointment of governors and civil servants, and the rationalisation of the taxation system. The political agreements reached at the 1997 Hargeysa conference, the 2001 constitutional plebiscite that adopted the constitution, and the elections have been particularly important in concretising the authority of the government across the territory. Its authority in eastern Sanaag and much of Sool, however, remained tenuous. The current structure of local government was formalised in 2002 with the adoption of the Regions and District Law, approved in advance of the district elections. Until that time functional local government structures had been established with responsibilities for revenue collection and municipal administration, but without a legal relationship with central government. The creation of district councils was often used by the President to curry favour and reward support. In 1991, for example, there were five regions and twenty-one districts in north-west Somalia. By 2002, another region and twenty districts had been created. The uncoordinated manner in which this was done led to such confusion over the exact number of districts and their demarcation that only twenty-three of the forty-one districts were actually approved for elections.

The Regions and District Law formalised the division of Somaliland into six administrative regions, with a governor appointed by central government who chairs a regional council comprising the regional government departments and district mayors. Regions are divided into administrative districts, administered by district councils. These are the lowest level of elected government and oversee revenue collection, town management, security, public works, the environment, sanitation, health and education. Mayors, who are appointed by the council, are responsible both to the district council and to the Ministry of the Interior. The presence in the council of an executive secretary appointed by the Ministry of the Interior formally ties local government to central government.

The presence of elected district councils that recognise the authority of the Somaliland government provides a means of judging the territorial reach of the state.[16] Prior to the elections, one way of judging the geographical authority of the government was to count the number of sultans and *caaqilo* receiving a government stipend. But with shifting clan alliances this is an unreliable way of judging the extent of government authority. In the wake of the elections, the authorities in Hargeysa could, by 2005, confidently assert that a Somaliland civil administration exists across 80 per cent of the territory. But, on the same basis, the authority of the government does not extend throughout the whole territory claimed for the Somaliland state – especially in eastern Sanaag and Sool regions. The 2002 elections established nineteen districts with directly elected councils (out of the twenty-three approved for election). In these districts a formal judicial and policing system operates, locally raised revenue is transferred to central government and the authority of centrally appointed governors is accepted.[17] The government provides funds to these councils for the salaries of civil servants, including teachers and health workers. Even in some districts of Sool and Sanaag where elections did not take place, the government supports some health and education services. In Las Anod some police continued on the Somaliland payroll even after Puntland established an administration there in 2002.

Prior to the district elections, state power and resources were largely concentrated in central government. With elections, the creation of

[16] For example, certain lineages in eastern Sanaag and Sool, for example, have changed their allegiances from Somaliland to Puntland.

[17] In 2003 the Ministry of the Interior listed a further eighteen councils where elections were pending, awaiting the delineation of their borders.

district and municipal councils that are accountable to the local electorate holds the potential for creating a form of government that is responsive to local needs. But the development of functional councils will depend on the ability of the new councillors to implement their responsibilities and a commitment by central government to support them in this task through appropriate legislation and resources. The elected councils face numerous challenges in carrying out their tasks.

First, the legal framework for district councils and the division of powers and responsibilities with central government needs further clarity. While district councils in theory have the power to plan economic and social affairs, the demarcation of central government, regional and district authority in levying taxes is unclear. As councils are dependent on central government subsidies, the extent to which local authorities are policy-makers or just implementers of central policy is similarly unclear. In line with the constitution, a city charter has been developed for Hargeysa to provide a comprehensive legal framework for the municipality, which should help provide more clarity on the structure and activities of all municipalities.

Second, the extent to which district councils can be resourced adequately will be a key test of decentralised government. Local councils are required to raise their own resources to support local services. Indeed, according to Article 3 of the Regions and District Law, a key criterion for conferring regional and district status on an area is 'the extent of self-sufficiency and of arrangements for social provision'. As the revenue-raising potential of councils varies, their capacity to deliver services to citizens is uneven, although central government subsidies are supposed to rectify this.

Third, the newly elected councillors who took up their posts in 2003 did so with little guidance on how to fulfil their roles, while council procedures were ill-defined. The mayor, for example, has no tenure of office and it was easy for council members to de-select and replace the person at whim, which happened in several places. The capacity of councillors was uneven, with most lacking experience in local government, and few having the requisite skills in management and administration.[18] This is partly a result of the political parties selecting candidates on the basis of clan rather than qualifications and experience; the sole qualification for some was to come from a major (*laan-dheer*) lineage. However, some skilled former administrators, businessmen and local politicians were brought into government who might otherwise have been involved in local NGOs or private business, and in places councils provided opportunities for a new cadre of civil servants and government officials. The ability of councils to attract skilled personnel was also dependent on rates of remuneration. This varied widely between districts. In 2003, for example, Hargeysa councillors received the equivalent of

---

[18] Interviews in Hargeysa, Borama, Berbera, Burco, Erigavo, August–September 2003.

9.1 Elected mayor and councillors at work in Erigavo, 2007 (M. Bradbury)

US$400 per month, compared to US$150 in Burco, and just under US$100 per month in Borama.[19]

Fourth, elections have produced councils that are generally representative of the major clans in a district. The interests of people who are not from the district, minorities and women are not directly represented. The councils also lacked mechanisms, such as town hall meetings, for public participation or consultation. The link between the political parties and their elected council members has also been tenuous. Councillors are more likely to be loyal to their local constituencies than they are to the party or central government. This may be positive for addressing local needs, but without stronger party structures the ability of the public to influence central government will be limited.

After the elections the public had high expectations of the district councils. Experiences in the first twelve months were mixed. In Burco, for example, the formation of elected councils had reportedly reduced disputes over land, an increasing source of local violence, while in Hargeysa there were indications that disputes increased. There was also some concern that the increased administrative cost of the new councils was diverting resources away from services. As one Somali put it, '[the elections have] brought in twenty-one naked people who need everything. Their allowances for one meeting absorb the equivalent of fifty

[19] Author's interviews, August 2003.

days' revenue collection.'[20] Nevertheless, most people were generally positive in their initial assessment, arguing that these councils were more accountable than the previous centrally appointed ones, that the management of finances has improved, and that because they were elected the public have the power to dismiss them if they do not perform well.[21]

Public administration

State-building in Somaliland has seen an inexorable growth in public administration. The first government of Somaliland had nineteen ministries. By 2003 this had risen to twenty-three sectoral ministries, all with deputy ministers and director generals, and eight ministers of state. By 2001/2 there were reportedly more than 26,000 people in public service employment, including 4,649 civil service staff employed by central government, some 4,000 district and municipal employees, 17,500 security personnel, plus employees of the Central Bank and Berbera Port (Civil Service Commission 2003). Aside from the security services, the ministries of Education, Health and Finance were the largest employers, accounting for 62 per cent of public employees.

In 2000, the Ministry of Finance, concerned to reduce the cost of public administration and improve efficiency, initiated a civil service reform programme to retrench the number of employees. The Civil Service Commission screened and graded 6,000 government employees through competitive examinations which nearly 80 per cent passed. But the reform was not enforced across all the ministries. Consequently, the administration is overstaffed, but short on qualified and experienced public administrators and managers at all levels. A clan bias in appointments means that women are under-represented, and mostly hold clerical or secretarial positions. Ministry capacities vary greatly, depending on a variety of factors – the strength of the minister and senior employees, his or her relationship to the President, the direct resources available to the ministries through taxation, the willingness of the clan to sponsor the ministry, and access to international resources. Some (Education, Health, Finance) are institutionally strong. Others are little more than a façade, with a minister and director general but no other employees, and no obvious function other than as addresses for their clans. Government salary scales were introduced in 1993, with the first state budget. But massive devaluation of the Somaliland shilling against the dollar has eroded their value. In 2002, a minister's monthly salary was equivalent to US$229, a parliamentarian's US$138 and a policeman's US$13. Consequently, public service workers do not earn a living wage from their employment, causing high absenteeism, corruption and the loss of skilled personnel to the private market, foreign aid agencies or overseas employ-

[20] Author's interview, Borama, August, 2003.
[21] Author's interviews, in Hargeysa, Borama, Berbera, Burco, Erigavo, August–September 2003.

ment. The importance of holding positions in the administration, however, lies not in remuneration that comes with such a position, but from the symbolic or political significance attached to it and the access it provides to other political networks and resources.

Financing government

The ability to establish and sustain an effective administration will depend on the ability of government to raise revenue. Since the first colonial administrations, themselves supported by colonial subsidies, successive Somali governments have relied heavily on foreign aid to maintain their institutions. As described in Chapter 2, this reached a peak in the mid-1980s. Somaliland has had a formal revenue collection system in place since 1993, which has funded the establishment of government and the maintenance of security. While foreign aid has financed much of the rehabilitation and development of social services, in contrast to the past very little of this has gone directly through government. Government administration in Somaliland has therefore been almost entirely supported through domestically generated revenue. In contrast donors have funded the establishment of the TFG, including allowances for sitting members of the National Assembly; at US$1,500 per month, these contrast starkly with MPs' salaries in Somaliland.

Government data show that revenue since 2000 has ranged between US$20 and US$30 million a year (see Figure 9.2). Public expenditure rose rapidly from nothing in 1991 to some US$19 million a year in 1999, after which it declined before rising again in 2004 (see Figure 9.3).[22] Up to

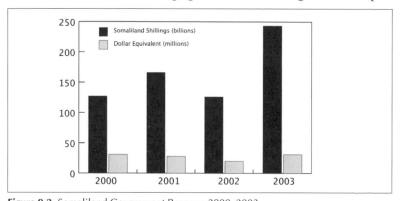

Figure 9.2 Somaliland Government Revenue 2000–2003
in Somaliland Shillings and Dollars Equivalent
Source: Government of Somaliland, Ministry of Finance

[22] Discrepancies exist in the data available from the ministries of Finance and Planning. The dollar figures shown here are somewhat lower than government figures, which were based on the official exchange rate.

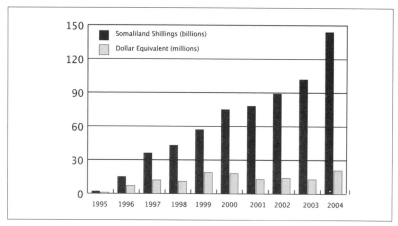

Figure 9.3 Somaliland Government Expenditure 1995–2004
in Somaliland Shillings and Dollars Equivalent
Source: Government of Somaliland, Ministry of Finance

2005, government finances, on the whole, appear to have been managed prudently, with only small fiscal deficits accumulated in 1998 and 2000, the years in which Gulf states banned the import of Somali livestock (Holleman 2002). But the government's revenue stream is precarious. Its main source of revenue is from customs tariffs and inland revenue, with the former accounting for 85 per cent of government revenue in 2002. Of this 30 per cent is from export tariffs, mainly on livestock. Government revenue is therefore highly dependent on a single export and is very vulnerable to changes in market conditions (Holleman 2002).[23] Furthermore, with levies on *qaad* imports accounting for over 10 per cent of the total government revenue, there is little government incentive to reduce the trade, despite its drain on national and household incomes and its impact on health. Although inland revenue makes up only a small part of government revenue, tariffs on imports represent an indirect tax on the remittance economy which sustains a high level of imports. Government fiscal deficits are partially financed by loans from businessmen, which are repaid in the form of tax relief. This form of financing, which has not been adequately monitored, has exposed the government to accusations of fiscal opacity and corruption.

Since revenue collection was introduced, the government's policy has been to maintain a light tax regime to assist recovery.[24] In the 1990s this helped to make the port of Berbera into a competitive alternative to

[23] In 2002 import tariffs stood at 43 per cent of government earnings, revenues from export tariffs at 30 per cent, and revenues from tariffs on *qaad* at 12 per cent. The government places a levy on fuel sales to support road maintenance and special levies have also been introduced by presidential decree, such as the additional 2 per cent customs tariff to fund the rehabilitation of Burco in 1996.

[24] Author's interviews with Ministries of Finance and Commerce, Hargeysa, August 2003.

Djibouti. Efforts by the government to increase its revenue through greater efficiency in revenue collection have met with resistance. In August 2003, for example, attempts to impose closer inspections on imported goods at Berbera elicited a negative reaction from traders and caused a shortage of basic food commodities. As we have seen, some Somaliland traders moved parts of their business to Bossaso, where tariffs were lighter.

Central government expenditure has changed little over time. Since 1993, the priority has been the maintenance of peace and security, with 50–70 per cent of the budget allocated to the National Security Services. Social spending has increased only slightly over the years. According to the government, in 2001/2, 55 per cent was spent on the security forces, 25 per cent on the political organs of the government, 8 per cent on health and education, and just 7 per cent went to ministries in the economic and productive sectors (Mohamed 2002). In 2004 expenditure on the health and education ministries again consumed a little over 8 per cent of total expenditure (World Bank 2006: 177). The overall increase in expenditure in 2004 is largely accounted for by increased military spending, possibly a reflection of the military tensions over Sool and eastern Sanaag. Most regular expenditure goes on salaries, administration and logistics, with little surplus generated with which to build up reserves and invest in development. In 2000 the government did invest in some infrastructural projects but the loss of revenue from livestock exports in 1998 and 2000 wrecked plans to increase its development spending. Nevertheless, it did manage to dedicate resources to the rehabilitation of Burco and ring-fenced sufficient revenue to partially pay for three elections.

One of the key challenges to sustaining the current state architecture in Somaliland is the financing of local government. Until 2000 local authorities collected revenue on all goods travelling through their jurisdictions, while different ministries also collected revenue to finance their activities and administration. In 2000 the government introduced Law 12 on the Unified Tariffs for Local Government which centralised all revenue collection. Under this arrangement all customs revenue was transferred to the Ministry of Finance and 12.5 per cent of this was redistributed to the districts; districts with customs posts also retained 10 per cent of the revenue they generated. The purpose of the revision was to stimulate commerce by reducing the multiple taxes on businesses, prevent the leakage of revenue and create a more equitable taxation system through the redistribution of revenues. It was also intended to offset the shortfall in central government revenue caused by the livestock embargo. The reform succeeded in stimulating trade, but it also reduced the revenue available for district authorities. And while local revenue declined, responsibility for the provision of social services shifted from central government to the districts, either directly or through the privatisation of services such as water.

District councils have various other sources of revenue. The primary source is taxing local resources, with land, animal slaughter and business tax providing the main revenue streams. As with central government, council budgets are largely earmarked for salaries and other recurrent costs. Importantly, the cost of maintaining security services is formally the preserve of central government. The main service that all councils provide is sanitation and rubbish removal, with some contributing to education and health. But the rapid pace of urban settlement means that services cannot keep up with demand.

The tax reforms of 2000 did not achieve the objective of creating a more equitable taxation system and increased the fiscal dependence of districts on central government. Delays in central government subsidies mean that councils become indebted to the local business community, who are reimbursed at high rates of interest.[25] Apart from Hargeysa and Berbera, and possibly Gabiley which benefits from *qaad* revenue, few councils are likely to become self-sufficient – raising questions of 'sustainable development'. To raise revenue, the under-resourced local authorities have sold off public assets like land, a policy with environmental and social consequences. The main revenue collection points of Berbera, Togwajaale and Zeyla are all in the west of the country. Consequently, the western regions receive the major proportion of government expenditure, which leaves populations in the eastern regions of Togdheer, Sanaag and Sool feeling neglected. To a degree the east-west disparity also reflects an inequality between urban and rural areas, which has been further exacerbated by the livestock bans. In 2000 the government did fund some small infrastructural projects in Sanaag Region to offset this disparity – until its funds ran out.

Corruption

Corruption has long been a complaint justifiably levelled by Somalis against their governments. The eradication of corruption and patronage in government was supposedly one of the aims of the coup in Somalia in 1969. But the mass embezzlement of state resources, the appropriation of foreign aid, the alienation of land and the use of parastatals to reward its supporters became a feature of the Barre regime and has left a legacy of public mistrust in government. In Somaliland corruption has again become a concern to the public and to some members of the government. Articles regularly appear in Somaliland's newspapers complaining about the corrupt practices in government (Gulaid 2003). In early 2007, for example, the editor of *Haatuf* newspaper was arrested over allegations made against the President and his family. Parliament has sought to investigate such allegations and some government ministers have voiced concerns about financial impropriety. In 2003, the Minister of Foreign Affairs remarked:[26]

---

[25] Author's interview with Mayor of Borama, August 2003.
[26] Interviewed by author, Hargeysa, August 2003.

It is accountability that we need to develop. We have to give priority to reversing corruption. It is no longer shameful to be dishonest. It is smart to steal. We need to reverse that and give rewards for accountability.

Petty corruption and graft is rife as public servants seek to supplement meagre salaries, but the biggest concern is institutional corruption and the lack of accountability in government. Two areas that have generated particular concern are the management of the revenue of Berbera port and government deals with international companies. The Berbera Port Authority was established in 1993 as an autonomous body directly under the office of the President. Although all customs revenue goes directly to the Ministry of Finance, only 10 per cent of handling charges is passed to it. The rest goes to the Port Authority and into an account for 'Presidential Payments'. In 2002, it is alleged that out of the US$1.7 million collected by the Port Authority, only US$158,000 was transferred to the Treasury (Gulaid 2003). Government handling of the contract with Total Mer Rouge for the management of its Berbera oil storage facilities was one aspect of the impeachment motion brought against Egal in 2002. The monthly fee paid by Total Mer Rouge for the lease of oil storage facilities in Berbera also allegedly goes directly to the account for Presidential Payments. As much as 50 per cent of the income administered by the Office of the President is said to be unaccountable.

The misuse of public office for self-enrichment reduces the amount of national revenue available to government for investing in development and redistribution. But corruption also has the potential to incite violence, particularly when it is combined with political manipulation. For example, opposition parties alleged that new Somaliland shillings printed in advance of the presidential elections were used to finance UDUB's campaign. As a consequence, the government was unable to pay public sector salaries for several months after the elections. As well as inciting dangerous levels of anger among opposition supporters, the introduction of new money causes inflation which further impoverishes the poor. On all sides, suspicion that public office has been used to advance party interests and for self-enrichment creates resentment among others who are unable to participate in the potential benefits of the new state.

State reform & the role of government

Since people in Somaliland broke with Somalia there has been broad public consensus on the need for some form of government to provide security, manage internal political competition and handle external relations. Post-war recovery in Somaliland has involved a significant degree of state 'reform', including the decentralisation of authority, the emergence of competing political parties, and the divestiture of public property to the private sector. Limited public revenue and international aid has also prevented government from taking on a developmental role. Communications, transport and banking services, for example, are all organised privately. While this has social costs, it has served to keep the centre of power weak. A large diaspora that engages in the politics and economy of Somaliland from beyond its borders also has implications for relations between state and society.

A fundamental change that has occurred in Somali politics as a result of the war has been the loss of a single overarching ideology or political programme to direct development. Under the former regime this was provided by Scientific Socialism which, in theory, vested leadership, security and welfare in the state rather than the clan. This political project was being eroded in the 1980s with the adoption of free-market liberal economic policies, and disappeared with the state as people looked to clan and kin for leadership and security. Scientific Socialism has not been replaced in Somaliland by any articulated political programme. Although the SNM manifesto sketched out a vision for post-Barre governance that embraced political pluralism, free enterprise and a decentralised form of government built on Somali cultural values and traditional Somali egalitarianism, when independence was declared in 1991 the leadership had no plans ready to turn the vision into reality. As a former SNM insider explained: 'When people wanted an independent state, they really had no idea about how that could be different [from the past].'[27]

As defined by its constitution, Somaliland's system of government is based on peace, cooperation, democracy and pluralism. However, political order is not maintained by subscription to a single ideology, but by a discourse on clan and lineage politics, mixed with concepts of multi-party democracy, human rights, civil society and the free market. In the absence of a political ideology, 'peace' and 'security' (that is, freedom from violence) and 'independence' (which for many people is their guarantee of peace) have been the main pillars of the 'political project' in Somaliland and the main task of government. This is evident in the power-sharing form of government that emerged in the early 1990s, the investments made in peace conferences, and the allocation of public resources – not only to security but also to the canvassing of public opinion through the constitutional referendum and the elections. To this, political concepts of multi-party democracy, human rights, civil society and the free market have been added.

With up to 70 per cent of the national budget spent on the maintenance of peace and stability and very little allocated for social spending, the government's role as a development actor has been decidedly weak. As described in Chapter 7, in 2000, having paid off debts to the business community and with a windfall from renewed livestock exports, the government did allocate surplus funds to development projects, including a new Parliament building, rehabilitation of the Hargeysa elec-

---

[27] Interview with Abdi Yusuf Duale, APD, Hargeysa, August 2003.

tricity plant, the rebuilding of Burco and some small-scale development projects in Sanaag Region. The government has also spent resources on the resettlement of returning refugees and, as noted, on the elections. Some better-resourced district councils also provide limited funds for education, in addition to policing and sanitation. Hargeysa municipality, for example, has supported the Hargeysa Group Hospital, the university, and several health centres. However, spending on reconstruction and development have largely come from non-state private sources, from individuals. collective family and clan initiatives, business, or foreign aid.

In many respects Somaliland is a policy-rich environment, with its constitution providing a legal framework for government, by-laws to guide the workings of Parliament, and a Civil Service Commission with guidelines for the workings of government departments. Several ministries, with international support, have also developed policies to guide and regulate work within their sectors of responsibility. But ministries, government departments and municipalities do not have sufficient financial resources or adequately skilled and paid staff to fulfil their legal responsibilities or implement well-intentioned policy. Somaliland's national plans for economic recovery and poverty reduction, written with the support of UN consultants, have not been implemented. Nor have they been articulated in the national budgets prepared by the Ministry of Finance and approved by Parliament. In part, this reflects a wider public ambivalence about the role of government. Public assumptions of what government should be responsible for are high, but expectations about what it is able to deliver are low. This also reflects global changes in ideas of government, from a model of state-led development to a neo-liberal, market-driven model in which the main development actors are the private sector and 'civil society' organisations, including international aid organisations.

Finally, it is worth reiterating that lack of international recognition and limited support for governance has meant that the post-war political system that has emerged in Somaliland has been largely a local creation. The political system and architecture of government evolved from a series of mass public consultations – clan conferences – that endowed the political system with a high degree of legitimacy. Since these conferences, the public has continued to discuss and debate political developments and has generally sought solutions to problems through dialogue rather than through conflict. If we return to Luling's description of Somalia in the 1980s (1997: 289) as a state 'suspended above a society that would never have produced it and did not demand it', Somaliland, by contrast, appears to be rooted in a popular consciousness and embedded in society rather than imposed from above.

10
Conclusions ▐ Rethinking
the Future

This book has sought to document how, from the rubble of war and the ruins of a state, a self-governing territory has been created in the Horn of Africa that fulfils most international criteria of statehood. Somaliland's modest state structure comprises a popularly elected constitutionally based government that exercises some control over its borders, manages certain public assets, levies taxes, intervenes in the market, formulates development policies and provides security for its citizens as competently as many better resourced and recognised states in Africa. A modest annual budget raised on customs duties and other local taxes finances an elected Parliament and municipal councils, sectoral ministries, a judiciary and security forces. The restoration of security has facilitated economic revival and enabled the rehabilitation of infrastructure and social services. Civic organisations have flourished and most people who took refuge in neighbouring countries during the war have returned. Rather than rejecting as irrational or impractical the aspirations of people in Somaliland for self-government, the task perhaps should be to understand the place on its own terms, to consider ways to support it, and to reflect on what it can tell us about state-building that is of relevance not only to Somalia, but also to other countries emerging from war. This chapter seeks to draw out some of the key features of the state-building process and considers Somaliland's future prospects.

State collapse & renewal

In historical terms, the modern state is a relatively new way of ordering social and economic relations; pre-colonial society in Somalia was famously stateless. Yet 'state collapse' (or the risk of it) and 'state fragility' evoke considerable anxiety among policy-makers in Western governments because of the perceived danger they are believed to pose to international security (von Hippel 2002). The US National Security

Strategy of September 2002 concluded that 'America is now threatened less by conquering states than we are by failing ones' (*Economist* 2002). In 2004 under Tony Blair the British Prime Minister's Strategy Unit (2005 February) identified 'weak' and 'failing states' as a threat to global stability. Since 1991, Somalia, perhaps more than any other country, has come to epitomise a 'collapsed state', and during the long period that it has been without a functional central government it has been the subject of foreign interventions aimed at curbing the threat it is perceived to pose.

In 1992, civil war and famine in Somalia were considered a danger to a peaceful 'new world order' and led to the intervention of the multinational peacekeeping force – UNOSOM – under US leadership. A decade later, in the wake of the September 2001 terrorist attacks in New York and Washington, there was speculation that Somalia would follow Afghanistan as the next military theatre in the US-led 'war on terror'. It was believed that materials and people involved in the bombing of the US embassies in Kenya and Tanzania in 1998 had passed through Somalia. To prevent the country from becoming a haven for transnational terrorism, an air and maritime surveillance regime was imposed by Western allies over the territory, while covert operations by US forces and paid proxies targeted suspects inside. In January 2007 the US government, for a second time since the state collapsed, dropped bombs on Somalia in support of the Ethiopian-backed TFG that was pursuing the forces of the Islamic Courts and suspected Al Qaeda operatives in southern Somalia (Reynolds 2007). Following the retreat of the Islamic Courts, the TFG was given a second chance to prove that it is capable of governing Somalia. But, as a body that was largely externally created and financed and had to rely on foreign military support to enter the capital, the challenges it faces are considerable. For fifteen years the mix of diplomacy, military intervention and humanitarian aid has failed to put the state of Somalia back together. There is a need, as Little (2003:162) suggests, to rethink old 'wisdoms'.

A starting point is to jettison the notion of state collapse in Somalia as simply a 'failure' of state governance or development, but to understand it also in the context of, and as a response to, global political and economic transformations that have been underway since the 1970s (Clapham 1996). While the human cost of state collapse in Somalia has been enormous and tragic, and Somali people continue to suffer the indignities of statelessness in their own country and abroad, the global threat that an ungoverned Somalia poses seems somewhat exaggerated. Criminal and terrorist networks have not flourished in the absence of government. Indeed, the number of named individuals in Somalia suspected of terrorist links is fewer than in several Western countries. And the mass flight of people from violence has not caused endemic insecurity across state borders. While the end of government in 1991 generated a range of destructive political and economic processes, the absence of government has not all been negative. Studies of 'post-modern' war economies illustrate how the exercise of power or participation in the global economy does not necessarily require a modern state (Duffield 1998; Nordstrom 2000). Elites in government, warlords and quasi-state authorities can survive without state institutions on extractive relations with populations in their own and neighbouring countries, or on economies that are linked through modern communications equipment into international trade and financial networks. Since the early 1990s the business class in Somalia has proven itself to be more than capable of running successful commerce without a state or regulatory authority (Marchal 1996; Little 2003). In many respects this is a continuation of conditions that existed before the war, when people were excluded from participating in the politics of the state and survived on an informal economy that the state did not control. Moreover, what collapsed was not a functional state, but what one long-term participant observer in Somalia has called a 'toxic state' (Bryden 2001:2) where the government had become an instrument of oppression rather than protection. While the quality of life for many people in Somalia is poor by any global standards, there have been some modest improvements in some indicators of human development (UNDP 2001). There are, for example, more children in primary school than there were before the war, the gross domestic product per capita compares favourably to other countries in the region, and the country can boast one of the most extensive telecommunication systems in Africa.

Furthermore, the consequences of state collapse differed in different parts of Somalia. While famine and war gripped Somalia's southern regions in 1991, in the north-west a decade of war was ended and a new political order was created. One of the paradoxes of international engagement in Somalia is that while efforts in diplomacy and state building have focused on re-establishing a sovereign government (in either a centralised or federal form) Somalis themselves have fashioned varied forms of governance within the territory of the former Republic. If Somalia is to emerge from its political crisis and aid strategies are to be effective, greater diplomatic creativity and international acceptance of alternative formulations of state governance may prove necessary. At the time of writing, more than a decade after the independence of Somaliland was declared, it should be evident that the varied needs in Somalia and Somaliland cannot be conflated within any single governance framework.

The foundations of political order in Somaliland

Since withdrawing from the union, the Republic of Somaliland has emerged as the most stable polity within the territory of the Somali Republic and since 1997 it has been one of the most stable areas in the Horn of Africa. It is worth rehearsing some of the reasons for this outlined in previous chapters.

Different societies have different ways of establishing political order. In Somaliland a distinguishing feature of post-war reconstruction was the role played by indigenous political institutions. In the twentieth century, it was assumed that the advent of the modern state presaged the passing of traditional society and in Somalia the aim of successive governments was to turn a nation of nomads into a modern nation state. But in post-war Somaliland, in the absence of effective government, people drew on non-state customary institutions of lineage elders and customary law to manage social relations and to re-establish rules and systems of law and order. It has been argued that due to the particular experience of British colonialism and the policy of light imperial rule – others have called it 'benign neglect' (Prunier 1998: 225) – these informal rule-based systems have remained more entrenched and stronger among northern pastoralists communities than in southern Somalia (Reno 2003). In addition, pastoralism retained a dominant role in the post-independence economy of Somalia and, beyond the urban centres and the south, penetration of the state was limited. In the aftermath of state collapse, in southern Somalia a range of factors including external interventions, warlord politics, economic interests and inter-clan rivalries, restricted opportunities for the numerous localised 'grassroots' reconciliation and peacebuilding processes that took place, to be scaled-up to a level much beyond the district or region.

In the immediate post-war environment in Somaliland, the primary roles played by customary institutions were in restoring inter-group relations, mediating relationships of power, re-establishing property rights, ensuring balanced political representation and demobilising the population. As government became established, 'tradition' was fused with the 'modern' to create a unique political system. The role of these customary institutions has evolved and, in the view of some, they have become corrupted as they have been incorporated into government. However, their importance in Somaliland's early years in ending hostilities and rebuilding relations between conflicting groups should not be underestimated. Somaliland's enduring stability owes much to the political consensus achieved at that time. The institutions of this 'pastoral democracy', with its inclusive and public meetings and the emphasis on consensus and dialogue, served to instil a high degree of accountability and local ownership in Somaliland's system of governance. The successes of the locally financed and managed peace conferences in Sheikh and Borama, and the numerous other clan peace meetings that took place in Somaliland between 1991 and 1996, contrast starkly with the failure of the multiple externally sponsored and managed meetings between warlords and power brokers, held in foreign capitals, that have characterised most international peacemaking efforts in Somalia.

It is important to recognise that the SNM did not announce Somaliland's independence with a blue-print, a set of 'objectives', a 'road map', a 'logical framework', a 'plan of action', 'benchmarks' or a 'reconstruction and development plan'. Neither was the state created by building the capacity of 'civil society' organisations. State-building is not a simple technical process of constitution-making, party formation and elections. Nor is it time-bound by project frameworks or funding schedules. In Somaliland state formation has been both a reactive and proactive process in response to internal and external events. It has involved political negotiation between numerous 'stakeholders' with varied interests and agendas, including the SNM, politicians, elders, business people, the diaspora, women, pastoralists, and neighbouring states. In the first decade these negotiations occurred in formal peace conferences, parliamentary debates and other public fora, making for a highly participatory form of politics.

For the past decade and a half, aid programmes have been the main prism through which the international community has engaged with Somaliland and has sought to understand it. But the assumption that state-building can be controlled through aid projects, logical frameworks and set timeframes is simplistic, if not delusional. State formation involves more than demobilisation, re-establishing the rule of law, or rehabilitating services and infrastructure. States are 'the outcome of complex sets of practices and processes [and] the result of myriads of situations where social actors negotiate power and meaning' (Krohn-Hansen and Nustad 2005: 12). And states in the making are subject to a range of internal and external political, social and economic forces that can affect the trajectory of development.

Another key factor underlying Somaliland's recovery and stability has been the interest of the elite in orderly politics. In the 1980s, in the wake of the Ogaden war, the political and economic elites in Somalia who were excluded from power went into exile or mobilised resistance against the regime. The SNM, which was founded by émigré communities, became a vehicle for the ambitions of northern politicians who had become politically marginalised by the regime. They found support among the northern business class who were excluded from Barre's patronage system and whose economic activities the state sought to regulate. In southern Somalia the atomisation of the state produced a range of powerful political and commercial parties, whose interests have conspired to oppose the restoration of government and the rule of law (Menkhaus 2004). In the highly volatile and insecure environment that developed there, the northern political elites found themselves again excluded from power and were left to pursue their interests through a separatist polity. While elite interests in the south appear to have invested in maintaining a situation of statelessness, it would seem that elite interests in Somaliland have been best served through state-building and investment in government, security and law. In Somaliland there has been a commitment to the restoration of a government and to address political problems through dialogue and institutions rather than through the force of arms.

To conclude from this that Somaliland is simply a project of a political elite, however, would be to deny its origins in the public pressure placed on politicians to revoke the union with Somalia. In many respects Somaliland is a 'people's project' rather than a project of an elite. A key factor behind Somaliland's political recovery was the existence of a broad political community which rejected the continuation of a unitary state. This community was shaped by the experience of colonialism in the British Somaliland Protectorate, a sense of political and economic marginalisation within an independent Somalia, the near genocidal oppression of the Isaaqs in the 1980s, the popular struggle against the military regime and the experience of self-organisation in the refugee camps. Although in 1991 and today Somaliland is based on the political unity of the Isaaq people, it has also developed into a more complex polity of 'orderly multi-communal politics' (Reno 2003: 12), with an elected president who is non-Isaaq. People of other clans in Somaliland have to different degrees and at different time accepted, contributed to or rejected it. Nevertheless, having rejected the union with Somalia, people in Somaliland through locally driven political processes have designed and financed a political system that has given the state and its government a high degree of local legitimacy.

In 1982 the SNM articulated a vision of a post-Barre government in its manifesto that in many respects describes Somaliland today, with a system that embraces pluralism, free enterprise and cultural values. If one takes Somaliland's constitution to be representative of the aspirations of Somalilanders, then this sets out the type of state which will deliver security. It is a state based on self-determination, participatory politics, equality and justice; Islamic *shari'a*; the separation of state powers, decentralisation, and fundamental rights and individual freedoms (Jama 2000). In the absence of a political ideology, 'peace' and 'security' and 'independence' have been the pillars of the state-building project. The developmental role of government has been constrained by its limited revenue, so the central function of the government, which was founded upon a peace agreement, is to preserve 'security' and 'independence'. Onto this foundation, concepts of multi-party democracy, human rights, civil society and the free market have been grafted.

Shaped by both local and global forces, state-building in Somaliland has also involved a degree of state 'reform', including the decentralisation of authority, competitive party politics and the divestiture of public property to the private sector. Limited international assistance has also meant that reconstruction has largely been achieved from the resources and resourcefulness of Somalilanders themselves, the main source of finance for which has been remittances from Somalis living overseas. Aside from internal conflicts in 1992 and 1994–6, Somaliland has largely avoided the protracted conflict and insecurity experienced in the south. This required establishing a system of government with an accepted balance of power and paying for the maintenance of a large number of militia. It is debatable where the real source of this security and rule of law lies, but given the poverty of the security forces and the judicial system, an argument can be made that law and order is really sustained by the citizens, rather than enforced by the government.

The challenges ahead

The issue of recognition
Somaliland's political system – and the internal legitimacy of that system – is closely tied to its citizens' desire for it to be recognised as an independent sovereign state. Legal arguments have been made in support of Somaliland's case for reclaiming the sovereignty it enjoyed on 28 June 1960.[1] These generally conclude that Somaliland has a high degree of internal legitimacy, that the government has demonstrated a capacity to govern and that Somaliland meets the criteria of a state in contemporary international law, namely: a permanent population; a defined territory; a stable system of government; and a capacity to enter into relations with other states.[2] Somaliland's territorial sovereignty is contested internally, and the government does not control all the territory over which it lays claim in the east. However, as Herbst (2000) has observed, there are few African states that exercise effective control over all their territory. The International Crisis Group (2006a: 11) also makes the point that Somalia's own claim to statehood could also be questioned, given the long absence of a locally accepted and effective body with the capacity and will to govern. There is an irony that while Somaliland has demonstrated a high degree of empirical statehood, it lacks juridical sovereignty. In contrast, while Somalia lacks empirical sovereignty, international political and development policies treat its juridical sovereignty as intact. But statehood in Africa has generally been more juridical than empirical, existing more on the assertion of state rulers than a proven capacity to govern and exercise power. At the end of the day, a resolution of Somaliland's status is likely to be influenced by 'realpolitik' and 'real-economic' rather than legal arguments in an international court.

The obstacles to recognition are considerable. At the same time, the prospects for Somaliland reuniting with Somalia are distant. Three issues are considered here: prospects for reconciliation and reunification with Somalia, the economic viability of an independent Somaliland and prospects for international recognition.

Prospects for reunification with Somalia
Western governments consider that the issue of recognition is a matter first for Somalis to agree upon, and secondly for Africans. For the majority of people in Somalia, and certainly the political leadership, the unity of

---

[1] For a review of these see: Rajagopal and Carroll 1992; Somaliland Ministry of Foreign Affairs 2002; Bermudez 2004; ICG 2006a.
[2] This definition of statehood was provided by the 1993 Montevideo Convention on the Rights and Duties of States.

Somalia is non-negotiable. The majority suspect that the push for Somaliland's independence is simply a consequence of foreign interests to keep Somalia divided and weak. The Federal Charter of the TFG states that Somalia's borders are 'inviolable and indivisible'. Public opinion in some places may be softening. Somaliland received messages of congratulation from southern civic activists after the parliamentary election, and in November 2005 the prime minister of the TFG, Mohamed Geedi, in an interview with the BBC, made the extraordinary statement that 'if the international community recognises Somaliland then we will have nothing against that'. His statement, however, caused a furore and was rescinded after he was accused of treason (Abdi Samatar 2005).

The commitment of successive Somaliland governments to the principle of independence has been queried by other Somalis, international diplomats and by Somalilanders themselves – and not unreasonably. The first Somaliland government foundered in part because its President, Abdirahman Ahmed Ali 'Tuur', was never fully committed to independence, as his subsequent alliance with General 'Aideed' and his support for federalism illustrated. Several prominent Isaaq political figures have declared their support for federalism and have held posts in various southern governments.[3] Many suspected that Tuur's successor, Mohamed Haji Ibrahim Egal, harboured ambitions to become leader of a 'Greater Somalia'.[4] President Riyale's commitment to the cause has also been questioned by some Somalilanders. Although this probably has more to do with Isaaq chauvinism, many people question his commitment to 'good government'.

Over the past decade and a half Somaliland nationalism has grown, at least among Isaaq people. This is apparent in Somaliland's national emblems, the remembrance days, the monuments to the 'struggle' and to those who fell fighting for the cause. A community project in Hargeysa to preserve the sites of mass graves of civilians slaughtered in the war is one of the strongest examples of this. For many Somalilanders, the evidence lying in these graves reinforces their belief that it was the south that shattered the union by attacking the north (Drysdale 1992: 35). Any reconciliation with Somalia would require some acknowledgement of the crimes committed in the name of the Somali state. Somaliland nationalism has been reinforced by the constitutional plebiscite and multi-party elections which in turn legitimise the political system. The political parties have reflected this populist mood in their common policies on independence and opposition to participation in the IGAD-sponsored talks on Somalia. An accusation of anti-Somaliland sentiments is an easy way to vilify one's political opponents. Consequently among most Isaaqs Somaliland's independence is *muqadas* (sacrosanct). This attitude,

---

[3] These include General Jama Mohamed Qalib 'Yare', Ismail Mohamed Hurre 'Buba' and Mohamed Jama 'Sifir'.

[4] With a political career that spanned colonial and independent Somalia, close associates suggest that he sought recognition as an elder African Statesman.

which is as strong, if not more so, among the diaspora, has had negative consequences, with the right to debate the issue publicly prevented by emergency laws.

Somaliland is no different from any state in incorporating different interest groups who take subtly different positions on the issues of independence and reunion. The Habar Awal, for example, are said to be staunchly anti-union, in part due to their dominance in Hargeysa and the economic benefits they have accrued over the past decade. Other Isaaq clans have benefited less. There is some indication that women may be stronger advocates of independence than men. A generation of people born after 1988 have no experience of a united Somalia. But political allegiances can change. Following Kulmiye's defeat in Somaliland's presidential elections, one of its senior members joined the TFG's national assembly. In 2003, following two elections, the Deputy Speaker of Parliament was of the view that 'democratisation must come before recognition. We will only know if it is working after three elections. If it fails then there is no point in seeking recognition.'[5] Among many Gadabursi, Harti and 'Iise, attachment to Somaliland is much weaker. Indeed, many non-Isaaq view it as an Isaaq 'project' from which they feel politically and economically excluded. But again, attitudes can change. The Gadabursi have become more supportive of Somaliland over time, and the incumbent President is from that region.

Independence terminated political ties with Somalia, but social and economic links were not totally severed. In many ways economic integration through trade, transport and communications is probably stronger than in the past. Somaliland business people are attracted by the economic potential in the south, with its larger market, lack of regulation and lighter tax regime. With Bossaso port competing with Berbera in terms of livestock exports, some big business people have increased their investments in Somalia, including Somaliland's biggest livestock trader and the remittance company Dahabshiil, which has many agents in Mogadishu. After the Arta conference in 2000 Somaliland businessmen began importing goods through El Ma'an port near Mogadishu. Shareholding companies link Somalia, Puntland and Somaliland through their franchises, while businesses linked with new Islamic orders provide another connection between the north and the south. Business people in Somaliland acknowledge the financial strength of businesses in Somalia, particularly those owned by Hawiye that dominate the Somali markets in Dubai and Eastleigh in Nairobi and are making inroads into other parts of Africa. Some business people in Somaliland are concerned that they cannot compete with the voracious entrepreneurial environment in the south[6] and that Somaliland would benefit from closer economic relations. Some professionals see limited opportunities for career development and personal advancement in Somaliland. A political settlement and a

---

[5] Author's interview with Deputy Speaker of Parliament, August 2003.
[6] Interviews by author, Hargeysa, September 2003.

reconstituted Somalia is likely to attract increased aid for reconstruction and attract foreign commercial investment.

But it would be wrong to assume that economic incentives would be sufficient to entice people to reunite with the south. Somaliland's 'new rich' have been accused in the media of turning their back on their country by investing in southern companies that are controlled by southerners, who are anti-Somaliland and charged with being linked to religious extremists (*Somaliland Times* 2003, September 13). Social standing, status and security are as important, if not more so, than financial inducements. This is one reason why the Somaliland authorities and some civic activists have been reluctant to participate in Somalia-wide aid projects promoting functional cooperation, such as livestock marketing boards, or civil society activities aimed at 'building bridges'. It is also why the authorities in Somaliland insisted that a UN and World Bank Joint Needs Assessment in 2005 and 2006 should deal separately with Somaliland.[7] Furthermore, the opportunities for people in Somaliland to regain a financial and political foothold in the south are slim. One consequence of the war has been to transform the regime of property rights, by strengthening territorial ties and increasing the exclusivity of territorial claims by clans. Northerners have not only lost physical assets in the south from looting, but also rights to social protection, economic rights and rights of access and ownership. In a reconstituted Somalia, with Mogadishu as its capital, Isaaqs and others who fled or were chased out of the south are likely to feel more marginalised than they were before the war.

There are also strong institutional barriers to reunion in a unitary or federated state. In the process of building a state people in Somaliland have developed their own government institutions, constitution, laws, municipalities, currency and political parties. The structure of government is different from the TFG. Somaliland's elections have served to reinforce the contrast between its elected government and the TFG, which has struggled from the start to retain support. None of this would be easily given up by people in Somaliland and formally it would require a referendum to reverse Somaliland's independence. Reunion would also see a change in the ethos of representative politics that has existed in Somaliland. A government of Somalia could not have the same level of representation of northern clans as currently exists in Somaliland and traditional leaders are unlikely to carry the same authority in Somalia.

Any moves to reunite with Somalia would also have to take into account the views of the Somaliland diaspora, who, since the mid-1990s, have invested heavily in the economy, infrastructure and welfare of the people in Somaliland. Many in the diaspora are likely to oppose moves

---

[7] The Joint Needs Assessment was initiated by the TFG and was a joint undertaking with the World Bank and the UNDP. An assumption that the authorities in Somaliland would simply accept funds for reconstruction to be administered by the TFG displays an ignorance of sensitivities in Somaliland.

that could jeopardise those investments. Reunion therefore offers few political incentives for people in Somaliland.

Finally, security and freedom from violence are key foundations of Somaliland. In the south criminal networks trafficking in arms, drugs and other contraband exist, often aligned with or controlled by faction leaders. Personal insecurity is a daily threat for people in many locations. People in Somaliland do not want to experience that again by reuniting with the south.

Many Isaaqs are ready for reconciliation with the south, especially if issues of justice can be addressed. But it is important to distinguish between reconciliation, dialogue and reunification, and between the views of Isaaqs, Dir and Harti. Some in Somaliland argue that in a global-ised world Somaliland cannot and should not isolate itself. Some influential Isaaq would like to see more dialogue with southerners. The poet Mohamed 'Hadraawi', a Somalilander, led a peace march throughout Somalia in August 2003, stating that as a poet he had the right to 'speak to all and for all Somalis'. Some Isaaqs may be open to dialogue with a southern government if a credible one is formed and no preconditions are set. But neither the TNG, the TFG nor the Islamic Courts, which have all claimed sovereignty over Somaliland, have provided a credible government. Somaliland began as a 'people's project', with the public and the SNM *mujahideen* demanding that the SNM leadership sever relations with Somalia. While the option of political association with Somalia in some form at some future date has not been totally ruled out, the popular mood remains against any dialogue that would cede that independence. Public opinion on this has been formally canvassed in the plebiscite on the constitution, which reaffirmed aspirations for independence, and the elections which in people's minds were linked with recognition. Consequently, while political debate in Somaliland has been opening up, the prospects for dialogue with the south are limited and the chances of reunion are minimal.

Can Somaliland be a viable state?
Somaliland's small economy and revenue base, amounting to between US$20 and US$30 million a year, is clearly inadequate to meet all the costs of public administration and Somaliland's social and development needs. For this reason, questions are raised about the economic viability of Somaliland and whether recognition of its independence would leave it eternally dependent on international largesse. For Somalilanders the Somali Republic was not a viable state either. In the 1970s and 1980s Somalia received more aid per capita than any state in Africa (Reno 2003: 15) but the public in the north (and other parts of Somalia) saw little benefit from this. With much smaller levels of foreign aid and an embargo on livestock exports, a basic system of public administration has been formed in Somaliland, security has been established, private and public infrastructure has been rebuilt and expanded, hundreds of thousands of

returnees have been absorbed and three elections have been held. During this period, major humanitarian crises have been avoided, although parts of eastern Somaliland have suffered from periodic drought. Much of the reconstruction and development that has taken place has been locally financed through the trade economy, remittances and taxation, and with the government playing a very limited development role. On this basis, while still poor, Somaliland's performance compares favourably with many wealthier recognised states.

The challenge facing people in Somaliland is to build on this. Political stability, a relatively light tax regime and diaspora remittances have enabled economic growth, a high level of imports and a boom in construction, particularly around Hargeysa. But this situation has served to disguise an economy dependent on a single export commodity and the continued inflow of remittances. The latter in particular has hidden high levels of unemployment. The new businesses that open daily in Hargeysa are financed by remittances and rely upon a remittance-dependent client base. Unless other forms of inward investment are forthcoming to regenerate and diversify the economy Somaliland's prosperity will be difficult to sustain. But Somaliland's *de jure* statelessness discourages foreign investment and constrains trading practices.

Limited levels of public revenue and the fact that much of the economy and sources of livelihood lie outside government control, especially in the remittance economy, serve to dilute political contest over the state. But it also means that Somaliland does rely on foreign aid to sustain some social services. In order to maintain and develop large-scale infra-structure, like roads and airports, Somaliland will certainly require larger sources of external finance than has been available to it through normal aid programmes. The most likely source of this would be international finance, but under current aid modalities this can only come with recognition. Recognition of sovereignty would bring additional costs that Somaliland would have difficulty meeting, such as the costs of support-ing foreign embassies and servicing at least part of Somalia's US$2.5 billion foreign debt. Any increase in foreign aid would also need to be managed in a way that does not undermine Somaliland's autonomy and the incentive to pay taxation.

Economic diversification has been occurring gradually, foreign investment has been slowly increasing, and there are areas where further growth could be realised. A proposal to develop Berbera into a free trade zone has been discussed for some time and has the potential to generate considerable income for Somaliland. It has long been speculated that prospects for oil extraction in Somaliland are good, a view encouraged by the geological similarities with Yemen, and several oil companies are reported to have applied for exploration licences in Somaliland (*Somaliland Times* 2002, October 19; Ali 2007). Other mineral deposits that could be exploited include coal, copper and gem stones. Pursuing the exploration and exploitation of these resources will eventually depend on a resolution of Somaliland's official status, especially as some speculated oil deposits are in contested areas of eastern Somaliland. In the absence of strong government-run or regulated institutions and a resolution of Somaliland's status, the discovery of commercial mineral deposits could have negative consequences for the region. But with a legal status enabling it to enter into foreign contracts, there is nothing inherent to Somaliland that should prevent it from enjoying higher levels of economic growth or developing a more robust economy that can sustain itself as a viable independent state.

International relations

Fulfilling the criteria for statehood or declaring *de facto* statehood counts for nothing unless it is recognised by another sovereign state, and sixteen years after breaking with Somalia, Somaliland's sovereignty is not recognised by any foreign country. During this time the diplomatic position of foreign governments has been fairly consistent. Despite some positive support to Somaliland from Britain, for example, its diplomatic position falls short of recognition, as was reiterated again by the British Prime Minister in early 2007 (*Somaliland Times*, 2007 March 24):

> Our policy has long been that the Somalis themselves should determine their future relationship and that their neighbours and African countries should take the lead in recognising any new arrangements which emerge from any dialogue.

Although diplomatic recognition has not been forthcoming, Somaliland has achieved a high degree of *de facto* acceptance internationally. It maintains representation in several foreign countries. Neighbouring Ethiopia has a trade office in Hargeysa and Somaliland has agreements of cooperation with Djibouti and low-key bilateral relations with IGAD and the African Union (AU). The presence of a South African observation team at all three elections illustrates a deepening relationship with South Africa. Somaliland has also signed bilateral agreements with the Danish and British governments on the repatriation of failed asylum seekers, there has been cooperation with Western intelligence services on counter-terrorism, and the European Community and UN agencies have offices in Somaliland to manage their aid programmes. Somaliland has also entered into agreements with foreign companies, including Total Oil and Ethiopian Airlines.

Increasing diplomatic interest in Somaliland was apparent in the funding provided for the elections from 2002 and assistance provided to the new Parliament, which contrasted with the lack of support to previous peace-making endeavours in Somaliland. Following the elections, the US, the Arab League and the United Nations, through the Secretary General's Special Representative for Somalia, all extended their congratulations to the people of Somaliland for what was one of the freest series of elections in the region. Of course, words will count for little unless they are followed by investment in the country's infrastructure and services and serious consideration is given to people's aspirations for statehood. A lack of such support for this new Islamic democracy is unlikely to go unnoticed in neighbouring countries and countries in the Middle East.

During the Somali National Peace Conference that produced the TFG, the strategy of regional and international mediators was to 'park' the issue of Somaliland in order to protect its stability. This demonstrated more pragmatic thinking than at previous peace conferences and acknowledged a growing respect for Somaliland's position that it would only enter into dialogue with a government in Somalia once one was formed. The formation of a TFG which has been accorded conditional recognition by the international community and has the backing of Somaliland's long-time ally – Ethiopia – means that Somalilanders may need to assess the options open to them. But equally, the international community will need to be creative in the way it deals with Somaliland.

In 1999, President Egal proposed that Somaliland should be given an observer status at the UN that would enable it to enter into direct links with international financial institutions. Others have suggested a confederal rather than federal architecture for the Somali entities that would accord recognition of Somaliland's independence, with a commitment to join with Somalia at an appropriate time to be defined (Drysdale 2000). The example of South Sudan provides an alternative model, whereby Somaliland could be granted an interim status for several years until a further referendum is held. All of these would release Somaliland from the diplomatic limbo that it has been in for over sixteen years. Given the position of Western governments, it has been suggested that the AU is the most appropriate body to take these ideas forward (ICG 2006a). Given the long held position of the Organisation of African Unity and its successor the AU on the inviolability of African post-colonial state borders, the possibility of recognising the break-up of a member state is extremely challenging. Nevertheless, moves by the AU to investigate Somaliland's claim for independence indicate that other African governments are not averse to giving this serious consideration. An AU mission to Somaliland in 2005 concluded that 'the AU should be disposed to judge the case of Somaliland from an objective historical viewpoint and a moral angle vis-à-vis the aspirations of the people' (African Union 2005). In late 2005, following the mission, the Somaliland government formally applied for membership of the AU. Of course, Western governments' line that 'Somalia's solutions lie with Somalis' appears somewhat disingenuous in the light of the support given to the TFG to overturn the Islamic Courts in 2006. If the political will and interest existed, non-African governments could do much to encourage the AU to take a stronger lead on Somaliland.

Many years of external support for state-building in Somalia have patently not worked and new approaches need to be considered. An understanding of state collapse as an adaptation or response by elites and societies to changes in the global political economy can help explain the failure of past efforts to restore a functioning state in Somalia. In considering the reasons why efforts to reconstitute a state in Somalia have failed for a decade and a half, Menkhaus (2005) has exhorted external actors not to import fixed state-building project templates, but instead 'to learn to work with local polities on their own terms'. Indeed, the imposition of former frameworks is likely to lead to resistance. People in Somaliland have demonstrated, in their own way and on their own terms, an alternative path to building a state and a system of government that is consistent with their own culture. In doing so, they have demonstrated that Somalis are no less capable of governing themselves than any other people. If it is possible in Somaliland then it can be feasible elsewhere in the Somali region. The process of state-building in Somaliland is not complete. As social scientists have argued, a state should be viewed as 'a work in progress' (Milliken and Krauss 2003:1). It is part of that dynamic work in progress that this book has sought to record.

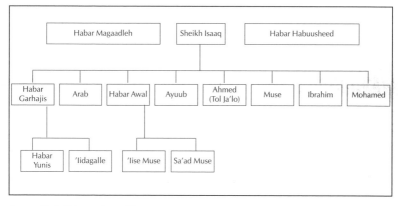

Appendix 1 Primary Isaaq Lineages

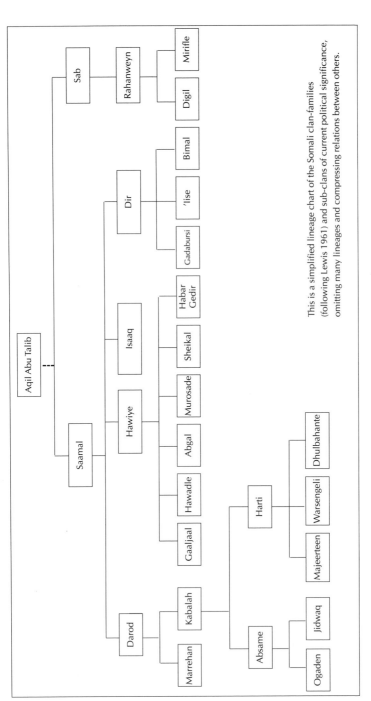

This is a simplified lineage chart of the Somali clan-families (following Lewis 1961) and sub-clans of current political significance, omitting many lineages and compressing relations between others.

Appendix 2 Somali Clan-Families

REFERENCES

Abdullahi, Mohamed S. (1996) *Somaliland NGOs: Challenges and Opportunities*. London: CIIR.

Abokor, Adan (2002) *20th February 1982: A Historical Day for the Somaliland Youth*. Paper presented to the Somaliland Youth Conference, 2002. ICD: Hargeisa.

Abokor, Adan *et al.* (2003) *'Very Much a Somaliland-run Election': A Report of the Somaliland Local Elections of December 2002*. London: CIIR.

Abokor, A.Y., Kibble, S., Bradbury, M., Yusuf, H.A. & Barrett, G. (2005*) Further Steps to Democracy: The Somaliland Parliamentary Elections September 2005*. London: Progressio.

Adam, Hussein (1994) 'Formation and Recognition of New States: Somaliland in Contrast to Eritrea', *Review of African Political Economy*, Vol. 21, No. 59: 21–38.

Africa Watch (1990) *Somalia: A Government at War with its Own People*. Washington/New York: The Africa Watch Committee.

African Rights (1993a) *Operation Restore Hope: A Preliminary Assessment*. London.

African Rights (1993b) *Components of a Lasting Peace in Sudan: First Thoughts*. Discussion paper no. 2. London.

African Rights (1994) 'Grass and the Roots of Peace: Pastoral Resources, Conflict and Conflict Resolution in Somalia and Somaliland', London: unpublished.

African Rights (2003) *Somaliland: Shadows of the Past as Human Rights Deteriorate*. Discussion Paper no 11. Hargeysa.

African Union Commission (2005*) Resumé: AU Fact-Finding Mission to Somaliland (30 April to 4 May 2005)*.

afrol News (2001, June 1) 'Somaliland Referendum Tainted by Arrest of Oppositional'. http://www.afrol.com/News2001/som010_somaliland_hrights.htm

Ahmed, Ali J. (1995) (ed.) *The Invention of Somalia*. Lawrenceville, NJ: Red Sea Press.

Ahmed, Ismail I. (1999) 'Understanding Conflict in Somalia and Somaliland', in Adebayo Adedeji (ed.) *Comprehending and Mastering African Conflicts*. London: Zed Books, pp. 236–56.

Ahmed, Ismail I. (2000) 'Remittances and their Economic Impact in Postwar Somaliland', *Disasters*, Vol. 24, No. 4: 380–9.

Ahmed, Sadia M., Ali, Hassan M., & Warsame, Amina. M. (2001) *Research Findings on the State of pastoralism in Somaliland*. Hargeisa: PENHA/ICD.

Ali, M.Y. (2007, March 24) 'Hydrocarbon Potential of Somaliland' in *The Somaliland Times*. Issue 270. Hargeysa.

Amnesty International (1988) *Somalia: A Long Term Human Rights Crisis*. London.

Amnesty International (2004, November 30) *Somaliland: Amnesty International Concerned about 16-year old Girl's Trial and Rape Allegations, and Summary Imprisonment of her Defence Lawyers*.

APD (Academy for Peace and Development) (2002, April) *The Judicial System in Somaliland*. Workshop Report. Hargeisa.

APD (Academy for Peace and Development) (2006 September) *A Vote for Peace: How Somaliland Successfully Hosted its First Parliamentary Elections in 35 Years*. Hargeysa/Nairobi: Academy for Peace and Development/Interpeace.

Barnes, C. (2006) 'U dhashay Ku dhashay: Genealogical and Territorial Discourse in Somali History', *Social Identities*, Vol. 12, No. 4: 487–98.

Bemath, Abdul S. (1992) 'The Sayyid and Saalihiya Tariga: Reformist, Anticolonial Hero in Somalia', in Said S. Samatar (ed.) *In the Shadow of Conquest: Islam in Colonial Northeast Africa*. Lawrenceville, NJ: Red Sea Press, pp. 33–47.

Berdal, M. & Malone, D. (eds) (2000) *Greed and Grievance: Economic Agendas in Civil Wars*. Boulder, CO: Lynne Rienner.

Besteman, C. & Cassanelli, L.V. (eds) (2000) *The Struggle for Land in Southern Somalia: The War Behind the War*. , Boulder, CO/London: Westview Press/Haan Publishing.

Bermudez, M.S. (2004) 'Somaliland: Time for Recognition'. Thesis. European Master's Degree

259

in Human Rights and Democratisation. Irish Centre for Human Rights.

Boutros-Ghali, B. (1992) *An Agenda for Peace*. New York: United Nations.

Bradbury, M. (1994a) *The Somali Conflict: Prospects for Peace*. Oxfam Research Paper No 9. Oxford: Oxfam UK/I.

Bradbury, M. (1994b) 'The Politics of Vulnerability, Development and Conflict: Exploring the Issues with Reference to Somalia and Somaliland'. MSc dissertation. School of Public Policy. University of Birmingham, UK.

Bradbury, M. (1996) '"Hostility and Hospitality": The Pastoral Dimensions of the Somali Civil Conflict'. Unpublished report for VetAid.

Bradbury, M. (1997) 'Somaliland Country Report'. London: ICD/CIIR.

Bradbury, M. & Coultan, V. (1998) *Somalia Inter-Agency Flood Response Operation Phase I November-December 1997. An Evaluation*. Nairobi: UNICEF Somalia.

Bradbury, M. (2002) 'Somalia: The Aftermath of September 11th and the War on Terrorism'. Unpublished report for Oxfam.

Bradbury, M., Abokor, Adan. Y. & Yusuf, Haroon A. (2003) 'Somaliland: Choosing Politics over Violence', *Review of African Political Economy*, No. 97: 455–78: ROAPE Publications Ltd.

Bradbury, M. Ryle, J., Medley, M. & Sansculotte-Greenidge, K. (2006) *Local Peace Processes in Sudan. A Baseline Study*. London: Rift Valley Institute.

Brons, M. H. (2001) *Society, Security, Sovereignty and the State in Somalia: From Statelessness to Statelessness?* Utrecht: International Books.

Bryden, M. (1994a) *Mission to Somalia*. A special report prepared for the UNDP Emergencies Unit, Ethiopia.

Bryden, M. (1994b) 'Fiercely Independent', African-American Institute in *Africa Report*, Vol. 39, No. 6: 35–40.

Bryden, M. (2001) 'Reviving the Somali Peace Process: Perspectives and Prospects in the Post-Arta Period'. Paper presented to the 8th Congress of the Somali Studies International Association, Hargeisa.

Cabdi, Sucaad I. (2005) 'The Impact of the War on the Family', in WSP International (ed.) *Rebuilding Somaliland: Issues and Possibilities*. Lawrenceville, NJ & Asmara: Red Sea Press/WSP International, pp. 269–326.

Cassanelli, L. V. (1982) *The Shaping of Somali Society: Reconstructing the History of a Pastoral People 1600–1900*. Philadelphia, PA: University of Pennsylvania Press.

Cassanelli, L. V. (2004) 'The Role of Diaspora Communities in Homeland Development' in R. Ford, Hussein Adam & Edna Adan (eds) *War Destroys, Peace Nurtures: Somali Reconciliation and Development*. Lawrenceville, NJ & Asmara: Red Sea Press.

Civil Service Commission (2003) *Project Proposal on Establishment of Somaliland Public Administration Institute*. Hargeisa.

Clapham, C. (1996) *Africa and the International System: the Politics of State Survival*. Cambridge: Cambridge University Press.

Clapham, C. (1998) *African Guerrillas*. Oxford: James Currey.

Clarke, W. & Herbst, J. (1997) *Learning from Somalia: The Lessons of Armed Humanitarian Intervention*. Boulder, CO/London: Westview Press/Haan Publishing.

Commission for Africa (2005 March) *Our Common Interest*. www.comissionfor Africa.org.

Compagnon, D. (1991 January-June) 'The Somali Opposition Fronts: Some Comments and Questions', *Horn of Africa*, Vol. XIII, Nos 1–2: 29–54.

Compagnon, D. (1998) 'Somali Armed Movements: The Interplay of Political Entrepreneurship and Clan-Based Factions', in C. Clapham (ed.) *African Guerrillas*. Oxford: James Currey.

Coultan, V., Davies, R., Jowett, A., & Mariano, N. (1991) *A Report of an Assessment Mission to Northern Somalia, March to April 1991*. London: Inter-NGO Committee for Somalia.

The Daily Telegraph (2001, September 28). '*Banks-to-Terror Conglomerates Faces US Wrath*.' London.

de Waal, A. (1993) *VioleNt Deeds Live on: Landmines in Somalia and Somaliland*. London: African Rights and Mines Advisory Group.

de Waal, A (1996) *Class and Power in a Stateless Somalia: A Discussion Paper*. London: Justice Africa.

de Waal (1997) *Famine Crimes: Politics and the Disaster Relief Industry in Africa*. Oxford/Bloomington, IN: James Currey/Indiana University Press.

Dixon, B. (2002) 'The Colonisation of Political Consciousness: States and Civil Society in Africa', in T. Zack-Williams, D. Frost, & A. Thompson (eds) *Africa in Crisis: New Challenges and Opportunities*. London: Pluto Press.

Drysdale, J. (1992) *Somaliland: The Anatomy of Secession*. Brighton: Global Stats Ltd.

Drysdale, J. (1994) *Whatever Happened to Somalia? A Tale of Tragic Blunders*. London: Haan

Drysdale, J. (2000) *Stoics Without Pillows: A Way Forward for the Somalilands*. London: Haan.

Ducaale, Boobe Y. (2005) 'Media and Political Reconstruction', in *Rebuilding Somaliland:*

Issues and Possibilities. Lawrenceville, NJ/Asmara & Geneva: Red Sea Press/WSP International, pp 123–88.

Duffield, M. (1990) *War and Famine in Africa*. Oxford: Oxfam.

Duffield, M. (1998) 'Post-Modern Conflict: Warlords, Post-Adjustment States and Private Protection', *Journal of Civil Wars*, Vol. 1, No. 1: 65–112.

The Economist (2002, September 28) 'Unprecedented power, colliding ambitions'. p. 51.

European Union (2002) *Report on the Somaliland Local Elections held on 15 December 2002*. Nairobi.

Ehret, C (1995) 'The Eastern Horn of Africa, 1000 BC to 1400 AD: The Historical Roots', in Ali Jimale Ahmed (ed.) *The Invention of Somalia*. Lawrenceville, NJ & Asmara: Red Sea Press.

Evans-Pritchard, E.E. (1974 [1940]) *The Nuer*. New York: Oxford University Press. 6th Printing.

The Famine Early Warning Network (FEWS Net) and Food Security Assessment Unit (FSAU) (2003, November 22) 'Emergency Alert: Sool Plateau Faces Alarming Deterioration in Food Security'. Nairobi.

Farah, Ahmed Y. (1994) *The Milk of the Boswellia Forests. Frankincense Production among the Pastoral Somali*. University of Uppsala.

Farah, Ahmed Y. (1995) *Salient Features of the Refugee Camps in Eastern Ethiopia*. UNDP Emergencies Unit for Ethiopia.

Farah, Ahmed Y. (1996 July 11) *Camp Abokor Peace Conference, General Observations: Geedi-Socodka Nabadda ee Beelaha Hargeysa: Progressive Peacemaking Process Among the Clans in Hargeysa Area*. UNDP/EU for Ethiopia.

Farah, Ahmed Y. (1999) 'Political Actors in Somalia's Emerging De Facto Entities: Civil-Military Relations in Somaliland and Northeast Somalia'. Presented at the Conference on Civil-Military Relations. Nairobi.

Farah, Ahmed Y. & Lewis, I.M. (1993) *Somalia: The Roots of Reconciliation*. London: ActionAid.

Farah, Nuruddin (2000) *Yesterday, Tomorrow: Voices from the Somali Diaspora*. London/New York: Cassell.

Federal Research Division (1993) *Somalia, A Country Study*. Washington, DC: US Library of Congress.

Forster, S (2002) *Somali UK Diaspora – Enterprise Survey*. Mid Yorkshire Chamber of Commerce and Industry Ltd. Nairobi: European Commission.

Fortes, M. & Evans-Pritchard, E.E. (eds) (1958), *African Political Systems*. London: Oxford University Press.

Fukui, K. (1994) 'Conflict and Ethnic Interaction: The Mela and their Neighbours', in K. Fukui & J. Markakis (eds) *Ethnicity and Conflict in the Horn of Africa*. London: James Currey, pp. 33–47.

Gaani, M. X (2005) 'Regulating the Livestock Economy of Somaliland' in *Rebuilding Somaliland: Issues and Possibilities*. Lawrenceville, NJ/Asmara & Geneva: Red Sea Press/WSP International, pp. 189–268.

Gardner, J. & el Bushra, J. (2004) *Somalia the Untold Story: The War through the Eyes of Somali Women*. London: Pluto Press.

Gebissa, E. (2004) *Leaf of Allah: Khat and Agricultural Transformation in Harerge Ethiopia, 1875–1991*. Oxford: James Currey.

Gers, M. & Valentine-Selsey, N. M. (2002 December) *Final Report of the European Union/GTZ Technical Advisory Team*. Nairobi: European Commission.

Gersony, R. (1989) *Why Somalis Flee: A Synthesis of Accounts of Conflict Experience in Northern Somalia by Somali Refugees, Displaced Persons and Others*. Washington DC: Bureau for Displaced Persons, US Department of State.

Gilkes, P. (1992) *Ethnic and Political Movements in Ethiopia and Somalia*. London: Save the Children Fund (UK).

Gilkes, P. (1993) *Two Wasted Years: The Republic of Somaliland 1991–1993*. London: Save the Children Fund (UK).

Gilkes, P. (1995) *Acceptance not Recognition: The Republic of Somaliland 1993–1995*. London: Save the Children Fund (UK).

Glick Schiller, N. & Fouron, G. (2002) 'Long Distance Nationalism Defined' in J. Vincent (ed.) *The Anthropology of Politics*. Oxford: Blackwell Publishers.

Griffiths, D. (2002) *Somali and Kurdish Refugees in London: New Identities in the Diaspora* (Research in Migration & Ethnic Relations Series) Aldershot, UK: Ashgate.

The Guardian (2007, January 12) 'Somali Islamists Held Meeting In Britain To Raise Funds'.

Gulaid, Ali (2003) 'Corruption, Corruption Everywhere', in *The Republican*, Vol. 7. No. 26, 23–9.

Gutherz, X., Cros, J.-P. & Lesur, J. (2003) 'The Discovery of New Rock Paintings in the Horn of Africa: The Rockshelters of Las Geel, Republic of Somaliland', *Journal of African*

Archaeology, Vol. 1, No. 2: 227–37.

Hannan, L. (2003) *A Gap in their Hearts: The Experience of Separated Somali Children.* Nairobi: UNOCHA.

Hansch, S., Lillibridge, S., Egeland, G., Teller, C. & Toole, M. (1994) *Lives Lost, Lives Saved. Excess Mortality and the Impact of Health Interventions in the Somalia Emergency.* Washington, DC: Refugee Policy Group.

Hansen, P. (2003) *Revolving Returnees: Return Migration in Somaliland.* Copenhagen: Danish Institute for International Studies.

Hansen, P. (2004) *Migrant Remittances as a Development Tool: The Case of Somaliland.* Copenhagen: Danish Institute for Development Studies (DIIS). Denmark Migration Policy Research Working Papers Series No 3. International Organisation for Migration.

Harris, H. (2004) *The Somali Community in the UK: What We Know and How We Know It.* London: Information Centre about Asylum and Refugees in the UK/Kings College London.

Helander, B. (1995 August) 'Some Problems in African Conflict Resolution: Reflections on Alternative Reconciliation Work and Research'. Internet edition: NomadNet.

Herbst, J. (2000) *State and Power in Africa.* Princeton, NJ: Princeton University Press.

Holleman, C. F. (2002 December) *The Socio-Economic Implications of the Livestock Ban in Somaliland.* Nairobi: FEWS NET Somalia.

Holt J. & Lawrence, M. (1992) *The Prize of Peace - A Survey of Rural Somaliland.* London: Save the Children Fund (UK).

Human Rights Watch/Africa (1995) *Somalia Faces the Future: Human Rights in a Fragmented Society*, Vol. 7, No. 2. New York, Washington & London.

International Crisis Group (ICG) (2002) *Somalia: Countering Terrorism in a Failed State.* Africa Report No. 45. Nairobi/Brussels.

International Crisis Group (2003) *Somaliland: Democratisation and its Discontents.* Africa Report No. 66. Nairobi/Brussels.

International Crisis Group (2004) *Somalia: Continuation of War by Other Means?* Report No. 88. Nairobi/Brussels.

International Crisis Group (2005a) *Counter-Terrorism in Somalia: Losing Hearts and Minds?* Africa Report No. 95. Nairobi/Brussels.

International Crisis Group (2005b) *Somalia's Islamists.* Africa Report No. 100. Nairobi/ Brussels.

International Crisis Group (2006a) *Somaliland: Time for African Union Leadership.* Africa Report No. 110. Nairobi/Brussels.

International Crisis Group (2006b) *Can the Crisis in Somalia be Contained?* Africa Report No 116. Nairobi/Brussels.

International Committee of the Red Cross/Somali Red Crescent Society (1997) *Spared from the Spear.* Nairobi.

Integrated Regional Information Networks (IRIN) (2001 April 3) *The Berbera Lifeline: Part I.* www.reliefweb.int

IRIN (2001 May 28) 'Somalia: IRIN Interview with Muhammad Ibrahim Egal, President of Somaliland'. www.reliefweb.int

IRIN (2001 July 10) 'Somalia: IRIN Special – A Question of Recognition – Parts 1&2'. Nairobi. www.reliefweb.com

IRIN (2001, August 22) 'Somaliland Leader Accused'. www.reliefweb.int

IRIN (2003 January 17) 'Somalia: Review of 2002'. www.reliefweb.int

IRIN (2003, March 26) 'Funding Somaliland's Poll'. www.reliefweb.int

IRIN (2004, October 15) 'Somaliland Leader Rejects Unity with Somalia'. Agence France Presse. www.reliefweb.int

IRIN (2004 November 1) 'Somalia: Over 100 Killed in Clashes between Somaliland and Puntland'. www.reliefweb.int

IRIN (2005 November 15) 'Somalia: Heavy Sentences for Murder of Aid Workers in Somaliland'. www.reliefweb.int

Jahzbahy, Iqba (2006) 'African Union and Somaliland: Time to Recognise Africa's Best Kept Secret?' *Sub-Saharan Informer.*

Jama, Ibrahim, H. (2000 June) 'The Revised Constitution of the Republic of Somaliland: Unofficial English Translation'. www.Somalilandforum.com.

Jama, Ibrahim H. (2003) 'The Somaliland Supreme Court and the Presidential Elections'. www.Somalilandforum.com

Jama, Ibrahim H. (2007 May) 'The Sheikh Concordat – Settling Constitutional Disputes in the Somaliland Way?' *Somaliland Focus UK Newsletter.* http://www.somalilandfocus.org.uk/

Jamal, Vali (1988) 'Somalia: Understanding an Unconventional Economy', *Development and Change*, Vol. 19, No. 2: 203–65.

Jan, Ameen (1996 July) *Peace Building in Somalia.* IPA Policy Briefing Series. New York:

International Peace Academy.

Jimcaale, Cabdiraxmaan (2005) 'Consolidation and Decentralisation of Government Institutions', in WSP International (ed.) *Rebuilding Somaliland: Issues and Possibilities*. Lawrenceville, NJ & Asmara: Red Sea Press/WSP International. pp. 49–122.

Kapteijns, L. (1994) 'Women and the Crisis of Communal Identity: The Cultural Construction of Gender in Somali History', in Ahmed I. Samatar (ed.) *The Somali Challenge: From Catastrophe to Renewal?* Boulder, CO/London: Lynne Rienner. pp. 211–33.

Kent, R., von Hippel, K. & Bradbury, M. (2004 November) *Social Facilitation, Development and the Diaspora: Support for Sustainable Health Services in Somalia*. London: Kings College.

King, A. (2003) *Hargeisa Urban Economy Assessment February-March 2003*. Washington, DC: Chemonics International Inc.

Kleist, N. (2004) 'Somali-Scandinavian Dreaming: Visions of Home and Return in Somscan and UK Cooperative Associations', Paper presented at Sussex Centre for Migration Research Seminar, University of Sussex.

Krohn-Hansen, C. & Nustad, K.G. (2005) 'Introduction', in C. Krohn-Hansen & Knut G. Nustad (eds) *State Formation: Anthropological Perspectives*. London: Pluto Press.

Le Sage, A. (2002) 'Somalia: Sovereign Disguise for a Mogadishu Mafia', *Review of African Political Economy*, Vol. 29, No. 1: 132.

Le Sage, A. (2004) 'Somalia and the War on Terrorism: Political Islamic Movements and US Counter-Terrorism Efforts'. PhD Thesis. Jesus College, Cambridge University, Faculty of Social and Political Sciences.

Le Sage, A. (2005 July) *Stateless Justice in Somalia: Formal and Informal Rule of Law Initiatives*. Geneva: Centre for Humanitarian Dialogue.

Lewis, I.M. (1961) *A Pastoral Democracy: A Study of Pastoralism and Politics Among the Northern Somali of the Horn of Africa*. London: Oxford University Press. 3rd edition 1999 James Currey/IAI/Lit Verlag.

Lewis, I.M. (1972) 'The Politics of the 1969 Somali Coup', *The Journal of Modern African Studies*, Vol. 10, No. 3: 383–408.

Lewis, I.M. (1990), 'The Ogaden and the Fragility of Somali Segmentary Nationalism', *Horn of Africa*, Vol. xiii, Nos 1 and 2.

Lewis, I.M. (1993) *Understanding Somalia*. London: Haan Associates. 2nd edition.

Lewis, I.M. (1994a) 'An Anthropologist at Large in the "Cinderella of Empire"', in I.M. Lewis, *Blood and Bone: The Call of Kinship in Somali Society*. Lawrenceville, NJ: Red Sea Press, pp 1–17.

Lewis, I.M. (1994b) 'The Rise of the Somali National Movement: a case study in clan politics', in I.M Lewis, *Blood and Bone: The Call of Kinship in Somali Society*. Lawrenceville, NJ: Red Sea Press, pp 177–219.

Lewis, I.M. (2002 [1965]) *A Modern History of the Somali*. 4th Edition. Oxford/Hargeisa/Athens, OH: James Currey/Btec Books/Ohio University Press.

Lewis, I.M. & Mayall, J. (1995) *A Menu of Options: A Study of Decentralised Political Structures for Somalia*. London: London School of Economics/EC Somalia Unit.

Lindeman, Berit N. & Hansen, Stig J. (2003) *Somaliland: Presidential Election 2003*. NORDEM.

Lindley, A. (2004) 'Somalia Country Study'. Commissioned for a report on Informal Remittance Systems in African, Caribbean and Pacific (ACP) Countries. Compas. DFID, EC, Deloitte & Touche.

Lindley, A. (2006) *Migrant Remittances in the Context of Crisis in Somali Society: A Case Study of Hargeisa*. London: Overseas Development Institute, Humanitarian Policy Group.

Little, P.D. (2003) *Economy Without a State: Accumulation and Survival in Somalia*. (African Issues). Oxford: James Currey.

Louis Berger S.A & Afro-Consult Plc. (2003) *Pre-Feasibility Study of the Regional Transport Sector in the Berbera Corridor*. Report for European Commission.

Luling, V. (1997) 'Come Back Somalia? Questioning a Collapsed State'. *Third World Quarterly* Vol. 18, No. 2: 287–302.

Luling, V. (2006) 'Genealogy as Theory, Genealogy as Tool: Aspects of Somali "Clanship"', in *Social Identities: Journal for the Study of Race, Nation and Culture*, Vol. 12, No. 4: 471–85.

Lyons, T. & Samatar, Ahmed I. (1995) *Somalia: State Collapse, Multilateral Intervention and Strategies for Political Reconstruction*. Brookings Occasional Papers. Washington, DC: Brookings Institution.

Macrae, J. & Shepherd, A. *et al.* (2003) *Aid to 'Poorly Performing' Countries: Critical Review of Debates and Issues*. London: Overseas Development Institute.

Mansur, Abdalla O. (1995) 'The Nature of the Somali Clan System'. In Ali Jimale Ahmed (ed.) *The Invention of Somalia*, Lawrenceville, NJ & Asmara: Red Sea Press.

Marchal, R. (1996) *The Somali Post-Civil War Business Class*. Nairobi: EC/Somali Unit.

Marchal, R. (1997) 'Forms of Violence and Ways to Control It: The Mooryaan of Mogadishu', in

Hussein M. Adam & Ford, R. (eds) *Mending Rips in the Sky: Options for Somali Communities in the 21st Century.* Lawrenceville, NJ & Asmara, Red Sea Press.

Marchal, R. (2001) *The Outcomes of US Decision on al-Barakaat.* Working Paper, Paris: CERI-CNRS.

Marchal, R. (2004) 'Islamic Political Dynamics in the Somali Civil War', in Alex de Waal (ed.) *Islamism and its Enemies in the Horn of Africa.* London: Hurst & Company. pp. 114–45.

Markakis, J. (ed.) (1993) *Conflict and the Decline of Pastoralism in the Horn of Africa.* London: Institute of Social Studies and Basingstoke, UK: Macmillan Press.

Medani, K. (2000) *Report on Internal Migration and Remittance Inflows: Northwest and Northeast Somalia.* Nairobi: UNCU and FSAU.

Menkhaus, K. (1999) 'Traditional Conflict Management in Contemporary African Crises: Theory and Praxis from the Somali Experience', in William Zartman (ed.) *Traditional Cures for Modern Conflicts: African Conflict Medicine.* Boulder, CO: Lynne Rienner, pp. 183–99.

Menkhaus, K. & Prendergast, J. (1995 May) 'Governance and Economic Survival in Post-intervention Somalia', in *CSIS Africa Notes No. 172.* Washington, DC: Centre for Strategic and International Studies. pp. 1–10.

Menkhaus, K. & Ortmayer, L. (1999) 'Somalia: Misread Crises and Missed Opportunities', in Bruce W. Jentleson (ed.), *Preventative Diplomacy in the Post-Cold War World: Opportunities Missed, Opportunities Seized, and Lessons to be Learned.* Lanham, MD: Rowman and Littlefield.

Menkhaus, K. (2003) 'Bantu Ethnic Identity in Somalia', *Les Annales d'Ethiopie* Vol. XIX: 323–40.

Menkhaus, K. (2004) *Somalia: State Collapse and the Threat of Terrorism.* London: International Institute for Strategic Studies.

Menkhaus, K., Bryden, M., le Sage, A. & Bradbury, M. (2005, January) *Somalia Programming and Policy Assessment,* Washington DC: Development Alternatives Inc./USAID.

Menkhaus, K. (2005, August 31) *Kenya-Somalia Border Conflict Analysis.* Washington, DC: USAID/Development Alternatives Inc.

Miller, N.N. (1981) 'The Other Somalia: Part 1 – Illicit Trade and the Hidden Economy' *American Universities Field Staff Reports.* Vol. 29. Oxford: Queen Elizabeth House. pp 1–17.

Milliken, J. & Krauss, K. (2003) 'State Failure, State Collapse, and State Reconstruction: Concepts, Lessons and Strategies', in J. Milliken (ed.), *State Failure, State Collapse, and State Reconstruction.* Oxford: Blackwell Publishing, pp. 1–21.

Mohamoud, M.S. & Hashi, A.M. (1988) *Somalia Livestock Sector Development: Interventions and Responses,* Mogadishu: BOCD (CIIR).

Mohamed, Saeed Sheikh (2002 October 16) *National Development Plan for 2003–2005: Framework for Recovery and Development.* Hargeysa: Ministry of National Planning and Coordination. Republic of Somaliland.

Mubarak, Jamil Abdalla (1996) *From Bad Policy to Chaos in Somalia: How an Economy Fell Apart.* London: Praeger.

NAGAAD Umbrella et al. (October 18, 2005) *A Joint Appeal of Civil Society Groups Towards Improving the Political Position of Women in Somaliland.*

Nair, K.N.S & Abdulla, Faisal (1998) *Somalia 1997–1998: A Status Report.* Nairobi: UNDOS.

National Electoral Commission (2005) Election Results. http://www.somalilandelectoralcommission.org

New Sudan Council of Churches (2002) *Inside Sudan: The Story of People-to-People Peacemaking in Southern Sudan.* Nairobi.

Nordstrom, C. (2000) 'Shadows and Sovereigns', *Theory, Culture and Society.* Vol. 17, No. 4: 35–54.

NOVIB (2003) *Mapping Somali Civil Society.* Nairobi.

Nyathi, P. (1995) 'Somaliland, Zimbabwe: Demobilisation and Development. The Tasks of Redesigning a Future without Conflict', in A. Shepherd & M. Bradbury (eds) *Rural Extension Bulletin: Development and Conflict,* No 8, December, pp. 26–28. University of Reading AERDD.

Omaar, Rakiya (1994) 'Somaliland: One Thorn Bush at a Time', *Current History.* Vol 93: 232–6.

Omar, Abdulsalam (2002) *Supporting Systems and Procedures for the Effective Regulation and Monitoring of Somali Remittance Companies (Hawala).* UNDP Somalia.

Pankhurst, S.E. (1951) *Ex-Italian Somaliland.* London: C.A. Watts & Co Ltd.

Peace Committee for Somaliland (1995) 'The Search for a Peaceful Solution to Fighting in Somaliland: An Interim Report'. Mimeo.

Peace Committee for Somaliland (1996) 'An Interim Report on the Search for a Peaceful Solution to the Fighting in Somaliland, report on main events from 22 March 1996 and other major activities planned to follow'. Mimeo.

Prime Minister's Strategy Unit (2005 February) *Investing in Prevention: An International Strategy to Manage Risks of Instability and Improve Crisis Response.* A Prime Minister's Strategy Unit Report to the Government. London: Strategy Unit.

Prior, J. (1994) *Pastoral Development Planning.* Oxfam Development Guidelines no. 9. Oxford.

Prunier, G. (1991) 'A Candid View of the Somali National Movement' in *Horn of Africa.* Vol. XIV, Nos 1–2: 107–20.

Prunier, G. (1998 May), 'Somaliland Goes It Alone', *Current History,* Vol. 97: 225–8.

Puntland Development Research Centre (2003) *Somali Customary Law and Traditional Economy: Cross Sectional, Pastoral, Frankincense, and Marine Norms.* Garowe: PDRC.

Rajagopal, B. & Carroll, A. (1992) 'The Case for the Independent Statehood of Somaliland'. Mimeographed report. Washington. DC.

Reno, W. (2003) *Somalia and Survival in the Shadow of the Global Economy.* Queen Elizabeth House Working Paper 100. Oxford and Northwestern University.

Reynolds, P. (2007, January 14) 'Twin US Aims in Somalia'. BBC News website.

Ryle, J. (1992) *Where There is no Border.* London: Save the Children (UK).

SACB (Somalia Aid Coordination Body) (2002) *Donor Report.* Nairobi: SACB.

SACB (2003) *Donor Report.* Nairobi: SACB.

Sahnoun, Mohamed (1994) *Somalia: The Missed Opportunities.* Washington, DC: USIP Press.

Samatar, Abdi I. (1985) 'The Predatory State and the Peasantry: Reflections on Rural Development Policy in Somalia', *Africa Today,* Vol. 32, No. 3: 41–56.

Samatar, Abdi I. (1989) *The State and Rural Transformation in Northern Somalia, 1884–1986.* Madison, WI/London: University of Wisconsin Press.

Samatar, Abdi I. (1994) 'Empty Bowl: Agrarian Political Economy in Transition and the Crisis of Accumulation', in Ahmed I. Samatar (ed.) *The Somali Challenge: From Catastrophe to Renewal?* Boulder, CO/London: Lynne Rienner, pp. 65–94.

Samatar, Abdi I. (2005) 'Somali Prime Minister: An Act of Betrayal, Venality, and Incompetence!' University of Minnesota. Hiiraan Online. http://www.hiiraan.com

Samatar, Abdi I, & Samatar, Ahmed I. (2003) 'International Crisis Group Report on Somaliland: An Alternative Response'. Mimeo. University of Minnesota & Macalester College.

Samatar, Ahmed I. (1995) 'Underdevelopment in Somalia: Dictatorship without Hegemony' in *Africa Today,* 32 (3). Indiana University. pp. 23-40.

Samatar, Ahmed I. (1988) *Socialist Somalia: Rhetoric and Reality,* London: Zed Books.

Samatar, Ahmed I. (1994) *The Somali Challenge: From Catastrophe to Renewal?* Boulder, CO/ London: Lynne Rienner.

Samatar, Ibrahim M. (1997), 'Light at the End of the Tunnel: Some Reflections on the Struggle of the Somali National Movement', in Hussein M. Adam and Richard Ford (eds) *Mending Rips in the Sky: Options for Somali Communities in the 21ˢᵗ Century.* Lawrenceville, NJ & Asmara: Red Sea Press, pp 21–48.

Samatar, Said S. (1991) *Somalia: A Nation in Turmoil,* London: Minority Rights Group.

Samatar, Said S. (ed.) (1992a) *In the Shadow of Conquest: Islam in Colonial Northeast Africa.* Lawrenceville, NJ: Red Sea Press.

Samatar, Said S. (1992b) 'Sheikh Uways Muhammad of Baraawe, 1847–1909: Mystic and Reformer in East Africa', in Said S. Samatar (ed.) *In the Shadow of Conquest: Islam in Colonial Northeast Africa.* Lawrenceville, NJ & Asmara: Red Sea Press, pp. 48–74.

Schlee, Gunter (2001) *Regularity in Chaos: The Politics of Difference in the Recent History of Somalia.* Working Paper No. 18, Halle: Max Planck Institute for Social Anthropology.

Schraeder, Peter, J. (2006 December 19) 'Why The United States Should Recognize Somaliland's Independence'. Center for Strategic and International Studies. Africa Policy Forum. Forums.csis.org

Simons, A. (1995) *Networks of Dissolution: Somalia Undone.* Boulder, CO: Westview Press.

Simons, A. (1996) 'Somalia: A Regional Security Dilemma', in E.J. Keller & D. Rothchild (eds) *Africa in the New International Order.* Boulder, CO/London: Lynne Rienner, pp. 71–84.

Somali National Movement. *Mujahid's Constitution, Political and Basic Facts.* (undated).

Somaliland Ministry of Foreign Affairs (2002). *The Case for Somaliland's International Recognition as an Independent State.* Briefing paper. Hargeisa: Somaliland Government.

Somaliland Ministry of National Planning and Coordination (MNPC) (2004) *Somaliland in Figures.* (5th edition). Hargeisa.

Somaliland Peace Charter (1993) *Somaliland Communities Security and Peace Charter.* (Translation by Mohamoud Hamud Sheik).

The Somaliland Times (2002, May 11) 'Tens Of Thousands Bid Farewell To Late President Egal'. Issue 18. Hargeysa.

The Somaliland Times (2002, July 6) 'Editorial: Judiciary Reform'. Issue 25. Hargeysa.

The Somaliland Times (2002, October 19) 'British Company To Start Exploration And Drilling For Oil Soon'. Issue 39. Hargeysa.

The Somaliland Times (2003, September 13) 'Dubai-based Businessmen Recruiting Delegates to Represent Somaliland at the Nairobi Talks'.

The Somaliland Times (2004, March 27) 'Editorial'. Hargeysa.

The Somaliland Times (2005, October 18) 'Somalia Says Range Resources Mineral and Oil Rights Deal is Invalid'. Issue 196, Hargeysa.

The Somaliland Times (2007, March 24) 'The UK Prime Minister's Office Reply To The "Somaliland E-Petition"'. Issue 270. Hargeysa.

Sommer, John (1994) *Hope Restored? Humanitarian Aid in Somalia, 1990–1994.* Washington, DC: Refugee Policy Group.

Spears, I. (2001) 'States-Within-States: Incipient Political Entities in the Post-Cold War Era'. Paper presented to the Eighth Congress of the Somali Studies International Association (SSIA), Hargeisa, 3–13 July.

Svedjemo, E. (2002) 'In Search of a State – Creating a Nation: The Role of the Diaspora in Somaliland's Pursuit of Recognised Statehood'. Master's Dissertation. University of Sussex, Brighton.

Swift, Jeremy (1979) 'The Development of Livestock Trading in a Nomadic Pastoral Economy', in *Pastoral Production and Society*, Proceedings of the International Meeting on Nomadic Pastoralism, Paris, 1–3 December 1976, Cambridge: Cambridge University Press, pp. 447–65.

Terlinden, U. & Hagmann, T. (2005 July 29) 'Faking a Government for Somalia: International Diplomacy Supports Fictitious Peace Process', *Sub-Saharan Informer.*

Thompson, A. (2004) *An Introduction to African Politics.* Second edition. Oxford: Routledge.

Turton, D. (1989) 'Warfare, Vulnerability and Survival: A Case from South Western Ethiopia', in *Cambridge Anthropology: Special Issue on Local Warfare in Africa, 1988–1989*, Vol. 13, No. 2: 67–86. University of Cambridge, Department of Social Anthropology.

United Nations (1999) *Report of the Secretary General on the Situation in Somalia*, S/1999/882. New York.

United Nations (2003) *Inter-Agency Assessment of Sool Plateau and Gebi Valley Sool & Sanaag.* Nairobi.

UNSC (United Nations Security Council) (2003) *Report of the Panel of Experts on Somalia in Pursuance of the Arms Embargo.*

UNCT (United Nations Country Team Somalia) (1998 June) 'Information and Issues for Possible Mention in the Security Council Ambassadors Meeting'. Mimeo. Nairobi.

UNDOS (United Nations Development Office for Somalia) (1998 July 18) *Emergency Programme of Action in Response to Livestock Import Ban.* Nairobi: Somalia Aid Coordination Body.

UNDP (2001) *UNDP Human Development Report, Somalia 2001.* Nairobi.

UNICEF (1991) *An Analysis of the Situation of Children and Women in Somalia.* Mogadishu.

UNICEF (2000) *End Decade Multiple Indicator Cluster Survey, Full Technical Report for Somalia, 2001.* Nairobi.

UNOCHA-Somalia (2002). *Study on IDPs and Minorities in Somalia.* Nairobi.

UNPOS (2005) *United Nations Special Representative to Visit Hargeisa, Somalia.* Media Advisory.

UNRC (United Nations Resident Coordinator) (2000) *First steps: An Operational Plan to Support Governance and Peace Building in Somalia (Sep–Dec 2000).* Nairobi.

Vaidyanathan, K.E. (1997) *Report of the UNFPA Consultant on Population Statistics of Somalia.* Nairobi: UNDOS.

von Hippel, K. (2002) 'The Roots of Terrorism: Probing the Myths', *Political Quarterly.* Vol 73, No. s1: 25–39.

Watson, M. (1990) *Collapse of Somalia and the Science of Governance.* Nairobi: Management Resource Limited.

Willis, Justin (2003) 'Violence, Authority, and the State in the Nuba Mountains of Condominium Sudan', *Historical Journal*, Vol. 46, No. I: 89–114.

Woods, R. & Mutero, J. (2002 September) *Somalia Urban Sector Profile Study.* European Commission Somalia Office/ UN-HABITAT Regional Office for Africa and the Arab States.

World Bank (2006) *Somalia: From Resilience Towards Recovery and Development.* A Country Economic Memorandum for Somalia. Washington, DC: World Bank.

World Bank/UNDP (2003) *Somalia Socio Economic Survey, 2002 Report No. 1. Somalia Watching Brief.* Nairobi.

WSP International (2001) *Rebuilding Somalia: issues and possibilities for Puntland.* London: HAAN Associates.

WSP International (2005) *Rebuilding Somaliland: Issues and Possibilities.* Lawrenceville, NJ & Asmara, Red Sea Press/WSP International.

Yusuf, Haroon A. (1996) 'The Role of Traditional Governance in Sanaag/Somaliland'. Unpublished mimeo.

INDEX

267

About Progressio

Progressio is an international development charity working to tackle poverty and injustice in developing countries. It has been working in Somaliland since 1995. Initially it focused on supporting nascent local organisations working in the areas of women's rights, disability, youth, minority rights and human rights. It has also played a key role in supporting the development of primary health care services. Progressio's current work in Somaliland includes helping to tackle HIV and AIDS, capacity building with local civil society organisations, and promoting sustainable environment initiatives. From its head office in the UK, Progressio has also been heavily involved in highlighting the progress the people of Somaliland are making towards democratisation and stabilising the country. It has been active in linking diaspora groups together to support Somaliland, and it led the international observation team for the 2005 parliamentary elections.

FOR MORE INFORMATION ABOUT PROGRESSIO SEE WWW.PROGRESSIO.ORG.UK
Progressio is the new name of the Catholic Institute for International Relations (CIIR) which is registered in the UK as a charity (number 294329) and a company limited by guarantee (number 2002500)